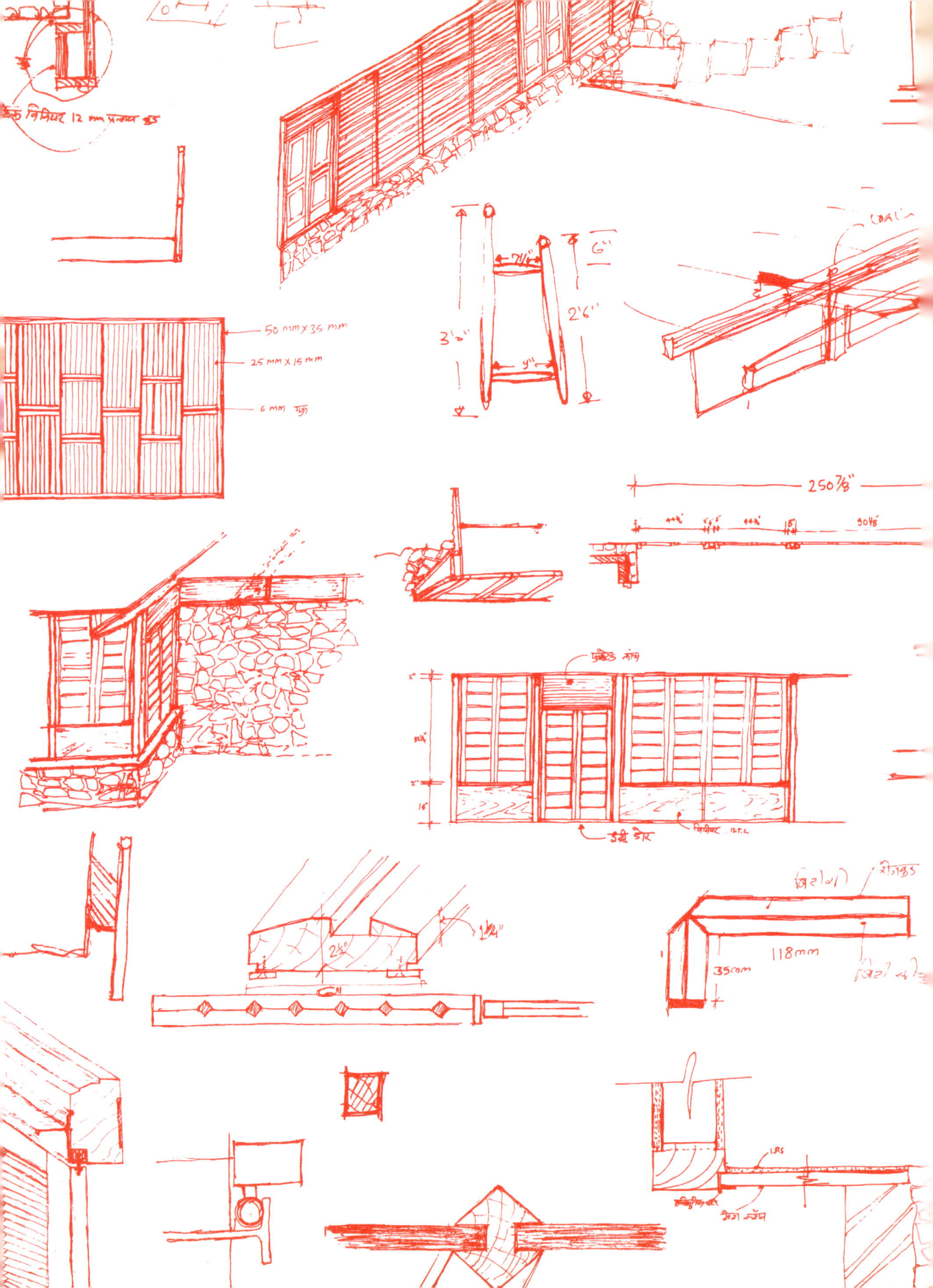

STUDIO MUMBAI : Praxis

With special thanks to my wife Priya.

STUDIO MUMBAI : Praxis

First published in Japan on July 11, 2012
Sixth published on June 10, 2024

TOTO Publishing (TOTO LTD.)
TOTO Nogizaka Bldg., 2F
1-24-3 Minami-Aoyama, Minato-ku
Tokyo 107-0062, Japan
[Sales] Telephone: +81-3-3402-7138 Facsimile: +81-3-3402-7187
[Editorial] Telephone: +81-3-3497-1010
URL: https://jp.toto.com/publishing

Supervision: Bijoy Jain and Joseph Van der Steen
Publisher: Akira Watai
Editing: TOTO Publishing
Cooperation: STUDIO MUMBAI
Art Director and Designer: ASYL Naoki Sato+Masataka Kikuchi
Printer: Tokyo Inshokan Printing Co., Ltd.

Except as permitted under copyright law, this book may not be reproduced, in whole or in part, in any form or by any means, including photocopying, scanning, digitizing, or otherwise, without prior permission. Scanning or digitizing this book through a third party, even for personal or home use, is also strictly prohibited. The list price is indicated on the cover.

ISBN978-4-88706-328-0

STUDIO MUMBAI:Praxis
スタジオ・ムンバイ:プラクシス

Contents
目次

006　**Praxis**
Bijoy Jain
　　プラクシス
　　ビジョイ・ジェイン

008　Interview with Bijoy Jain
　　Living and Working, Studio Mumbai
　　Interviewer: Erwin Viray (Professor, Kyoto Institute of Technology)
　　ビジョイ・ジェイン氏に聞く
　　暮らしながら働く、スタジオ・ムンバイ
　　インタビューアー：エルウィン・ビライ（京都工芸繊維大学教授）

026　**Inspiration**
　　インスピレーション

036　**Studio Mumbai Workshop**
　　スタジオ・ムンバイ・ワークショップ

046　**Interviews with Staff and Collaborators**
　　Interviewer: Wolfgang Fiel (Architect)
　　スタッフや共働者に聞く
　　インタビューアー：ヴォルフガング・フィール（建築家）

　　Jeevaram Suthar: Head Carpenter
　　ジェヴァラム・シュシャー（大工棟梁）

　　Jean-Marc Moreno: Master Roofer
　　ジャン＝マルク・モレノ（屋根葺きマスター）

　　Pandurang: Head Mason
　　パンデゥラング（石工リーダー）

　　Dr. Muirne Kate Dineen: Colour Artist
　　ムイルネ・ケイト・ディニーン（カラーアーティスト）

　　Samuel Barclay: Associate Architect
　　サミュエル・バークレイ（共働建築家）

　　Works
　　作品

058　**Reading Room**
　　リーディング・ルーム

068　**Tara House**
　　ターラ邸

084　**Leti 360 Resort**
　　レティ360リゾート

100　**Palmyra House**
　　パルミラの住宅

120　**House on Pali Hill**
　　パリ・ヒルの住宅

134　**Belavali House**
　　ベラヴァリの住宅

152　**Utsav House**
　　ウスタヴ邸

168　**Copper House II**
　　コッパー・ハウス II

188　**1:1 Architects Build Small Spaces**
　　V&A Museum
　　「1:1 建築家がつくる小さな空間」展
　　ヴィクトリア＆アルバート博物館

194　**Workplace, Venezia Biennale**
　　ワークプレイス ― ヴェネチア・ビエンナーレ展

200　**META Chile**
　　METAチリ

206　**Saat Rasta　561/63**
　　サート・ラスタ　561/63

212　**Studio Mumbai, Seeing and Knowing**
　　Erwin Viray
　　スタジオ・ムンバイ　見ることと知ること
　　エルウィン・ビライ

217　**Profile**
　　略歴

218　**Credits**
　　クレジット

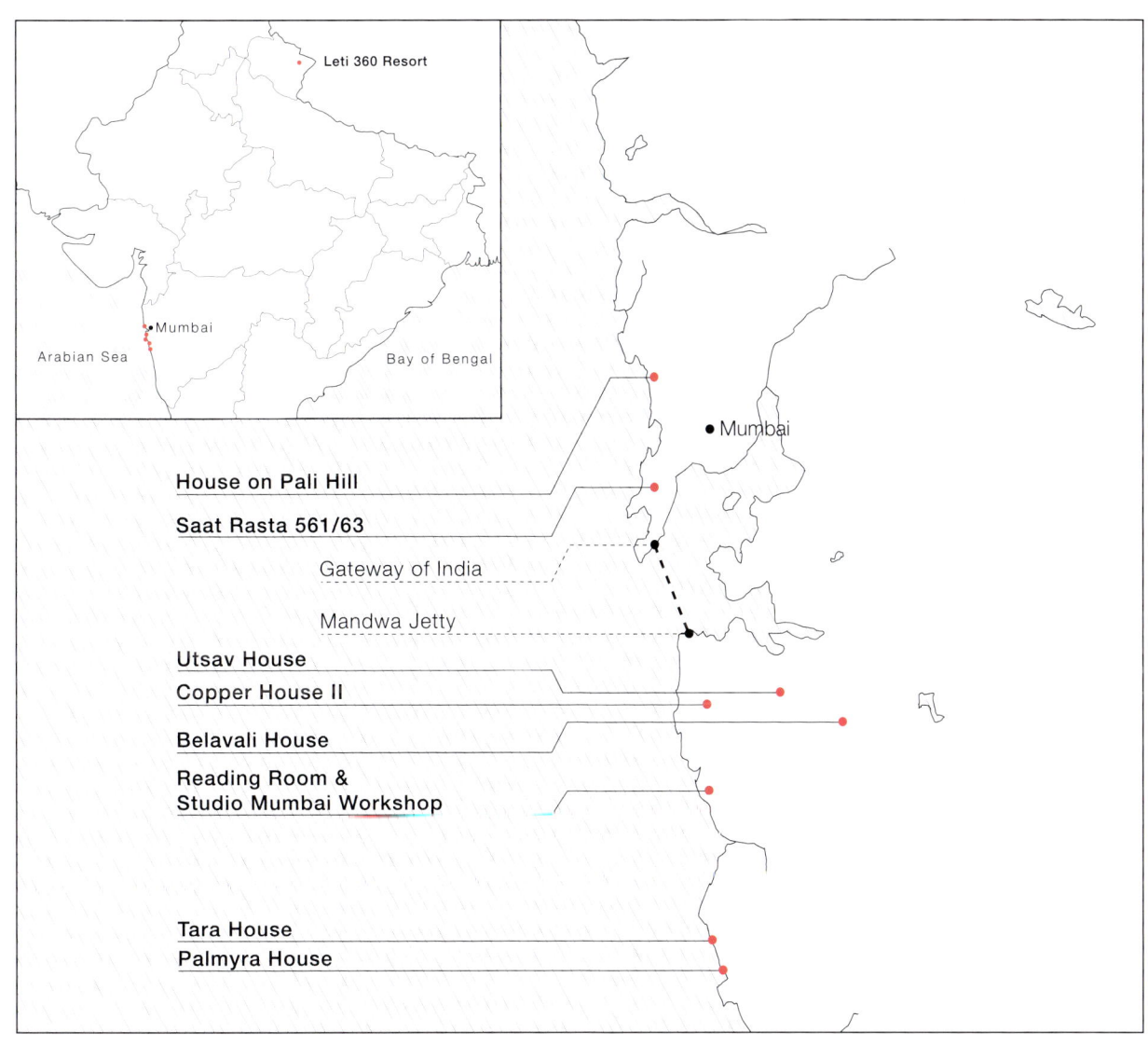

インド国内プロジェクトマップ
Project location map in India

プラクシス

「Praxis（プラクシス）とは、理論や知識や技能を実演や実行に移すこと、体現すること、あるいは実現することである。場合によっては、考えを実行、応用、行使、実現、あるいは実施する行為を指す」

建築家の仕事には、あらゆるものが含まれる。具体的なものもあれば、漠然としたものも理論的なものもある。つまり人間の存在に関わることなら基本的になんでも含まれる。「Praxis」というものをこのように存在論的に解釈すると、スタジオ・ムンバイの仕事がなぜ反復作業によって成り立っているか、なぜ案を検討するために、大型モックアップやスケッチや図面を作成し、素材のスタディを重ねるのかが見えてくる。それはすなわち独自の思想を練り上げ、自発的に組織を形成していくためなのだ。

プロジェクトに取り組む間は、場所を念入りに検討し、そこにある環境や文化、人びとが身も心も捧げてきたことに目を向けるようにしている。なぜならそこには、限られた資源を相手に人間が創意工夫を凝らして編み出した建設技術と素材があるからだ。

ビジョイ・ジェイン

Praxis

"Praxis is the process by which a theory, lesson, or skill is enacted, practiced, embodied or realized. It may also refer to the act of engaging, applying, exercising, realizing or practicing ideas."

All encompassing, the practice of the architect, whether tangible, ambiguous or theoretical, is primarily concerned with the nature of being. This ontological understanding in 'Praxis' may begin to express how the work at Studio Mumbai is created from an iterative process, where ideas are explored through the production of large-scale mock-ups, material studies, sketches and drawings to form an intrinsic part of our thought and body.

Projects are developed through careful consideration of place and a practice that engages intently in an environment and culture, the physical and emotional engagement of the people involved; where building techniques and materials draw from an ingenuity arising from limited resources.

Bijoy Jain

ビジョイ・ジェイン氏に聞く
暮らしながら働く、スタジオ・ムンバイ

インタビューアー：
エルウィン・ビライ（京都工芸繊維大学教授）

エルウィン・ビライ（以下、「**EV**」）　このたびは対談の機会を設けてくださり、たいへん感謝しております。さっそくですが、まずはスタジオ・ムンバイとはどういう組織か、そしてなぜ「スタジオ・ムンバイ」と命名なさったのかをお聞かせください。

ビジョイ・ジェイン（以下、「**BJ**」）　こちらこそ、今日はわざわざお越し頂きありがとうございます。さて、スタジオ・ムンバイにはいろんな人たちがいます —— 建築家もいれば、職人も大工も石工もいる……　その彼らが建築を建てる、あるいはつくるためにここに集まってきました。スタジオ・ムンバイという平凡な名前にしたのはつまり、ここが私たちの作業場となる「スタジオ」であり、昔ながらの工房のようなものだというのと、それが地理的には「ムンバイ」にあるというだけのことです。事務所の所在地は厳密にはアリバグですが、ここからムンバイはさほど離れていませんから。
　もう少し説明すると、ここは建築の研究・開発の場ということで、材料に関する事柄であれ、つくり方であれ、それらすべてをひっくるめた哲学であれ、なんでも扱います。スタジオ・ムンバイでは、つくりながらアイデアを練る、という筋書きを辿ります。たとえばアイデアを練りながらその場でそれを試したり、あるいは現物を相手にアイデアを組み立てていったり。大まかにいえば、そんなところです。

EV　スタジオには大勢の人間がいて、その中には職人や建築家やエンジニアがいる。こうした特殊技能をもつのは、いったいどういう素性の人たちなのでしょう。

BJ　それはね、たとえば身近なところでいうと、ケイト・ディニーン博士という女性の協力者がいるんですが、彼女はロンドン在住で、アライシュ（Araish）という特殊な左官技術の博士号を取得している。でも彼女の強みはなんといっても色づかいの巧みさにあり、だからこそ彼女はうちの仕事には欠かせない存在となっています。同様に、私たちの仲間には、インドに住みついたフランス人ジャン＝マルク・モレノもいます。彼のおかげで、このスタジオでも非常に高度なスキルが使えるようになりました。
こうした共同作業を何年か続けていくうちに、進展もありました。また、先祖代々大工であった人たちも仲間に引き入れました。彼らはもともとラジャスタンの出身で、大工の伝統の中でその継承者として訓練を受けてきたので、工匠の技術をもっています。この地方には切石技術に長けた石工もいます。業種も出身地も異なる人たちが、ひとところに集まって仕事をするのが、スタジオ・ムンバイです。これが事務所の原点です。もうひとつの特徴は、常に外部からの参加に対して開かれていること。まずは建てるという行為がありきですから、そこに複数の人間が関わる以上、必然的に共同作業になります。これがいちばん肝心な点かもしれない。建築について考えよう、建築をつくろうという人なら、誰でもこのスタジオに加われます。

EV　建築をつくるためには、専門分野も関心も業種も異なる人たちを受け入れる。これだけの人が集まって、いったいなにをするんですか。

BJ　具体的になにをするとは言えませんが、ある意味ではそれ［を考えること］が私の役割かもしれません。私自身はあくまでもまとめ役に過ぎない。オーケストラでいえば指揮者にあたります。こうした人と人とのつながり、交流を担保するためにも、私自身はコミュニケーションが円滑にいくよう心がけています。あとは方向づけをすること。ただし縛り付けてしまっては議論や会話がしにくくなるので、あくまでも緩い方向づけです。それでも運転手がいないと自動車は動きませんから、私がその運転手役を務めます。この方向性は、ある程度明確にしておきます。アイデアがいったんかたちになれば、あるいはコンセプトが一定の表現なり動きとして現れるようになれば、あとはそのコンセプトの実現に向けてこれを守り抜く。アイデアの原点あるいは核から逸脱しないようにね。共同作業はこの核を中心に進められるので、皆の意識がその核から離れることはありません。私の任務はそこ、つまりコンセプトを育てることにもある。アイデアというものは所詮、心と身体を通じて経験されるものですから。

EV　アイデアは具体的にどこからどういうふうに湧いてくるのですか。

BJ　答えにくい質問ですねえ、なにしろアイデアの出所はいつも同じではありませんから。私自身が直観的に（これまで培ってきた経験などから）ひらめくこともあるし、日常の体験からひらめくこともあります。私の場合、そうした経験を、あるいは車での移動中に気づいたことなどを、写真や映像やドローイングに記録していきます。旅に出るといろんな体験や出会いがあるでしょう。意識にじわじわと「浸透」していくものもある。印象づけられる、という感じですね。ではそれがプロジェクトにどう具体的に現れるか、どんなアイデアとなって現れるかが、これまた面白いところです。というのも何年も潜在意識に眠っていたものが、ここぞ

Interview with Bijoy Jain
Living and Working, Studio Mumbai

Interviewer:
Erwin Viray (Professor, Kyoto Institute of Technology)

Erwin Viray (EV) Thank you very much for giving us the great opportunity to have this conversation with you. Maybe you could start by talking about what Studio Mumbai is, and why "Studio Mumbai" is the name that you chose for this studio.

Bijoy Jain (BJ) Firstly, thank you for your generous participation. Studio Mumbai is formed by a group of people – made up of architects, artisans, carpenters, and masons, …brought together in the idea of building architecture or making architecture. The idea behind Studio Mumbai as a name is a more generic one: "Studio" being the place that we work in, much like a traditional atelier, and "Mumbai" to locate ourselves geographically. Alibag is where we have the practice, but it is in very close proximity to Mumbai.

To elaborate a little further, it is also a place for research and development towards building and architecture, whether it is materials, matters of making, or philosophical ideas of how they all come together. Studio Mumbai presents a scenario where ideas can be explored through making. While one thinks about or conceives the idea, there is immediacy in the experimentation or in the process of physically conceiving it, and then in responding to it in a way. This is broadly what we do.

EV You mentioned that it is a group of people and that there are craftsmen, artisans, architects and engineers among others, who are all these special people are?

BJ For example, I collaborate very closely with a lady called Dr. Kate Dineen. She lives in London and has a PhD in a particular lime plaster technique called Araish. But her strength is in the utilization and the understanding of color, so she is very much an integral part of the practice. Likewise, we have a Compagnon from France who has now settled in India – Jean Marc Moreno. He brings a very refined set of skills into the studio.

Our collaboration has spanned over several years, and there has been an evolution within that. Another extension is the carpenters who come from a long lineage. They are primarily from Rajasthan and all have a traditional background and training in carpentry, so they bring their skill sets. There are the stonemasons of this area working and practicing the art of cutting stone. It is a close collaboration with several different kinds of people, from different locations. Studio Mumbai is a place where they begin overlapping with each other. This is primarily the nature of how we are set up. Another important aspect is that we are always open to participation from the outside. When I say that, I mean that the idea or the act of building is primary, and to participate in it entirety, is to have that collaboration. I think that is most critical for us. The studio is open and allows for people to come in with the idea of exploration and of making architecture.

EV In these explorations of making architecture, you have all these people coming from different disciplines, different interests, and different occupations. What is the role of this coming together of people in making architecture?

BJ It is not so specific, and yet it is in some ways in terms of what I do. First and foremost I am a facilitator; like the conductor of an orchestra. It is pivotal for me to ensure that these connections or overlaps occur, and that there is a fluid communication between all these conditions. It is also important for me to give it direction, which is more of a loose framework that is open for discussion and dialogue. Somebody still needs to drive the car and that is the role that I have to play in the studio. The direction has some sort of clear definition. Once an idea is given form, or a concept has been articulated or activated, then the rest of the time is actually spent protecting and then supporting the concept to its fruition, so that the origin of the idea or the core of the idea remains central. The participation must occur around this core in order to see it in its full experience, I think that that is one of the roles that I play; nurturing the concept, because the idea is finally what needs to be experienced emotionally, physically, and experientially.

EV Can you talk about these ideas and how they come about? Where they come from?

BJ That is a difficult question to answer because they come from several different places. One is my own intuition (i.e., experiences that I have had), but also from every day experiences. Much of the documentation that I do is through photography, film, drawing and driving from place to place. There is a lot that one experiences and encounters through travel. There is an "osmosis"

という瞬間に現れたりするんです。

EV つまり、ばらばらにあったものが、あるとき納まるべきところに納まって、かたちとなって現れるということですか。

BJ そうです。でもただ漫然と待っているだけでは、そういう瞬間は訪れない。だから私たちは太陽観測なんかもしているんです。たとえばプロジェクト「ハミード邸」では、マンゴーの美しい木立があの場所の決め手になっていたので、それをどう活かしていくかという話になります。いつからか入植が始まった——敷地が平らに均され、段丘がつくられている——土地ですから、そうした造成の痕跡を残し、継承していきたいと考えたわけです。

EV 既存のものを活かし、なおかつ敷地そのものを活かすということですか？

BJ ええ、敷地には長年かけて培われたものがありますから。私たちはその場所の世話人というわけです。だからそこにあるものを育て、欲をいえばその土地のポテンシャルをもっと引き出していきたいとも思っている。そこからプロジェクトの構想が始まります。私たちはどんな措置を講ずるにも、どんな物理的な介入をするにも、こうしたポテンシャルを伸ばすつもりでやります。これに関しては集団としての見解が一致している必要があります。「そうだね、これは大事にしなければ」、「これをもっと活かそう」、「どう介入すれば、ここにある物の良さや情緒を損ねないだろうか」という具合にね。そこには歴史、時間、参加……の感覚がある。そうした蓄積の上に現在と将来を重ねていく。さまざまな思想、さまざまな時間を複雑に縒り合わせて共存させるためにも。

EV それを享受する側の人びとは、以前より良くなったと感じるのでしょうか。

BJ であってほしいけどね。少なくともいろんな状況が想定されていなくてはなりません。心地良いだけではなく、時には寂しくなるようなところもあったほうがいい。これはなにも否定的な意味ではなく、いわゆる「人生」におけるあらゆる場面を喚起するようなもの、「人生」を内包したものであってほしい。それが建築に求められる役割ではないかと。建築には人生そのものが詰まっている。以上ふたつは、ほんの基本的なことですが、ほかにもいろいろ可能性はあるでしょうね。結局ね、私たちはそこを目指しているんです。私たちが繰り返しこの問いに立ち戻るのは、仮に問いを誤ったまま突き進んでしまうと取り返しのつかないことになるからです。そもそもの出発点がどこにあったかをその都度確認しながら、自分たちの行為がそこから外れていないかを再確認していく。問いの核心に何度も立ち返るうちに、プロジェクトは徐々にできあがっていく。あと、なにかを着想するときには判断力がものをいいますね。つまり取捨選択の判断が。

EV 調整も必要でしょうね。

BJ ええ、判断力と調整、そして共有することが、集団としての意思決定の決め手になります。もちろん人数が多すぎてもなかなか決まらないので、コアメンバーだけで決定します。なにが語られ、そして語られなかったかという微妙なニュアンスも判断材料になる。ここでは少なくとも3名が合意しなければ、その案は却下されます。責任逃れというのではなく、三者三様の立場をどうすり合わせるかという、もっと複雑な話なのです。

EV ここにはこれだけの数の人間が働いています。ここにいても作業場の活気が伝わってくるし、賑やかな音も聞こえてきます。彼らにはどんな言葉をかけるのですか。あるいはどんなふうに指揮をすれば、各人のパートがきれいに奏でられるのでしょうか。ちなみにお手元にはスケッチブックが積まれているし、こちらには模型があり、向こうでは皆が作業をしているのが見えますが。

BJ ひとつコツを言うと、物語仕立てにして話すことですね、対話を成立させるためにも。これは万国共通でしょうけれど、物語のほうが話が通じやすいということがあります。物語は人の心に残ります。日本であれインドであれイタリアであれ、人間の経験というのは場所が変わっても似たり寄ったりですから。表現は違えど、ある状況に置かれた人間の心理は普遍的です。だから、議論をするためにはそれ相応の雰囲気をつくっておく。たとえばこのプロジェクトについて語るなら、この美しいマンゴーの木立のおかげで木陰もこの環境もあるのだから、これを使わない手はない、といった雰囲気をつくっておく。これがギリシャならオリーブの木立になるかもしれない。つまりマンゴーの木にこだわるのではなく、そこから生まれる状況や光景を思い浮かべてみる。これを会話の糸口に、銘々の頭にそのイメージを喚起させる。まずはこうしたイメージや体験、あるいは雰囲気を共有しておいて、つぎにそれをどう表現するかという議論に進んでいく。あとはそれをスケッチやドローイングに起こしたり、あるいは身振りで示したり、写真に撮ったり、物語に仕立てたりするわけです。こうすれば各自が自らの体験や記憶や想像に重ね合わせることができる。ほかには実際に建てるという方法もあって、やはり現物があることが議論のきっかけになります。たとえば素材に関する話なら、この素材ならなにができるかとか、どんな表現ができるかといったことを説明できる。相手が大工さんなら話は早い——長年木を相手に仕事をしてきた人たちですから。それをそのまま実践にもち

that creeps into your awareness; it is more of a registration. How that then physically manifests itself in projects, or how ideas come about is what is fascinating, because sometimes they remain latent for several years until they find an appropriate moment to express themselves.

EV So, everything somehow would be in a certain condition, everything would simply fall into place and allow for things to emerge?

BJ Yes, and I think that is important. But it also comes from a lot of work that one has to do: one of the things that we do is surveying the sun. For example, in this particular project - Hamied Residence, what was very critical was how to develop a project where the key to that place was the organization of these beautiful mango trees. It had been colonized at some point in time – there are levels and terraces – and the idea was to maintain a part of this creation that continues to exist on the site.

EV So, it's taking what the site has and then maybe dwelling the site?

BJ Yes. There is something that exists on site that has been nurtured over a period of time. We are now the new caretakers of the place, and must continue to nurture what has been set, but also our hope is to take it further and to realize a new potential along with what has been set on the ground. That becomes a critical basis of the conception of the project. All the actions that are taken, all the physical movements that occur, are done with the intent to nurture this fundamental core, which is one that we collectively agree upon as saying that, "yes, this is of value," "this is something that we take forward," and "how do we participate in this process in a way that extends, or takes further what is physically and emotionally there." There is a sense of history, of time, of participation… all of these overlays, of our time, of what the future is, of what can occur. It is woven in a complex way, where potentially all these points of view or points in time can co-exist.

EV People enjoying it and being in that place would somehow feel better?

BJ Hopefully. I think it must carry within itself all kinds of conditions. Not just feeling good, but feeling sad from time to time. I am not saying that in a negative way, but to conjure up all the possibilities of what we call "life" and to hold within it, "life". I think that is foremost the role of architecture: to contain life itself and everything that is within it. Those are just two very fundamental ideas, but potentially it has all these possibilities. In a very simple way, that is what we work towards. We continuously ask those questions, because asking a wrong question and then walking towards it, could take you farthest away from what you are trying to do. The idea is to continuously inform the starting point, and every action thereafter, to reevaluate the origin of what we are doing. We keep returning to the core of the question, and through that the project will evolve. I think discretion is also critical in the process of conceiving something; in what you keep and what you take out.

EV Do you think that it requires adjustment too?

BJ Yes, discretion, adjustment and sharing are also critical when a decision has to be made collectively, of course when there are too many people it is difficult; but with a core group, It is in the nuances of what is said and what is not said. This is how we work, where a minimum of three people collectively get together in agreeing to an idea. It is not so much to not take responsibility, but I think what we achieve is a far more complex relationship with three different points of view.

EV In a place like this, you have all these people here. One can actually feel the energy that is in the workshop, hearing the sound of this work going on. How do you go about having a conversation with them? Or how do you go about orchestrating so they play their music very well in this whole process? You have here some sketchbooks and we also have some models here, and behind you we can see them working?

BJ I think one of the critical points in all of this is story telling, which is central to the idea of a dialogue. I think it is a universal condition where we can all connect with stories, because they have had an impact in some way, whether you are in Japan, India, or Italy, you will find similarity in certain experiences. Their expressions might differ, but the spirit of the condition is universal. One way is to discuss it through creating an atmosphere. Like I spoke about in this particular project, the atmosphere was the idea of nurturing these beautiful mango trees, which provide the shade, and create a particular environment. Now this can be

込めば、手間取らない。ここでもやはりドローイングは用いずに、記憶と口承に頼って作業を進めます。面白いことに、ある程度曖昧な部分があっても話は通じるんですね——臨機応変に解釈される。そのときどきの状況に応じてちゃんと話は通じるんです。木切れさえあれば対話は始まる。あとはそれをどう切って、どう組み立て、かたちにするかを追々詰めていけばいいんです。

EV 第1段階というものがない?

BJ ありません。作業はリニアには進まないし、物語は開かれています。誤解もあるので、必ずしもすんなりとはいきませんが。いちばん根気がいるのは、相手の言葉に聞く耳をもち続けること、共有することです。スタジオの運営でいちばん重要なのは、共有の意識をもち続けること、つまりコミュニティの動向に敏感であることです。透明性が保たれていなければ、私たちの仕事はうまくいきません。

EV その透明性というのは物の透明不透明ではなく、人間の心構え、意識、考え方、仕事に対する姿勢のことですね。このひとりひとり個性の異なる集団に、協調性を求めたり、こちらの思い通りに動いてもらうのは難しくありませんか。

BJ たしかに、建築は単独行動でつくれるものではありませんからね。建築の規模に応じて、関わる人間の数も増減します。農業がそうでしょう?

EV タイミングを逃すと、人はついてきてくれないものですよね。

BJ あれこれと気をまわさないとね。建築をつくるということはとりもなおさず、その場所でなにが起こるか、そこで誰がなにをするのか、というところまで先読みをすることですからね。

EV ええ、そこでどんな展開があるのか……。

BJ それを念頭に置いて建築をつくれば、建築は自然とまとまっていきます。その場所のもつ精神に建築が馴染んでいくというか。たしかに、プロジェクトが完成してみると、あれっと驚くこともままあります。そこが面白いところで、最終的にどんなかたちになるのかは、この私にもおおよその見当しかついていない。なにが出てくるかわからないから、わくわくする。

EV いろいろな状況が想定されるときほど、思いがけない展開が起きるものですよね。

BJ そういうものを大切にしたいんです。だから、あえて予測不能な部分をいくらか残すようにしています。本心ではそれは避けたいところではあっても。でもそれがあるから人生は面白い。人生なにが起こるかわからない。建築は人生を内包するものでないといけない、というからには、そこに予測不能なものも含めなければならないんです。ところで、建築の「弱さ」という概念があるでしょう。あれは建築が人間に近づく感じがしていいですね。

EV お手元にあるのはなんですか。ドローイング、それともスケッチですか。

BJ ドローイングです、大工たちの。このスタジオではたいてい誰もが自分のスケッチブックを持っています。このドローイングは、たしか更新されたものかな。この大工は毎日10〜15枚のドローイングを起こします。ドローイングの良いところは、これを描く習慣をつけておくと、プロジェクトの進捗状況に敏感になれることです。つまり、適宜微調整を加えることができる。すでにフィックスされたものにさらに手を加えて、予定していたプロポーションやディテールを改良することだってできる。こうしたスケッチブックを描きためていけば、実施図面の代わりにもなるし、設計図書にもなります。

EV 記録にして資料でもある、と。そうしてこの記録をヒントに、適宜調整を加えていくのですね。

BJ ええ、それどころか、これは議論の記録でもあるし、建物の進化の軌跡でもあります。このドローイングを残しておけば、過去の議論を再構成したり、判断の決め手となったスケッチに立ち戻ったり、変更の過程を思い出したりできるんです。

EV すばらしい。そのスケッチブックがすべてを物語り、ひらめきを与えるわけですね。

BJ それにね、スケッチブックを見れば、その住宅や建物の建設過程を辿ることもできます。プロジェクトの辿った時間と道筋の記録でもある。

EV ドローイングだけで1冊の本ができてしまうんですね。ひとつの建物、ひとつのプロジェクト、そしてアイデアの展開にまつわる本が。

BJ そう、スケッチブックのおかげで。たとえばこのプロジェクト「コッパー・ハウスⅡ」ひとつをとっても、12〜15冊くらいになります。アイデアも議論も会話もディテールも一切合切記録してあ

replaced by olive trees maybe in Greece. So it is not the mango itself but the quality of what this condition creates, and being under this insight, under this environment. That becomes one of the bases to initiate the conversation, which conjures up images in everyone that are particular to themselves. Conversation then is the sharing of these images or experiences, or the sharing of these atmospheres and how they are then expressed, whether it is through sketches or drawings, a gesture, a photograph or through storytelling. This will then connect them to their own experiences, their memories and their possibilities.

Another way could be a physical construction, a physical object can also be the start of a discussion. To talk about the material, to understand what the material can do or how it can be expressed, this is something that the carpenters are extremely familiar with – they have spent most of their lives working with wood. So they bring to the practice, a very intense understanding of making. Again, these are done without drawings. This is all done through memory, and through what has been passed on orally. What is interesting is that there is an ambiguity that allows for interpretation – an appropriate interpretation that is relevant to the situation that we are dealing with at that moment. It then becomes responsive to a certain point in time. The conversation can start from just a piece of timber, from the process of cutting it, planing it, and giving it shape and form; something can be conceived.

EV There is no step one?

BJ No, it is a non-linear route and an open narrative. But it also has its difficulties because there can be misunderstandings in those interpretations. So what is key and requires a lot of internal energy is to remain attentive to communication, and to sharing. I think the most critical part for our studio to be successful, is to remain open to sharing, in a sense what a community would do. It is this constant idea of transparency that is critical to our practice.

EV When you say transparency it is not the object itself, but the spirit of the person and how the person feels, how they think, how they work. Is there an issue of rapport and proper action in order to have this group of individuals?

BJ Yes, I think it is important because architecture is not a singular act. It requires a collective participation of several people depending on size and scale, no different from farming.

EV Being sensitive to working with the timing, in how they feel.

BJ There is a consideration that needs to be taken into account in the making of these things. I think architecture is about considering what is going to occur in a particular place and holding it in a way that supports the actions of the occupant through the occupancy.

EV Right, that is to begin to unfold…

BJ If this consideration is central to the making, then I think it naturally weaves itself; we can invite it into the spirit of that place. So yes, I think we are often surprised by the outcome of the project. For me what is exciting is not fully knowing the final shape, but having a sense for it. This sense is the most exciting part because you do not quite know what to anticipate.

EV Sometimes we may anticipate a variety of conditions, and then something totally unseen before may happen.

BJ For me, that is the important part. Our intent and what is central to the idea is to maintain a certain quality of unpredictability, and I think that is what we do not like. But this is what activates life. Life is unpredictable in every which way, and so when we say that it needs to contain life, it needs to contain unpredictability, as one of many things. I like this idea of "vulnerability" in architecture because it humanizes it.

EV What is this in front of you? Are they drawings or sketches?

BJ These are drawings of the carpenters. Most of the people working in the studio maintain a sketchbook. I think in this case, the carpenter has taken it to another level. He produces ten to fifteen of these drawings every day. Also what is important is that it is a way to remain alert and attentive while the projects are being made: it gives enough space to make small adjustments at a very specific point in time. To take it further than where it had been fixed: for it to be pushed to the limit in terms of proportion, or a detail that might have been overseen. These are sketchbooks that we maintain and in many ways are our working drawings and make up a drawing set.

EV So it is a record and documentation, and through the documentation one is able to see things and then they make

ります。

EV どの本も赤い表紙に統一されていますが、これにはなにか理由があるのでしょうか？

BJ これはインドではよくあるタイプの布表紙です。帳簿にも台帳にもぜんぶこの廉価な赤い布表紙が使われています。丈夫で汎用性があるので、昔から使われてきたんでしょう。遡ること——懐古趣味はありませんが——数百年かな。本の表紙は赤、と決まっていました。だからそれに倣っただけのこと。スタジオ・ムンバイには専用のゴム印もあります。インドでは公式文書にはゴム印がつきものなんです。パスポートにもなんにでも。

EV スタジオ・ムンバイは、実に自在な発想で建築をつくっていますけど、それもこの職場環境だからこそできることなんでしょうね。

BJ ご明察。ポイントは、どこででも成立しうる普遍的な環境があること、かたやここでしかできない仕事をすること、です。その兼ね合いですね。いろいろなものの寄せ集めでありながら、特定の時と場所に応じること。帯域幅って言葉があるでしょう？　面白いことに、帯域幅がその物理的な限界を超えることもあるし、かたやその限界にも揺らぎがあるんです。

EV なぜ建築の道に進まれたのですか。なぜまた建築を？

BJ ずるい質問だなぁ（笑）。うちの家族は皆医者なんです。それで、自分は医者にだけはなるまいと思った。そうなっても仕方ありませんね。さて、卒業後は選択肢がふたつありました。9歳から始めて18歳までの間は、遠泳の代表選手として国際大会にも出場していました。それが今の自分とどう関係があるのだろう？　関係があるような、ないような。そうですねぇ、なぜ建築の道に入ったのか。
思えば昔から、空間に惹かれるというか、興味はありました。1972年に、家族で北インドにドライブ旅行に出かけたんです。チャンディガールが完成したころです。毎年夏になると家族（両親と弟）でヴァンに乗り込んで2か月ばかり全国各地をまわりました。チャンディガールは、たしか広いプロムナードを下っていった先にあった——コンクリート・スラブがどかんとあって、オープン・スペースがあって、そして目の前にあの巨大な建物が現れた。車を外に停めて、さあこれからル・コルビュジエの議事堂を見物しようという時でした。幼い私は車から出たくないといってべそをかき、結局、皆ですごすごと引き揚げました。なにしろ、あんなに巨大なものは見たことがなかったんです。いまでもあの日のことは鮮明に憶えています、あれはちょうど昼前でした。もちろん（当時7歳の私は）ル・コルビュジエなんて知りません。それでも強烈な体験については憶えているものです。やはり4歳のときに、アウランガーバードのアジャンタの石窟寺院を訪れました。あそこの階段も空間も、今でもこの目にありありと浮かびます。
さて、医者になりたくなければ、海洋生物学者はどうだろうとも思いましたが、当時のインドにはその分野の教育環境がまだ整っていませんでした。建築も好きでしたが、ただ漠然と、本能的にそう思っていただけでした。だから勘ですね、建築の道に入ったのは。建築学部に入って1週間と経たないうちに、世の中にこんなに面白い学問があったのか、と思ったものです。それでなんの疑いもなく、もちろん深く考えもせずに、この道に進んでしまったのです。医者並みに、懸命になって勉強しましたよ。

EV 医者より大変かもしれませんね。

BJ ええ、医者よりずっと大変だったりします。昔はあまり深入りしないようにしたものですが、最近はむしろ自ら進んで深みにはまっていきます。

石窟寺院　Cave temple

EV 建築の道に入る際に、誰かの言葉がそれを後押ししたということはありませんか。特に影響を受けた人物はいませんか。

BJ ヴァヌ・G・ブータ[*1]は建築家としてはあまり有名ではありませんが、私は彼に間接的に影響を受けました。昔よく泊まりに出かけた建物があって、それは製薬会社のゲストハウスなんですが、心臓外科医だった伯父がこの会社に勤めていたので、夏になると私たちはその伯父一家を訪ねたんです。私は、1960年代か70年代ごろに建てられたこのゲストハウスに泊まるのを毎年心待ちにしたものです。あそこには一種独特なもの——そこを抜ける空気といい、丁寧なつくりといい——があった。設計者の名前を知ったのは、だいぶ後になってからのことです。代表作の「ガン

adjustments where they need to be fixed?

BJ Yes, but it is also a record of discussions that have occurred, and the evolution of parts of a building, or the building itself. And by looking at these drawings, one can go back and reconstruct in many ways the discussions that took place, how decisions were made from a particular sketch, and the evolution of that change.

EV It is wonderful, because the book itself tells a story, and is the unfolding of certain ideas.

BJ Yes, and it is interesting because you can trace the construction of the house or the building in the sketchbooks. It is an archive of the time and the evolution of the project itself.

EV So then one book can be made from all of these drawings: maybe one building, one project and then the evolution of the idea.

BJ Yes, through these sketchbooks. For this particular project (Copper House II) we have between twelve and fifteen books, that contain all the ideas, discussions, dialogues, details… They are all embedded in these books.

EV All the books all have red covers. Is there a particular reason?

BJ This is a very generic cloth that you see commonly used in India; all accounting books and ledgers are covered in this very inexpensive red fabric. It is quite robust and has been around for years. This goes back – I do not want to sound nostalgic – but several hundred years. Books would be covered in red. So we have adopted the same idea. Studio Mumbai has a rubber stamp, and in India, everything is rubber stamped, to make it official: your passport, everything.

EV In many ways, Studio Mumbai has all these universal ideas about making architecture, but at the same time I think that it is also very specific to the conditions in which you work.

BJ I think that is key. One is a universal condition that can be applicable anywhere, but it is also important to locate oneself very particularly. It can be a hybrid; something that is a collection of many things, but it also needs to be responsive to place and time.

We are very much interested in that idea of a bandwidth that can exceed its own physical limitations, but it is also appropriate that these limitations are allowed to oscillate.

EV Why did you decide to do architecture? Why architecture?

BJ That is not a fair question (laughs). In my family everybody was a doctor, and what I definitely did not want to do was become a doctor. So I think it was a natural selection. When I graduated I had two choices. I used to swim professionally, and from the age of nine to eighteen I did a lot of long-distance marathon swimming for the country. But how does that connect to what I am doing today? There is and there is not a connection. I will try to answer this question about how I came into architecture.

Now when I look back, I had an affinity or an inclination towards space. It is an interesting story. In 1972 I traveled with my family in our car to the North. Chandigarh had just been completed, and every summer my family (my brother and my parents) would get into the van and travel for two months experiencing different parts the country. Visiting Chandigarh, I remember we drove down a big promenade –with large slabs of concrete, the open space, and then this very large building up front. I remember the car being parked outside; we were going to visit Le Corbusier's parliament building. I refused to get out of the car, and I started crying until I finally had to be driven away. I had never experienced that scale. I distinctly remember that, it was just before mid-day, naturally I did not know (I was seven years old at that time) Le Corbusier, but what is interesting is that I remember very particular experiences. Similarly at the age of four, I visited the Ajanta Caves in Aurangabad, a cave temple and monastery. I can vividly visualize all the conditions – the steps, the space…

What I am trying to get at is that I knew I did not want to be a doctor, I thought maybe I would explore being a marine biologist, but we did not have an infrastructure in India at that time to support this kind of education. I liked architecture, but not in a formal way, and it seemed to be an instinctive choice. So I think that is what lead me to architecture. Within a week of joining architecture school it was the best thing I had experienced in its method of learning, at that point, it just seemed a natural choice and I have not thought about it any further. It is something that one does with as much rigour as practicing medicine.

EV More than a doctor maybe?

ディ・サマディ」は、ブータがコンペで勝ち取ったものです。しかしこの有名な慰霊碑の後、彼はあまり実作を残していません。ともあれこの建物こそ、私に建築体験を与え、ブータのこだわりを物語るものであった —— 彼はいろんな意味で時代の先を行っていたように思います。

スリランカのジェフリー・バワ[*2]もそうです。彼は庭のロマンティシズム、庭と建物の関係に従って、建物が主役か、それともそれを取り囲むものが主役かというように、物事の優先順位を決めていった。東南アジア地域の風景は独特ですから。

EV 内が外で、外が内で……。

BJ 風景や樹木に圧倒的な存在感があるので、モンスーン地方に行ったりすると樹木の伸びる音まで聞こえてきます。それだけにヴァヌ・G・ブータのつくる建築は、地味ではあるけれども、とても貴重な体験をさせてくれました。

ヴァヌ・G・ブータ設計のゲストハウス　Guest house by Vanu G. Bhuta

EV 建築をつくろう、あるいは建築の道へ進もうと思ったきっかけが、そうした個人的体験にあったとおっしゃるときに、たとえば子どものときに見たチャンディガールの話といい、今おっしゃった、家の中にいると空気が違った、空気が通り抜けていった……という話といい、聞いているこちらにも、その通り抜ける空気が肌で感じられ、戸外の景色が目に見えるようです。

BJ なるほどね。ところで、人間の記憶はどこにしまってあるのでしょうか。ここ、と決まってもいないし、だいいち記憶がどこにあるかなんて知る必要もない。むしろそれがどこかにあるというだけで十分なんです。私はね、絵画、音楽、詩、数学などに興味がありますけど、そのひとつひとつには専用の場所があって、起源もある。その起源はばらばらですが、いずれも必ずどこかにあるはずで、無から生じたわけではない。同様に、今ここでかたちについて話しているうちに、建築のアイデアがひらめいたりします。そこで本来なら漠然としたものでしかない空間について、私は説明をすることになります。でも相手はその空間を、己の体験を通してしか理解できません —— だから体験が重要になってくるんです。

さて、ジェフリー・バワの作品ですが、こちらもすばらしかった。ほんの短い時間とはいえ運よく本人に会うこともできたし、なによりそのタイミングが絶妙でした。スリランカを訪れたのは1996年のことで、バワの作品については予備知識もありました。彼の空間づくりの仕方というのがこれまた独特でした。なんというか、力みがないんです。空間の位置も構えもさらさらっと決めているような感じで……。ちょうど武術や柔道・柔術の型に無理がないのと似ています。しっかり構えて、相手の動きから目を離さないのに、動きは滑らか。そのほうが身体は動く。

EV 最小限のエネルギーで、最大限の効果を上げる……。

BJ 最小限のエネルギー。まさしく。そこに —— エネルギーの少なさに —— 感銘を受けたわけです。私が駆け出しの頃に担当したプロジェクトというのが、やたらとディテールに凝っていて、もう目を覆いたくなるような代物でした。あの手のものとは金輪際関わるものか、と心に決めたものです。あんな思いは二度としたくありませんね。勉強にはなりましたけど。

ところでジェフリー・バワに話を戻すと、1996年にスリランカを訪れた私たちは、彼の建てたとある住宅（現在はホテル）に泊まりました。嬉しいことに、そこへ翌朝バワ当人が現れたので、こちらから挨拶をしました。私の義姉が、ニューデリーの自宅の設計をバワに頼んだという縁もありましたしね。さてそのバワが自動車を降りると、そこにたまたま門柱が2本立っていました。それは彼が30年前にルヌガンガに建てたプロジェクトだったのですが、そこにこの新しい門が付け加えられていたんです。彼は私に聞いてきました「どう思う？　このプロポーションでいいのかな」。「私は〇〇と申します」「初めまして」のあと、まだ二言三言しか言葉を交わしていないのに。この不意打ちに、私はすっかり当惑してしまって、なにも答えられず —— せいぜいしどろもどろに答えたか、肩をすくめたか。でもこの体験は衝撃的でした。いきなり自分の見解を求められたのですから。結局自分の意見は述べなかったけれど、あの瞬間のことは深く心に刻まれました。

その晩、彼はお茶菓子を用意して私たちをルヌガンガの自宅に招いてくれました。同行した友人たちは、建築にはまったく不案内な人間ばかりでしたが、その彼らでさえこの美しい作品については、なめらかなつながりだの、空間がどうの、ディテールがどうの、と言っていましたっけ。なるほど門外漢の人間の目にも、この建物はそう映るのか —— この建物には、彼らにもちゃんと伝わるだけの普遍性がある、と思ったものです。いっぽう私は、間取りも

BJ Yes, sometimes much more than a doctor. It is interesting what I was trying to move away from is the very intensity, which I currently enjoy.

EV In this beckoning into architecture, is there also a dialogue with the people that interested you first of all? Were there a few people that were influential to you?

BJ Vanu G. Bhuta[*1] is not very well known, but I think he was influential to me very indirectly. There is a building that we would go and stay in, a guesthouse for a pharmaceutical company. My uncle was a doctor (a heart specialist), with this company and we would go to visit them in the summer. I would particularly want to stay in this guesthouse, which I think was built in the late 60's or 70's. There was something about it – just the air that moved through it, the quality of its making… – that made me look forward to visiting it every year. It was much later that I found out who had actually built it. One of the important projects that he did was the Gandhi Samadhi, a competition that he had won. It is well known, however he did not build a lot after that. This particular building, very much in the way that I experience architecture, shows the influence of the things that were of importance to him – and I think that in many ways he was ahead of his time.
Another person like that is Geoffrey Bawa[*2] in Sri Lanka. With the romanticism of the garden and its relationship to the building, he questioned which one is more critical, the building or what envelops it, because the presence of the landscape is very particular in this Southeast Asian region.

EV Inside is actually outside, outside is actually inside…

BJ There is a great presence of the landscape, the trees, and you actually hear the growth, especially in the monsoon. So, Vanu G. Bhuta in a very quiet way was important in terms of the experiences that I had through the architecture that he made.

EV When you talk about these personal experiences as the driving forces in you making architecture and making the choice of architecture: For example, the childhood experience in Chandigarh, and then even now the experiences that you have mentioned: You in the house, in terms of the quality of the air, the flow of the air… It is something that one can almost feel, with the air passing through and having the outside environment so immediate?

BJ I think that is an interesting question. Where do memories lie? It does not have to be specific; we do not need to know where they actually lie, but the fact that they actually exist is important. For me the interest is that paintings, music, poetry, mathematics; have a place, and an origin. That origin can also be independent, but it has to be physically located somewhere; it cannot exist in a vacuum. So in the same way, what we are talking about shapes and informs these ideas of architecture specifically to me. I have to claim space, which is otherwise endless and vast. This is important, but I can also only understand it through my own experiences – that becomes critical.
I have enjoyed Geoffrey Bawa's work. I had the good fortune of being able to meet with him, briefly, but it was a very important point in time. We were in Sri Lanka, in 1996. I had seen and studied his work already, and there was something very particular in the way that he made his spaces. There was an ease I would say; the position and the posture it took seemed effortless… If you look at martial arts and forms of Judo and Jujutsu, it is all about effortlessness; taking a position, paying attention, but being relaxed. You are able to move.

EV Move in the most optimal way with the minimum energy…

BJ Minimum energy. Exactly. And for me that is extremely important – the amount of energy expended. I did projects initially where the details were made in such a way that it used to pain me to see them being built, and I did not want to be part of that, to be the maker or the instigator of this. It was extreme pain that I do not want to experience again, and it was a learning process for me.
Coming back to Geoffrey Bawa, in 1996 we were in Sri Lanka, staying in one of the homes he had built; now a hotel. To my good fortune, he happened to be visiting it that morning, so I introduced myself. He had designed a house for my sister-in-law, which was to be built in New Delhi, and we made a connection. Just randomly, he got out of the car and there were these two gateposts. He had built this project 30 years ago in Lunuganga, but there was a new gate that had been built. So he asked me, "What do you think? Do you think it is the right proportion?" This is four sentences after saying, "I am so-and-so", and "Hello." I was perplexed because I was caught unaware. I did not answer the question – I grunted maybe, or gestured in a non-committal way – but that experience stuck with me. There I was, put into the situation of taking a position. I did not take a position, but for me,

ジェフリー・バワの自邸　Geoffrey Bawa's own house

木立の風景もすべて頭に入っているつもりでしたが、しかし現物は想像以上に良かったです。

EV　想像力を働かせる余地が残っていたんですね。

BJ　もうひとつ、バワの発言で印象的だったのは、風景の見せ方をたえず意識し続けること、そしてそれは終わりのない仕事だ、というものです。当時の私にはぴんときませんでした。日々そこに注意を払って──微妙な変化をとらえ、どの枝を下ろし、木のどの面を見せるか、といったことを決めていく。それは一生涯かけて行うプロセスなんです。

EV　プロセスそのものですね。

BJ　その考えと言葉を、しかと胸に刻みました。この歳になってようやく彼の言わんとしていたことがわかるような気がします。彼とはほんの短い時間しか接していませんが、その数分間に実に多くのことを学びました。時間の長短は関係ない。たったひとつかふたつの事柄が、その人の思想を左右することもあるんです。ただしその効果が現れるのは15年先のことかもしれない──「その瞬間」がいつ訪れるのかはわかりません。それが私のいう物事の「潜在能力」です。ずっと眠っていたものが、あるときふとその能力を発揮する、というように。
ルイス・バラガンの抽象的な作品も好きですね。彼の表現の源泉は、きっとメキシコの広大な大地の風景や環境にある。いっぽうインド国内のアノニマスな作品もたくさん見てきました。その雑然とした風景も……。

EV　住宅のタイポロジーには昔から関心がおありとのことですが、アノニマスな住宅の良さとは？

BJ　住宅は、私たちにとっては外すことのできない研究テーマです。だからアノニマスな建築はたびたび取り上げます。アノニマスというのは否定的な意味ではなく、作者が誰かわからないというだけ──どのプロジェクトにも当然つくり手はいるはずですから。インド国内の建物の半数以上が、非正規に建てられています。そのインドの人口は12億人。国土の景観の大半がそのようにしてつくられている。この雑然とした風景にはね、あなどれないものがあるんです。なにしろ経済状態が悪かろうが資源が限られていようが、それを素直に受け止め本能的につくった風景ですから。どんな与件にも几帳面に応えていく私たちにとって、こうした市井のプロジェクトは、物の考え方や見方を教えてくれるものなのです。そうしたものをヒントに、私たちは進行中のプロジェクトについての判断を下していく。だって現物があるということは、すでにモックアップが用意されたも同然ですからね。

EV　見るのも経験のうち。

BJ　そう、プロポーションとか、そのつくり方とか、寸法とか……。実際に見たり体験したりすることで、現状からなにかを学び、そこから自分たちのしていること、あるいはこれからすることを理解するのです。

たとえば街中には石造りの大型建築があるでしょう。インドには、謹厳で真面目な建築文化もあるんです。地中には、私たちには計り知れないいろんな事情が隠されている──そういう建物はたいてい空に向かって伸びています。私が影響を受けたものは実にさまざまで、特定のなにかというわけではありません。レム・コールハースにせよペーター・ツムトーにせよ、どちらが良い悪いではなく、世の中の人がそれをどう見ているか、なにを見ているのか、なぜ見ているのかが気になるんです。あるいは、いったいなにが彼らをそうさせたのか、と考えてみたりする。そこから得るものは必ずあります。彼らの目を通して初めて見えてくるものもある。彼

ジェフリー・バワの自邸　Geoffrey Bawa's own house

it was extremely important. That moment is something that I will never forget.

Later on in the evening he invited us to his home, Lunuganga, for tea and cakes. I was with friends that had nothing to do with architecture and we were sharing this beautiful project that he had built. They made comments on the quality of seamlessness, the space, the details… It was interesting to see it from a non-professional point of view – how universal the condition was that they could respond in such a particular way. I had seen the plans and I knew the trees, but it is interesting that everything you thought you knew, or anticipated, was even better.

EV It left room for your own imagination.

BJ Another comment that Bawa made was that it is a relationship of maintaining the idea of a view of the landscape, and that it is a work-in-progress. I did not understand at the time. The participation is every day – you see nuances, how to prune a branch, what a tree opens up to, so on and so forth. It is a process that is a commitment to a lifetime's interaction.

EV It is a process itself.

BJ I registered that thought and comment but only now can I see what he was talking about. Although the encounter was very brief, it has filled me in many more ways than those few minutes that we spent together. I think these are very important because sometimes it is not about the amount of time spent but about one or two things that could become critical in the way you think. It could happen fifteen years later – you do not know when the right moment will occur. So I use this word, "latent potential" in things, where they lie quietly and there comes a point in time when there is the possibility for an appropriate response that is unexpected.

I have enjoyed Luis Barragan very much in his abstraction. Where his formulation must have occurred, where it was coming from, through the landscape and environment, and his greater topography. Simultaneously, I have enjoyed a lot of the anonymous work that we see in India. One is the informal landscape…

EV You mentioned that you were always interested in house typology. It is interesting to see what anonymous houses can offer.

BJ Yes, that has been very important in our studies. We continuously use these anonymous pieces of architecture. I say anonymous not in a negative way, but that you do not know the maker – there is clearly a maker in the production of these projects. More than fifty percent of India is informally built. We are living in a country of a billion two hundred million people. The vast majority of the landscape is built in this way. My interest and curiosity is also in this informal landscape because there is an intuitive response and an honesty as a result of economics and limited resources. We respond very precisely to the conditions that we need to meet. These projects are very particular in shaping our thinking and the way we look at things. We use them to understand the projects that we are making because they also physically exist, and we are able to use them as mock-ups.

EV Seeing becomes an experience.

BJ Yes the proportions, the way they are made, the dimensions of structure… We can learn from these existing conditions using what we see and experience as a way to understand what we are doing, or are going to do.

Take for example some of the bigger projects in a city, one that is built mainly of stone. Here my interest lies in the fact that we have this very rigorous, intense culture of building, which is inclusive of many conditions that far exceed our limitations to see under the ground – usually, they extend themselves to the sky. I am influenced by many things it is not one specific thing. From Rem Koolhaas, to Peter Zumthor, and it is not that one is better than the other it is about how everyone sees, what they see, and why they see it. It is important to ask what it is that motivates them to do the things that they do. I think in that, there is learning, and in there lies the potential to see through their eyes. It is all about agreeing or disagreeing, good or bad. How do you take from that, and make parts of it your own.

EV Make it always your own as a proposition.

BJ It makes it that much more full. While they might seem to be in conflict, they can actually work together. To give you an idea that the influences are several, Laurie Baker[*3] is another one. I am inspired by his commitment, because it was to build for the poorest section of society in India. He developed an architecture that addressed very specifically their conditions, and the shape of that architecture was derived from the central idea of housing

らに同意したり、しなかったり、彼らが参考になったり、ならなかったり。そこから自分の血となり肉となるものを吸収していくのです。

EV　なんでも自分自身の問題としてとらえてみる。

BJ　自分の栄養分としていくわけです。互いに相容れないものだって、大丈夫です。影響を受けた人物といえばもうひとり、ローリー・ベイカー*3がいます。彼の献身ぶりに感銘を受けましてね。なにしろインドの最貧困層のために建てたんですから。彼は貧困層の境遇を本気で改善するつもりで建築をつくった。どうしたらお金をかけずにこの貧困層に住まいをあてがうことができるか、その一心で彼はつくったんです。

EV　テーマが具体的ですね。

BJ　非常に具体的。しかもそれに真剣に取り組んだ。

EV　実現に向けて。

BJ　そして実現させたんですよ。そこが彼の偉大なところであり、彼のプロジェクトの理念でもあります。その理念を貫くためならなんでもする。「ローリー・ベイカー・スタイル」を目指すのではなく、まずは思想ありき、そしてその思想があらゆることの根拠にもなる。材料もずばり漆喰と煉瓦だけなので、安上がりです。目的は、質と価値の高い建物を極力廉価に建てること。それにはまず居住機能を満たし、シェルターとなる場所を提供し、さらにそれを家らしくすることだったのです。

EV　おかげで彼らは自分たちの空間をもつことができた。

BJ　そう。

EV　記憶と生きるための？

BJ　ああ、それは建築のとても重要な役割ですね。単なるシェルター以上のものにならないといけません。

EV　それで思い出しましたが、恩師のロバート・マングリアン教授*4のおかげで、世界観が変わったとか。

BJ　観察と探求のことですね。たとえば目の前にあるものでも、その本質は肉眼には見えません。そういえばあの頃から徐々に物の見方が変わり──ある物を別のなにかに見立てるのではなく、それがいったいなんであるかを見抜けるようになっていった。仮に植物を輪切りにして、その断面を顕微鏡で覗いても本質は見えてきません。たしかに肉眼にはそう見えますが、輪切りにした段階で、もうそれは抽象化なんです。私たちは科学者ではありませんから。観察には精度が求められます。物事の本質を見極める能力とは、いわば観察力のことです。つまり、なにをどう見るか、見た結果をどう処理するか、観察からなにが言えるか。あるいは、観察からなにを取捨選択して、それをプロジェクトに反映させるか。眼力ですね。見るということは、好奇心があるということでもある。好奇心がなければ「いったいこれはなんのために存在するのか」、「これはどんな位置づけにあるのか」、「妥当性はあるのか」といった疑問も湧きません。

EV　子どもの目線で世界を見る。

BJ　そういうことです。子どもの、というのは、先入観がないという意味です。先入観は、物を見る際に邪魔になる。子どもというのは無垢で、なにかに対して評価を下したりしません。その時分ならふつう、感情と体験に基づいて物事を観察します。見たままに反応する、つまり素直なんです。どうしたら先入観抜きに物を見ることができるでしょう？

EV　一歩引いて見る……。

BJ　でもどうやって？　プロセスとはなにか、どうしたら人は前に進むことができるのか。プロセスは実践とセットになっている。模型をつくるのでもいいし、図面を引いたり、本を読んだり、映画を観るのでもいい……、それだって建築家にとっては実践のうちです。医者だって、似たようなことをしながら医者としての洞察力を養っていくわけです。

EV　正しい診断を下し、正しい予後を立てるために。

BJ　そう、しかもそれをさらりとやってのける。そういうことをロバート・マングリアンの下で学んだわけです。模型づくりもそうです。どの材料が模型向きかを知っていれば、模型表現がうまくなります。スタジオでの模型制作も、マングリアンの教えの延長にあります。

EV　ほかには誰から影響を？

BJ　ルイス・カーンには、間接的にも直接的にも絶大な影響を受けています。実は私、建築の勉強を始める前に「IIMA」（アーメダバードのインド経営大学）を訪れているんです。あれは一時代を画した名作で、そのときの私もなんだかわからないけれど、え

them in a way that was extremely frugal.

EV So there is a specific question.

BJ A very specific question, and he worked with it.

EV In actualizing it.

BJ He actualized that. I think that is what is important and is the concept of the project. Everything is done to support that concept. It is not about the "Laurie Baker style". It is about the idea itself and why it is done that way. It is very specific, made of plaster and brick; so very inexpensive .The idea was to build dignified, quality buildings in an extremely economical way that addressed: one, their function to live, and a place for shelter, but also beyond the place for shelter, to become something much more pertinent.

EV It actually allowed them a space of their own.

BJ Yes.

EV The living of memories?

BJ Yes, I think that is a very important role that architecture has to play. It has to go beyond the potential of just shelter itself.

EV When you talk about this way of working, you mentioned one of your professors, Robert Mangurian.[*4] How did he influence the way you look at the world?

BJ I think observation and seeking, because many times what is physically in front of oneself is not necessarily the nature of its manifestation. I think it was the early part of being within something that I observed – the ability to see things precisely for what they are, not to imagine them to be something that they are not, like cutting a section of a plant and looking at it under the microscope. It is what you actually see, because there is an abstraction when you make that sectional cut; much like a scientist, the observation needs to be very precise in what one sees. I think the ability to have an insight, is like the art of observation. It is based on how one sees, how we process what we see, and how you claim the observation that is made; or one then appropriates the observation that is made into the intervention of the project. It is important to have the ability to see. Seeing also means curiosity, without which, questions such as "why do they exist?" and "what is its position," "It's appropriateness".

EV Seeing the world like a child.

BJ Yes. When we say child-like, it is because it lacks prejudice, and I think prejudice is what prevents us from seeing things. This child like quality has a certain openness that does not make judgment. It makes an observation based on an emotion and a physical experience that is precise at that point in time. It is responding to what it is, and there is an honesty in that response. How does one see without prejudice?

EV Being able to step back and look at it…

BJ But how do you do it? What is the process and the means by which one is able to move? That comes with practice. Whether it is making a model, a drawing, reading or seeing a film… these are all parts of the practice of an architect. A doctor would do similar things that give him insight into what he or she does as a professional.

EV In order to make a good diagnosis and write a good prognosis.

BJ Yes exactly, and they do it in the simplest way . I think that is what I learned by being with Robert Mangurian. Even making models. Knowing what is the appropriate material for the model; in order to express it best. The models that we make are a continuity of what I learned from him.

EV Who else are influential to you?

BJ Another extremely important influence has been Louis Kahn, indirectly and directly. It is interesting because I visited IIMA (the Indian Institute of Management Ahmedabad) before I began studying to be an architect. It was a seminal piece, and it did something to me. I could not explain precisely what it was at that time, but now I have visited the building several times. One of the important things was the sense of weight and grounding, sort of earth-bound. The idea of gravity in those projects – you can feel the sense of weight, but also simultaneously it is not a limitation. It

らく興奮したものです。あれから何度か訪れるうちに、気づきました。あの建物の偉大さは、その重量感、まるで大地から生えてきたかのような接地の仕方にあるんです。重力の扱いが——重さを感じさせるのに、それが制約になっていない。そういう次元を超越してしまっている、それがこの作品には特に顕著です。

ここからは廃墟の話をします。建物が過去と現在と未来の間を揺れ動く、それが廃墟です。これはごく最近になって——この1年半前あたりから——気づいたことですが、建物というのは、すでに起こった出来事と、これから起こることと、今起きていることの間を揺れ動いている。逆にいえば、この3つの時間の間を建築が行き来できるだけの余地が残されている。ある意味では時間をずらすということでもあります。建物は、作者の肉体的限界を超えて存在し続けるでしょう？ そんなわけで、私にとってルイス・カーンは特別な存在です。彼にはこうした無時間性を自在に表現できたし、時間を超越した建築がつくれた。

EV では、スタジオ・ムンバイも変わりつつあるのですね。ここで今、あたり前のように見えているものも、以前はそうではなかったかもしれませんね。ところでご自身にとっては、今なにがいちばん面白いですか。

ルイス・カーン設計のIIMA　IIMA by Louis I. Kahn

BJ いい質問ですね。進化することと予測不能性を信条にしているからには、私たちは1か所に留まり続けるわけにはいきません。それが事務所の、また集団としての方針なのです。変化から道が開けることもある。よって事務所の再編成も避けられません。インドの成長率は年間8〜9％の値に達しています。この時勢に後れをとらないためにも、私たちも議論を通じて変わっていかなければならない。たとえば私たちの仕事の仕方も、数年前と今とでは同じではありません。もう以前のやり方には戻れないでしょうね。適応していかなければならないから。この私も、言うべきことはもっとはっきり言わないといけない。変化と成長の必要性を伝えるためにも。ところでインドの伝統は、この仕事にも色濃く表れています。といっても古き良き伝統でも有形の伝統でもなく、むしろ次世代に伝えるべき方法論とか先人の知恵です。ただしこちらには迷信がつきまとう。だからそれを振り払うためにも、新たに橋を架け渡すことを考えなくてはいけない。私たちは、方法論を体系化しつつ、かたや世界と足並みをそろえるためにも事務所を発展させていかなければなりません。だから自分たちなりの方法で、相互に協調できるような今どきの組織をつくるつもりです。自分たちなりにというのは、まだ私たちは昨今の変化やコミュニケーションのスピードにはついていけない——そのための機器や体制が整っていない——からです。これからは、このふたつを両立させ、補完し合うようにしていかなくてはなりません。それが今後のスタジオの課題です。もうひとつは、これを徹底的に推し進めていって、物理的環境の限界を乗り越えるということです。よくよく考えると、スタジオの壁の外でも、国内にはこれだけ豊富な職人技術や工法がそろっている。では、それをどう活用するか。うちの事務所には、それ相応の実績があるし、おまけにそうした伝統の中で育った人間が15〜16名もいる。その彼らは先人の知恵を継承しているだけでなく、ここに来てからまた別のものを身につけている。だったら物理的な境界を取り払って、外部にあるものを取り込んでいくべきでしょう。インドの近代化に比べれば、私たちなんておよそ非力な存在です。この近代化についていくには、壁を取り払うしかない。閉じこもっていてはだめなんです。それがこれからの課題になってくるし、もちろんそのつもりで仕事を請けています。実際に前々からその予行演習のようなものはしてきています。たとえばヒマラヤ山脈の「レティ360リゾート」プロジェクトは、規模は小さいけれども、地元の人たちと一緒に手がけました。この両者の組み合わせが功を奏しました。おそるおそる試した実験のようなものですけどね。問題は、どうしたらもっと規模を拡大できるか、どうしたらほかでも展開できるかということです。

EV スケールは変わってくるでしょうし、むしろ大きくなるでしょうね。それにコンテクストも変わってくるでしょうし。

BJ たぶんね。要はコミュニケーションの問題です。あとは実作勝負です。過去の実作をツールなり見本にして、今回はどんなプロジェクトになっていくかを伝える。いかに相手の好奇心に火を点けるか、いかにこちらに共感してもらえるか。時間はかかりましたが、興味のない人を無理に誘っても仕方ありません。だから、そのための仕掛けをしておく必要があります。模型やモックアップを使えば、話は早い。相手はそれを自分の目で見て、手で触れ、反応することができるから。模型は、施主にとっても、施工業者にとっても、私自身にも役に立ちます。リアルですからね。

extends beyond this, which is particularly expressed in the work. I am coming to this idea of ruins. Where the buildings oscillate between the past, present, and future. This is something that I have observed very recently – within the last year to year-and-a-half. I am curious to explore the idea of building, where they oscillate between the idea of anticipation and of something that has occurred, might occur, and is occurring now: To position architecture in a space where it can oscillate between these three conditions of time. In a sense you displace time, because it extends beyond the physical limitation of the creator. And so for me, Louis I. Kahn is of extreme importance because I think in many ways he is able to articulate and then achieve this quality of timelessness.

EV In thinking about all these things, we can see that Studio Mumbai is transforming. So that means that there are certain things that we are seeing now, that were maybe not so apparent before. What are you seeing that is interesting for you now?

BJ I think that is an important and a good question. We cannot remain static if evolution and unpredictability remains central to the core of our thinking. As a practice and as a group of people, we have to also move with that idea. Transformation is something that is key. Reconfiguring is imperative to the success of our practice. India's rate of development increases eight to nine percent a year. To be abreast or in parallel, we also need to continuously, through discussion, reconfigure ourselves. For example, the nature or the manner in which we practiced a few years ago, we may not be able to practice in exactly the same way now. We have to make adjustments, and I am going to try to be more specific in what I mean, to better articulate this idea of change and growth. We have traditions that are very much a part of the nature of practice; tradition not in a nostalgic or a physical way, but the methodologies and classic knowledge that are being taken forward. But along with that, come the superstitions. To support this movement, one has to think of other ways to form new bridges. I think part of the practice is to organize a methodology, with the idea of developing in parallel, the practice of an architectural studio that you would see in the rest of the world. We are trying to construct, a mutually integrated practice of architecture as it is produced worldwide along with our method of practice, because the rate of change and communication is something that we are not equipped with yet – we need an armature or framework to support this. Both of these conditions now need to co-exist and support each other. That is something that we will have to bring into the studio. The other is to extend this beyond the limitations of our physical environment. To make the observation that this craftsmanship or this method of building is available in this country by thousands, so they exist outside the envelope of our studio. How do you tap into that? Today we have the years behind us, and we have fifteen or sixteen people who come from that tradition and are now also equipped with other aspects that reinforce this classic knowledge that they have. Part of the responsibility is to extend it beyond our physical boundary and take advantage of what exists externally. The position of modern development in India far exceeds our strength. The only way to keep abreast or in parallel is by extending this idea and opening it up. It cannot remain exclusive to us. I think that is going to be an important part of how we are able to move towards this, and we have accepted projects on that basis. I did a few experiments earlier on, so that we can calibrate precisely how to work in this way. For example, the Leti project in the Himalayas was a small project with a group of local people working along side our group. It was the combination of the two that enabled us to produce that project. It was a controlled environment, an experiment. Now the question is how do you scale that up? How do you further that idea?

EV It will become a different scale now, and you will have even bigger scales. Maybe you will also have different contexts now.

BJ I think it can. It is fundamentally about communication. It is also through the work that we do; using it as a tool or a method to communicate the potential of the project; to instigate and initiate curiosity on the outside, and engage in the same way as we have been. This process has taken its own time but I think what is critical is to engage it with a certain curiosity; hence it is a device that we will have to make up. The models and mock-ups are a very immediate way for people to connect because they are able to visualize, touch, feel, and respond. Whether it is for the client, the person building the project or myself. It becomes real.

EV So you are saying that communication is essential and crucial to this operation going beyond what you have now.

BJ I think so. What I have experienced and seen outside our practice is that a lot of times our projects are remarked upon for their lack of communication. They become compartmentalized.

EV　今以上のことをしようと思ったら、コミュニケーションは絶対に欠かせないということですね。

BJ　そう思います。現に、外部の人たちからはよく、うちのプロジェクトにはコミュニケーションが足りないと言われるんです。作業が縦割りだって。施工業者vs.建築家vs.施主……経済性だけでつくられていると。ごもっとも。経済性も必要だけれど、それが原動力になってしまったら、仕事に対する共感は湧きません。

EV　ある程度選択をしておいて、あとは成り行きに任せる。

BJ　そのとおり。

EV　原寸大のモックアップをつくったのは、そのほうが施主や関係者にご自分の意図が即座に伝わるからですか。

BJ　ええ、そうです。これにはいくつか理由があります。まず、木を1本1本記録していくのは大変な作業です——枝振りとか輪郭とか、木の植わっている間隔まで逐一記録できません。いろいろな要素のある敷地を、仮に縮小模型で再現しようとしたら、スタジオ内での作業だけでもけっこう時間がかかります。いちばん手っ取り早いのは、原寸大のモックアップをつくることです。それなら1週間あれば十分で、現地で原寸大の図面を引いて、その上に木の骨組みを立てて布を張って立体に仕立てていけばいい。木の植わっている間隔も正確に記入できるし。これをコミュニケーション・ツールにすれば、私も含めて皆が会話に加われる。施主だって、これを見ればプロジェクトがおおよそどんなふうになるかを疑似体験できる。ともかく、これは人を会話に引き入れるための仕掛けであり、またある意味では、彼らが互いに口を利かずにはいられない状況をつくるツールでもある。現地にいるのに、この原寸大のモックアップが目に入らないはずがないでしょ？　だからこれが、コミュニケーションや会話や参加のきっかけをつくるツールなんです。

EV　ありがとうございました。最後になりますが、これから建築の世界に足を踏み入れようとしている人たちに、なにかお言葉をお願いします。

BJ　謙虚さ、慎み深さ、そしてなぜと問いかける好奇心を忘れないことかな。でないと——あるいは知識を身につけないと——イマジネーションは湧きません。問いかけること、諦めずに問い続けること。なにごとも根気が必要です。忍耐強くあれ。今の世の中、とかく安易に物事がすんでしまう。でも忍耐強い人は、融通が利くし、耐性もある。したがって帯域幅も増え、そのぶんゆとりができる。ポイントはそこ——そうした資質を培うこと——で、それさえあれば、残りは自然と納まるべきところに納まります。技術や技能も重要ですが、こちらはその気になれば身につけることのできる類のものです。かくいう私も、挫折を繰り返してきました。一歩進んではまた後戻り、の繰り返し。でも学びに終わりはありません。建築学科を卒業したからといって、一人前の建築家にはなれない——建築家への道をようやく歩み始めたばかりですから。この私たちだって、まだ勉強中なんです。学生時代と同じように、本も読まなくてはならないし。終わりのないプロセスなんです。自分はなにもかもを知り尽くしていると思うようになったら、おしまいです。

2011年5月　スタジオ・ムンバイにて

*1. Vanu G. Bhuta, an American-trained Indian architect who won the Government-sponsored competition to create a suitable memorial to Gandhi, the Raj Ghat, 1956-1957, in New Delhi.
ヴァヌ・G・ブータは、米国で建築教育を受けたインド人建築家。政府主催のコンペに勝ったことから、ニューデリーに［マハトマ・］ガンディの慰霊碑「ラージ・ガート」（1956-57）を手がけている。

*2. Geoffery Bawa, (23 July 1919 – 27 May 2003) was a Sri Lankan architect. He is the most renowned architect in Sri Lanka and was among the most influential Asian architects of his generation. He is the principal force behind what is today known globally as 'tropical modernism'.
ジェフリー・バワ（1919年7月23日－2003年5月27日）はスリランカの建築家。スリランカを代表する建築家で、同世代のアジアの建築家に多大な影響を与えた。いまや世界的に広まった「トロピカル・モダニズム」の第一人者。

*3. Laurie Baker, (2 March 1917 – 1 April 2007) was a British-born Indian architect, renowned for his initiatives in sustainable and organic architecture. He obtained Indian citizenship in 1989 and lived in Trivandrum, Kerala, since 1970, where he set up COSTFORD (Centre of Science and Technology for Rural Development), for spreading awareness for low cost housing.
ローリー・ベイカー（1917年3月2日－2007年4月1日）は英国生まれのインドの建築家。環境配慮型の有機的建築の先駆者として知られる。1989年にインド国籍を取得し、1970年以降はケララ州トリヴァンドラムに定住し、同地にCOSTFORD（Centre of Science and Technology for Rural Development：農村開発技術研究所）を設立し、低廉住宅の啓蒙に努めた。

*4. Robert Mangurian, He is a founding member of STUDIO WORKS Architects where he has served as a Principal since 1969. Mr. Mangurian has also served as the Director of the Graduate Program at the Southern California Institute of Architecture from 1987-1997.
ロバート・マングリアン（1994年－）は、スタジオ・ワークス・アーキテクツの設立メンバーであり、1969年以来その代表を務める。1987-97年南カリフォルニア建築大学（SCI-Arc）大学院長。

The contractor versus the architect versus the client… and it is only driven by economics; fair enough, that is also required, but if that becomes the driving force, and there is no empathy towards the work, then it is very difficult.

EV   To make selections and an open set of things to unfold and nurture.

BJ   Yes, Absolutely.

EV   You were building a one-to-one scale mock up so that it was immediate for clients and others involved in the conversation to understand what you were doing in the project.

BJ   Yes, that is right. That decision was taken from several different standpoints. One was that it was very difficult to document a tree – all its branches and its edges, the space between the two trees. It was a shortcut considering the time that it would take to develop a model in the studio given the complexity of the site. We worked out that the most efficient process was to develop a full-scale model mockup. We were able to construct enough within a week's time through physically drawing full-scale on site, and appropriating it in three-dimensions through fabric and wooden frame. In that way we were able to register the spaces between these trees. It became a tool or a means of communication for me and for everybody who was making it, to participate, register and hence have a dialogue. And also for the client, they were then able to experience the potential of what the project would become. It was also done very particularly to draw them into a conversation. It was a tool that in a sense passively ensured that they would interact, because now they could not stand there and be invisible to the physicality of this full-scale mockup. It was an instrument to initiate communication, dialogue, and commitment.

EV   Thank you. Lastly, Can you say words of advice to people who are embarking in this world of architecture?

BJ   I think modesty is important, a sense of humility, of how, and of curiosity. I think they allow for the imagination to flow or to occur – through that process or gaining of knowledge. It is important to question, and in the questioning, to work rigorously. I think that very fundamental is patience. Be patient. We are living in a world where everything is instant. When one sees that there is a vast amount of patience it gives you an elasticity, which creates this idea of tolerance. It opens up the bandwidth that has the ability to hold infinite space. I think these are key – developing and nurturing this quality – because other things will fall into place naturally. Techniques, skills… all of that is meaningful and can be gained, but this is something that we have to nurture consciously. I think that is what I have tried to do and failed several times. You gain and you fail, and you gain and you fail, but the learning is constant. Once you are out of architecture school, it does not qualify you as an architect – it is just the beginning of a process of learning to be an architect. We are still in the process of learning. You have to continue to read, and to do all the things that you did in school. It is a continuous process. The moment you think you know everything, there is a problem.

Studio Mumbai, May 2011

Inspiration
インスピレーション

インド国内を旅してまわる中で私たちがたびたび遭遇したのは、制約のある環境下で空間を機能させるという必要から生まれた、ある特色をもった空間である。限られた空間や資源しか利用できない人びとは、生活の必需を満たすために自発的にそうした空間をつくる。それらは人と人との交流を決して妨げない、慎ましくも自由な空間である。

During our travels in India, we come across conditions where spatial qualities arise out of the need to function in restricted environments. It is a spontaneous act to resolve all basic requirements where available space and resources are limited. These spaces are considerate to human interaction. They are modest and free.

Mosquito Net Colony
Surat, India

蚊帳の集落

地方の村々に暮らす農夫たちは、夏の間だけ日雇労働者として都会へ出稼ぎにやって来る。都市風景のなかで彼らの存在が認められるのは、夜に現れ朝になると消えてしまうこの蚊帳でできた集落のみである。

Farmers from small villages migrate to cities to work as daily-wage labourers in the summer months. Their only physical presence in the urban landscape is these ephemeral mosquito-net colonies, which emerge at night, only to disappear every morning.

026

Collage Housing
Ahmedabad, India

コラージュ・ハウジング

個人の領域が、微妙な色の違いによって互いに区切られ区別されている。廊下などの共用領域ですら、ここは誰々が使うとの線引きがされている。つまり住居の内部が外部に持ち出され、公と私の境界線が引き直されている。

Personal territories are defined and manifested through careful distinction in colours. Even the common areas like corridors are marked for personal use. This brings insides of the dwellings to the outside and the public-private thresholds are re-adjusted.

Gopitalao
Surat, India

ゴピタラオ

この集落は、墓地を浸食しながらじわじわと呑み込んでいく。墓石が街路を囲い、さらには塞いでしまう。やがて生と死が隣り合わせになるという異様な光景が生まれる。今ここに暮らしている人びとは、死んだらどこかよその場所に埋められる。

The settlement encroaches upon a graveyard and gradually absorbs it. The tombs define and occupy the streets. This results in an uncanny juxtaposition of the living and the dead. People living here now are buried somewhere else when they die.

Typo-Graphic 'Lunatic'
Surat, India

「狂気の」タイポグラフィー

地元では変わり者のその男は――壁に、扉に、看板に、ゴミ入れに、中央分離帯に、とにかく手当たり次第に――書きつける。自分のつくり出した文字のタペストリーでおよそ500メートルの範囲を埋め尽くした彼のことは、巷では都市伝説として語り継がれている。

A local lunatic writes - on walls, doors, sign-boards, dustbins, road-dividers and every possible object in his reach. He has generated a tapestry of type across a stretch of about half a kilometre and has become a subject of urban folk-lore.

Sunken Temple
Surat, India

沈める寺

この小さな寺は、地面が幾度も均されるうちにいつしか地中に沈み、さらに道路拡幅にともない、中心寄りに移動していった。おかげで高架下の空き地は、いまや公共空間的な雰囲気を漂わせている。

Over time this small temple has sunk below ground due to repeated re-carpeting and has shifted to the centre from the edges due to road-widening. Now it imparts a sense of public space to the residual space of the flyover.

Temple on a Turning
Surat, India

曲がり角の寺

T字路に面したその寺は、歩道に鎮座している。寺はインドボダイジュの木に寄りかかりながら、壁をカーブさせ、その階段は街路めがけて下りていく。その街路は、寺の前庭を兼ねている。

The temple on a T-junction sits on the sidewalk. Anchored to a Peepal tree, it turns with the wall and steps right on to the road. In an informal way, the road becomes the forecourt of the tenple.

Immediate Shelters
Gujarat, India

即席シェルター

放浪者らは、女性が身につけるサリーを使って、シェルターや入浴用の目隠しや赤ん坊の揺りかごをつくる。同じく流しのほうき売りたちは、ナツメヤシの葉を使って売り物のほうきをつくるだけでなく、自分たちの寝場所もつくる。

Nomads use sarees, that the women wear, to make shelters and bathing partitions and to cradle the children. Similarly, wandering broom-sellers use date-palm leaves to make brooms to sell and use the same material for making their hutments.

Pocket-Man
Nagaur, India

ポケットマン

ありきたりの物も、そこに少し手を加えれば地方色が備わる。地元では正装の印とされる懐のポケットをTシャツに縫い付けるのも、近くに生えている木の小枝や皮を熊手の材料に使うのも、その種の工夫である。独自の環境というものは、発明ではなく即興によってつくられる。

Generic objects are localized through minor modifications. T-shirts are altered to have a belly pocket, an essential part of the local attire and rakes are assembled using twigs of surrounding trees and leather. A personalized environment is thus achieved through improvisation rather than invention.

031

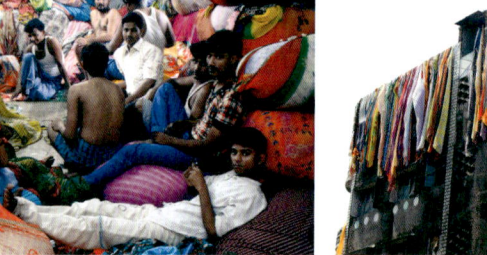

Saree Building
Surat, India

サリー・ビルディング

ある共同住宅は、インド女性の伝統衣装サリーを仕上げる作業場代わりに使われている。仕立ての終わったサリーが外に干されて建物に満艦飾を施している。本来とは異なった用途に充てられることで、建物はまた別のアイデンティティを獲得する。

A residential building is appropriated and used for finishing sarees, traditional attire for Indian women. Once finished, they are hung out to dry veiling the building. The building gets a renewed identity due to modification in its function.

Dhobi Ghat
Mumbai, India

ドビ・ガート［洗濯場］

市内全域から集められた洗濯物は、各指定地区に運ばれる。洗濯屋はコミュニティを形成し、先祖代々こうした洗濯地区に暮らす。コミュニティの生活は、この洗濯場を中心に営まれている。

Laundry from all over the city is collected and brought to central locations. Communities of clothes washers have lived in these laundry districts for generations. The lifestyle of the entire community is woven around this occupation of washing clothes.

Cloth Shop
Ahmedabad, India

生地屋

布地はこうした露店で、じつに簡便かつ大っぴらに売られている。店内は布で埋め尽くされているので、商品と空間が一体化している。これなら客寄せにもなるし、客のほうでも手軽に買い物ができる。

Fabrics are sold in these roadside shops in the most functional and candid way possible. The shop is entirely lined with fabric, thus the product and the space are unified. This makes the experience of shopping effortless and engaging.

Demolition
Surat, India

解体工事

開発途上にある都市ではたえず建物が取り壊されており、ふとしたことで建物の古い層が顔をのぞかせていたりする。瓦礫には無数のヒントが詰まっている。だからそれがなにとつながり、絡み合い、どう適応し、どんな可能性を秘めていたかも見えてくる。もし時計の針を逆戻りさせたとしても、この状態から難なく建設工事を続行できそうだ。

Constant demolition in developing cities inadvertently exposes the layers of their past. The debris contains myriads of clues about associations, adaptations, complexities and possibilities. If reversed at any given point, this could very much be a work in progress.

Studio Mumbai Workshop
スタジオ・ムンバイ・ワークショップ

1995 Nagaon, Maharashtra, India

アリバグのワークショップには、建物をつくるのに必要であろうものならなんでもそろっており、至るところにそうしたものや上質なものが置かれている。ここはいまや私たちにとって、アイデアを練るための場、自分たちを取り巻く世界の成り立ちと根拠を教えてくれる場となっている。

この同じ空間で大工、石工、電気工、配管工、建築家、技師が共に働き、暮らしながら、建築の物理的な殻を突き破るために、建築に携わり、建築を営み、実践している。

仕事場には物があふれている。屋外では建物のさまざまな部分が組み立てられ、壁には大判ドローイングが立てかけられ、棚やテーブルは道具と作品に埋め尽くされている。まさにこの果てしなき前進と反復のプロセスによって、アイデアは引き出され、建物に具現化されるのである。

By surrounding ourselves with all that may be necessary to produce buildings and objects of quality, the workshop in Alibaug has become a place where we are able to develop ideas and begin to understand the formation and reasoning of the world around us.

Carpenters, masons, electricians, plumbers, architects and engineers work together, inhabiting the same space; engaging in, exercising and practicing architecture in a way that aspires to transcend its outward physicality.

Objects proliferate the work place, with parts of buildings being constructed in the open spaces, large-scale drawings resting against walls and artifacts filling shelves and tables. It is through this iterative and constantly evolving process that ideas are explored, drawn and built.

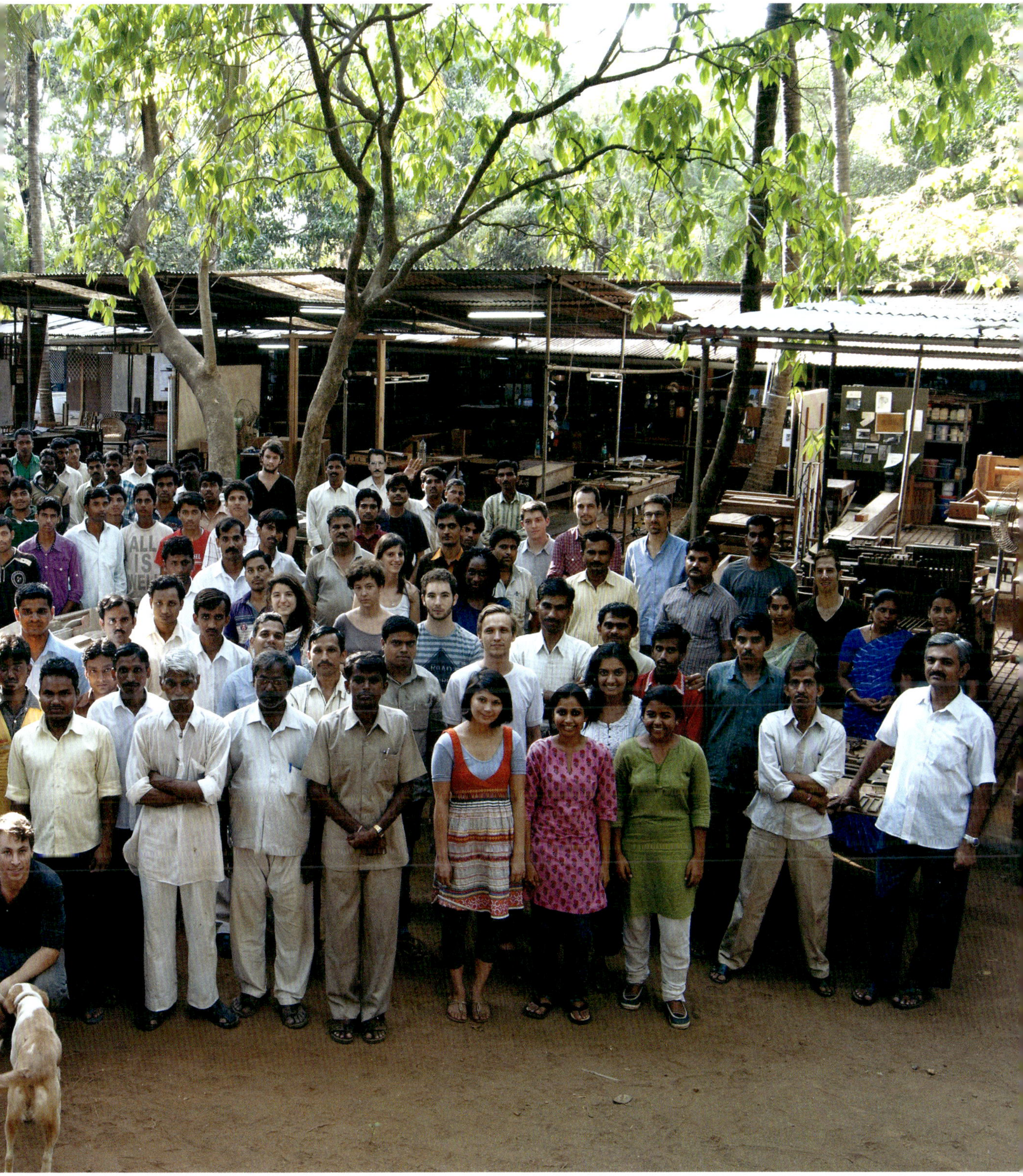

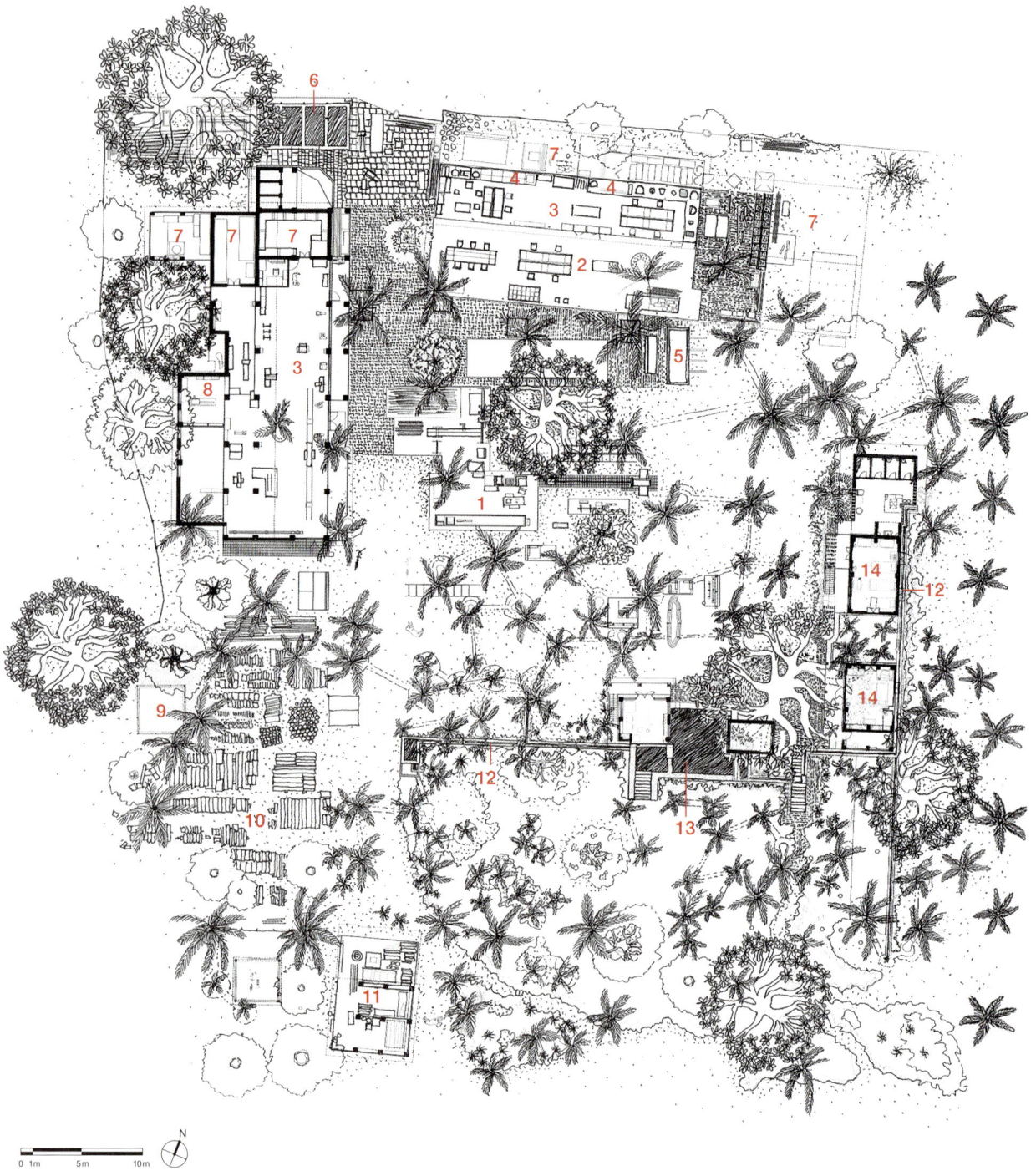

Overall plan

1 outdoor work area
2 drafting, drawing and discussion area
3 indoor work area
4 prototypes and models
5 curing tank
6 lime tank
7 storage
8 lathe machine
9 incinerator pit
10 stone samples
11 colour sample room
12 aquaduct
13 well
14 staff quarters

039

040

スタジオ内で作業をする大工たち。　Carpenters working in the studio.

041

（上）Mac Lyon［リヨン現代美術館］の「スタディ」展に向けた模型制作。
（右頁上）工作機械室。（右頁中）色見本の制作。
（右頁下）「コッパー・ハウスⅡ」のデザインの打ち合わせ。

(Above) Fabrication of 'Studies' exhibition at Mac Lyon.
(Opposite page) Machine room (above), preparation of colour samples (middle), discussion and design development of Copper House II (below).

043

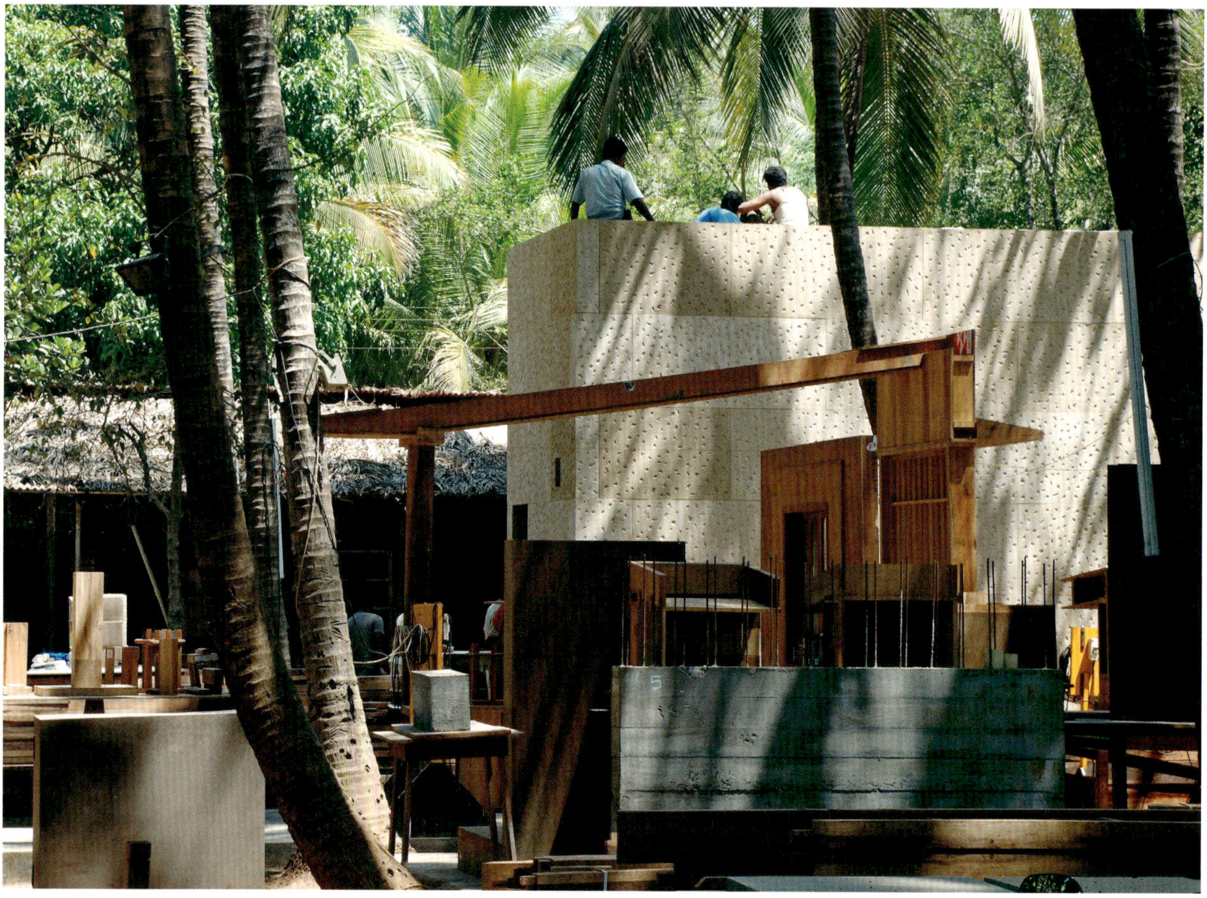

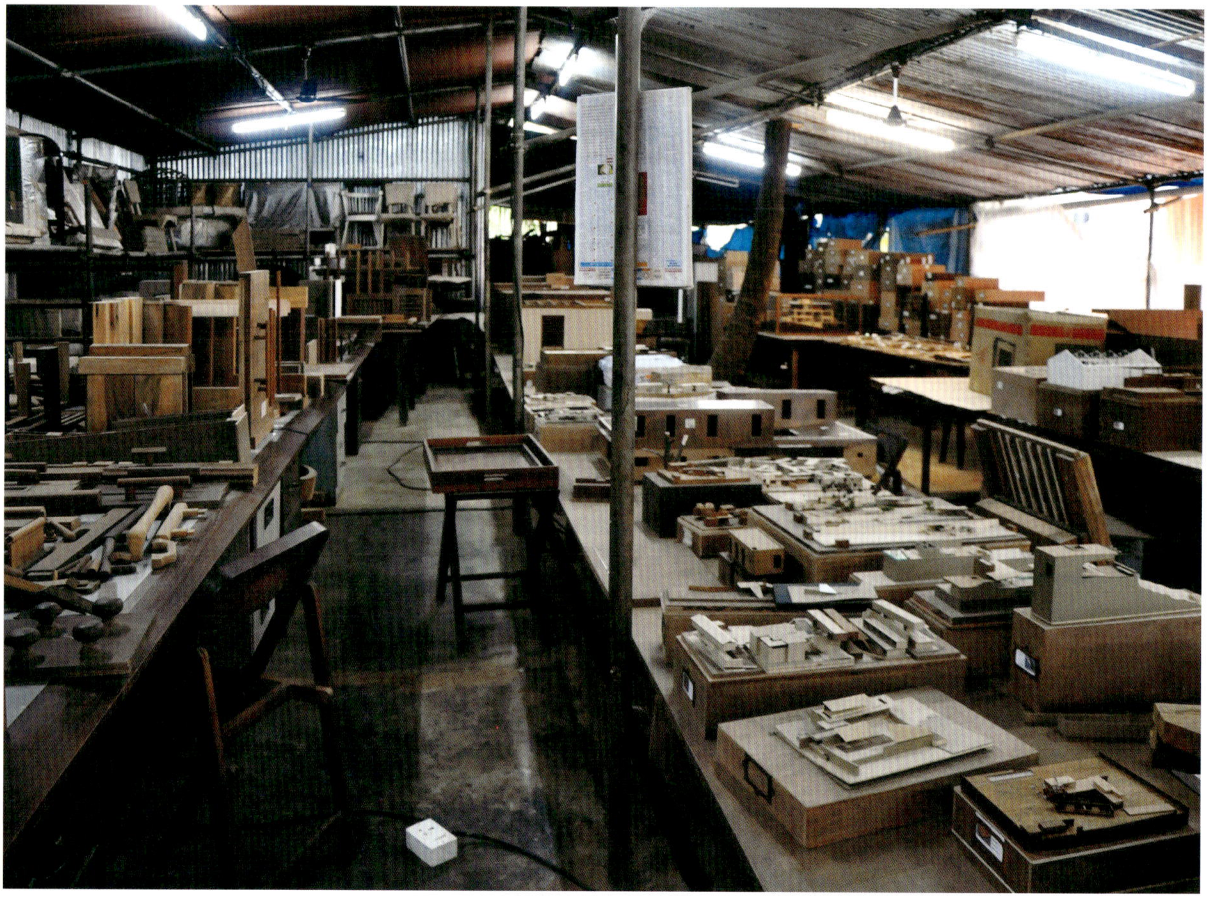

(上)石工用の資材とモックアップ。
(下)模型と細部のモックアップ。
(左頁上)敷地中央のモックアップ置き場。
(左頁下)模型やサンプルが並んだスタジオ内部。

(Above) Masonry tools and mock-ups.
(Below) Models and detail mock-ups.
(Opposite page) Central open space with full-scale mock-ups (above), Covered studio with models and samples (below).

Interviews with Staff and Collaborators
スタッフや共働者に聞く

Interviewer: Wolfgang Fiel (Architect)
インタビューアー：ヴォルフガング・フィール（建築家）

Jeevaram Suthar: Head Carpenter
ジェヴァラム・シュシャー（大工棟梁）

ヴォルフガング・フィール（以下「WF」）あなたの職業はなんですか。またどのようにしてスタジオ・ムンバイに来たのでしょうか。

ジェヴァラム・シュシャー（以下「JS」）私はインド北西部の州ラジャスタンから来た大工で、以前はグジャラート州のアーメダバードで働いていました。私の叔父のひとりがビジョイ氏の所で働いていたので、一緒に働くために2002年にこちらに来ました。非常に重要で繊細な模型を家具とともにつくる仕事でした。私の仕事の質を認めてくださったビジョイ氏が、私の叔父に私を続けて雇い一緒に働きたいとおっしゃってくださいました。

WF スタジオ・ムンバイで大工になってから、あなたの仕事はどのように変わりましたか。

JS 初めてスタジオ・ムンバイに来たとき、私たちは伝統的な働き方をしていました。職人はみんな指示に従って働いていました。その後スタジオが発展するに従い、ビジョイ氏はデザイン・プロセスを押し広げ始めました。アイデアを発展させようとする時、ビジョイ氏は「もし私のことを理解したのなら、あなたから提案をしなさい。あなたならこの仕事をどのようにしますか」と言い、私たちに早い段階から設計に関わるよう求めました。対話が私たちのプロセスになりました。これが、大工である私たちが、紙に図面を考え描くことで、ビジョイ氏との間に相互作用が生まれる可能性があると気がついた瞬間でした。図面を通してビジョイ氏は私たちの思考プロセスをより理解できるようになり、私たちは彼とより深く議論することができるようになりました。実際に木工作業を行う前には、いくつもの変更を重ねました。図面を描くことによって紙の上でさらに発展させ、良い結果を生み出すことができるようになりました。スケッチは大工である私たちと建築家であるビジョイ氏とをつなぐものであり、コミュニケーションのための接点でした。この仕事の進め方を見てたくさんの大工が図面を描き始めました。現在ではスタジオ・ムンバイのすべてのスタッフがスケッチブックをもち、どの段階であっても、なにを議論するにあたっても、常に図面化しています。よってこの数年は特に、スケッチを描くことは、私たちの基本的な仕事のプロセスの一部となっています。

WF この手法はスタジオ・ムンバイ特有のものだといえると思います。この独特な手法の採用によって、あなたの職業との関係や身近な環境の扱い方は、劇的に変化したといえるでしょうか。またさらに、これらの方法は昔ながらのやり方へ戻ったといえるのでしょうか、それとも、そこにはさらに発展させ改良するべき余地があると思われますか。

JS 古い時代へ遡り、昔ながらの方法へ戻るという選択肢は、私たちにはありません。私は物事が年月をかけて発展していくということが好きです。図面を描き、原寸大の模型をつくり、試行錯誤し、新しいことをする。私はあまり外国に関する見識がないので、世界の中にこのような方法で働いている人がほかにいるのかはわかりませんが、インドでは誰も、これほど、このような手法を用いて働くことに力を注いでいる人はいないと確信しています。私は間違いなく、前進し、できうるすべてのことを学ぼうと試みることができる、今のこの方法を続けたいと思います。このスタジオに

Wolfgang Fiel (WF) What is your occupation and how did you come to be at Studio Mumbai?

Jeevaram Suthar (JS) I am a carpenter from Rajasthan, the northwestern state of India and I have also worked in Ahmedabad in Gujarat. In 2002 I came to work with one of my uncles who was doing some work for Bijoy. There was a very important and delicate model to be made along with a freestanding piece of furniture. I did a good job and Bijoy told my uncle that he would like to continue working with me as a permanent employee because he recognized the quality of my work.

WF How has your work changed since you have been a carpenter at Studio Mumbai? Can you tell us about the evolution of the working process since you started to work here?

JS When I first came to Studio Mumbai, we were working in a traditional manner. People were told to do something, and they followed these instructions. As the studio evolved, Bijoy started to push the design process. When developing ideas he would seek to involve us at an early stage, saying: "If you have understood me, put in your suggestions. How would you do this job?" Dialogue became our process. This was the moment when we realized that if we as carpenters put our thoughts on paper in the form of a drawing, there was a possibility of further interaction with Bijoy. Through these drawings he could better understand our thought process and we could discuss things with him in greater depth. There were modifications and changes made before any physical woodwork was done. This enabled things to be further developed on paper, producing a better result. It is this interaction that encouraged us to begin drawing. Sketches were a connection and an interface for communication between us as carpenters and Bijoy as an architect. Having seen the advantages of this method of working, more of the carpenters started making drawings. Today everybody at Studio Mumbai has a sketchbook and at whatever level, whatever is discussed is always put down in a drawing like this. So to sketch in this way has been a fundamental part of our process especially in the last few years.

WF It could be said that this kind of methodology is unique to Studio Mumbai. Would you say that your relationship with the profession, the way you are dealing with your immediate environment, has changed dramatically because of the application of this specific methodology? Would you say that this is a way back to the old way of doing things or would you say that there is even more room to develop and refine the methodology?

JS Going backwards and trying to work with old methods is not an option for us. I like the way things have been developing over the years; working with drawings and mockups, experimenting, doing new things. Since I don't have much international exposure, I don't know whether anybody else in the world works like this, but I am convinced that nobody else in India puts in as much effort working in this

たくさんの可能性を感じています。

WF あなたの背景について教えてください。大工の伝統、あなたの出身地や家族、そしてスタジオ・ムンバイに来て最初の頃に経験したことなどについてお話しください。

JS 私たちは、地域に伝わる神話の中の神のひとりであるヴィシュヴァカルマンの子孫である、と信じるラジャスタン州から来ました。その私たちの歴史や文化が、先祖代々大工をしてきたということを伝えています。私はほかにはなにも知りません。私の祖父はまだ存命で今でも簡単な大工仕事をしています。彼は家庭用の小さくてシンプルな物や農耕道具をつくったりしています。それらは高度な技術は必要ではありませんが、実用的であり、強度が不可欠です。私はここに来ることができ、家族の伝統を追求する機会を得ただけではなく、村に残り基本的なことだけをする、という選択をしなかったことで、もっとたくさんのことを学ぶことができて幸せに思います。私の息子がこの伝統を引き継いでいくのかはわかりません。私は彼に正当な教育が与えられるように、できうるすべてのことをしていますが、もし彼がより洗練された方法と、より良い機会を得て大工になるというのならとても幸せです。

WF あなたの意見では、これは近代的な方法へ進歩するための移行でしょうか、それともあなたが受け継いだ何世紀という長い間の伝統のさらなる成長とみなされる純粋な延長でしょうか。あなたの伝統のライン上にあるこの変化をどのように捉えていますか。

JS 昔、人は牧草を採るために牛車を使っていました。そして建物に木が必要なら、木は人手によって伐採されていました。それはその時代には合っていたし、また人がそれを引き継ぐのも良いのです。というのも、人手によって伝わる技術は伝統として生き続けます。もしすべてがテクノロジーによって置き換えられてしまったなら失われてしまうであろう経験や勘に基づく知識が手仕事に残っている限り、私たちがアクセスすることができるのですから。手仕事は私たちを過去へとつないでいます。しかしながら現代において、名作をつくる職人にとって、すべて手仕事でするということは必要ではありません。機械は

way. I would definitely like to continue in this way, progressing and trying to learn everything that I can. I see a lot of potential in the studio.

WF Could you talk about your background, your tradition of carpentry, your area and family and what you experienced at the beginning of your time at Studio Mumbai?

JS I come from Rajasthan where we believe that we are all descendants of Lord Vishwakarma; one of the mythological gods in our region. Our history and culture tell us that we have been doing carpentry since the first generation. I do not know anything else. My grandfather, who is still alive today, does very simple carpentry work. He makes small simple things for households as well as farming equipment. It is not high technology, but is necessarily basic and strong. I am happy that I have been able to come here and have this opportunity to pursue the family tradition, but also to learn more by not being in the village only doing basic things. I do not know if my son will carry on the tradition. I am doing everything that I can to give him a formal education, but I would be very happy if he were to become a carpenter, perhaps in a more sophisticated way and with better opportunities.

WF In your opinion is the transition to a modern way of doing an improvement or is it purely an extension that you consider a further growth of the centuries long tradition that you are continuing? How do you perceive this change in your line of tradition?

JS In earlier times people used a bullock cart to go to the fields where they would harvest their crops. If wood was required for building, trees would be cut by hand. That was good for its time, and that people still do it is good

スピードの面だけではなく、精度が要求される場面においても、私たちの技量を向上させることができます。それらはわれわれの手で何世紀にもわたって行われてきた特定の技法の改良です。この種の進歩は正当で普通のことです。牛車を引いていた私の祖父は今バイクに乗っています。私たちの伝統を残すことは大切です。しかしながら同様に、私たちは私たちの時代と関わり続けなくては、すべてを失ってしまいます。

WF あなたにとって木とはなんですか。

JS 動物が私たちのために殺されたり死んだりした場合、彼らは私たちに体を提供してくれています。私たちは先史時代から、その骨を使い、皮を使っています。それは動物が人間のためにしてくれる最終的な犠牲です。樹木はその寛大さで、生と死、両方の場面において私たちに自身を提供してくれています。私たちは樹木の木材の提供者としての犠牲を尊敬しなくてはいけません。インドでは、人は生まれたときには、素早く木の揺りかごの上におかれ、そして死んだときには、薪で焼かれるといわれています。この生涯を通じての木との関係は木を使う私たちにある種の救いを与えます。これが私にとって木が意味するものです。

because it keeps traditions alive and enables us to continue to have access to the tacit knowledge which is lost if everything is replaced by technology. This is what links us to the past. For a craftsman to make a masterpiece, however, it is not necessary to work only by hand. Machines can enhance our workmanship, not only in terms of speed, but also where accuracy is required. They are an improvement for certain methods that we have been doing for centuries with our hands. This kind of progress is legitimate and normal; my grandfather with a bullock cart rides a motorcycle today. It is important to retain our traditions, but equally, we have to keep in touch with our time or we will lose everything.

WF What does wood mean to you?

JS When animals are killed or die for us, they offer us their remains. We have used their bones since prehistoric times, we use their skin as leather, and so it is the final sacrifice that an animal does for a human. The tree in its generosity offers itself to us in life and death. We have to respect this sacrifice of the tree as a provider of wood. In Indian tradition, when you are born, you are very quickly placed somewhere on wood, such as a baby's cradle and when you die, you are burnt on a funeral pyre. This relationship offers us a kind of salvation. This is what wood means to me.

Jean-Marc Moreno: Master Roofer
ジャン＝マルク・モレノ（屋根葺きマスター）

WF あなたの背景を教えて頂けますか。どのようにしてスタジオ・ムンバイとコラボレーションを始められたのでしょうか。

ジャン＝マルク・モレノ（以下「JM」） 1970年代後半、私は電子工学とコンピュータを学んでいましたが、技術を学ぶために勉強をやめようと考えていました。当時は「ヒッピー」の時代であり、私はイエス・キリストの父、ヨセフのように大工になりたかったのです。そこで、フランスのとても歴史ある組織コンパニオン・デュ・ドヴォワールに参加しました。この組

WF What is your background, how did you start collaborating with Studio Mumbai?

Jean-Marc Moreno (JM) In the late seventies I was studying electronics and computing when I decided to stop my studies in order to learn a craft. It was a "hippie" period and I wanted to become a carpenter like Jesus Christ's father, Joseph so I joined a very old school in France called Compagnon du Devoirs. It is more like a guild; they are the people who built the cathedrals in Europe in the 11th century. At the

織はどちらかと言うと11世紀にヨーロッパで大聖堂を建てたギルドのような人たちによって構成されています。当時、大工には仕事がなく、私は他の地域で屋根工事の仕事を探すことにしました。ギルドの原則では、仕事を学ぶ方法はフランス国内を巡ることです。すなわち、地方から地方へ移動し、異なった工法を学ぶのです。現在その行き先はドイツのケルンやカナダへもおよんでいます。世界にはさまざまな種類の家があるので、その範囲は広がっています。2004年当時、私はすでにインドに6年間住んでおり、15年前にビジョイ氏とともにトレーニングしていたという建築家のプーナム氏を知っていました。ビジョイ氏と妻のプリヤ氏がポンディシェリ近郊のオーロビルに彼女を訪ねたとき、彼らはコミュニティのためにつくられた食堂と、私が建てた堅ハゼ葺きの屋根がかかった上階のコーヒーショップを見ました。ビジョイ氏はそれを見たとき、この屋根をつくった人を紹介してほしいと彼女に頼み、丸一日私を探したそうです。その時私がどこにいたのかは覚えてはいませんが、後にビジョイ氏はどうにか私に辿り着きました。そして私はここに来て一緒に働き始めたのです。

WF これまでにいくつのプロジェクトでコラボレーションしてこられたのでしょうか。

JM 私がビジョイ氏と最初にした仕事は、カシッド（Kashid）にある「ターラ邸」です。そして数年後には、「パルミラの住宅」を。これに続き、彼とはヒマラヤにある「レティ360リゾート」を手がけました。これはとても小さなスケールの仕事で、つまるところ私がやるべきところは煙突だけでした。煙が上がるのを防ぐため、煙突のようなものを銅でつくったのです。さらにはジャロカーという、インドで見られる一種の出窓をつけ、その上部と横をアルミニウムで覆いました。

WF どのようにほかの方々とコラボレーションしているのか教えてください。あなたはコンサルタントとして雇われたエキスパートですが、しかしほかの人の仕事も請けていますね。

JM 私は職人です。自分の仕事を学び、少しずつトレーニングをして職長になり、チームを統括するようになりました。インドに来る前は文化省の

time there was no work for carpenters, so I decided to search for roofing work elsewhere. The principle of the guild is that the way to learn a trade is by doing a Tour de France: going from one region to another and learning different ways of working within the country. Now the tour also goes to Cologne in Germany and to Canada. There are different houses all around the world now; it is extending.

In 2004, I had already been living in India for six years and I knew an architect named Poonam who had been training with Bijoy fifteen years before. When Bijoy and Priya visited her in Auroville, near Pondicherry, they saw a canteen there for the community and on top of that a coffee shop with a standing seam aluminium roof that I had built. When Bijoy saw it he said that he wanted the guy who had done it. He asked Poonam and the story is that they spent a whole day trying to find me in Auroville. I don't remember where I was at the time, but later he finally got in touch with me. I came here to the studio and we started to work together.

WF How many projects have you collaborated on since then?

JM The first job that I did with Bijoy was Tara House south of Kashid and then a few years later we did Palmyra House. Following this I collaborated with him on the Leti 360 Resort in the Himalayas. It was a very small job for me, essentially just a chimney. In order to avoid the smoke rising, we did something in copper. There was also a jharoka, a kind of projecting window, whose top and side I covered with aluminium.

WF Describe how you collaborate with people. You are an expert who is hired as a consultant but you also execute other people's work.

JM Originally I am a craftsman. I

ためフランス領西インド諸島にいて、教会や大聖堂、古城、植民地時代の住居などの歴史的建造物の仕事をしていました。そこでは屋根部門の担当でした。とても大きな会社でしたので、木枠の職人や彫刻などを担当する石工部門、そして私の屋根のチームなどがありました。

90年～98年の間、私はカリブのグアドループとマルティニークにいました。そこで8年間働き、チームを指揮していました。いくつものプロジェクトを同時に抱えていたので、15～20人を監督するため、現場から現場へと動きまわっていました。

98年カリブを離れ、フランスを離れ、ヨーロッパを離れ、インドへ来る決意をしました。そのためには自分で事業を始めなければなりませんでした。当初、私にはプロジェクトがあったので、村から数人の働き手を集めました。彼らを数年間トレーニングしたところ、そのうちの数人が、やがて自分たちで現場を管理できるようになり、自分たちでお金が稼げると感じ始めました。彼らは十分なスキルをもって私から離れ、そして事業を立ち上げました。その後、私は会社を立て直し、また別のチームをトレーニングし直さなければなりませんでした。そんなことが4度も起きました。私は大きなチームは物事を複雑にするため、チームは5人に保ち、仕事の質を保つため、一時期には1プロジェクトのみを受けていました。

WF スタジオ・ムンバイにいないとき、あなた自身のチームを指導しているのですか。彼らはあなたのトレーニングに従って働いていますか。

JM 常にではありません。「パルミラの住宅」では、ポンディシェリからチームと一緒に現場に行きました。最近

learned my trade and slowly with training became a foreman, supervising a team. Before coming to India I was in the French West Indies for the Ministry of Culture, working on historic monuments such as churches, cathedrals, castles and colonial dwellings. I was in charge of the roofing department. As I was working for a very big company, there were carpenters for wood framing, a stone department with people doing sculptures and my team doing roofing.

Between 1990 and 1998, I was in Guadeloupe and Martinique in the Caribbean. I was working there for eight years also directing a team. We had different projects running concurrently so I was going from one site to another to supervise fifteen to twenty people.

In 1998 I decided to leave the Caribbean, leave France, and Europe to come to India. For that I had to start my own business. In the beginning, I had a project, and gathered some guys from the village. After training them for a few years some of them began to feel that they were able to manage themselves and to earn their own money. They felt that they had good enough skills so they left me and started their own businesses. I had to rebuild my own company and train another team. This happened four times. I do not want a big team because it makes things more complicated. I keep a team of five people and we work on one project at a time, in order to retain quality in our work.

WF When you are not at Studio Mumbai, are you directing and guiding your team? Do they work according to your training?

のスタジオ・ムンバイでの私の役割は技術を職人に教えるトレーナーで、どちらかというとコンサルタントという感じでしょうか。私のチームはポンディシェリとバンガロールで仕事をしていますが、スタジオ・ムンバイでは私はひとり、コンサルタントとして活動しています。私は大工が銅を扱えるようトレーニングをしました。ビジョイ氏はもっと私から独立したいのだと思います。私は自分の仕事が忙しく、ここにいつもいることができないので、スタジオ・ムンバイの大工をトレーニングするのです。大工たちはすでに自分の専門については熟練の域に達しているので、非常に飲み込みが早い。どの分野においても技術をもっている人は、新しいこともすぐ身につくということなのでしょう。

WF あなたの仕事に対する哲学を教えて頂けますか。「仕事（work）」は「仕事（job）」以上のものだということですが、なにか特別な哲学的意味を含んでいるのでしょうか。あなたの職業に対するお考えを教えてください。洞察が重要ということでしょうか。

JM ちょっとほかの事例をお話ししてから、ご質問にお答えします。人はなぜインドに来たのかと問いますが、私はそれに対して精神的な理由で、と答えます。そうすると、皆その理由を聞きたがります。しかし、それに対しては覚えていないし、理由はわからない。でもここに来る運命だったんだ、と答えるのです。あなたがおっしゃるように、仕事のために勉強をしました。そんなに高度な勉強ではありませんでしたが。しかし20歳の時事故に遭ってしまい、学校を辞め、ほかのことを学ばなければならなかった。そこで私は手に職をつけようと決めました。仕事との関わり方、仕事の性質、そしてそれが私に与えるものを理解しようとしました。
例を挙げるなら、トレーニング中は教会の先端や、そのほかでも非常に高い場所にいることが多いのですが、そこにいるのは私と鳥と風だけでした。それはある種の救済だと、今ならいえます。なぜなら、今、私はインドにいて、ある種の精神的なものに触れているからです。職人の仕事は、瞑想のように感じられます。仕事ややるべきことに没頭しているとき、そのほかのまわりのことを忘れる。これは本当の瞑想です。誰もが瞑想と集中は内なる平和をもたらすと知っているのです。技術を学ぶという選択は、間違っていなかった。なぜなら、私の内なる探求に合致しているからです。

WF あなたの技術はここに根付くと思いますか。価値があり、さらにこの技術を教えた人たちが研鑽していくことで、決して失われないと思われますか。

JM そうは思いません。しかしインドでは、いささかヨーロッパで起こっていることから切り離されています。ヨーロッパでは、人は常に新しい技術やシステム、事業機会を求めています。なにかを売らなければなりません。人件費が非常に高いので、それを抑え建設費を安くするために、皆扱いやすい素材を使うよう努め、常に新しい製品を求めています。
私が伝統的な方法から学んだことはインドにありました。ただ、ここでは停電などなにか不都合が起こるかもしれないけれども、機械を使わない方法を常に見つけることができました。木の道具を使って金属を曲げる方法や道具を自分でつくること。それらを伝統的手法で学んだのです。それは私にとって自然ななりゆきでした。コンパニオン・デュ・ドヴォワールのギルドで勉強したとき、すぐさまフランスの優れた会社の情報を集めました。その分野のトップで働きたいならば、政府が発注する歴史的建造物の現場で働くのがいちばん良い方法だからです。働く期間も、しっかりした仕事をする時間も十分ある。歴史的建造物の仕事をするときは、プラスチックやシリコンではなく、銅や鉛、スレートなど非常に高価な素材を使います。現代的な素材を使うことも可能ですが、屋根では難しいと思います。幸運にも私は施主に恵まれ、ビジョイ氏とのように建築家と

JM Not all the time. At Palmyra House I came from Pondicherry with my team and we did the job. Nowadays, my role here is training, more like consultation work. My team is doing work in Pondicherry and in Bangalore, but here I am alone acting as a consultant. I trained the carpenters to work with copper. I think Bijoy wants to be more independent. I am busy with my own jobs and I can not come all the time, so I train the carpenters here. They learn very quickly as they are already skilled people. When you have a skill in any trade you pick up new skills very quickly.

WF Can you tell us a little bit about the philosophy of your work? You said that for you work is more than a job, it has certain philosophical implications. Can you tell about your views on craft. Is it important for you, the way you interpret it?

JM I would like to mention something else very quickly and then I will come back to the question. When people ask me why I came to India and I tell them it was for spiritual reasons, they then ask me why. I say I do not remember, I do not know why, but I know that I am meant to be here. For my work, as you said, I did some studies, not very high level studies, but because I had an accident when I was twenty, I had to quit school and learn something. I decided to learn craftwork. I am trying to understand the way I am involved with work, the nature of the work, and what it is giving me.
Just to give an example, during my training, I was often at the peak of a church or somewhere very high and I was all alone with only the birds and the wind. It is a kind of salvation, I can say it now, because I am here in India and because I am involved in the spiritual part. I feel that doing craftwork is like meditation. When you are into your job, into what you have to do, you forget the rest of the world. This is real meditation. Everybody knows that meditation and concentration lead to an inner peace. I feel that my choice to learn craftwork was a good one because it also matches my inner research.

WF Do you think that your craft is here to stay, do you think that it will never disappear because of these values, and because you are training other people who are learning these skills and continue to practice?

JM No, but in India I am somewhat removed from what is happening in Europe. There people are always searching for new technologies, systems and business opportunities. You have to sell something. People are always searching for new products and because labour is very expensive, people try to use materials which are easy to build with, in order to reduce labor and construction costs. What I learned in the traditional way is that in India, while there may be a power cut or something, I am always able to find a solution without needing a machine. I know how to bend metal by hand with wooden tools, tools which I can also make myself. I learned in that way.
This came naturally for me. When I studied at the Guild of the Compagnon, I immediately tried to collect information about the best companies in France. If you want to practice at the top of the trade, it is best to work on historical monuments for the government because there is always money. You have time to work and do a proper job. With historical monuments one works with very noble materials like copper, lead and slate, not with plastics or silicon. You can use modern materials but with roofing I think it is difficult. I am

も良い関係をもつことができました。いっぽうで、インドでの建築の市場は難しいです。ビジョイ氏は「コッパー・ハウスⅡ」のような建物は最初で最後になるかもしれないと言っています。というのも、インド人の精神構造はヨーロッパとはけして同じではないからです。ここではみんな短い工期で建てたがります。そして、カシッドの家（パルミラの住宅）のように銅葺きの屋根にするプロジェクトでは、なぜ屋根にこんなにお金をかけなければならないのかと、施主はある日突然問い始めます。インドでは、もし雨漏りがあれば、その下にバケツを置くだけです。誰も屋根を直そうとはしません。バンガロールの施主のときの私のいちばんの心配事は、屋根から雨漏りをさせないことでした。しかし施主は私にこのように言いました。「私たちには屋根からの雨漏りが必要なのです。さもなければ、ヨーロッパで起こっているように、インドでも自然との触れ合いが少なくなってしまいます」と。私たちは雨の存在を忘れてしまいます。そして私たちは完璧ではないということも忘れてしまうでしょう。日本では完璧な仕事をしますが、その結果、日本人はなにかを曲げ、なにかを破壊してしまいます。神のみが完璧な存在です。そのような意味では、日本人も神に降伏しているのです。私たちは間違いをおかさなければならないのです。

WF 古代ヨーロッパの手仕事への理解と、その手仕事がどのように素材を理解することで行われていたのか、もう少し教えてください。あなたは古代より受け継がれてきた技法においてどのような経験をしましたか。私には非常に特別で美しく思えます。約千年前の伝統の技をもち、それらはまだ受け継がれています。そのことに

lucky because I have some good clients and I have a good working relationship with architects like Bijoy. In India the market is difficult. Bijoy said that Copper House II could be the first and the last one of its kind, because the Indian mentality is not moving in the same direction as Europe. Here people want to build fast, and with a project like the house in Kashid (Palmyra House) where

the roof was supposed to be built in copper, the client suddenly questions why he should spend so much money on a roof. In India if you have a leakage on the roof they put a bucket under it, nobody is going to repair the roof. I had a client in Bangalore and my main worry was how to make the roof waterproof. But what the client said to me is that we need a leak in the roof because otherwise what is happening in Europe, the lack of contact with nature, will happen here. We will forget that there is rain, that we are not perfect. In Japan when they do a perfect job, just at the end, they bend something, they break something, because only god is perfect. They are surrendering to god in that way. We have to make a mistake.

WF Could you tell us a bit more about this ancient European understanding of craftsmanship and how it goes beyond the true material? What is your experience of this skill? I find it quite special, it is beautiful. The tradition started almost a thousand years ago and is still being practiced in this way. Could you give us an insight into this world?

JM To start I will outline a brief history of European craftsmanship. In the eleventh century some European

ついて説明してください。

JM まず最初にヨーロッパの手工業の歴史についてざっとご説明します。11世紀に数人のヨーロッパの王たちがモーゼが十戒を書いた碑を探しにエルサレムに行きました。彼らがエルサレムから戻ったとき、大聖堂を建造しイエス・キリストを讃えることにしました。石に加え、王たちはギリシャ人やイスラム教徒から教わった幾何学や数学の知識ももち帰りました。イスラム教徒の幾何学的知識は非常に高度でした。一方、当時のヨーロッパではまだ基礎的なレベルの理解にしかすぎませんでした。現場の職長や建築家は、まだ精通してはいませんでしたが、基礎的な幾何学に非常に長けていました。さながら哲学者のように。そして、彼らは数学的原理を用い、最初にローマン、そして後にゴシックのアーチを建造しました。彼らが数学を利用していたのは、宇宙の創造主である神と同じ方法で構築したいという思いからでした。形態は黄金比のみを用い、つくられました。今日までに物事は進化していますが、現在私たちがしていることは価値がない、それに対し昔の人のほうがずっとうまく行っていた、という人がいます。しかし、私はそうは思いません。14世紀や、さらには12世紀の建物でさえも、間違いは見られるのです。先人は現代のような高度な幾何学の解析知識がありませんでした。よって、その時代においても間違いは起こっていたのです。私たちは前時代よりもずっとうまくやっていると思います。もちろん材料は変わりました。さらには働き方も。つまり、手仕事との関係も変わったということです。手工業を行う職人は学術研究についていくことができないので、皆この方法でトレーニングをするのです。私が思うに、職人たちの多くは、一歩下がり、自分たちが行っている仕事や、その仕事がどのように彼らに影響しているのかを見つめる余裕がないのです。見習い期間中、私は掃除をし、観光客の案内をしていました。コンパニオン・デュ・ドヴォワールでの見習いは「ラビット」と呼ばれていますが、いつも走りまわっているのがその所以です。1年か2年「ラビット」をすることになるのですが、その間、至る所を走りまわらなければなりません。同時に職長がすることを見ていなければなりません。職長に道具を持って行くとき、彼がなにをしているのかを盗み取

kings went to Jerusalem to search for the tablets on which Moses wrote the ten commandments. When they were coming back from Jerusalem, they decided to honor Jesus Christ by building a big cathedral. In addition to bringing the stones, they also brought back knowledge of geometry and mathematics which they had learned from the Greeks and the Muslims. Muslim writing on geometry was quite advanced at that time but in Europe we were still at a basic level of understanding. The foremen and architects on the site were not enlightened, but they were very skilled in geometry. They were like philosophers. They used mathematical principles to build arches, first Roman and later the Gothic. They were using mathematics because they were saying that the architect of the universe was god, so we wanted build in the same way as him. They used only the golden ratio to establish proportions. Nowadays, things have evolved. People have said that what we are doing today is worthless, that previously people were working better than we are now. This is not true. In some buildings from the fourteenth or even twelfth century people were also making mistakes. They did not have knowledge of geometry, so mistakes were made at that time as well. We work much better now, this is my feeling. Of course the materials have changed, and the way of working is changing, so this means that our relationship with the trade is also changing. people train in this way because they are not able to follow academic studies. I think that many of these people do not have the time to step back and look at the work that they are doing, and how the job is influencing them. At the beginning of my apprenticeship I was cleaning and showing around tourists. An apprentice with the Compagnon is called a rabbit, because he is running all the time. For one or two years you are a rabbit, you have to run everywhere. At the same time you have to watch what the foreman is doing. When you bring the tools to him you have to catch a glimpse of what he is doing, so you learn that way also. I tried a few times to quit the trade because I was tired. I was thinking maybe I should do something else with my life. I can not, it is in my

るのです。そのようにして学ぶのです。何度か仕事を辞めようとしたこともありました。疲れてしまっていたのです。自分はなにかほかのことをすべきなのではないかと考えることもありました。しかしできませんでした。これは私の血です。説明するのは難しいです。数年前、私は仕事を辞めようとしましたが、私が辞めたことを誰も知らなかったので、依然として多くの人が仕事を頼みにきて、非常に驚いたことがありました。私はそれが嬉しくて、それらの頼みを断ることはできませんでした。

WF あなたがヨーロッパで行ってきたことは、ここインドでは一般的な、または普通のことだといえますか。はたまた、あなたはインドに新しい知識をもたらしたのでしょうか。

JM 基本的にはインドにはないものです。南インドのケララにあるいくつかのお寺の屋根には、銅葺きの屋根を見ることはできますが。屋根にはタイの塔を連想させるディテールのふたつのスロープがあり、たぶん2mm厚の小さな銅のタイル状のものが、釘で固定されて使われています。時には釘を銅のタイルの真ん中に打っているので、重ね合わされる部分は非常に小さくなります。水が屋根を伝うとき、銅板にあいた釘穴から水が入ることもあるかもしれません。私がここで言いたいのは、仕事（技）を学ぶときには、技術があり、やり方がある、ということです。実践も必要ですが、理論もまた必要なのです。従って、数年の間は、屋根の各要素の方向について理論を学ぶのです。ルーフィングの重なりを設計するときは、風や雨の方向を考慮しなければなりません。このような理論は学ばれなくてはならないし、それらは計算で導き出せるのです。ケララの寺院での方法は良くはありませんでした。木のフレームは腐り、そんなに長くはもたないでしょう。しかしながら幸運なことは、材料にチークが使われていることです。チークはこのように使うには適している木です。そんなにすぐには腐りません。もしこれがヨーロッパでパインやオーク材だったなら、10年後にはフレームはなにも残っていないでしょう。世の中には技術と正しい建設法があります。それらの技術は、ビジョイ氏を含む新しい建築家によって探求されています。私はビジョイ氏はヨーロッパの技法を使っているのではなく、ヨーロッパの知識を使っているのだと言いたいのです。私たちが「コッパー・ハウスⅡ」で行ったことは、私が以前学んだことに近いのです。私たちは、古い技法を再考するために組み合わせた、基本的な知識と理論を使っているのです。

私が「コッパー・ハウスⅡ」で頼まれたことは、経験のないことで、ヨーロッパでは誰もやろうとはしないことでした。私たちは、実験を行うことによって進めていきました。銅を使い、建物のまわりに布のように延ばしたのです。これにより建物上部は上から下まで一体のものとなります。通常ヨーロッパでは、角にはコーナー材を使うのです。伝統的なやり方のように、私たちは道具を考案しなければなりませんでした。そして、新しい方法と道具を考えながら、私たちは過去へと戻っていったのです。

blood. It is difficult to explain. It is in the heart somehow. Some years ago I tried to stop and it was amazing because nobody knew I had quit, yet somehow a lot of people came to me for work. I could not turn it down because it made me happy.

WF Would you say that what you have done in Europe is common or normal here in India? Or would you say that you have brought new knowledge to India?

JM It generally does not exist here. There are a few copper roofs in Kerala in the south of India, on temples. They have two slopes with a detail reminiscent of a pagoda in Thailand. They use small copper tiles, maybe two millimeters thick that they fix with a nail. Sometimes they put the nail in the middle of the piece so there is very little overlap. When water runs off the roof, it may go through where the nail punctures the metal. What I want to say is that, when you learn a craft, there is technology, there is a way of doing things. There is a practice, but there is also theory. So for a few years, you learn all these theories about the orientation of the elements of a roof. You have to consider where wind and rain will come from when designing the overlaps. All of these things have to be learned and there are calculations which can be done. What they did here in those temples is not good. The wooden frame is rotten and will not last for long, although luckily they were using teak wood. Teak is good in this way, it does not rot very fast. If you did this in Europe with pine or oak, in ten years there would be no frame left. There is technology and a proper way of building. These technologies are being explored by new architects including Bijoy. I do not want to say he is using European technology, but European knowledge. What we did for Copper House II is similar to what I learned before. We have basic knowledge and theory which we have combined in order to rethink old techniques.

What I was asked to do for Copper House II was something that I had never done before and nobody would do in Europe. We did it by making an experiment; to take the copper and stretch it like a fabric around the building. For example, the head is one single piece from the bottom to the top. Usually in Europe we have a locking piece somewhere in the corner. Like the traditional way, we had to invent tools, and by inventing new ways and new tools we came back to the past.

Pandurang: Head Mason
パンデゥラング（石工リーダー）

WF あなたの背景について少し教えてください。どこからいらっしゃったのですか。なぜスタジオ・ムンバイに来たのですか。

パンデゥラング（以下「P」） 私はこのスタジオ・ムンバイがある地域の出身です。私がビジョイ氏にお会いしたのは、17年〜18年前のことです。私は建物の井戸づくりや大工工事、石工などなんでもこなす請負人でした。ココナツの木は、この辺りでは大変よく利用され普及しており、私の両親はココナツの小さな農場を所有していました。この辺りでは、材料としてこの木が多く利用されます。建材として使われ、果実は売るために収穫されます。ある日ビジョイ氏は、私に自転車で移動して仕事をするのではなく、1か所に留まり働くことができるようにと仕事をくださいました。私は移動しながらいつも仕事を探し歩いていましたので、継続的な仕事をもち、ひとりの人の下で働くということは都合が良いことでした。今は私はスタジオ・ムンバイの石工の棟梁として働いています。

WF 今の話によると、あなたはスタジオ・ムンバイで約18年も働いているということですが、技術や取り組み方はどのように変わりましたか。

WF Can you tell us a little bit about your background, where you come from and what circumstances brought you to work at Studio Mumbai?

Pandurang (P) I am local to the area where Studio Mumbai's workshop is. It must be between seventeen and eighteen years ago when I first met Bijoy. I was a contractor doing things like building wells, carpentry and masonry. I was more of an all-rounder Coconut trees are very prevalent in this area, and my parents ran a small farm harvesting them. A lot of things are done with the trees here; the wood is used in construction and the fruit is harvested to sell. One day Bijoy offered me a job which allowed me to work in one place instead of traveling around on a bicycle. I was always searching for and traveling to work in this way and it was a little more convenient to have a permanent job and to work for one person. I am now head of the masons here.

051

P　私が思うに、良い方向へ変化したと思います。私がここに来たとき、この場所にはなにもありませんでした。当時私たちは木の下に座ったものですが、そこが唯一の作業場でした。私は作業場をつくるのを手伝いましたので、ここにあるすべての壁のことを知っています。そしてさらに、私たちが今抱えている、チーム員のほとんどを集めることも手伝いました。以前私たちは、チームをつくらず、すべての工程の仕事を分担していました。たとえば電気工が必要な場合、それは少し複雑な作業ですので、外注し、下請け業者を使っていました。私は組織が発展したことを嬉しく思っています。現在、私たちは恒久的な作業場をもっていますし、信頼できるチームもあります。私たちは、もう同じ品質をつくることができない外部の人びとに頼る必要がないのです。もっと効率的に物事が進められるように設備投資や作業プロセスに対して投資されたこ

とも喜ばしいことです。おかげで、仕事のペースは速くなり、またそれは、私たちが同じ時間内でより多くの物事が行えるよう役立っているので良いことだと思っています。私にとってこの進歩を実感することは重要なことです。私のふたりの息子もここで働いていますし、スタジオは私の生活の大きな一部です。息子たちは現場監督として管理業務を行っていますが、それも私をこの地に留まらせる理由のひとつです。私の家族がこのような機会をもてたことが私を幸せにしてくれます。ここはボンベイ（現在のムンバイ）からたった30kmのところにありますが、アリバグは、インドのもっと急速に発展している地域に比べたら、人里離れたところです。私たち家族にとって、生活費を稼ぎ、そして現在も生まれ育った土地に残れるということは、非常に恵まれたチャンス

WF　Given your background and the fact that you have worked for almost eighteen years at Studio Mumbai, how has the work changed, the technology and the way you are doing things?

P　I think the change has been positive; when I started here there was nothing on the construction sites. We used to sit under the trees; that was our only workspace. I helped build up the workshop and I know every wall that is here. I also helped in assembling most of the teams that we have today. Previously there were no fixed teams and we would share all of the work across trades. If we needed an electrician for example, it became a little complicated. We would then use contractors or subcontractors. I am happy that the system has developed. We now have a permanent workshop and teams that we can rely on. We no longer have to count on people who cannot work to the same quality. I am happy that investments have been made in machinery and methodology so that things can be done more efficiently. I think the pace has quickened, and that it is good because it helps us to do more things in the same time span. It is important for me to see this progress. The studio is a big part of my life as my two sons also work in the studio. They are both site managers, looking after construction, so that is also something that is holding me here. It makes me happy that my family also has this opportunity. Although it is only thirty kilometers away from Bombay, Alibag it is still remote compared to other parts of India that are developing more rapidly. It is a good opportunity for my family to earn a living and still remain

だったといえるでしょう。

WF　使われている技法の中に特有な質があるとお伺いしたことがあります。その独特な側面や、もしくはあなた個人の仕事や技術の中で、飛び抜けて秀でた特徴を挙げて頂けますか。それは品質でしょうか、設計過程に対する関わり方でしょうか、それともあなたがビジョイ氏やほかの人と図面を用いてコミュニケーションをとり始めた方法でしょうか。

P　IPS〈Indian Patent Stone〉はビジョイ氏が現場でよく使うひとつの特別な製法です。それは石のようで石ではありません。よく見られる仕上げではありますが、私たちはその技術を発展させ改良してきました。これは少なくとも200年前の伝統的な製法ですが、私はこの芸術を完成させた職人のひとりであることを大変誇りに思っています。この仕上げを施した床や壁の各部分はとても美しい仕上がりだと思います。それはとてもシンプルであり、機能的である。それが最も重要なことなのです。

WF　もう少しIPSとその改良や完成させた製法について教えて頂けますか。製法にはどのくらい時間がかかりますか。

P　それは完璧に近い精度をもたなければなりません。私が好きなのは、IPSの継ぎ目のなさです。それが大きな領域に施されたとき、継ぎ目が見えないため一体となったように感じます。タイルはIPS以前から存在していますが、常に目地ラインが出てしまいます。目地があるものは一体的な表層をつくり出すのは非常に困難です。また普通の壁の場合、色を塗らなければならない。そしてこれを定期的にするともっとコストが上がり、このような壁は頻繁に補修が必要です。IPSは2年ごとに壁を清掃し、ワックスをかけるだけです。タイルでは、自然石と同じように入手可能なものに従わなくてはなりません。IPSはあらゆる濃淡をつくることができ、コントロールしやすく、継ぎ目なくつくることができる。そしてもっともすばらしいのは色です。スイミング・プールには継ぎ目がありません。すべてを覆い、接合部分がない。それが私がIPSを愛するところです。

where they were born and where they had the chance to grow up.

WF　We have heard about qualities that are specific to the methodology that is being imparted. Would you be able to single out one specific aspect or feature of your personal work, your craft, which really stands out among other issues or features of the work? Is it quality, is it your involvement in the design process, is it the way that you started communicating with Bijoy and others using drawings?

P　IPS - Indian Patent Stone - It is one of the special processes that Bijoy uses at a lot of his sites. It looks like stone, but is not stone. It is a finish that can be seen commonly but we have worked to develop and refine the technique. This is a very traditional process which is at least two hundred years old and I am very proud to be one of the craftsmen who has perfected this art. I am very proud of each piece of floor or wall that I do with this finish and I think it is very beautiful. It is simple and it works, that is the most important thing.

WF　Could you tell us more about IPS and the process of refining it or perfecting it? How long does the process take?

P　It has to be extremely fine, nearly perfect. What I like about IPS is the seamlessness. When it is done on large areas it feels seamless. Tiles existed before IPS, but with tiles you always have lines, you have grooves and it is very difficult to create a seamless surface. If you do a normal wall you have to paint it, and doing this regularly is more expensive and requires s lot of maintenance. With IPS you just have to clean and wax it every two years. In tiles you succumb to what is available, as with natural stone, but what I love about IPS is the colours. You can have any shade, control what you are doing and make it seamless. The swimming pool is seamless, it covers the whole pool, there are no joints, and that is what I love about it.

Dr. Muirne Kate Dineen: Colour Artist
ムイルネ・ケイト・ディニーン（カラーアーティスト）

WF あなたがスタジオ・ムンバイに来た経緯を少し教えてくれませんか。

ムイルネ・ケイト・ディニーン（以下「KD」） 私は色を扱うアーティストでロンドンを拠点としています。インドには30年程の長い間、たびたび訪れています。私とビジョイが会ったのは、私が勉強していたロンドンのロイヤル・カレッジ・オブ・アートで15年程前のことです。私はラジャスタン州の熟練職人の元でアライシュ（Araish）と呼ばれる製法を学び働くために、インド政府から奨学金を受けました。アライシュとはマルワリ語で「反射」の意味で、製法を通して得られる表面の質に起因しています。ロンドンに戻ってから、私はスタジオベースの博士課程を取得するように言われ、このために約7年を費やしました。博士課程では60％は実践で、ほかの40％は製法について記述する必要がありました。私は1997年にそれを終え、その後ビジョイに会いました。彼は私についてのなんらかの記事を読んでいましたが、それとは別に、このフレスコの製法に興味をもっていました。私と同様、ビジョイはこのアライシュをラジャスタン州で目にし、その美しさに心を打たれていました。アライシュはとても特殊な製法でつくられており、非常に複雑で、インドでもごく限られたギルドやカーストの男性のみが、この仕事に従事することができるのです。

WF このアライシュの製法は、かつて歴史を通して発展してきた方法で、まだ受け継がれているのでしょうか。

KD 人びとはこの製法について知っ

WF Can you tell us a little bit about how you came to work with Studio Mumbai?

Muirne Kate Dineen (KD) I am an artist based in London working with colour and have been coming to India for a long time, about thirty years. I specialize in a particular process that comes from Rajasthan, which I discovered through various trips here. Bijoy and I met about fifteen years ago in London where I was studying at the Royal College of Art. I received a scholarship from India to learn and work with a master craftsman in Rajasthan, learning a process called Araish. This is a Marwari word meaning reflection; it has to do with the quality of the surface produced through this process. After returning to London I was asked to do a studio-based PhD which took about seven years. It was sixty percent practical, and for the other forty percent I had to write about the process. I finished in 1997 and first met Bijoy then. He had read something about me and, entirely separately I think, had been interested in this fresco process. Like me, he had seen this in Rajasthan and had been struck by the beauty of it. It is a very particular process, quite complicated, and only a specific guild or caste of men are able to do this kind of work in India.

WF Is the process still alive the way it has been developed through history?

KD People are aware of the process but much less than before. It was a way

はいますが、以前に比べるとそれを習得している人はとても少なくなっています。この製法は床の仕上げや、建物の壁や天井面で使用されていました。セメントやコンクリートが伝えられた時、コンクリートはより実用的で安価だったため、この製法の使用は少なくなりました。この技法は非常に骨の折れるもので、多くの手作業を必要とします。その時代の国境線が曖昧だったため、どこから来た技術かははっきりとはわかりませんが、12世紀頃に始まったと考えられています。職人はペルシャやイランから来ましたが、インドの北部から来た職人もいました。
私に教えてくださった人はすでに亡くなっていますが、私は彼と15年ほど一緒に働いていました。彼はこの製法がラジャスタンから来たこと、そしてマルワリの人びとが発展させたということを確信していました。ラジャスタンには、とても美しい白大理石と天然石灰で有名なジャイプールと、その郊外にあるマクラナを含む、大きな大理石の採掘場があります。お寺の彫刻や彫像はここで主につくられ、これが大量の大理石の粉塵を生み出します。彫刻からの副産物はアライシュをつくるため石灰に加えられます。そしてさまざまな大きさで砕かれ、積み上げられた約21の層になります。まずこの層を木のブロックで削ることから始め、最終的には瑪瑙（めのう）でつくられたとても繊細な道具をつかって整えられます。以前、彼らはこの製法によって広いエリアを施行していたので、その人手と品質に対する注意の払い方は並外れたものでした。ジャイプールでは300年〜500年前の仕事を見ることができます。とても驚かされます。これがビジョイが見たものであり、彼が再現しようとしているものです。そしてそれは私が見たものでもあり、幸運なことに、私はその製法を教えてくれる人を見つけていたのです。ビジョイと私は同時に同じことを考えていたのです。私たちが出会う前、私はインドで3年間、熟練職人の下で働いていました。そして私はロイヤル・カレッジ・オブ・アートに戻り、博士号を取得したのですが、これは現代建築のコンテクストに伝統的な製法を再導入することを模索したものでした。私は壁、色、そして寸法に興味がありました。ロンドンまたはイギリスでは誰ひとりとしてこれをすることはできません。イギリスでは私が一度にできるのは5フィート×5フィートの、真ん中に繋ぎ目のあるブロック

of finishing floor, wall or ceiling surfaces in buildings. When cement and concrete were introduced, the application and the use of this process declined because concrete was cheap and practical. This technique is very laborious and requires a significant amount of manual labor. It is thought to have started in the twelfth century, although where it came from is slightly ambiguous because borders at that time were flexible. Craftsmen came from Persia and Iran, but there were also craftsmen in the north of India.
The man who taught me has since passed away but I worked with him for about fifteen years. He was very clear that this process came from Rajasthan and that it was developed by the Marwari people. The careful use of resources has always been a consideration here in India. There are large marble quarries in Rajasthan including one called Makrana just outside Jaipur which is very famous for its beautiful white marble and natural lime deposits. The temple carvings and sculptures were mainly produced here, and this guaranteed large amounts of marble dust. This byproduct from the carving is added to lime to make Araish. There are about twenty one layers which are ground in varying proportions, and gradually built up. You start by grinding these layers with a block of wood and by the end you are using a very fine tool made from agate. In the past they would make huge areas, so the manpower and the attention to quality was phenomenal. In Jaipur you can see work that was done three to five hundred years ago. It is astounding. This is what Bijoy had seen and had tried to reproduce. This is also what I saw and fortunately I found a man who was prepared to teach me how to do it. Bijoy and I were thinking along parallel lines. Before we met I had been living in India for three years working continuously for the master craftsman. I then returned to the Royal College and did my Ph.D. which explored

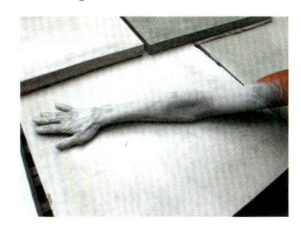

053

だけです。インドに来ることによって私はアートだけではなく、こちらに来ることでしか実現できなかった大きなスケールのものも実践することができました。敷地、興味、そして同じ情熱をもつビジョイとのコラボレーションは、大きなプロジェクトを行うことを可能にしたのです。私たちの最初の仕事を振り返ってみれば、それはとても実用的なものとは言えません。当時は顔料を粉にするのは女性たちの家内工業だったのです。その作業は数か月にもおよびました。実用的ではありませんが、最終的に非常に美しいものとなりました。

WF 私は色がもつほかの側面に関心があります。ここにはたくさんの色があります。私たちは今、技法について語ったばかりですが、いつの間にかもっと複雑なものになり始めています。

KD 色をつくることこそ、私が行うことの理由です。私は布地と染めの勉強もしていました。色が表面と一体化しているということが私にとっては重要です。色は後付けするものではないのです。私がしていることは色を構築することであり、それは分量や材料だったりします。それは私の情熱です。そして興味深いことに、ビジョイも統一された空間という考えに関心があることです。色の固まりになることで、あたかも壁や家がひとつの作品としてつくられたかのように現れます。私たちは今コンクリートを使用しています。それは非常に骨の折れる作業であるフレスコの製法よりもずっと安価なものです。安く、普遍的な材料であるコンクリートを使用することはすばらしい。すべての人がそれを知ってはいます。しかし、もし私たちがそれをフレスコの製法と同じように扱い、同様な色の品質を保持させたなら、そこには私たちが行っている移行と変革があるのです。

WF あなたは同様な品質でなにかを達成するため、コンクリートとフレスコの技術を融合させようとしているのでしょうか。

reintroducing a traditional process into a contemporary architectural context. I was interested in walls, colour and scale. As no one else in London or England is able to do this, the most I can do at any one time is a small five foot by five foot block with a seam running down the middle. By coming here I was able to practice not only an art form but to do it on a huge scale which would be otherwise impossible. Collaborating with Bijoy, who has the sites, interest and the same passion as me, enables us to do bigger projects. Looking back on our first job together, it was very impractical; essentially a cottage industry of women grinding colour. It took months, but what we ended up with was very beautiful.

WF I am interested in the different aspects of colour, you see a lot of colours here. We just talked about the technique, and at some point it started to become more complex.

KD Colour is why I do this. I used to study textiles and I would dye fabrics. It is important to me that color is integral to the surface. It is not something you apply afterwards. What I do is to build colour; it is a volume and a substance. That is my passion and what is interesting is that Bijoy is also interested in the idea of monolithic spaces. Becoming a solid block of colour; it appears as if the wall or the house were made as one single piece. We are now working with concrete. It is much less precious than the fresco process, which is incredibly laborious. It was nice to use concrete because it is a cheap and universal material. Everybody knows about it, but if we treat it in the same manner as the fresco process, and with a similar quality of colour then there is a transition and a transformation in what we are doing.

WF Are you in a position to combine concrete and fresco technology in order to achieve something with a similar quality?

KD Not the technologies because the processes are different. The common factor is the quality that Bijoy creates in his buildings, and the quality and passion I have for colour. Putting these

KD 技術ではありません。というのもお互いのプロセスが違うからです。共通の項目はビジョイが彼の建築の中でつくり出した質と、私が色に対してもっている質と情熱です。これらをコンクリートに一緒に投入し、建材をつくると、よりリアルになります。現在私たちが手がけているプロジェクトは非常に巨大で、アライシュで製作することは不可能です。何年もの時間がかかり、そして費用は計り知れません。私たちは高価ではなく、入手可能な安い材料を使用し、そして、時間、労力と配慮の下、品質を与えています。このようにして、私たちは非常にうまく共働しています。私は今まで、ビジョイのように私と同等に色彩に対する感性をもった建築家と仕事をしたことがありませんでした。ですからビジョイと共働することで、仕事をする余地が生まれ、これまでの創作とは大きな違いが生まれるようになりました。

WF あなたが使っている略称のIPSは、この製法を表しているのでしょうか。

KD IPSはIndian Patent Stoneの略で、私たちが「コッパー・ハウスⅡ」で使用したものです。IPSはこて塗りの漆喰のことで、流し込みのコンクリートとは違います。それは打設されたコンクリートの上にこて塗りした漆喰のことを指しますが、一方、私たちが行っているほかのプロジェクトでは、すでに着色したコンクリートを流し込んでいます。
IPSを使用することによって私たちが目指した色の質は、アライシュの製法で試していたものと等しくすることができるようになりました。これによって表面の質感と、表面に着色されているのではなく一体的になった時に生まれる色合いがもたらされました。初めてビジョイがこの製法を試した

together into concrete and making a building material becomes much more feasible. The project we are doing at the moment is enormous and it would not be possible with Araish. It would take years, and the expense would be beyond what is even possible. We are using a cheap material that is not precious but is accessible, and we are giving it that quality in terms of time, effort and consideration. In that way we work together very well. I have never worked with an architect who has as much empathy for colour as I have. That makes an enormous difference, because it allows you space to work.

WF Is the abbreviation IPS what you use to describe this process?

KD IPS stands for Indian Patent Stone. This is what we have used at Copper House II. It is a trowelled cement plaster and is different from poured concrete. It refers to the cement plaster screed that is trowelled on top of in-situ surfaces, whereas with the other project we are working on, we are pouring the concrete with the colour already mixed in.
With that, the quality of colour that we are trying to achieve is the same as we are trying to do with the Araish process. This is what brought us together, the quality of surface, and the fact that the colour was not on the surface, it was integral. When Bijoy first did it the workmen were not entirely honest because he did not know how to do the process. When you are doing twenty-one layers it is very complicated, so unless you know what you are doing, it becomes difficult to keep track of. For the job we did at Indigo (a restaurant in Mumbai) Bijoy got some men from

時、彼はその技法を知らなかったため労働者たちは完全に誠実ではありませんでした。21の層をつくるのはとても複雑なことです。自分でなにをしているのかきちんと理解していなければ、精度を上げることは困難です。その後、インディゴの仕事（ムンバイのレストラン）ではビジョイはラジャスタンから数人の男を呼び、その仕事をさせました。職人らはこの仕事にとても精通していましたが、最初は私と働くことが困難だったようです。私は師匠から譲り受けた道具を持っていました。これらの道具は店で購入するものではなく、譲り受け、得るものなのです。そして、〈白人の女性〉である私はその製法が、通常、父から子へ受け継がれるものであると理解していることを彼らに示しました。私が道具を出した瞬間、その道具を私がどのように使うのか知っていると彼らは理解し、それから展開が変わりました。その後すべてはうまく行き、最終的にとても美しい仕上がりを得ることができました。

WF これはインドに特有の製法ですが、これをほかの地にて行うことは可能だと思いますか。

KD この製法を採用する時には、労働力と資源、そして品質を達成するという意志が必要です。ほかの地で見つけることはできるかもしれませんが、とても稀でしょう。

私は運命を信じていたかどうかわかりませんが、私が行ってきたことの水平線上にビジョイが突然現れたことは、特に不思議に思えます。ほかの方法で、このような大規模なスケールの仕事を行うことができたのかはわかりません。この製法は非常に多くの労力を必要とします。金銭的献身ではなく、時間と行動が求められるのです。私は博士課程での7年に加え、熟練職人と14年間働いてきました。壮大なスケールでこの技法を使うには、私と同様のスキルをもったチームが必要です。それなりの規模を実現するには、10人〜15人の男手を必要とするでしょうし、そして私はひとりきりです。ロンドンでそれを行おうとした場合、15人の男はロンドンに来なければならず、私と11年間、どのようにこれを行うかを学ばなければならないでしょう。可能性は小さいです。この技術を知る男たちはここラジャスタンにいます。そしてもし彼らがこの仕事をするために努力したければ、私たちはそれ

Rajasthan to come and do the work. The craftsmen were well versed with this process, but had difficulty working with me. I have a set of tools which I was given by the man who taught me. You do not buy these tools off the shelf, you earn them, and when I came - a white woman - I showed that I understood this process that is typically handed down from father to son. The minute I got the tools out, the story changed because they saw that I knew what the tools were for. I said: 'why are you not using this, why are you using this, you need to do it like this.' Suddenly it was a different story. They understood that I knew what was going on, and that I knew how to do it. From that moment on it was fine and in the end it was a beautiful job.

WF This is a process specific to India. Do you think that it is possible to transfer these techniques elsewhere?

KD You need the workforce, resources and the will to achieve quality when doing this process. It is possible that you could find this somewhere else, but it is unlikely. I did not know if I believed in fate, but it seemed particularly strange that Bijoy suddenly appeared on the horizon as I was doing this. I do not know how else I would have been able to do this on such a large scale. This process is very demanding in terms of effort. It is not so much the financial commitment, but the time and effort that is required. My Ph.D. was seven years and I was working with the master craftsman for fourteen years. I would need a whole team of people who were as skilled as me to be able to do this on a grand scale; to do anything of a reasonable size, you need a row of ten or fifteen men and there is only one of me. Fifteen men would have to come and sit with me for eleven years in London and learn how to do this; the likelihood is small. They are here in Rajasthan, and if they want to make the effort to do the work then we can. It takes this combination to make it happen.

WF Can you tell us about the relationship that you have with Studio Mumbai?

を可能にすることができるのです。それを実現するために、ここでの、この組み合わせが必要なのです。

WF あなたとスタジオ・ムンバイとの関係を教えてください。

KD 私はここに来て、そして去ります。私はロンドンのアーティストなのです。私のギャラリーとスタジオはロンドンにあり、そこが仕事をするところです。ビジョイが、色彩と表層にかかわるプロジェクトに携わっているときが、私が呼ばれるときです。その意味で私はコラボレーターです。しかしながら、私が来るとき、彼にはすでに心に思い描いているものがあるといえるでしょう。アーメダバードにある住宅のプロジェクトの例では、どの色を建物に使うかという議論はなされませんでした。彼はだいたいどの色が適しているか、砂岩の種類やすでにアーメダバードの建物で使用されている美しい石について深く理解していました。私の役割は洗練させることです。私はビジョイが話したことと、私がうまくいくだろうと思うものを基にサンプルをつくります。私はもっとたくさんの色調を使ったほうが良いと提案もするかもしれません。私たちは、自然の石がもつようなグラデーションを、一連のブロックを用いてつくることができます。作品では、コンクリートでは起こりえないそのグラデーションを人為的につくる必要があるのです。

KD I come and go; I am an artist in London. My galleries and my studio are there, so that is where I do commissions. When Bijoy is working on a project that requires anything to do with colour and surface, that is when I get called to work with him. I am a collaborator in that sense, but I would say also that he already has a vision in mind when I come in. For example in Ahmedabad, there was not a discussion about what colour we were going to use in the building. He already knew what color roughly, a type of sandstone, a very beautiful stone that is used in some of the buildings in Ahmedabad. My role is to refine that. I make samples based on what he has told me and on what I think would work well. I might suggest that we should introduce more tones. We could do this by pouring a series of blocks in order to have a gradation of tone, as natural stone does. We would have to artificially manufacture that gradation, because it does not happen otherwise with concrete.

Samuel Barclay: Associate Architect
サミュエル・バークレイ（共働建築家）

WF スタジオ・ムンバイの仕事がどのように始まるのか教えて頂けますか。方法論や、なにが初めでなにが終わりなのか、プロセスはなにを伴っているのでしょうか。

サミュエル・バークレイ（以下「**SB**」）ビジョイにとって、仕事の始まりはとても直観的なプロセスで、それがいったいどのような方法で、またなにを意味するのかを導き出すために、私たちは参加者として、ともに多くの時間を費やしているのだと思います。彼があるプロジェクトに対して構築しようとしている雰囲気や世界を理解するため、参加しながら、私たちは会話や模型、図面などを用いて、試行錯誤し

WF Can you paint a picture of how a project comes about at Studio Mumbai; the methodologies, what is the beginning, what is the end, what does the process entail?

Samuel Barclay (**SB**) For Bijoy it is an incredibly intuitive process and I think for us as participants in that, a lot of the time is spent figuring out ways and means for us to extract our understanding of it. Through this participation we have to try and develop, by means of conversations, models, and drawings a way to be able to understand the atmosphere and the world that he is trying to build up in a

つつそして発展させなければなりません。私たちが行うすべてのプロジェクトでは、まず敷地がとても重要であるため、度重なる敷地への訪問や施主との打ち合わせを通して、私たちは施主の願望や不安、さらには彼らが、欲しいかもしれない物事までも描き出そうと試みます。彼らは頭の中に、建物に対してある特定のイメージはもっていますが、私たちは彼ら自身も設計に参加できるようなプロセスを通じて、そのイメージを導き出せるように努めています。継続的な対話を続けることは非常に重要です。スタジオの中であれ、施主と敷地に行き、ただその場にいるだけであっても会って時間を共有することは重要です。それは心の一部になり始めます。私たちは地形との関係において、規模やプロポーションを理解するため、よく測量を行います。それは非常に基本的なプロセスとなります。そのプロセスには一貫性と矛盾があり、漠然とした方法論があります。しかし、それは同時に、とても直観的なプロセスでもあり、かつそれぞれのプロジェクトにおいて独自に発展させられたものでもあると思われます。私たちには、9か月で構想と施工を終えたプロジェクトもありますし、3年前に考えられ、未だ建っていないプロジェクトもあります。プロセスはそれぞれに唯一無二であり異なったものなのです。

WF 建物がスタジオ・ムンバイの人びとの手によって建設されるということも異色なことだと思います。設計プロセスは施主との対話を伴うものだということはわかりましたが、施工に関して、ほぼすべてのものをつくるということは、建物全体に対してもいえることなのでしょうか。

SB はい、その通りです。ヒンジやハンドルなどの小さなものや、外装材や構造にいたるまですべてです。私にとってそれは、ここに留まる非常に魅力的な理由のひとつです。欧米、少なくとも私がいた国では、建築図面は指示書や法的書類の様相に成り下がってしまっています。施工業者、施主、建築家がそれぞれ相容れない立場をとります。建築家と施工業者の関係は、相互的に生まれる利害関係があるため好戦的になります。ある人には一連の関心があり、またある人には別の関心があるという状況です。施工業者が悪いということではありませんが、このような関係が根本的な構造として

particular project. In every project we do, the site is absolutely critical and through a lot of site visits and meetings with the client, we try to draw things out in order to reveal all of their aspirations, fears, anxieties, even the things that they might want. They have certain images in their head, and we try to draw that out through a process that allows them to participate in the design as well. It is really critical to have a continuous dialogue. Whether it is within the studio itself or with the clients by going to site and just by being in that environment. It begins to be injected into you. We take a lot of measurements ourselves as a way of understanding scale and proportion in relationship with the landscape. It is an incredibly organic process. There are consistencies and inconsistencies. There is a vague methodology, but I think it is a very intuitive process and one in which each

project develops particular to itself. We have done projects that were conceived and built in nine months and then we have projects that were conceived three years ago and still are not built. The process is unique to each one.

WF What is also unique is that the building is being constructed by Studio Mumbai itself. We know it entails the design process and dialogue with the client, but also the making of almost everything that ends up being implemented in the building?

SB Yes, absolutely, all the way down to hinges and handles, and all the way up to the scale of cladding and structure. For me that is part of what is incredibly attractive about being here. In the West, at least where I come from, an architectural drawing has deteriorated to the state where it has become an explicit set of instructions and a legal document. The contractor is one party, the client is another, and the architect is a third. The relationship between the architect and the

あるため、一定の仕事の品質を維持しようとするとき、別の内在的問題が発生するのです。

ビジョイはこの問題を避けるために、知識が豊富な石工と大工、そして人びとを集め、人的な基盤をつくり上げることで、仲介業者である施工業者を排除しました。これが、インドで私たちが求めてきた一定の品質を得るために、とられた方法です。私はほとんどの大工、特に棟梁であるジェヴァラムとは、本当にすばらしい関係を築いています。私は時々一緒にランチをし、彼の家にも行きますし、お互いの家族のことを知っています。欧米においてもこのような関係をもつことは可能です。ただし多くの場合、先に述べたような建築家と施工業者という関係性があるため、求めることを達成するということは、建築家にとっては闘いとなるのです。

WF この方法はインド以外の国でも応用が可能だと思いますか。それはインドの状況に合わせて特別につくられているように思われますが、このような実践をほかの地で行うことは考えられませんか。それとももっと世界的な規模で応用することは可能でしょうか。

SB ほかの国で同じようにできる一面もたしかにあります。たとえば欧米の例を見てみると、建築家で施工業者の免許をもっていて、独自の働き手をもち、設計施工をしている人もいます。私が考える真似できないものとは、物質的な条件や人件費の実情です。もしかしたら、ある部分についてはインド以外の地域で見つけられるかもしれない、しかしほかの部分は見つけることはできないでしょう。この状態（環境）はインド固有のもので、ビジョイが築いてきたものです。同時に、私たちが実践している方法は、インドのどの建築家にも可能なことですが、実は誰ひとりとしてそれを行ってはいません。誰もこのような方法で働こうと思っていない、少なくとも私は一度もそのような例を見たことがありません。私は、ほかの誰かが、ほかの地でこのような働き方をする方法はあると信じていますし、私たちがほかの地でこのように働く方法を見つけられることに期待しています。私たちは、ロンドンのヴィクトリア＆アルバート博物館で小さな規模の仕事を行いましたが、その時は職人たちをこちらから一緒に連れて行きました。今後、私

contractor is a contentious one because there is money to be made. One person has one set of interests, and the other person has another. This is not to say that contractors are bad, but because of the fundamental construct of this relationship, there is inherently a problem when it comes to facilitating a particular quality of work. The way that Bijoy has avoided that is to build up an infrastructure of human resources. He has collected masons and carpenters and people with a wealth of knowledge. In the process he has eliminated the middleman; the contractor. That is what it takes in this situation, working in India, to achieve the particular quality that we are after. I have a fabulous relationship with most of the carpenters and especially the head carpenter Jeevaram. I go to his house for lunch from time to time, he knows my family and I know his. It is possible for people to have those relationships in the West, but a lot of the time it is a struggle for the architect to achieve what they want to achieve because of the way this relationship is constructed.

WF Do you think that this model could be applied outside of India? It is so specifically tailored to the things you have here. Is this kind of practice unthinkable elsewhere or can it be applied on a more universal scale?

SB There are aspects of it that do transfer. If you look at examples in the West, some architects have contracting licenses, hire their own workers and do design-build work. What I think is not transferable is the realities of material conditions and labor costs. You might find a part that exists in China, but another part of it will not. Equally you might find a part of it that exists in Australia, but then this other part does not exist. This situation is unique to India and what Bijoy has built up. At the same time, the way we are practicing is available to any architect in India and nobody else is taking it on. Nobody else is thinking about working in this way, at least I have not seen any examples of it. I believe that there are ways that one can work in this fashion elsewhere and what I am excited to find out is how we are going to work in this way somewhere else. We have done it

たちがスタジオで国際的なプロジェクトを手がけることもあるでしょう。問題は、ほかの地で同じように行うのに最適な機会を見極めるということ、それのみです。

WF 同様にスタジオ・ムンバイにおいて顕著なこととして、対話がなされるということがあります。家には地元の技術や手工業が使われている一方、やや普遍的な建築的言語も用いられています。ここで発展したその種の建築的言語についてお話し頂けますか。その多くは世界的に用いられている建築家を教育する手法によるのでしょうか、そしてどの程度、その地方の土着的な建物の状態によるのでしょうか。

SB 私は、利用可能なすべてのものから、最大限を利用するように試みています。ビジョイは都市の歴史の過程のとてもユニークな時期にボンベイで育ち、アメリカで学び、ロンドンに住み、そしてここに事務所をもちました。彼が学んだある習慣や物事は、私たちのスタジオの仕事の進め方において大きな役割を担っていますが、しかし、私たちはある特定の言語にのみ従っているとは思いません。私たちは、妥当性を求めていると思います。それはその場所の社会環境によるかもしれませんし、作業方法や気候に対する素材の使い方かもしれません。私たちは環境デザイン面で世界を救おうとしているわけではありませんが、しかし同時にそこには素材の使われ方の確かな妥当性があります。効率性と利便性があるのです。誰もが利用できるよう、まさにここにある5000年にもわたる伝統的な建築知識を完全に無視することは、私は愚かだと思います。私たちは、知識や経験の妥当性を認めながら設計プロセスに貢献してくれる人びとに大きく依存し、私たちが建築家としてもっている訓練で得たもの、技能や思考法などを融合させています。もし私たちが伝統的な物のみを選択し使用するなら、それは施主のライフスタイルに関係がなくなってしまいます。しかしながら、もし私たちが現代的なデザイン面のみをとるのなら、それは環境の中ではうまくいかなくなってしまうでしょう。

ビジョイがすばらしいのは、それをレイヤーのように考えることだと思います。彼は彼の内部においてたくさんのレイヤーを同時に保持することができ、そしてこれらをどこに使うべきか、

また使わざるべきか、的確な決定をするために非常に正確な洞察力をもっています。このじっくりとしたプロセスを通してのみ、古いとか新しいとかではない、現代的で、ふさわしいなにかにたどり着けるのだと思います。外に出て私たちが使ったディテールを見れば、そのとても伝統的な一面を見ることができるでしょう。しかしそれらの多くは、すぐにはそれとわからないような方法で使われています。私が思うに、その抽象化や要素の抽出は対話を通じてのみ生み出され、実現することができるものなのです。

WF 次の5年後、10年後のスタジオ・ムンバイはどうなっているでしょうか。この期間にあなたが行う最も重要だと思われることはなんでしょうか。

SB それらは、今、私たちが扱っている物事と同じだと思います。ひとつ、私がわかっていることは、スケールが変わってくるだろうということです。もうそれはすでに始まってはいますが、作業の品質を達成するための管理と物流の面での規模の飛躍です。そこには空間と時間という建築家が常に扱ってきた普遍的な問題があると思います。発展された手法はもっと洗練されたものかもしれませんし、ある意味でもっと素朴なものかもしれません。私たちが扱っている物事の本質は、たとえまったく同じではなくても依然として似たものだと思います。たとえばアルバロ・シザは、プロジェクトをその本質にまで削ぎ落し、劇的に細部の複雑さや素材、色を減らすことで、ある規模においてそれを達成しました。私たちはSANAAを同じように見ています。私たちの事務所でどのようにそれを達成するのか、また複雑性の上においてどのように一歩を踏み出すのか。それらはこれまで以上に複雑になるようなプロジェクトではありません。むしろ私が思うには、ある点においてもっとシンプルになる。しかし、ある特定のスケールにおいては複雑性を備え始めています。どの状況でも私たちはそれを扱う方法を考え出せるでしょう。車輪はビジョイのためにすでに動き出しています。私はそのうしろを走り続けるだけです。

at a small scale in London, at the V & A, but we brought people there with us. There will be a time in the studio when we have international projects, it is just a matter of finding the right opportunity.

WF What is also remarkable is the dialogue that takes place. Between local crafts used and applied to build houses, and, on the other side, the architectural language which is somewhat universal. Can you talk a bit about the kind of language that is being developed here? Does it owe to a more international way of educating architects, and to what extent does it owe more to the local vernacular building conditions?

SB I think it tries to take the best out of everything that is available. Bijoy grew up here in Bombay at a very unique time in the city's history, studied in the US, lived in London and had a practice there. Certain habits and things that he has learned along the way play a big part in the way our studio works, but I do not think we are after a particular language. I think we seek an appropriateness, which may have to do with the social circumstances of a particular site, the way that work is done or the way that materials respond to climate. We are not out to save the world in terms of environmental design, but at the same time there is a certain appropriateness in the way in which materials are used. There is an efficiency and ease of means. To completely ignore five thousand years of traditional building knowledge that is sitting right here for anybody to take advantage of, I think is silly. We rely heavily on people to contribute to the design process in a way that allows us to take the appropriateness of the knowledge and experience that they have and combine it with what we, as architects have, in our training, skills and way of thinking. If we were to only take the traditional part and apply that, it would not relate to the client's lifestyle. If we only took the contemporary design aspect of it, it might not work in the environment. I think what Bijoy is good at is thinking about it in terms of layers. He is able to hold so many layers in his internal space at the same time and then use very acute discretion to make appropriate decisions about where those things are applicable and where they are not. I think just through this slow-cooking process comes something that is not old or new, it is contemporary and appropriate. You can look at very traditional aspects of it, drive down the road and see details that we have used, but I think a lot of time they are used in a way that one might not immediately recognize. That abstraction, or distillation I think is what we are able to achieve through dialogue.

WF If I could ask you to predict what is on the horizon for Studio Mumbai within the next five or ten years, what do you think will be the most important issues you will take on within this period?

SB I think they are the same issues we deal with now. One thing that I know is that the scale is going to change. It is already beginning to. It is a jump of scale in terms of managing and logistics while still achieving quality in the work. I think there are the things that we do which are universal issues of space and time that architects have always dealt with. We will deal with the same kind of issues, but the methods that we apply and develop may be somewhat more sophisticated, or less sophisticated in some ways. I think the nature of the things that we are dealing with will still be similar if not the same. If you look at somebody like Siza, he has figured out how to distill a project down to its essence and achieve it at a particular scale by radically reducing the complexity of details and the material and color palette. We look at a studio like SANAA in much the same way. How do we achieve that in our practice and take that step in terms of complexity. It is not that the projects will be more complex, in some ways I think they will become simpler, but it is about addressing complexity at a particular scale. I think we will figure out a way to manage. I know the wheels are already turning for Bijoy and I am just trying to run behind and keep up.

Reading Room
リーディング・ルーム

2003 Nagaon, Maharashtra, India

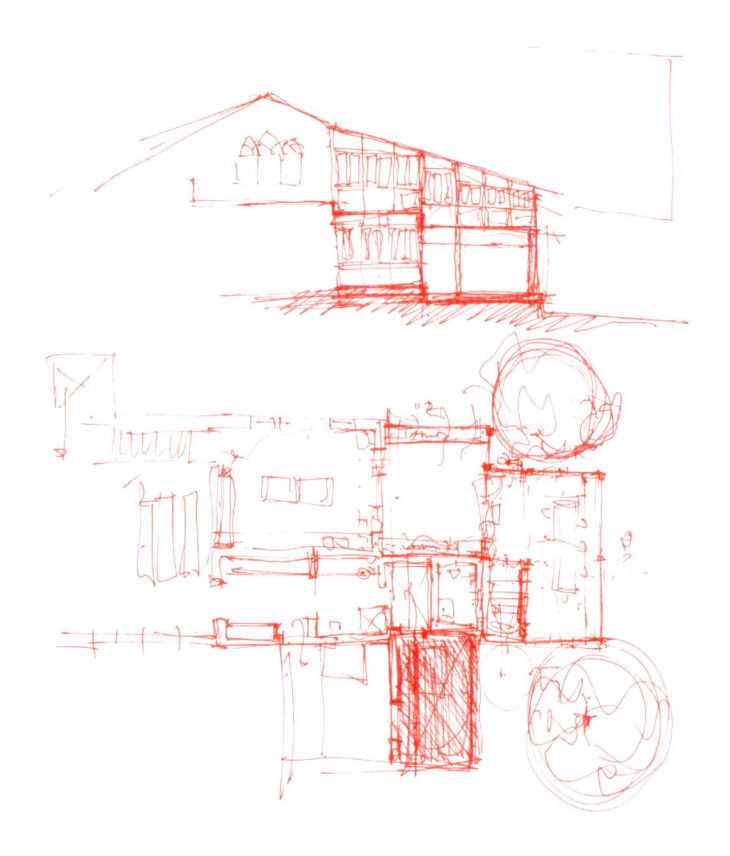

既存の住宅を建て増したこの翼部の1階には台所と予備室が、2階には書斎と居間が設けられた。この控えの間ならぬ控えの棟が、施設全体を引き立て、その全貌を知る手がかりとなる。

建物は布——白いスクリムカーテンなどに用いる軽くて丈夫な粗い平織りの綿布・麻布風の農業用ネット——を基調にしてつくられている。この素材の選択には、スタジオ・ムンバイの方針が反映されている。その方針とはすなわち、自然の力を建築に取り込みつつ、室内をその脅威から守ることである。

この網は、個室を覆う半透明の膜と化して、室内に光と風を通したり、隣に立つバンヤンノキ*の動きや変化を見せながら、室内を覗き見ようとする好奇の視線を遮る。このバンヤンノキは、増築翼部の雨除けと日除けにもなる。

建物の北西角に増築されたこの翼部は、見晴らしのきく位置合わせの目印となる——おかげで作業場も、職人と建築家の暮らす住居も、スイミング・プールも、共通の中心に顔を向けるようになる。その中心とは、翼部の台所や読書での作業と同様に素材やアイデアの発酵から始まる作業場での工程の中心である。

*クワ科イチジク属の常緑高木。

Built as an extension to the existing house, housing within its extended self the kitchen and its ancillary spaces at the ground level and private study and living spaces above, the ante-building becomes the foil off of which the entire complex of the workshop can be understood.

The primary material of the building is fabric–a white scrim-like version of agricultural net used in commercial farming, and this material decision reflects a core approach that the studio operates with: an intention to include the elements, invite them to become part of the architecture while protecting the interior from their potential extremes.

The mesh acts as a semi-permeable membrane on a cell might, allowing in light, air and the registration of movement and life on the banyan tree at its junction, while disallowing an inquisitive eye from witnessing life on the inside. The tree on its part protects the extension from the incident rain and sun.

Situated at the northwest corner of the extant house, the extension becomes a point of lookout and registration–it alerts the workshop yard, artisans' and architect's housing and the swimming pool to orient themselves to a common centre–that of the processes of the workshop, stemming as they do, from the fermenting of materials and ideas, not unlike the activities of the kitchen and reading room housed within the extension.

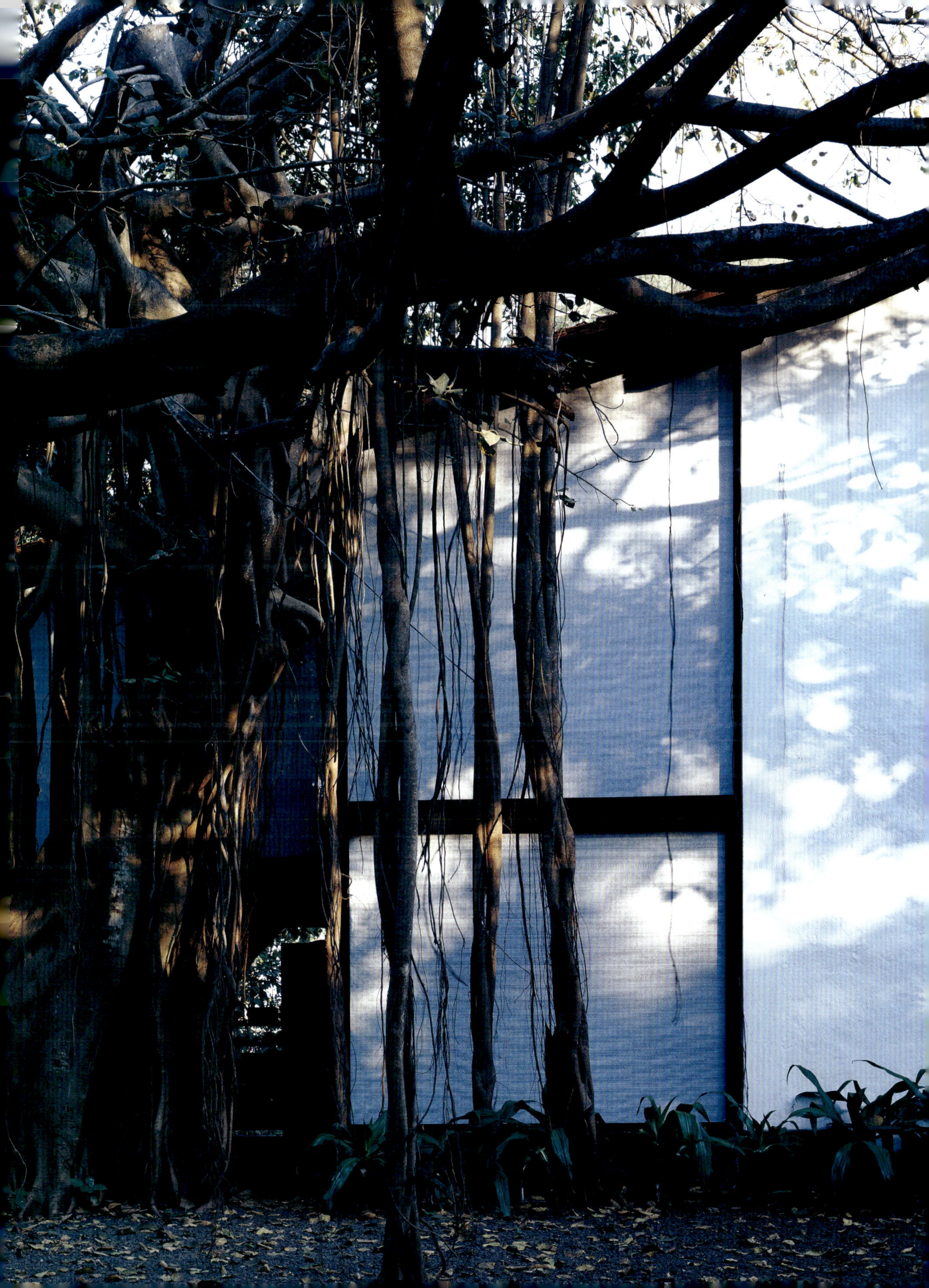

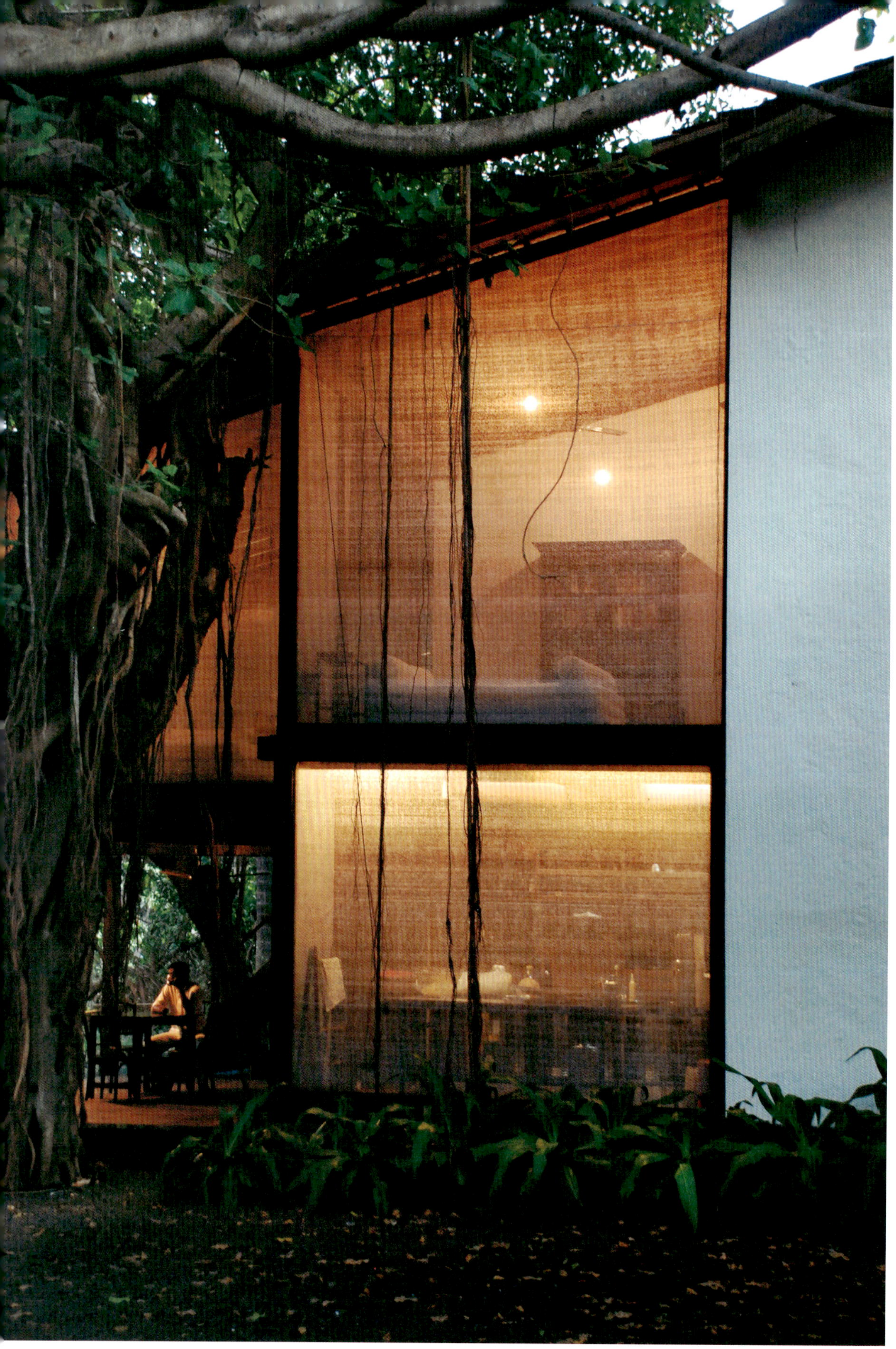

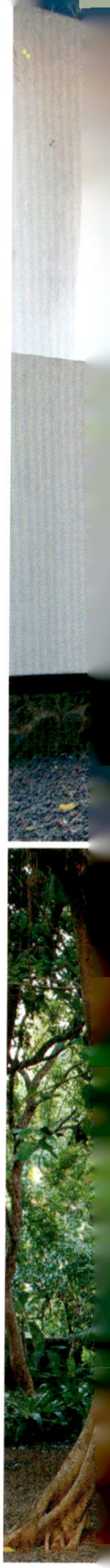

（上）ベランダ近景、リーディング・ルーム外観。
（左頁）住宅正面からのリーディング・ルーム夕景。
(Above images)Close-up of the verandah and exterior views of the reading room.
(Opposite page) The reading room seen from the front of the house at dusk.

Section north

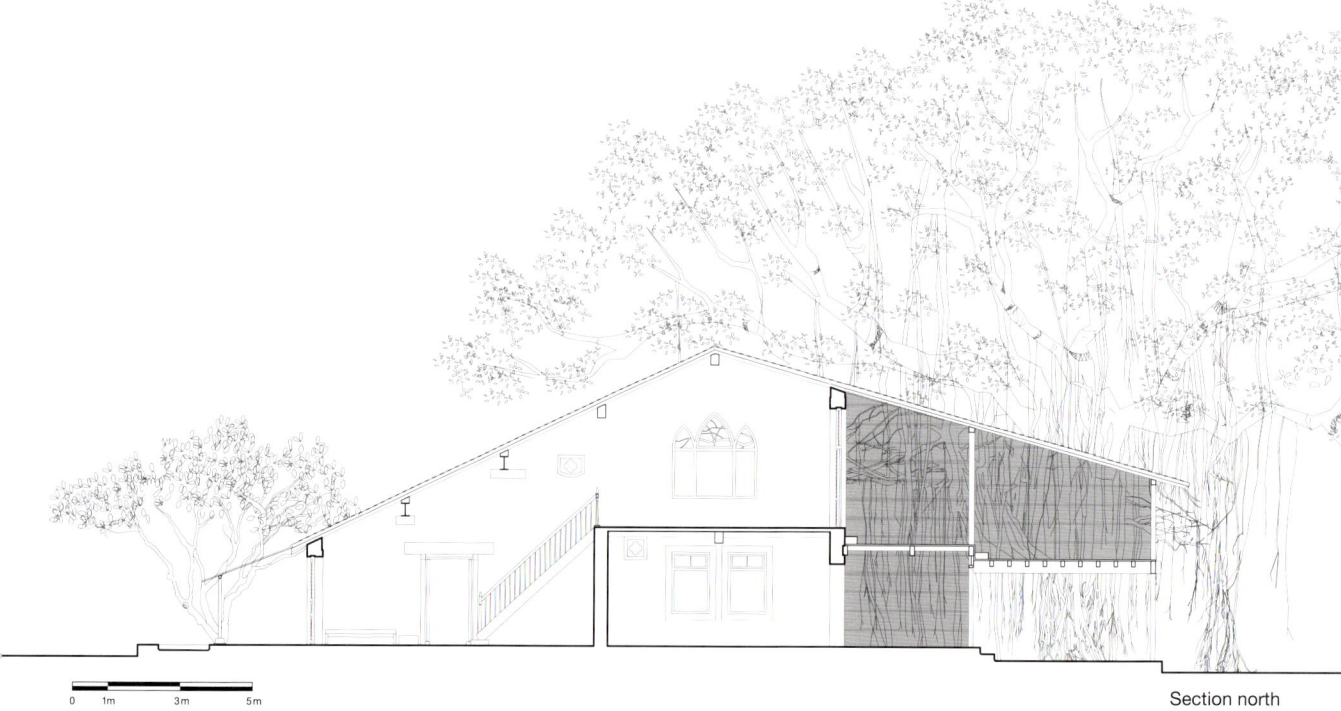

0 1m 3m 5m

062

リーディング・ルーム内観。
Interior views of the reading room.

First floor plan

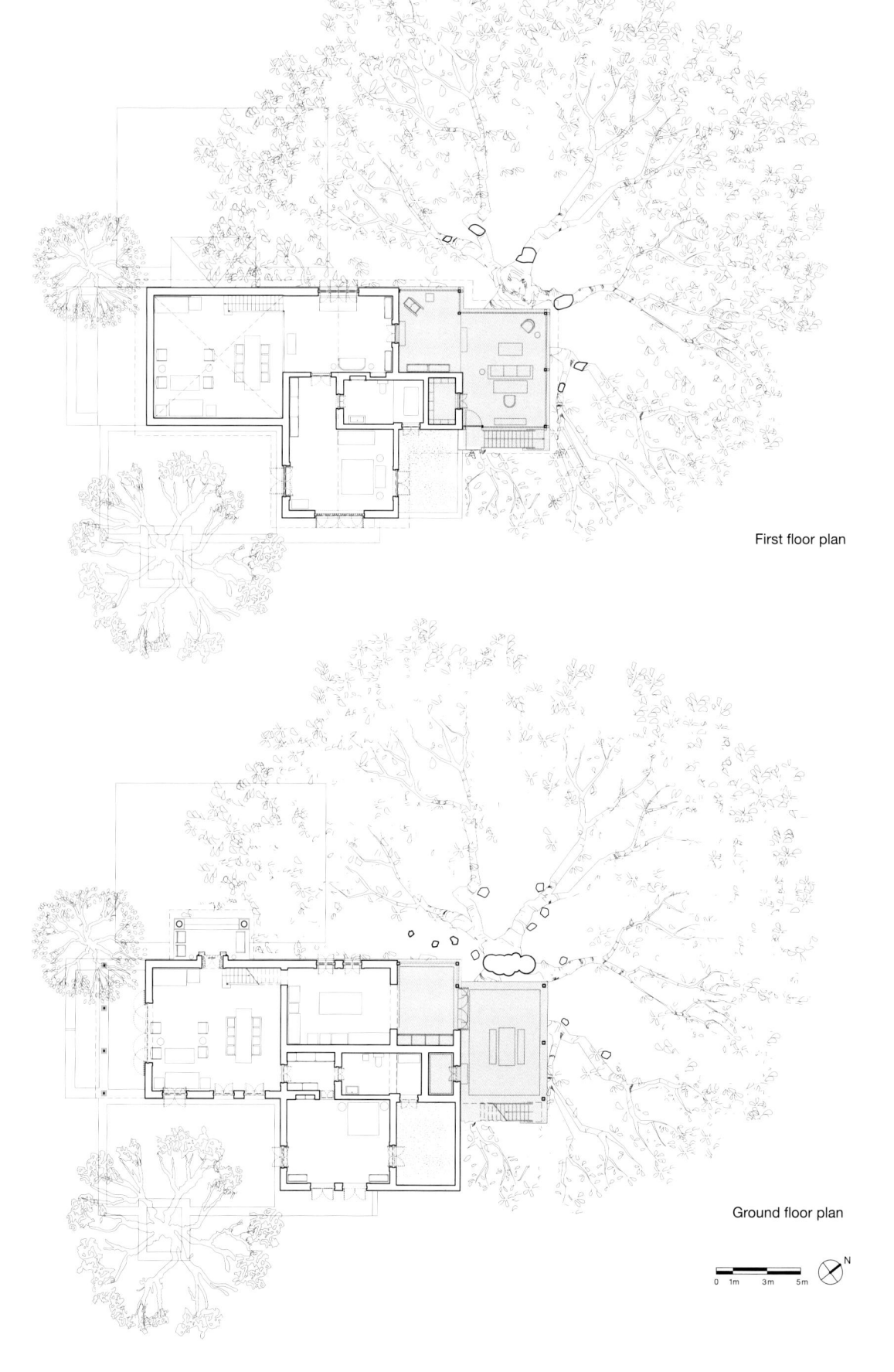

Ground floor plan

0 1m 3m 5m   N

リーディング・ルームから見たバンヤンノキ。　The banyan tree seen from inside the reading room.

コーナー部詳細。木製の枠に農業用ネットが張られている。
Detail of corner where agricultural netting sits in wooden frame.

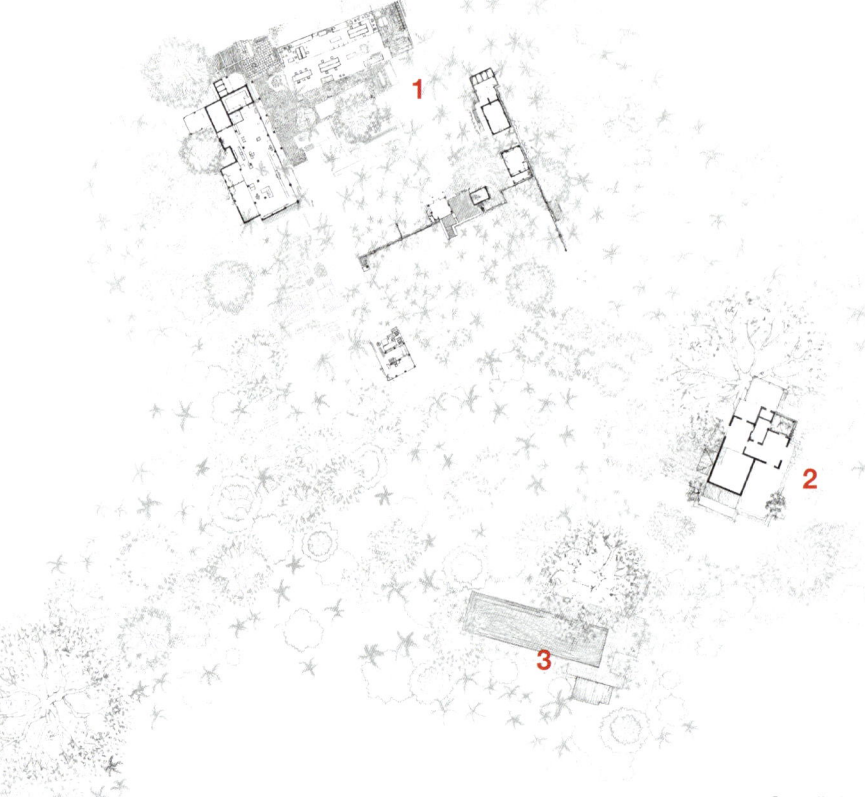

Overall site plan

1 Studio Mumbai Workshop
2 Reading Room
3 swimming pool

私道から眺めた既存住宅ならびに増築されたリーディング・ルームの夜景。
The reading room addition and existing house seen from the driveway at night.

Tara House
ターラ邸

2005 Kashid, Maharashtra, India

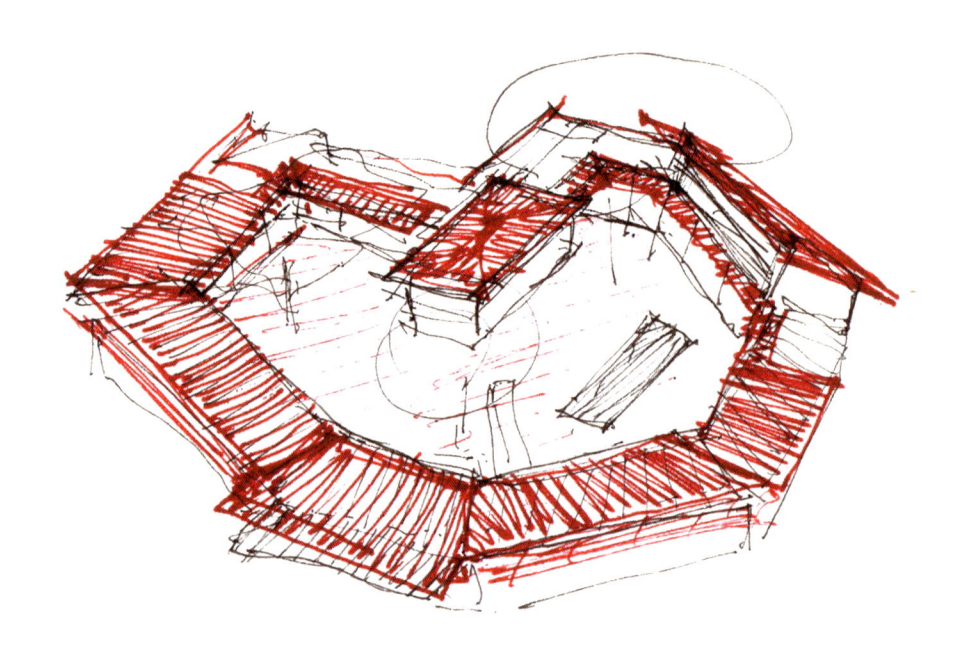

この住宅は、地面に伏せられた架空の風車から立ち上げられている。多角形の中庭の縁に各部屋が環状に並んで、家の中心に空洞をつくっている。

庭には、通路やベランダや窓から出入りできる。各住空間は、それぞれ異なった仕様で外界から守られているが、ひと続きの木造小屋組みの屋根がこれらを統一している。縦格子の間仕切り、持出し蝶番付きのジャロジー式扉、光沢のある黒鉛色の壁が、同心円状に層をなしながら、多世代が同居するこのカントリーハウスに溶け込む。黒く分厚い漆喰壁は、頭上から射す光を、ルリマツリ*に縁取られ同心円状に配されたベランダに投げかけ、また中庭の緑が室内に染み込んでいるようにも見せる。中庭から石段を下りて地下に潜ると、石の水槽ならぬ水を湛えたプラネタリウム風の空間がある。天井には円窓がほどよい間隔で穿たれており、ここから地上の光や風が入り、雨季には雨が落ちてくる。地面に浸み込んだ雨水は帯水層を潤し、そこからプールや庭に撒かれて夏の猛暑を和らげる。荒々しい石の壁面に射す光の点が、地中に星座を描く。部屋は巻き貝のごとく、波の音を立てて海の気配を感じさせる。

*イソマツ科の常緑低木。瑠璃茉莉。

Tara House unfolds as if from a notional planar pinwheel, with the multi-faced courtyard garden approached from a ringed arrangement of discrete rooms, forming the ventricular centre of the experience of the house.

The garden is approached through walkways, verandahs and window arrangements, and a wood-framed roof forms a unifying plane for the variously protected living spaces. Vertically slatted partitions, parliament-hinged, adjustable-louvered doors and burnished graphite-coloured walls together enable concentric layers of enclosure and mingling in this multi-generation country house. The dark, rich plastered walls impart a suspension of light into the concentric plumbago-edged verandahs and absorb the viridian courtyard as if into the house. Accessed by a stone staircase which descends beneath the courtyard, there lies a stone-lined, water-filled room like an aqueous, subterranean planetarium. Carefully arranged circular openings in the courtyard above draw in light, air and the monsoon rain. The percolating rainwater replenishes the aquifer which waters the pool and gardens and provides respite from the thick heat of the summer; intense points of light on the hewn stone walls form an underground stellar map. The room acts like a building conch, with oceanic reverberations to remember the nearby sea with.

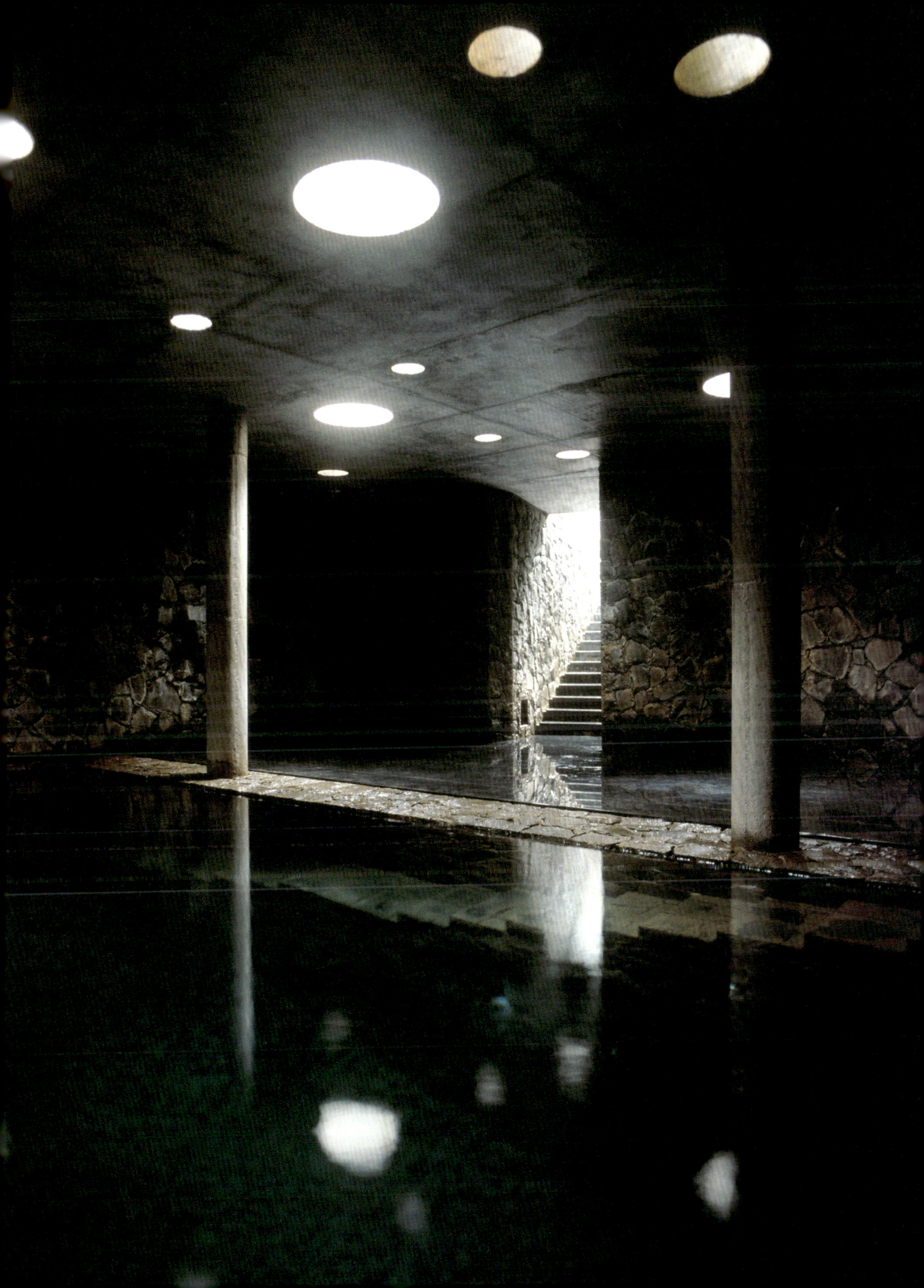

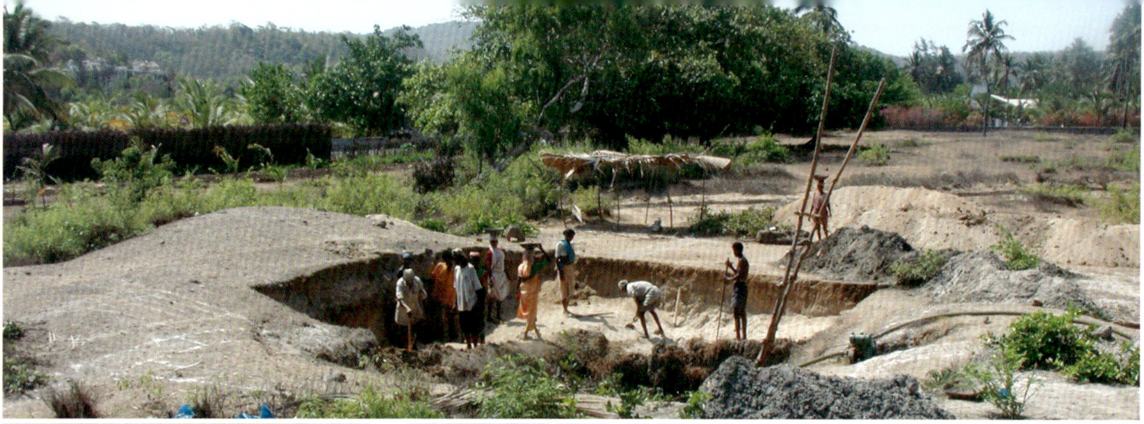

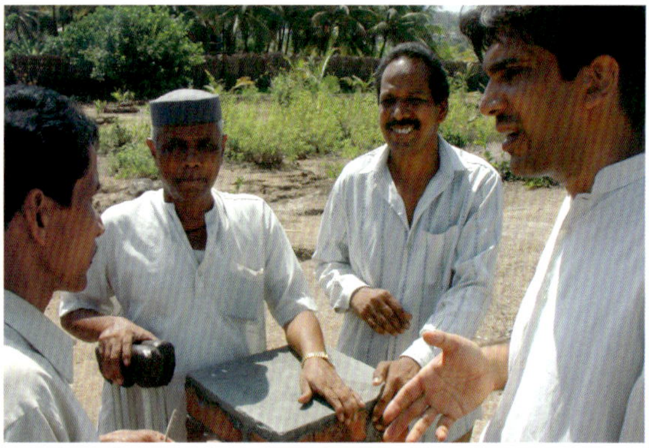

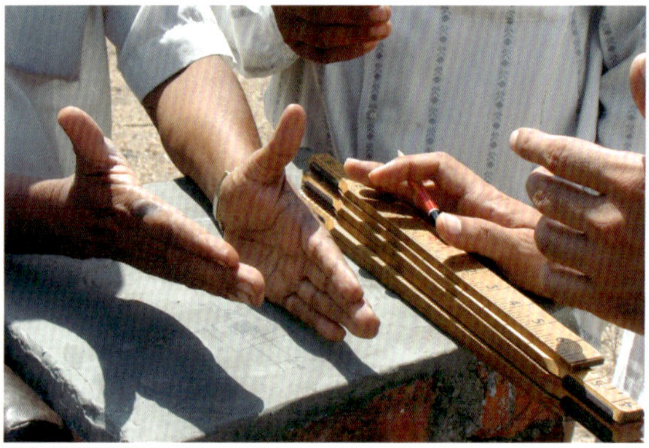

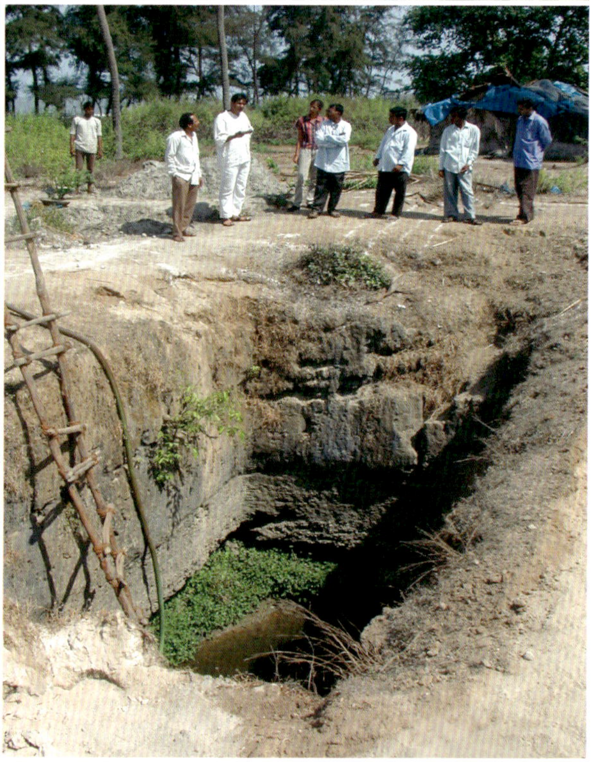

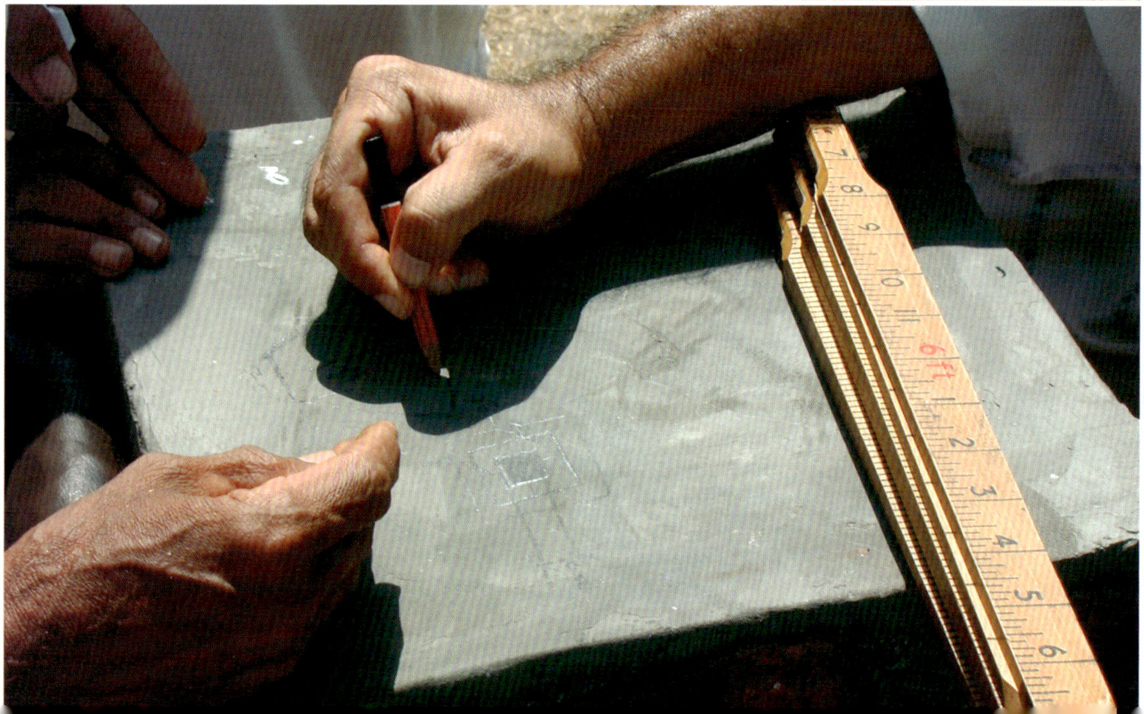

(上)バオリ(階段状井戸)の掘削と建設。
(左頁)現場にて井戸工事の技師とデザインの検討。

(Above images) The excavation and construction of the Baoli/step well.
(Opposite page) Design development discussion at site with master well builder.

0 1m 5m 10m N

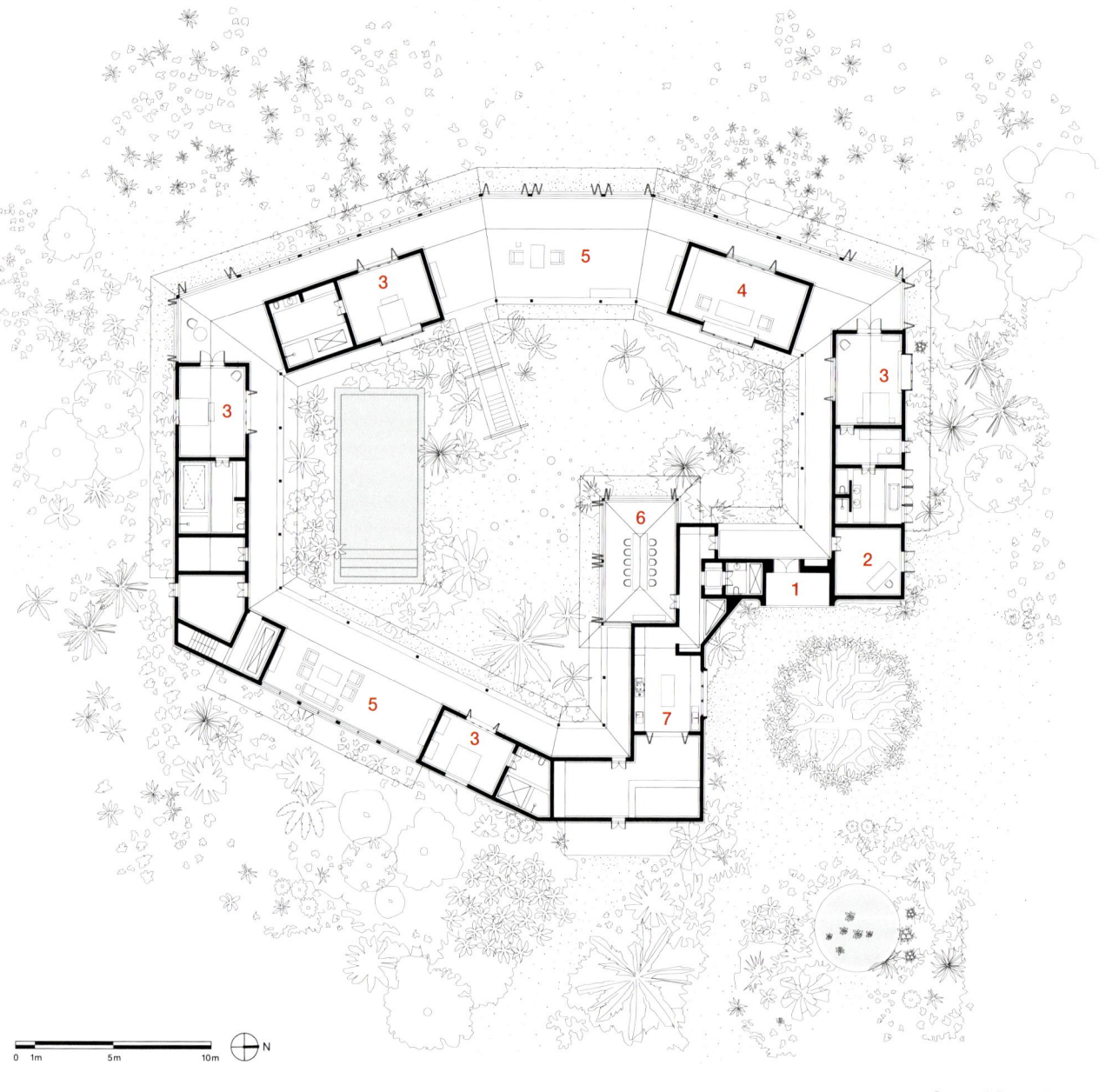

Ground floor plan

1. entry
2. study
3. bedroom
4. living room
5. veranda
6. dining
7. kitchen

072

住宅の西側外観。　View of house from the west.

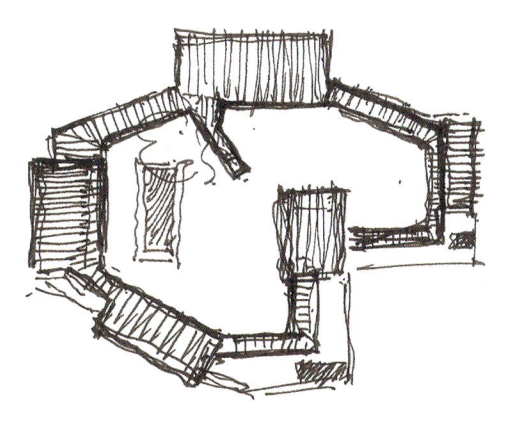

北側の廊下より居間のベランダを見る。
The main living verandah seen from the north passage.

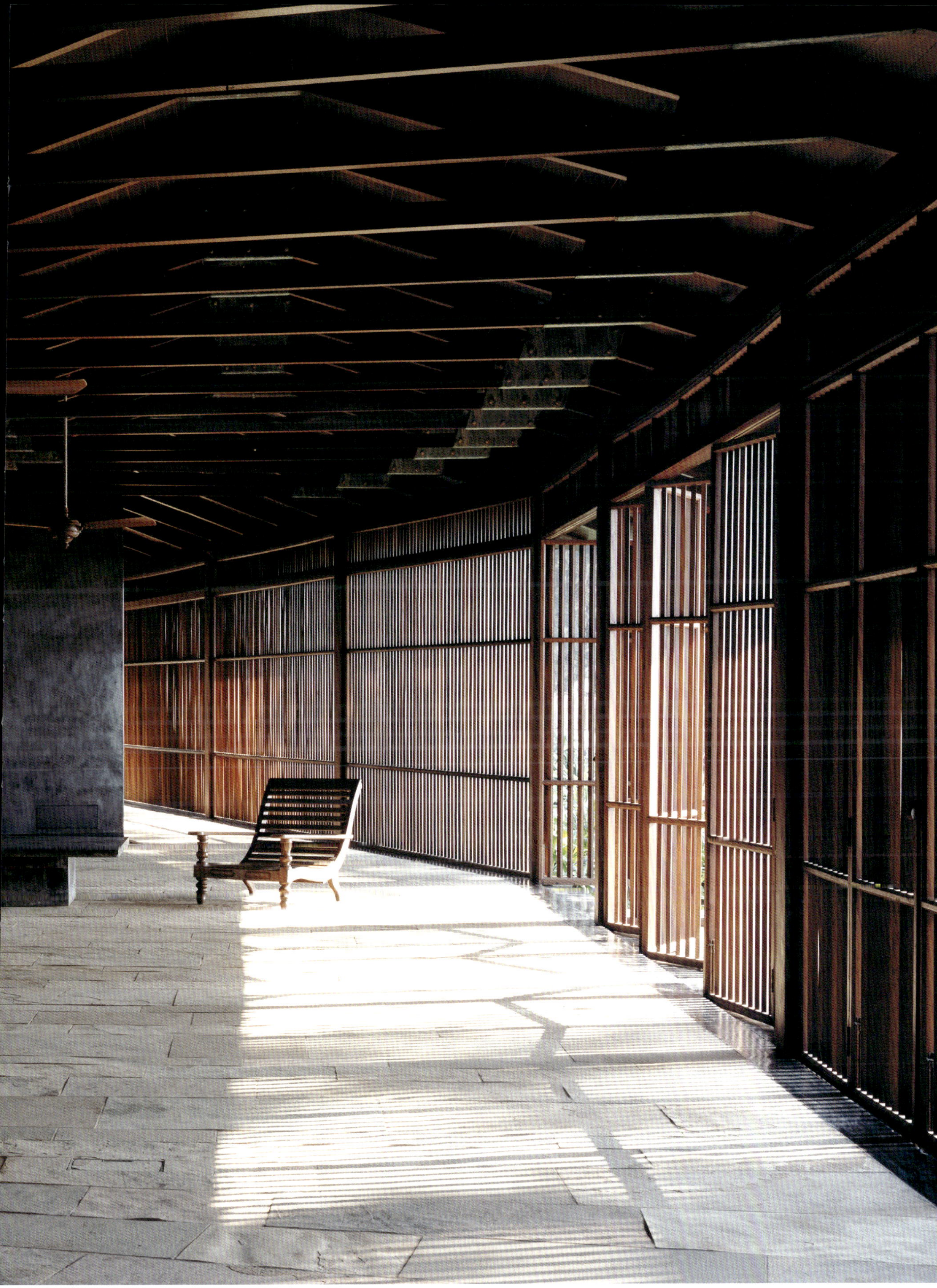

（上）バオリと中庭の断面。（左）地上の風、音、光、水は、円形トップライトから帯水層を抜けて地下に落ちる。（右頁）潮の干満が月・日周期を知らせる。

(Above) Section through the Baoli and courtyard.
(Left) Circular skylights puncture the courtyard above the subterranean aquifer allowing air, sound light and water to enter the space.
(Opposite page) Lunar and diurnal cycles are experienced through the rise and fall of the tide.

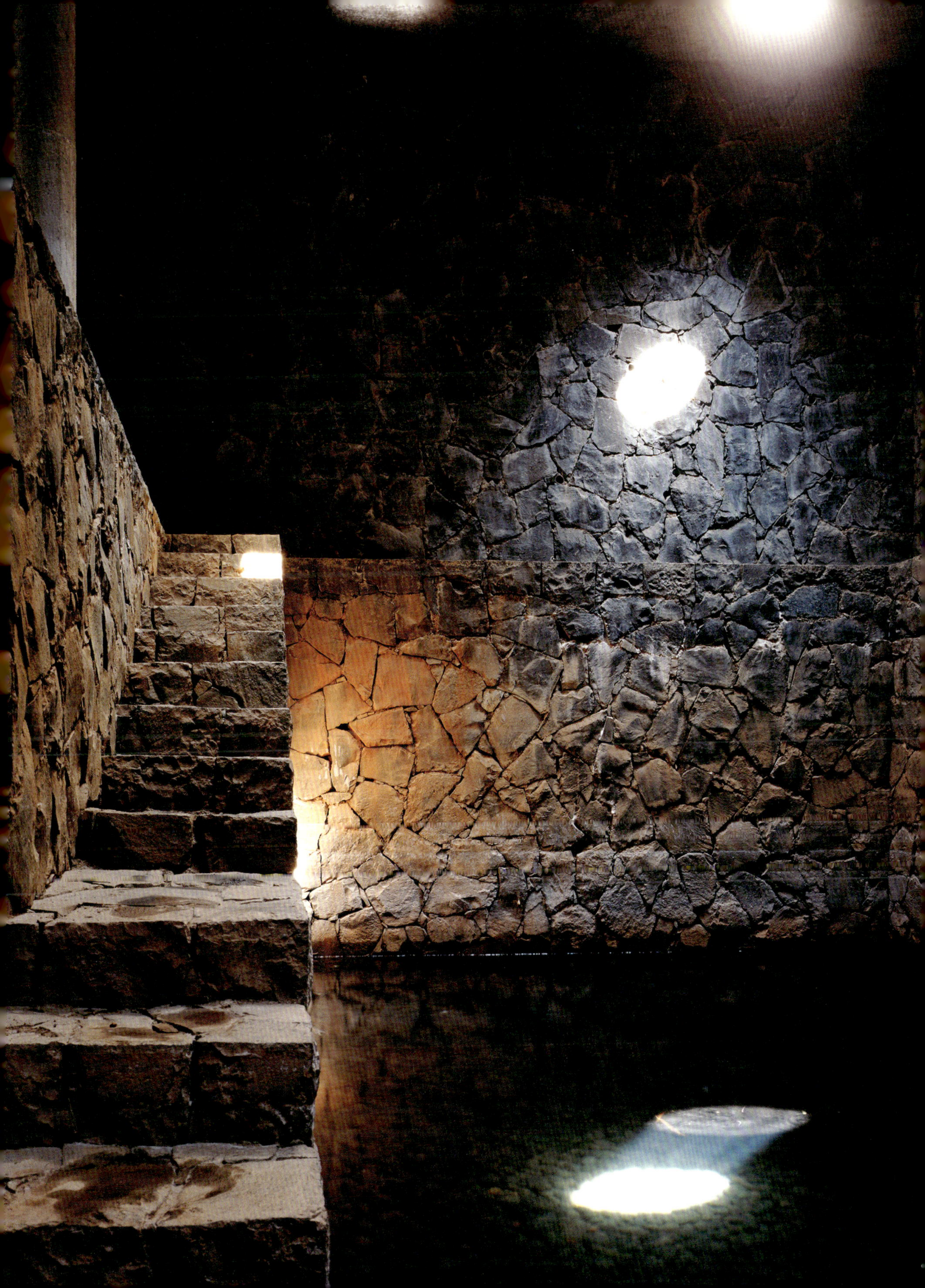

078

（上、左）縦格子のスクリーンが光を透過させつつ、外から廊下への侵入を防いでいる。
（左頁上・左下）定規摺りの着彩磨き仕上げのコンクリート壁に、中庭の緑が映り込む。
（左頁右下）黒いプラスターに縁取られた表玄関。

(Above, left) Slatted wood screens filter light and provide security around the main passage.
(Opposite page) Polished pigmented cement screed reflects the colours of the landscape from the central courtyard (above images, left).
Main entry to the house framed in black plaster (below right).

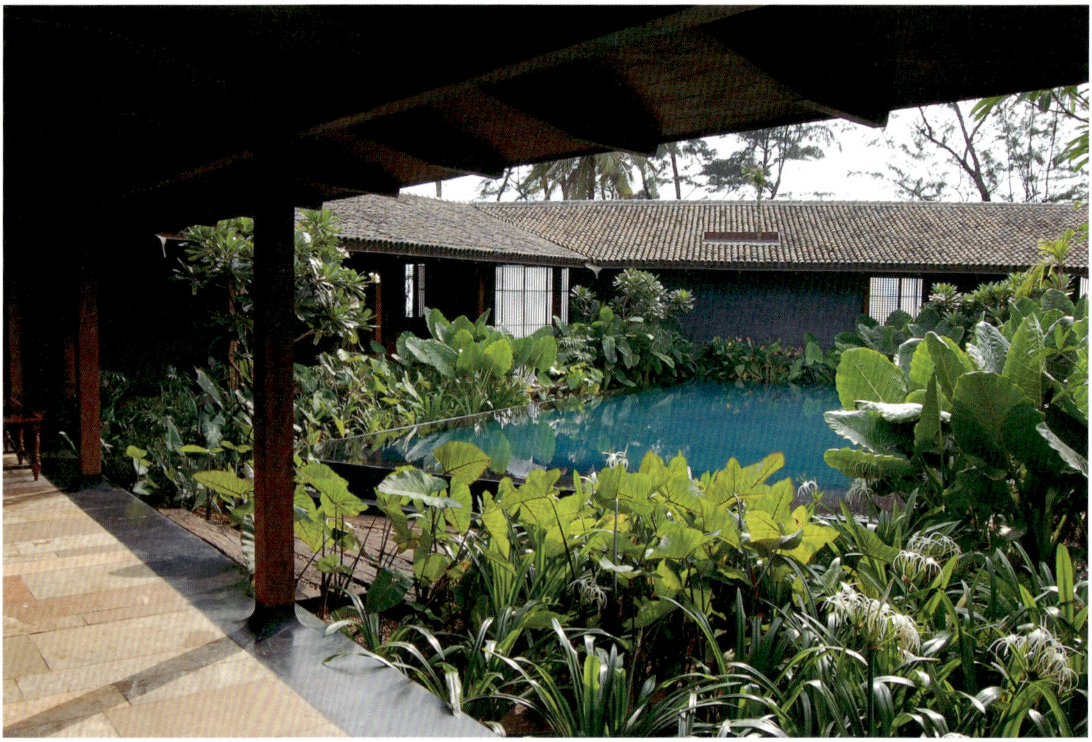

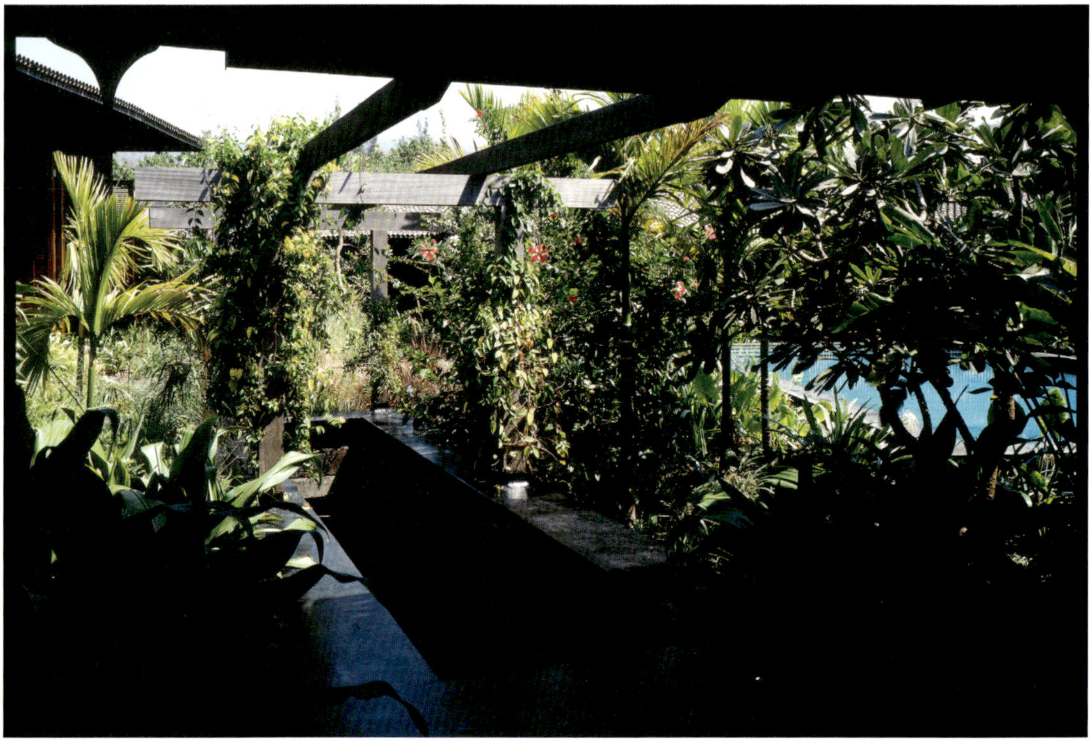

東から眺めた中庭。地面に穿たれた穴は地下空間用のトップライト。 The interior of the courtyard seen from its eastern edge showing the round skylights to the space below.

Section east

Section south

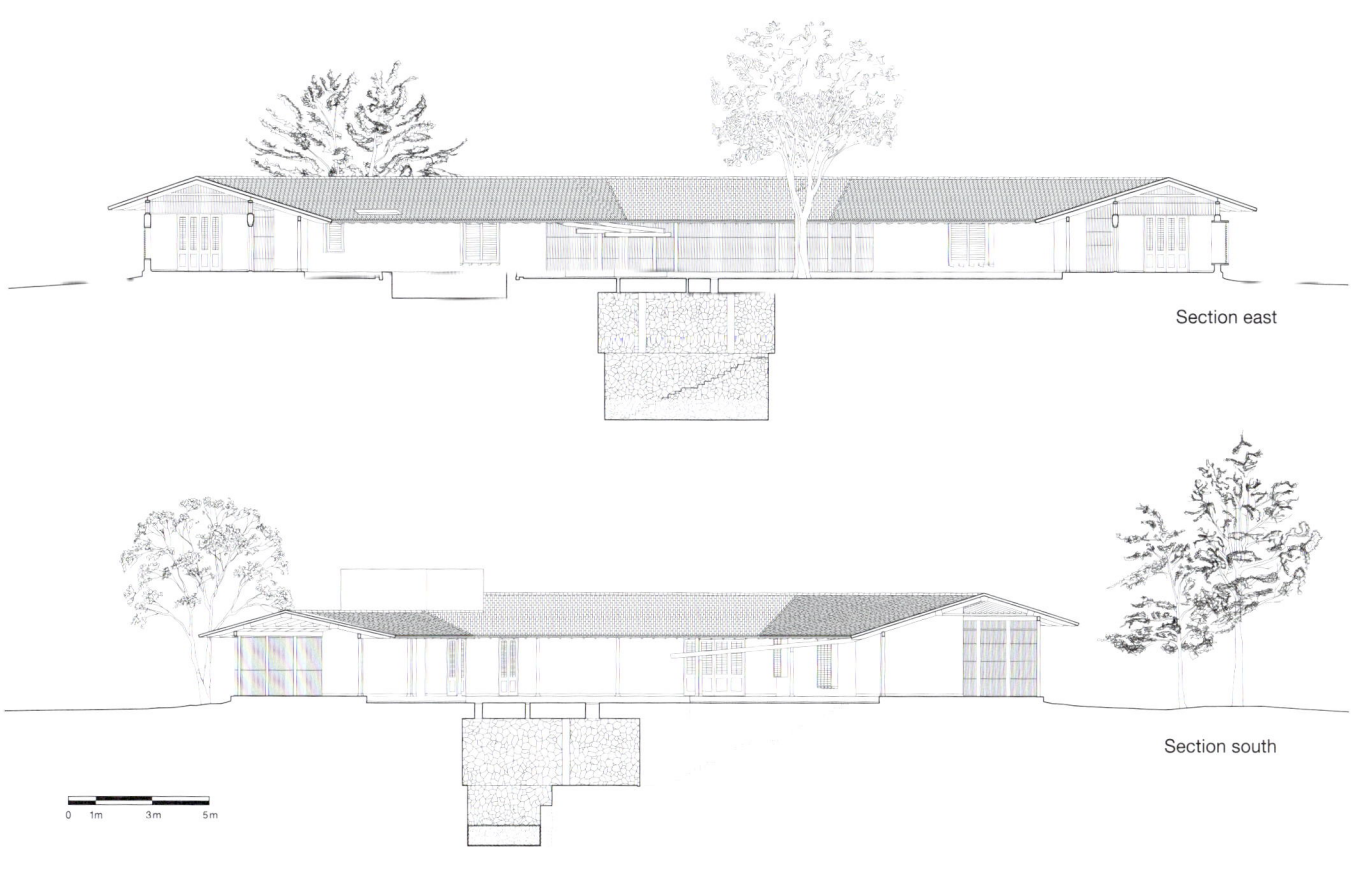

081

(下)海に面した西側ベランダ。
(右頁)西側ベランダ外観。
(Below) View from the western verandah towards the sea.
(Opposite page) View into the western verandah.

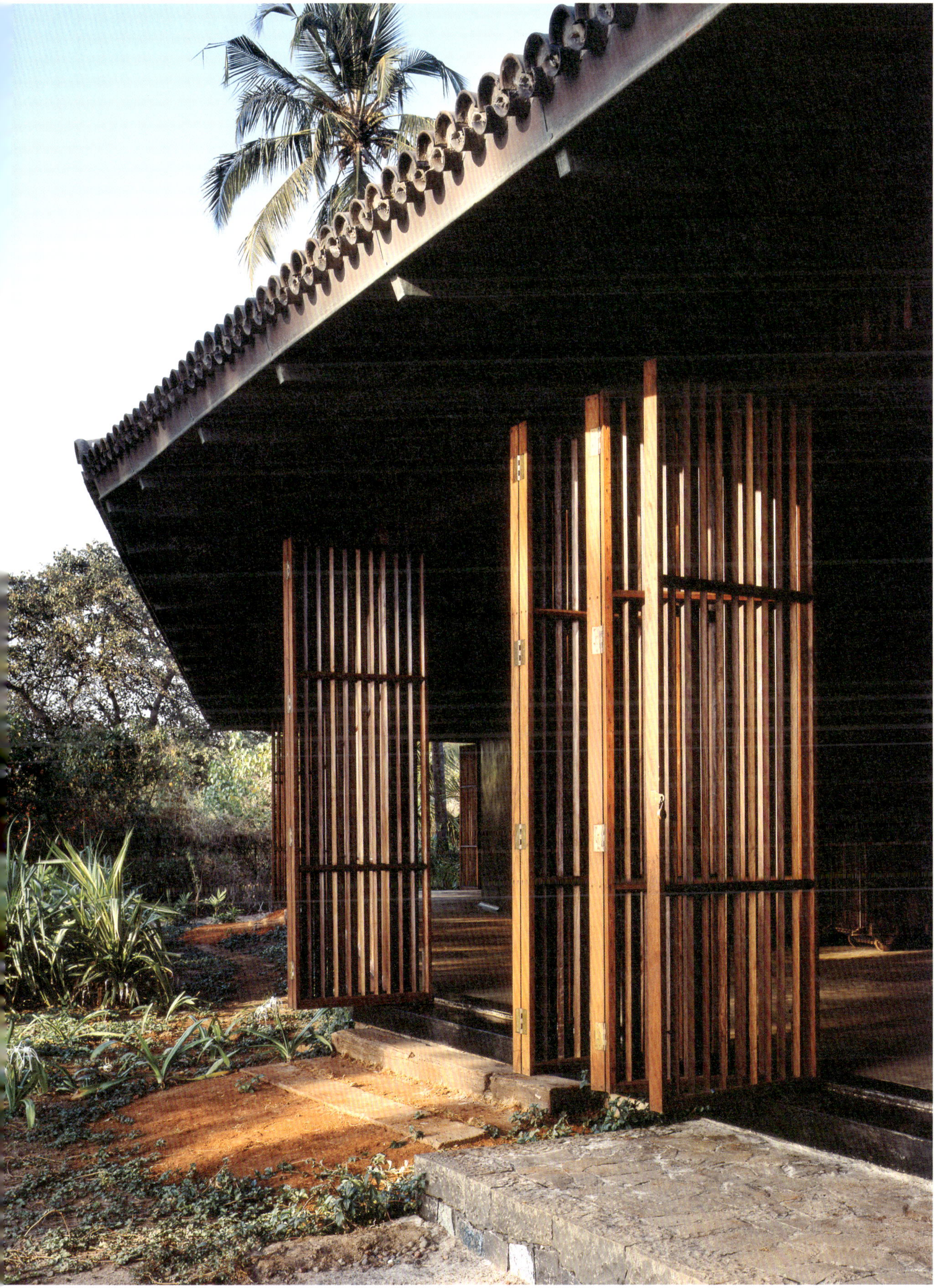

Leti 360 Resort
レティ360リゾート

2007 Leti, Uttaranchal, India

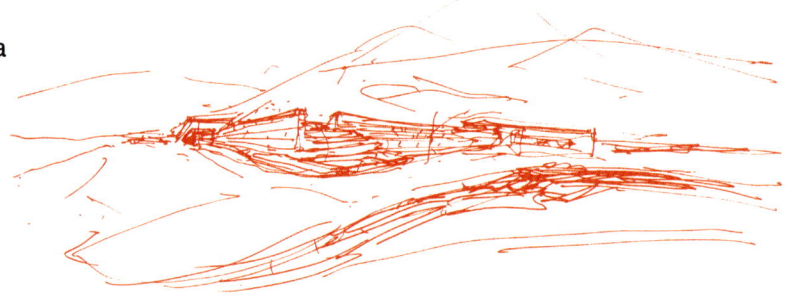

この一風変わったリゾートの設計では、単に与えられたプログラムをかたちにするのではなく、むしろ敷地を丹念に観察し、その風土を尊重するつもりでプログラムを一から組み立てることにした。

インド・ヒマラヤ山脈の麓、海抜2,350mの高みには、宿泊棟が居間と食堂棟を取り巻くようにして建っている。地元の村道のうちの1本の細い山道が、ここに直接通じている。北にはヒラモニー氷河とナンダコット山（標高6,861m）を、東の地平線にはネパール国境上の峰々を望み、南には峠や渓谷の間を切り開くようにしてラムガンガ川が流れている。

4棟の宿泊棟は、山裾の段々畑の段にもたれるようにして建つ。畑の農作物や家畜の世話をするのは、この地で逞しく生きる堅忍な山人たちだ。ここでは土着の工法と地場素材を用い、さらに土地の慣習に従うことで、プロジェクトを建築面でもそのほかの面でも管理しやすくした。7か月の工期で仕上げるために、総勢70名の地元の石工や大工や職人に協力を求めた。この工事には、ひとつ付帯条件があった。それは、建築家は土地の風習と農民大工（土地を借りる代わりに労働力を提供する人びと）の習わしに従って、モンスーンと冬の時季は作業を中断せよというものである。

現場は最寄りの車道から9km離れており、徒歩では2時間がかりの道程になる。当然、この地の利の悪さと、限られた人手と資材の範囲で可能なことを考えた。そこで空積みの石壁に、山の鋭い陽射しを取り込むために木製の格子窓をはめた。地元で切り出された石は、運搬人夫がラバを使って現場に搬入した。そのほかのチーク材、ガラス、アルミ、銅、キャンバス地といった資材も——特注の家具とともに——やはり同じ方式で搬入された。給湯用にソーラー・パネルを取り付け、またグリッドから遠く外れた位置にある客室用にソーラー・ランタンも用意した。

建物に与えられた寿命が10年である以上、このプロジェクトでは〈時間〉が主役を担う。したがって、いずれはこの場所を原状復帰できるような設計にした。そしてその効果はすでに現れている。自然はじりじりと建物に忍び込み、石壁や床の隙間にその姿を覗かせている。家畜は一面に茂った草を食み、段々畑では今も変わらずに作物が栽培されている。スタジオ・ムンバイは、このユニークな「受動的な修景」プロジェクトのまとめ役として、地元の人びとの助けを借りつつ、日常に磨きをかけ、それをたぶん崇高と呼べるものに仕立てていった。

The architectural parti for this atypical resort was defined not as an interpretation of programme as much as the creation of it, through careful observation and respect of the site and its cycles of climate and culture.

Perched in the foothills of the Indian Himalayas at 2350 metres (7700 ft.) above sea level, the group of guest buildings is centred on a public living/dining pavilion to which a narrow mountainside footpath, part of a network of local village trails, leads directly. Hiramony Glacier and the peak of Nanda Kot (6,861 m / 22510 ft.) are visible to the north; the peaks of Nepal line the eastern horizon; and to the south, the Ram Ganga River carves its way through steep terraced valleys and mountain passes.

The four guest structures are located in the folds of the agricultural foothill terraces, where food crops and livestock are tended to by the tenacious mountain people, fiercely tuned to the rhythms of the mountains. Using indigenous building techniques and materials, and adopting local custom as the key to managing the project, both architecturally and otherwise, the studio enlisted 70 village masons, carpenters and craftspersons to build the resort in a period of 7 months. A concomitant condition for the building of this project was that the architects follow the stricture laid down by the farmer-builders (who leased out the land and provided the labour), that work be halted during the monsoon and winter as is the custom in the region.

As a two-hour, 9 kilometre walk from the nearest motorable road, the project was conceived keeping in mind limited access, human and material, and was designed as a combination of dry-stacked stone with glazed wooden insertions, to let in the sharp mountain light. Stone was quarried locally and carried to site by porters and mules, all other building materials, including teak wood, glass, aluminium, copper, and canvas - along with custom-made furniture - arrived on site in the same manner. Solar panels are used to generate energy for hot water and solar lanterns for the guest units, owing to its remote location which is off the grid.

Designated to maintain a ten-year lifespan, Time is a primary protagonist in this project, which is designed to be reversible in timeline and form, and its effects are already visible, as the landscape creeps back into the buildings, appearing in the crevices of the stone walls and floors, local livestock partake of the grassy surroundings and terraced plantations continue to be cultivated. The studio played a facilitating role, unique and gratifying in the 'passive reworking of the landscape', enlisting the local and specific in order to hone the quotidian towards what could cautiously be called sublime.

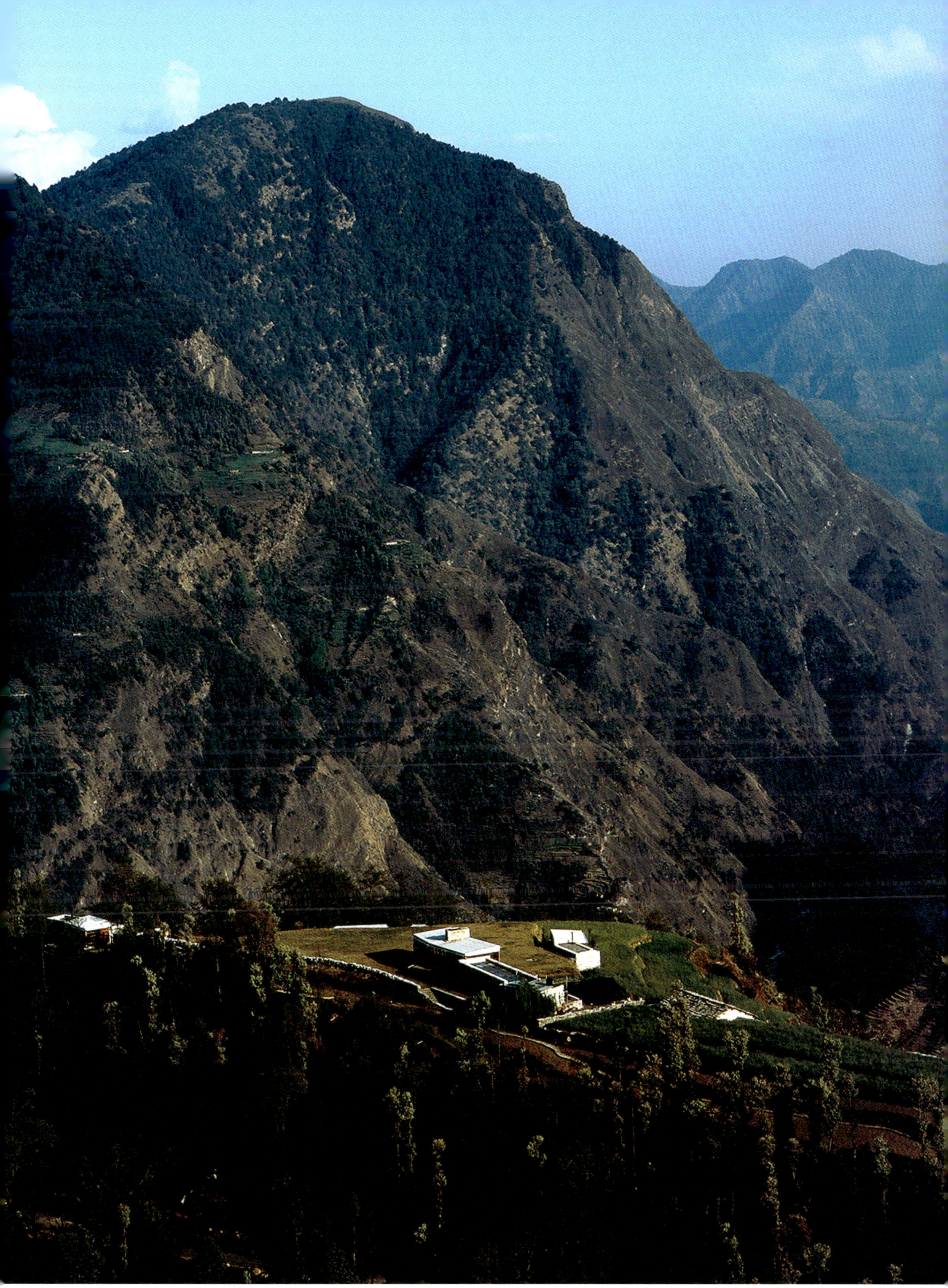

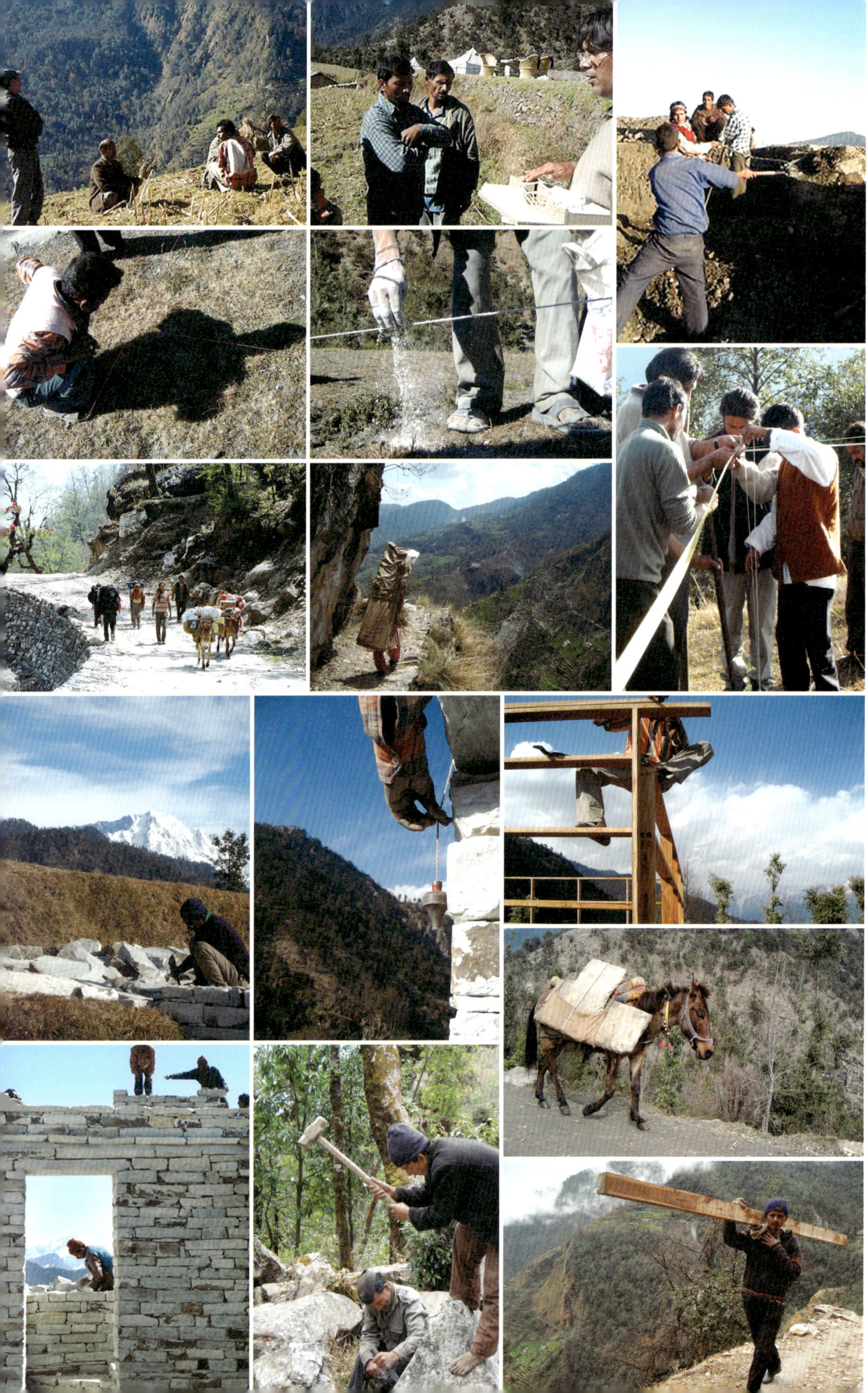

087

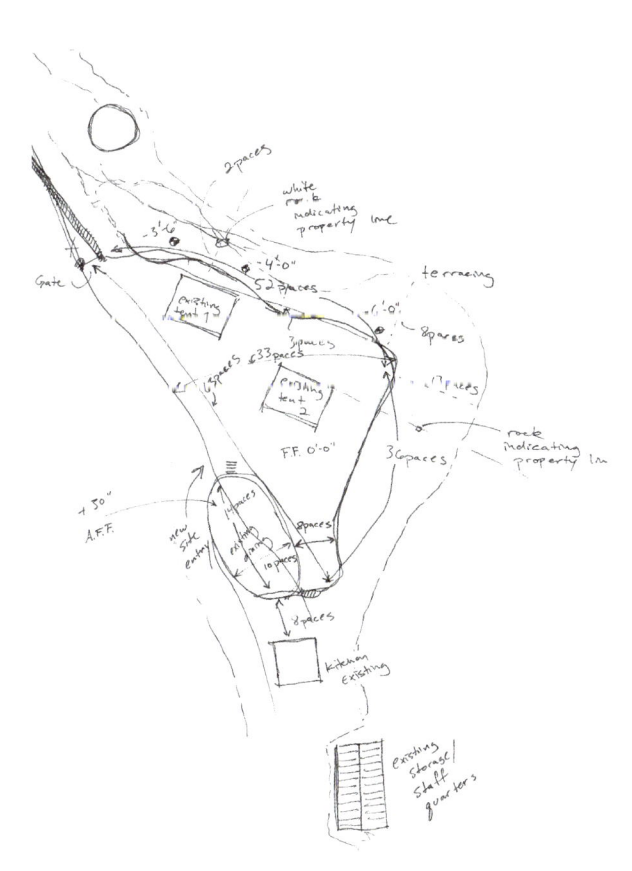

北側の景色。手前の台地が今回の敷地、奥に見えるのがヒラモニー氷河とナンダコット山の峰。

Looking north across the plateau on which the buildings are sited, towards the Hiramony glacier and the peak of Nanda Kot.

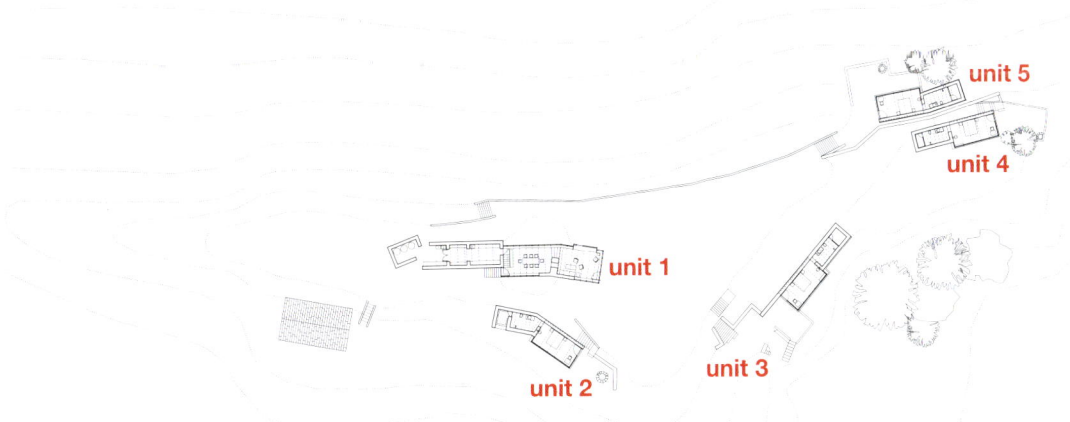

Site plan

unit1 main building
unit2-5 guest structures

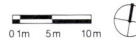

0 1m 5m 10m

089

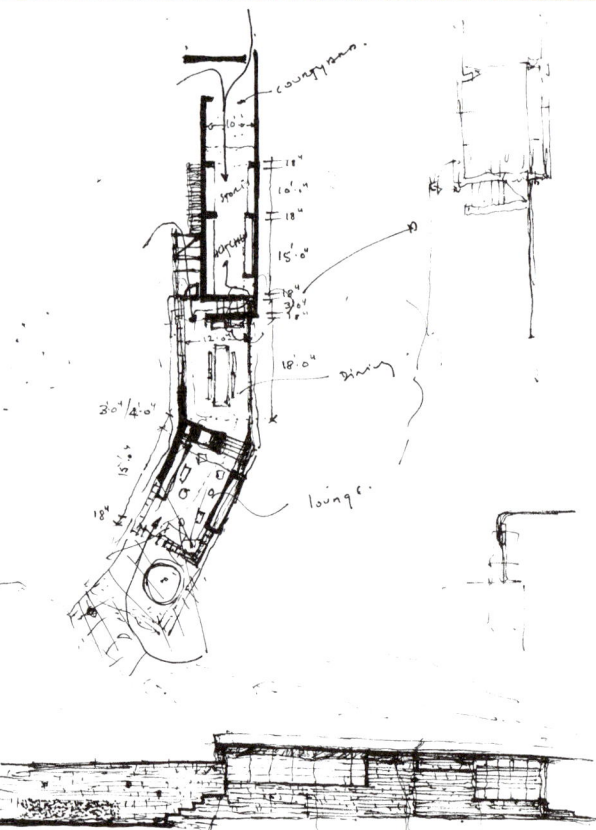

（上）東側のユニット4［宿泊棟］とそのテラスを望む。
（右頁上）本館［ユニット1］の北側をつたって敷地に入る。（右頁下）本館外観。

(Above) Looking east towards unit four and its terrace.
(Opposite page) Arrival at the site along north edge of the main building(above). Exterior views of the main building(below).

091

Site section: unit 1

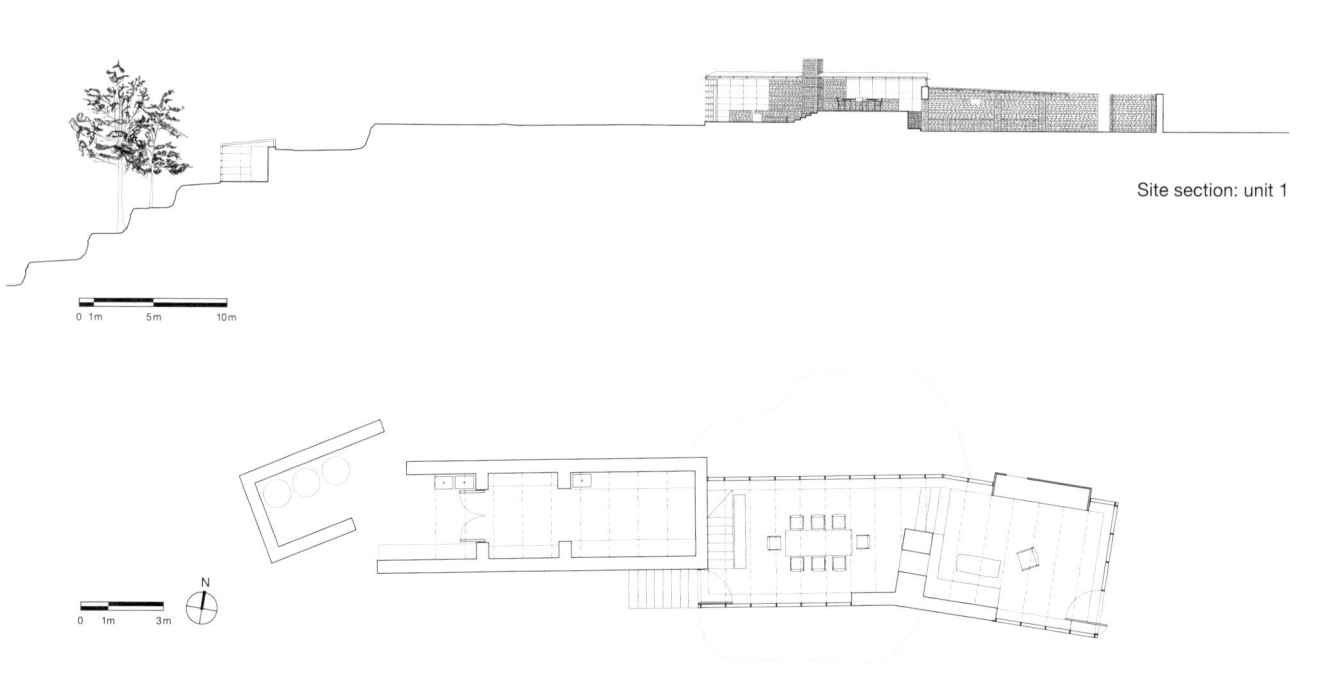

Floor plan: unit 1

（上、左2点）本館内部から外の景色を望む。
（下右）ユニット1の夜景。
（左頁）本館食堂から居間を見る。
(Above, left images) The surroundings viewed from within the main building. (Below right) Unit one seen at night.
(Opposite page) View from the dining room in main building towards the living space.

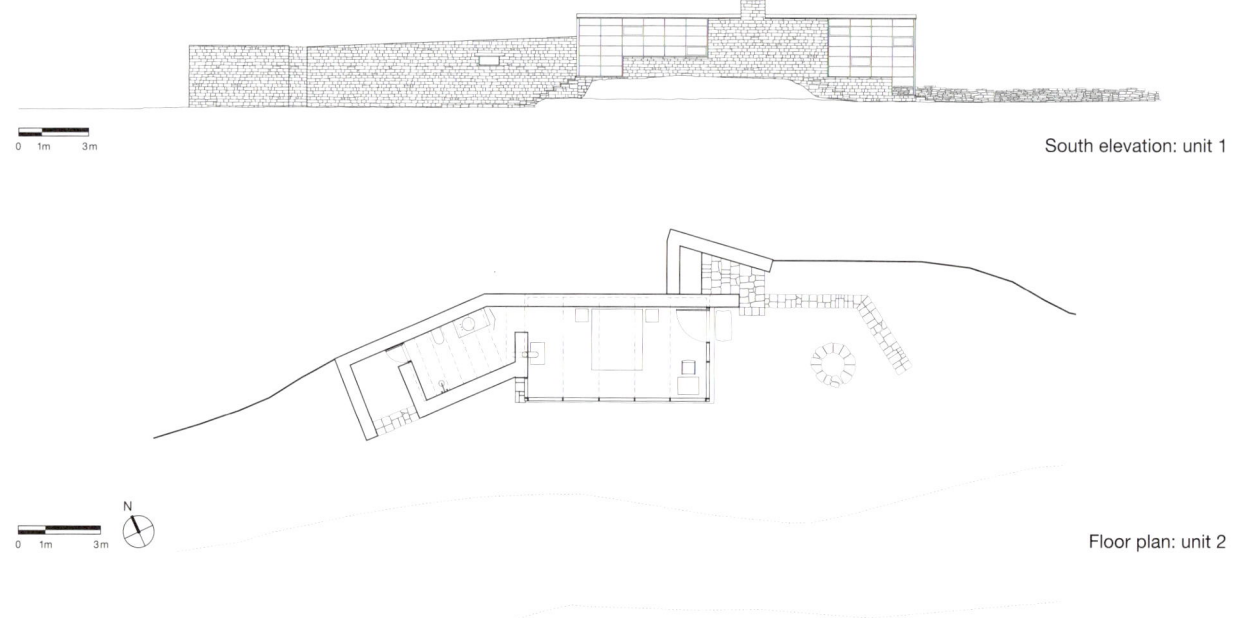

South elevation: unit 1

Floor plan: unit 2

(左上から時計回りに) ユニット2越しに南を見る。ユニット1の石垣。西にユニット1と2を見る。ユニット2の石垣。
(左頁) 南東よりユニット2を見る。

(Clockwise from top left) Looking south across unit two, unit one stone wall, looking west towards units one and two, stone walls of unit two.
(Opposite page) View of unit two from southeast.

（上）高台からユニット3越しに東側のユニット4と5を見る。
（右頁左）南東からのユニット3全景。
（右頁右）北東からのユニット3全景。

(Above) View from the plateau looking east across unit three towards units four and five.
(Opposite page) Views of unit three from the southeast (left image) and northeast (right image).

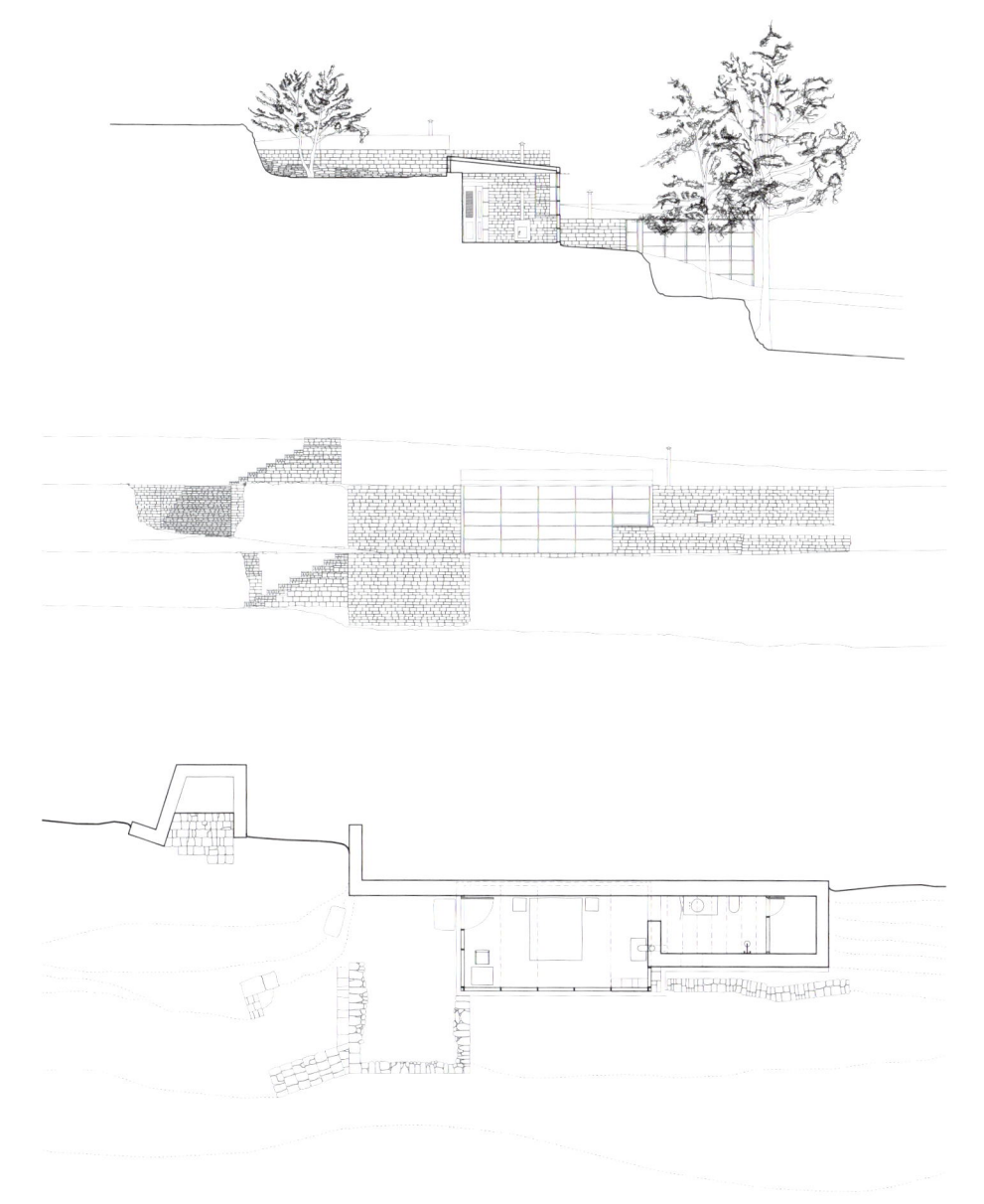

Section, south elevation and plan: unit 3

097

(上）ユニット4と5越しに北東を望む。彼方にはネパール・ヒマラヤが控えている。
(右頁）台地に面したユニット5の南側ファサード。

(Above) The distant Nepali Himalaya to the northeast viewed across units four and five.
(Opposite page) View unit five south façade looking towards the plateau.

Floor plan: units 4 and 5

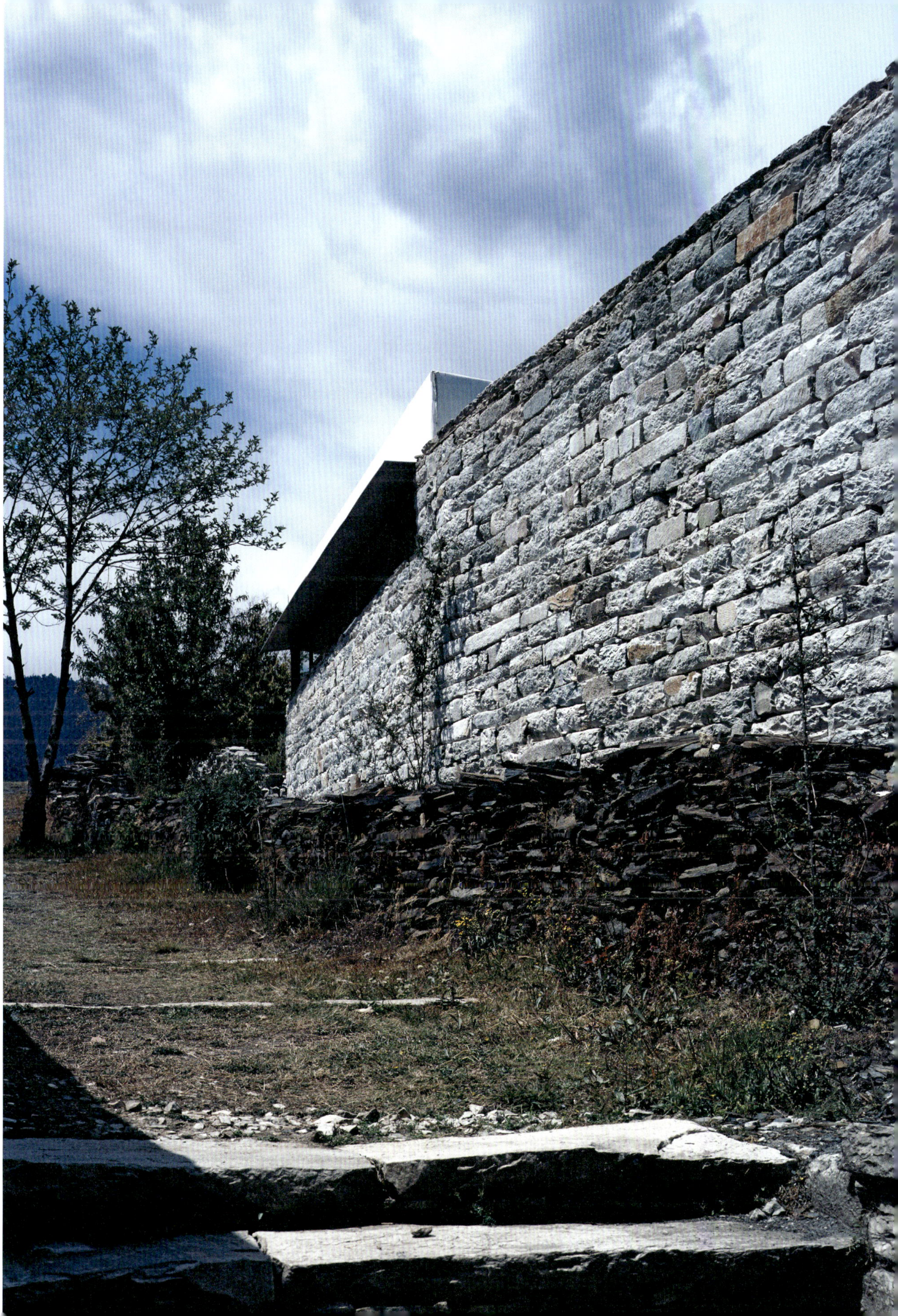

Palmyra House
パルミラの住宅

2007 Nandgaon, Maharashtra, India

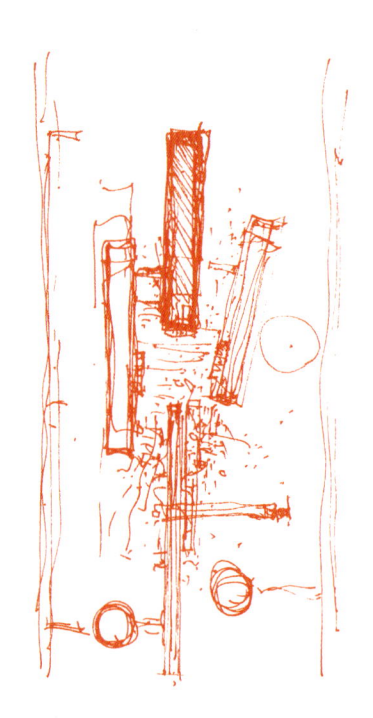

苔むした石造の水路づたいに歩いていくと、鬱蒼としたヤシ林の奥深くに21棟の木造住宅が建っている。この配置は、ヤシの木を極力切らずに済ませるためである。石壇の上に載ったこれら木箱から庭を見下ろすと、井戸や水路やヤシの林が見える。このように複雑なランドスケープまでもが住環境の一部に取り込まれている。

光と風が、木細工の壁を抜け、ゆっくりと室内にまわる。光が照り返したり、影が落ちたり、あるいは辺りが明るくなったりほぞ暗くなったりするたびに、家は表情を変える。居間と読書室は北側の棟に、台所と食堂は南側の棟に振り分けられているが、寝室と浴室はどちらの棟にもある。また、棟間のスペースも含めたこの2棟を臨機応変に使えば、種々のイベントにも対応できる。棟間のスペースには、スイミング・プールが設けられている。プールの東にはヤシの木立がどこまでも続き、西には海の眺めが広がる。

周りには木が密集しているため、建設重機が使えず、結局工事はすべてスタジオの職人たちが手作業で行った。住宅の骨組みについては、アインウッドという地場の硬材を、予め作業場でほぞ接ぎにできるように加工しておいてから現場で組み立てた。外壁のルーバーには、在来種のパルミラヤシの幹の外層を材料に、これを一定間隔に並べて、日除け、風除け、雨除け、さらには目隠しにした。外装は、銅板金の雨押えと南京下見、いっぽう内装は、チーク材と定規摺りのモルタル仕上げである。ちなみにこのモルタルは、地衣類の模様をつけたココナツの樹皮を模してモスグレーに着彩された。敷地内の4か所に掘られた井戸の水は、生活用水として使われるほか、土地の風習にならって水路から引かれて植物の水やりにも使われる。こうしてランドスケープは日々の暮らしに組み込まれる。伝統の継承にして、日常の儀式の始まりでもある。

Accessed by foot along a moss covered stone aqueduct, the house is constructed as two timber-framed volumes and sits at the heart of a dense coconut plantation, positioned carefully to preserve as many trees as possible. The wooden boxes are anchored to stone platforms which overlook wells, water channels and a field of palms, weaving and absorbing this complex landscape into an inhabitable whole.

Light and air filter through the handcrafted wood structures, gently inundating the spaces. Alternating reflections, shadows, brightness, and semi-darkness enliven the way in which the house is revealed. The house disperses living and reading in the north volume, while the south contains cooking and dining; sleeping and bathing functions are shared in both structures. Events oscillate between these two volumes, involving the space in-between, and the infinite in this performance. Set within this space is the pool, a channel for swimming towards endless vistas of palm trees to the east and the sea to the west.

The density of the trees prevented the use of heavy equipment and all phases of work were executed manually by artisans from the studio. Structural framing for the house was fabricated of ain, a local hardwood, and prepared in the workshop. It was later assembled at site using interlocking joinery. The external louvers were made from the outer part of the palymra trunk, a local palm species and were carefully calibrated to provide protection from the sun, wind, and rain and privacy to the interiors. Exteriors were detailed with hand-worked copper flashing and ship lapped wood siding while interior surfaces were finished with teakwood and gray-green coloured cement plaster screed, mimicking lichen that pattern the bark of coconut trees. Four wells on the site supply the house with water and irrigate the plantation using aqueducts typical of the area, involving the landscape in an ongoing and reciprocal relationship with inhabitation: the continuation of tradition, the beginning of a ritual.

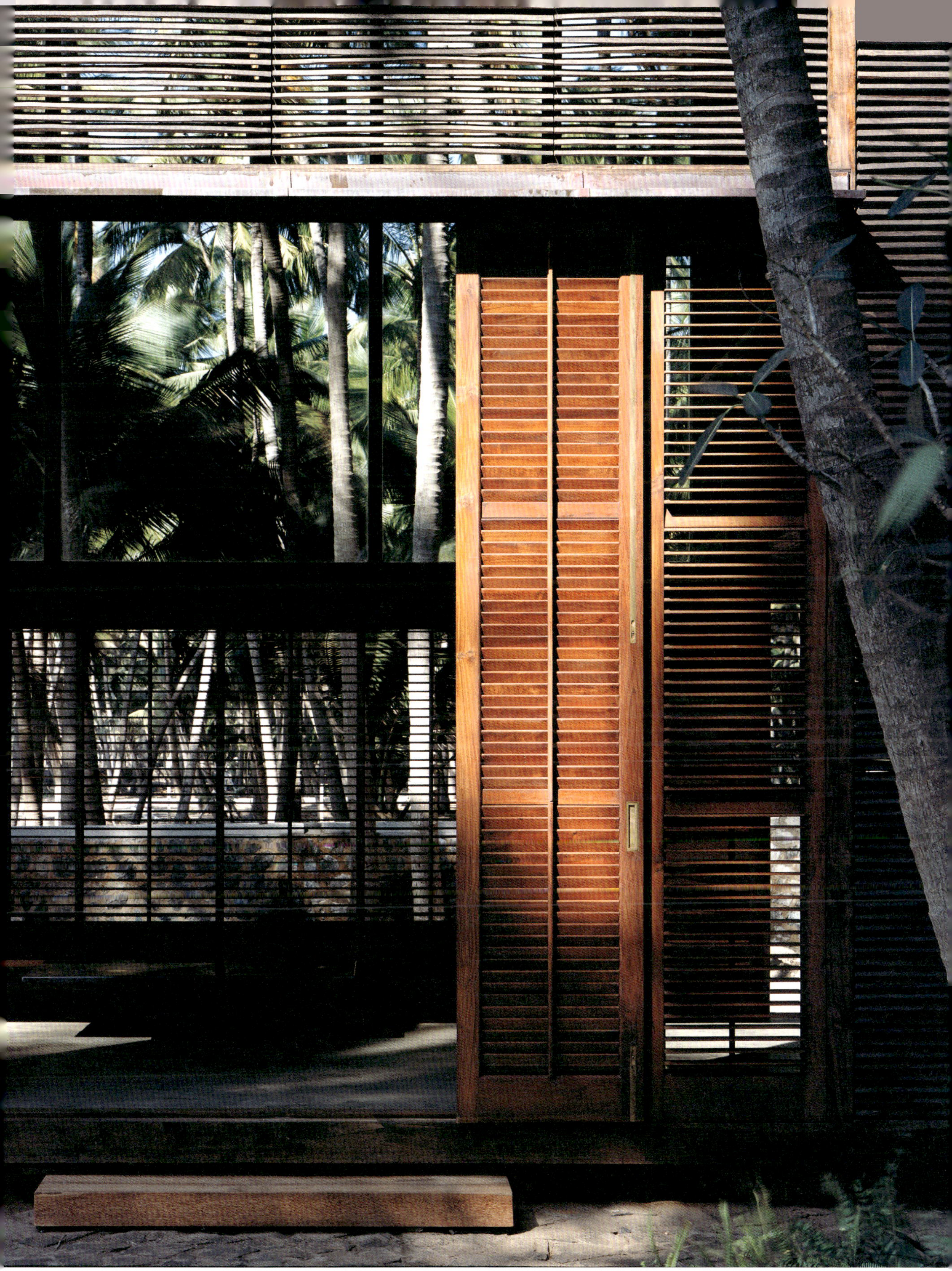

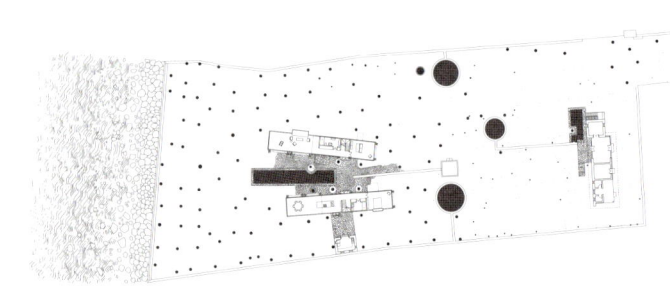

Site plan

102

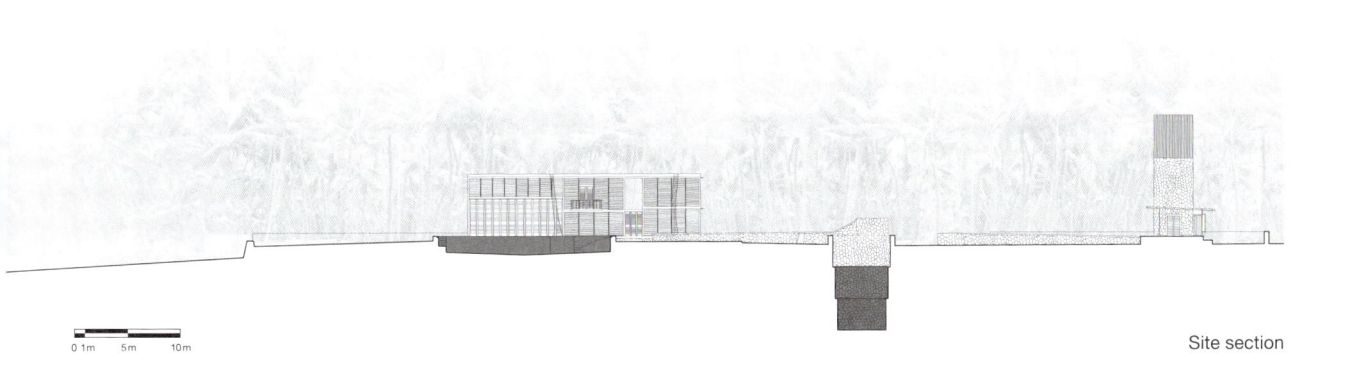

Site section

104

(上)棟間スペースの夕景。
(下)石造の水路と既存の井戸。
(左頁上)海側から眺めた西側立面。
(左頁下)木造架構の組み方ならびにルーバーにヤシの木を用いるヒントになった写真。

(Above) Central space between north and south blocks at dawn.
(Below) Details of stone aqueduct and existing wells.
(Opposite page) Western elevation from the beach (above). Inspiration images for method of timber framing and use of palm louvers (below).

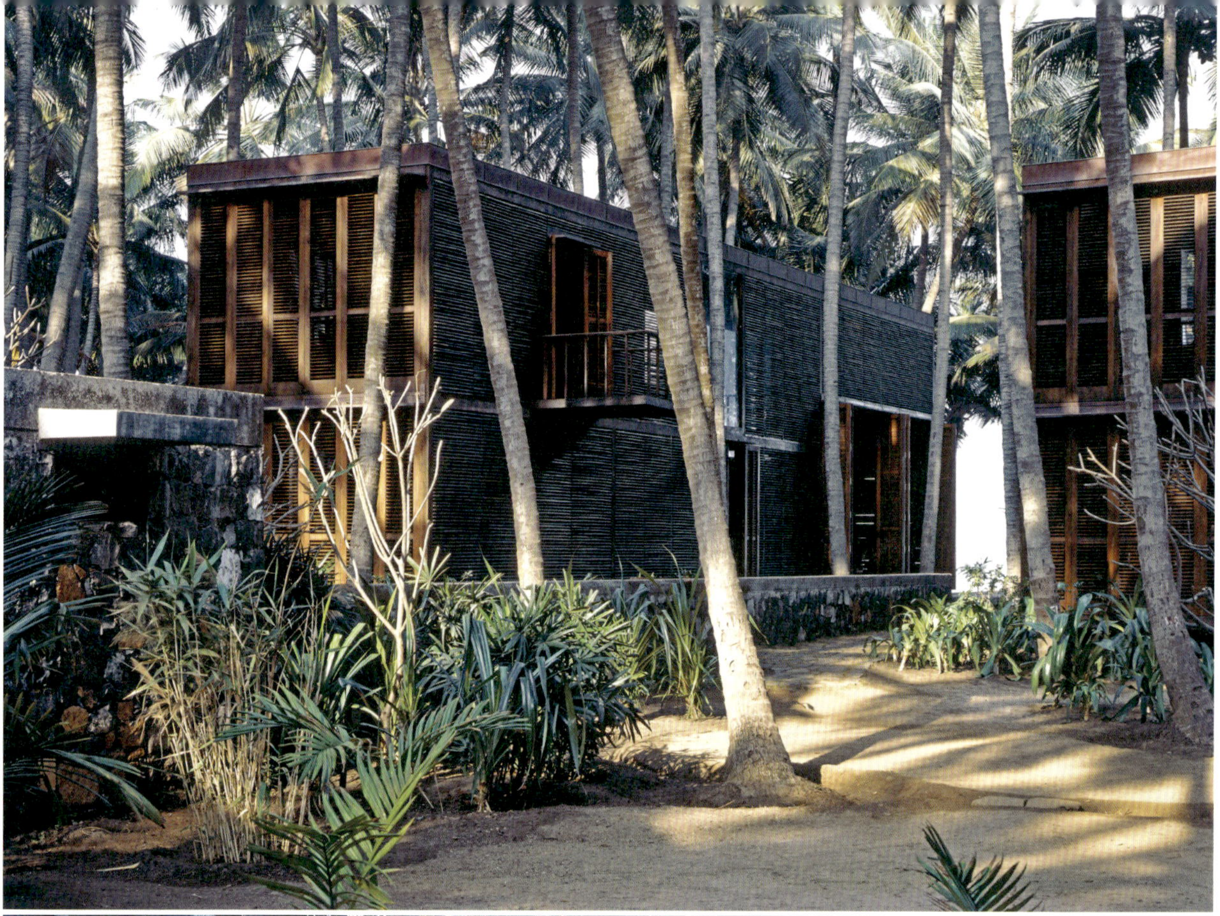
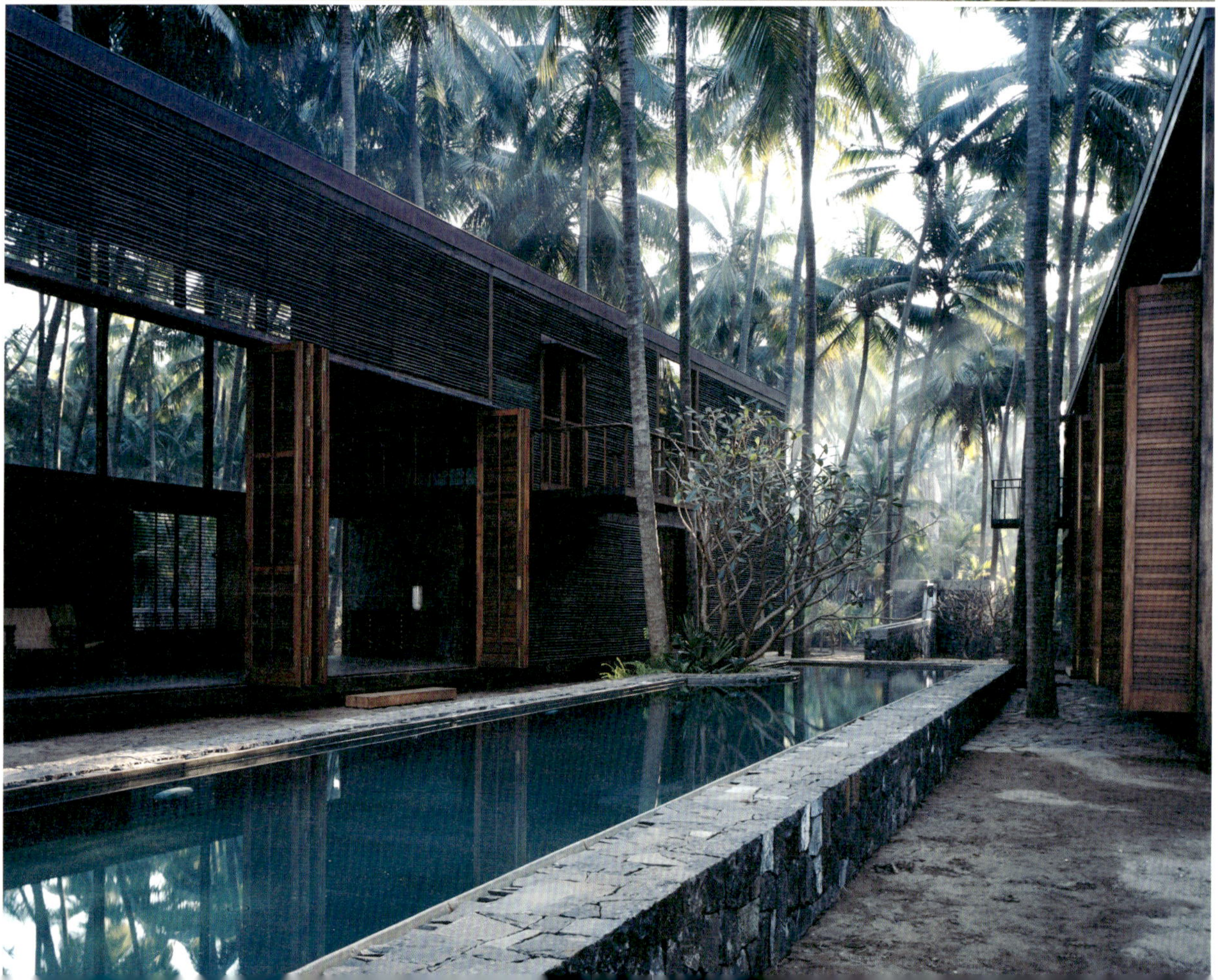

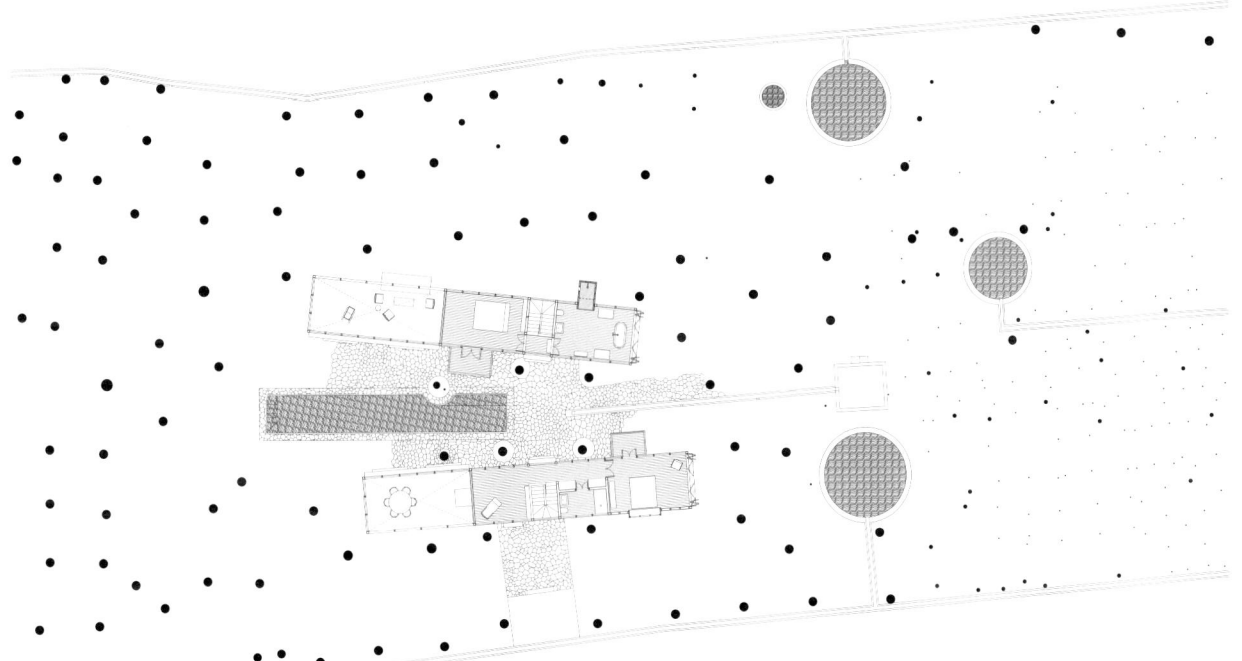

First floor plan

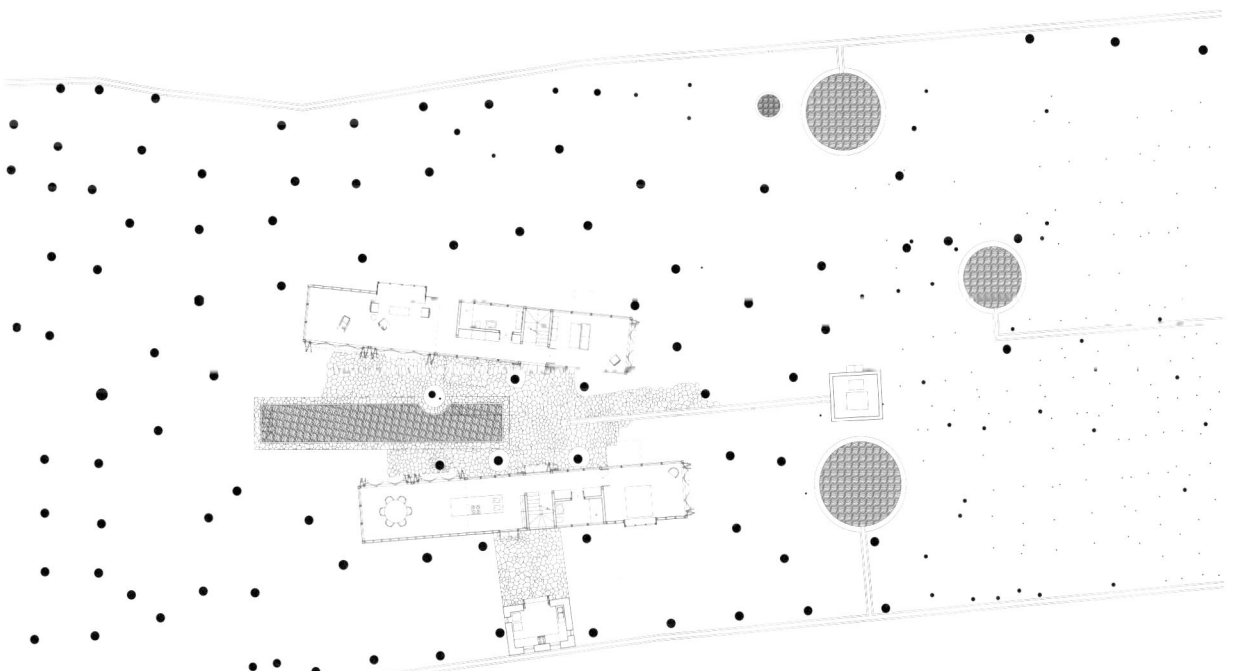

Ground floor plan

0 1m 3m 5m　N

107

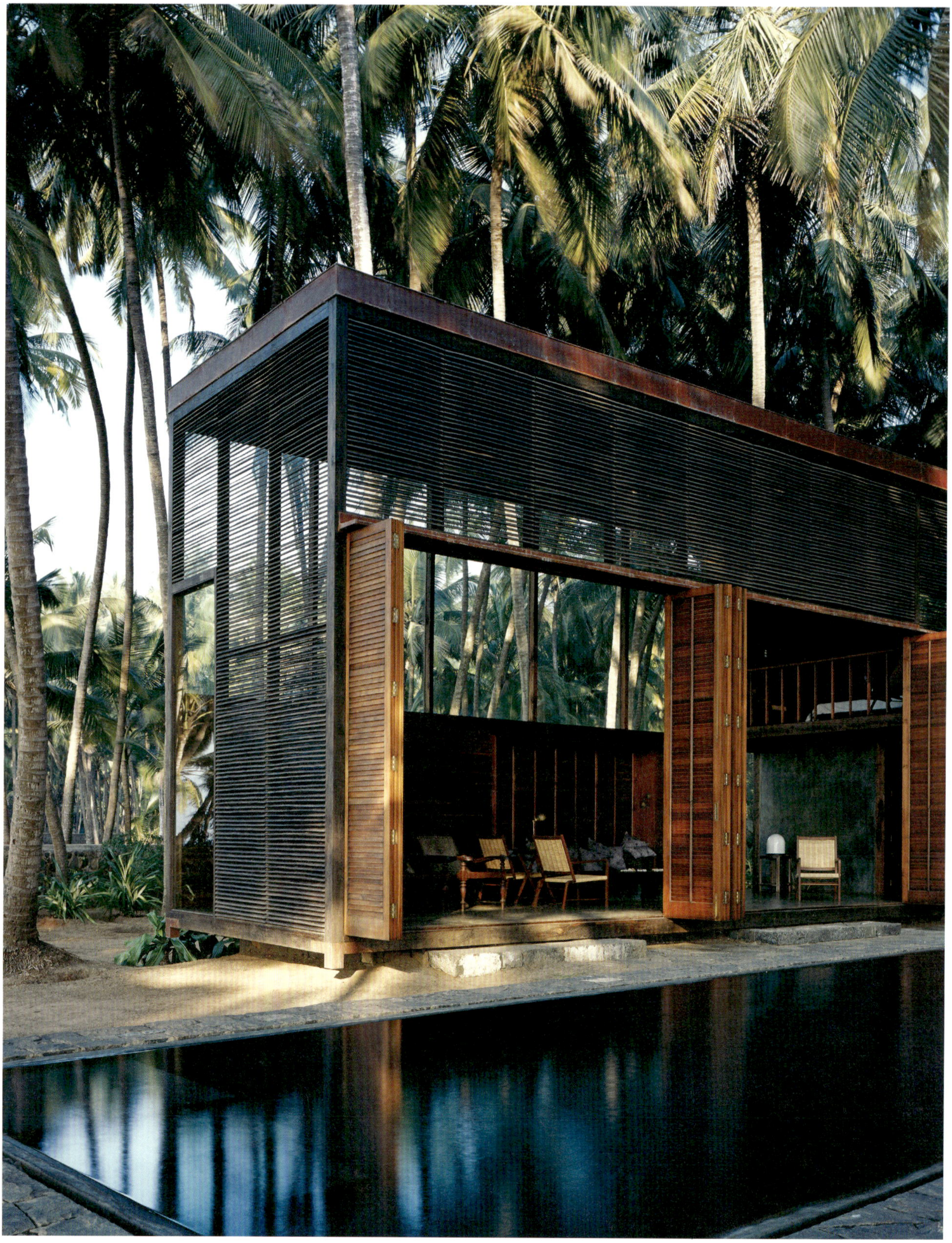

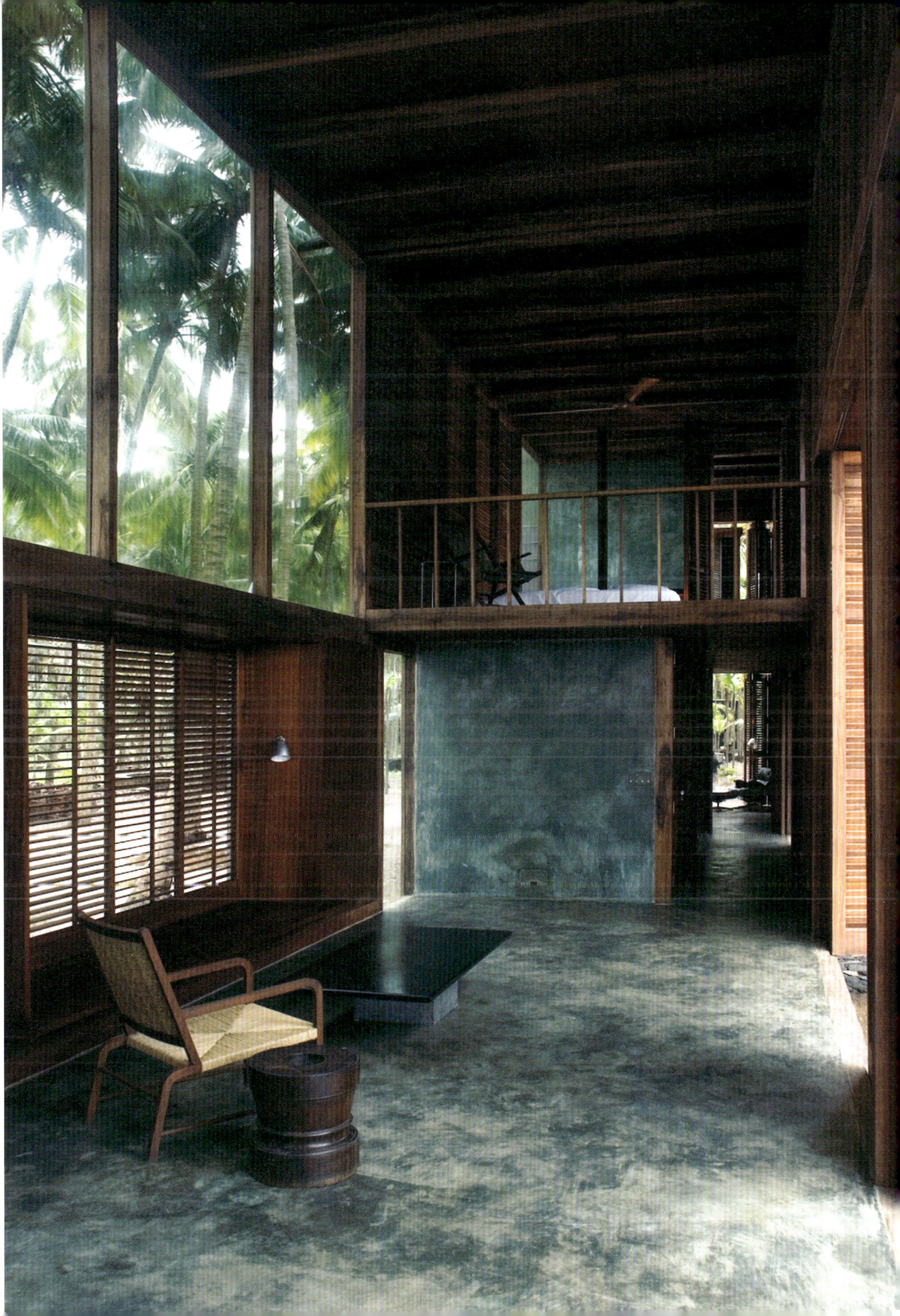

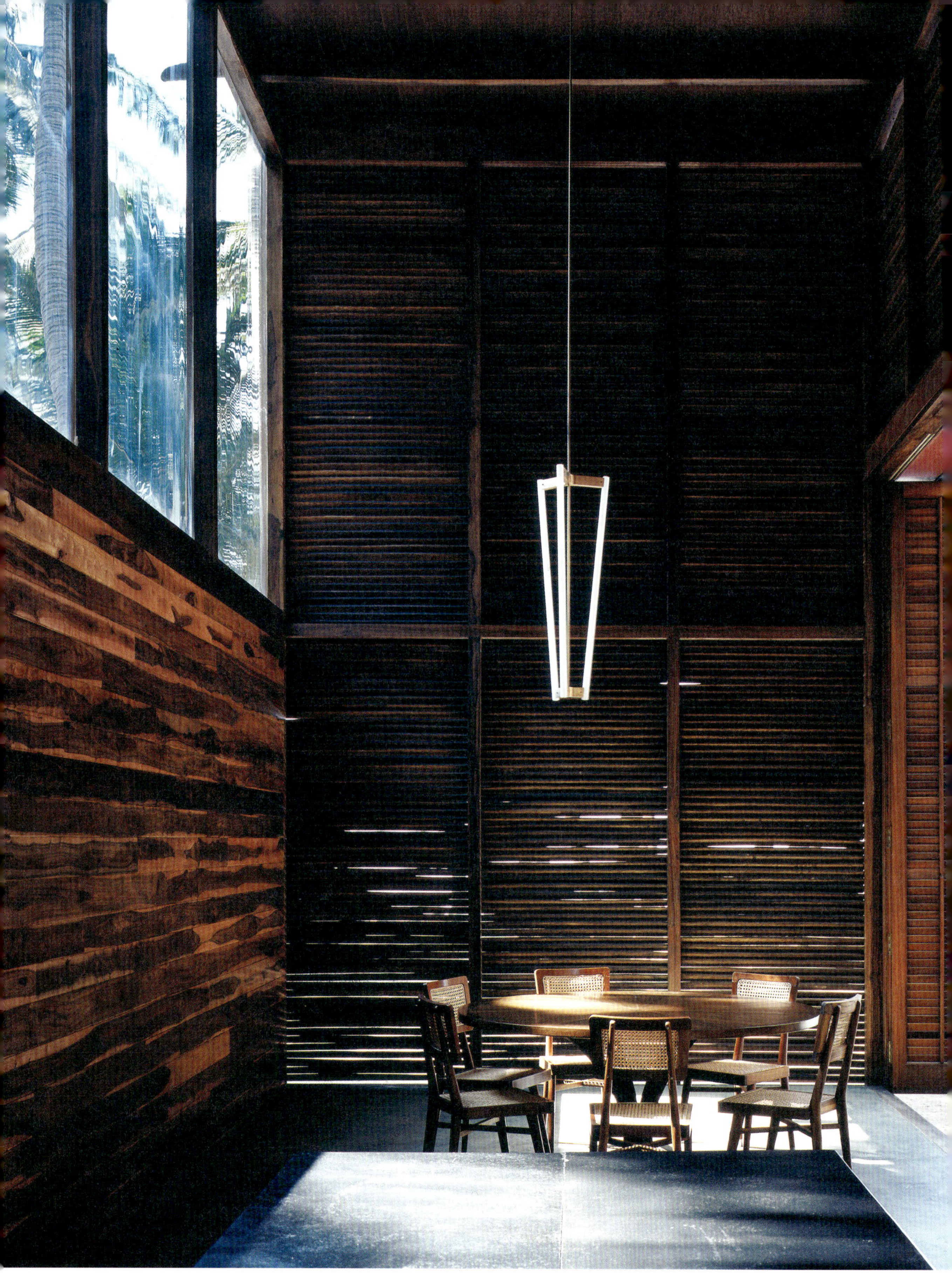

111

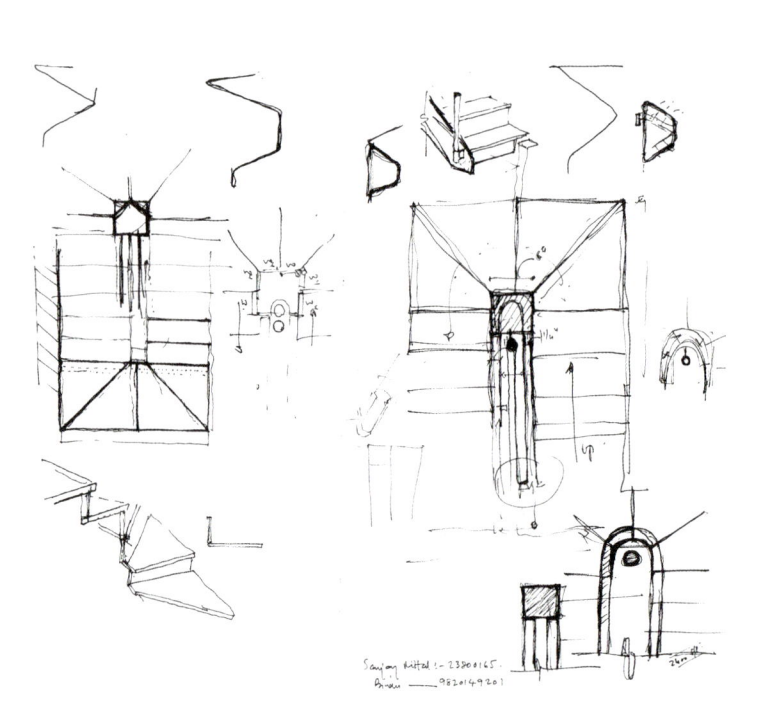

（左上より時計まわりに）プールの縁、チーク製の窓枠、パルミラヤシ製のルーバー、チーク製の階段。

(Images clockwise from top left) Edge detail of pool, teak wood window frames, Palmyra wood louvers and teakwood stairs.

112

(上) 南棟の勝手口越しに台所を見る。その奥の階段は2階へ続いている。
(右) 階段下から食堂を見る。

(Above) View of the rear entrance to the south volume, looking into the kitchen and the stair leading to the first floor.
(Right) View from the bottom of stairs towards the dining space.

（左）海に面した主寝室。
（下）南棟1階の客室。
（右頁上）主寝室から居間を見下ろす。
（右頁下）南棟1階のメディア・ルームから客室方向を見る。

(Left) View of master bedroom looking towards the sea. (Below) Guest bedroom on first floor of south block.
(Opposite page) Overlooking living room from master bedroom (above). Media room looking towards guest bedroom on first floor of south block (below).

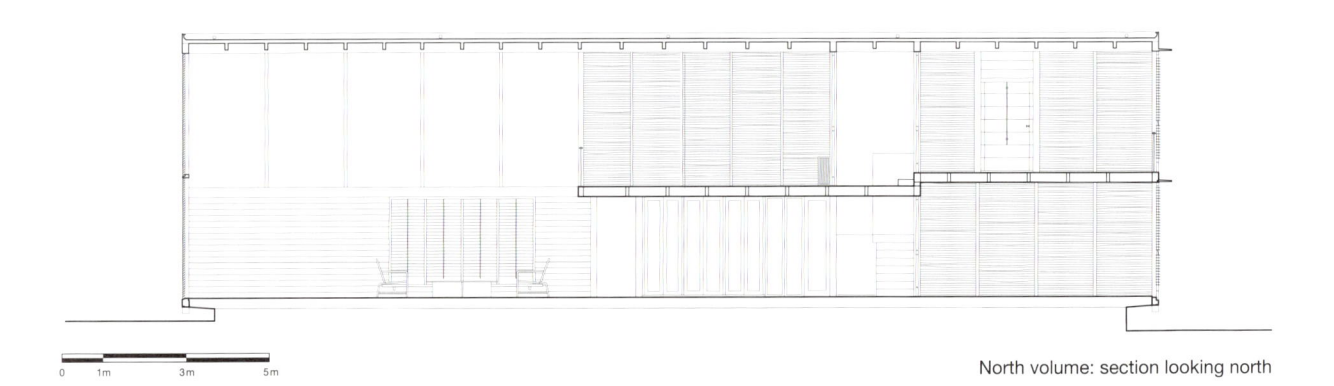

North volume: section looking north

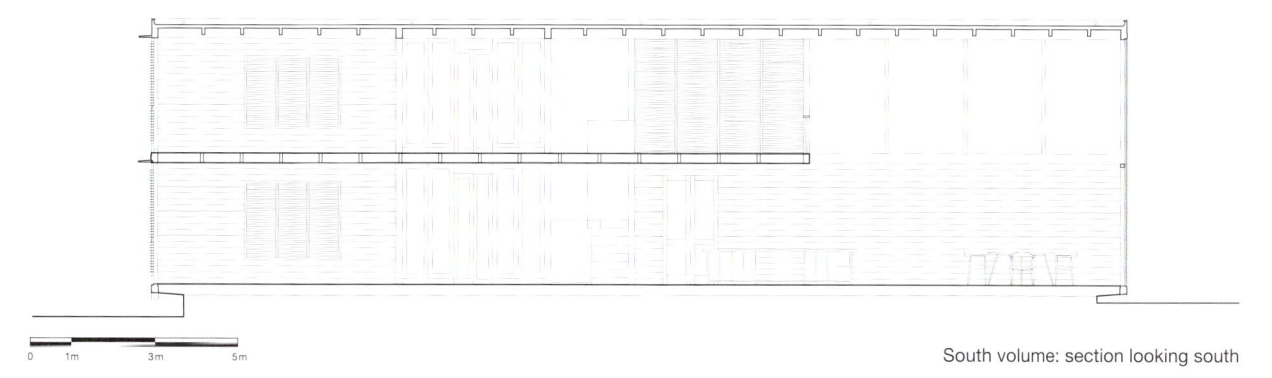

South volume: section looking south

115

大工によるデザインや収まりのスケッチ。

Design and detail development, sketches made by carpenters.

（上）資材と費用の見積りに使われた軸組模型。
（下）軸組模型、ルーバー、銅板金、接合部のモックアップ。

(Above) Framing model used for material calculations and cost estimate.
(Below) Framing model, louver, copper and connection mock-ups.

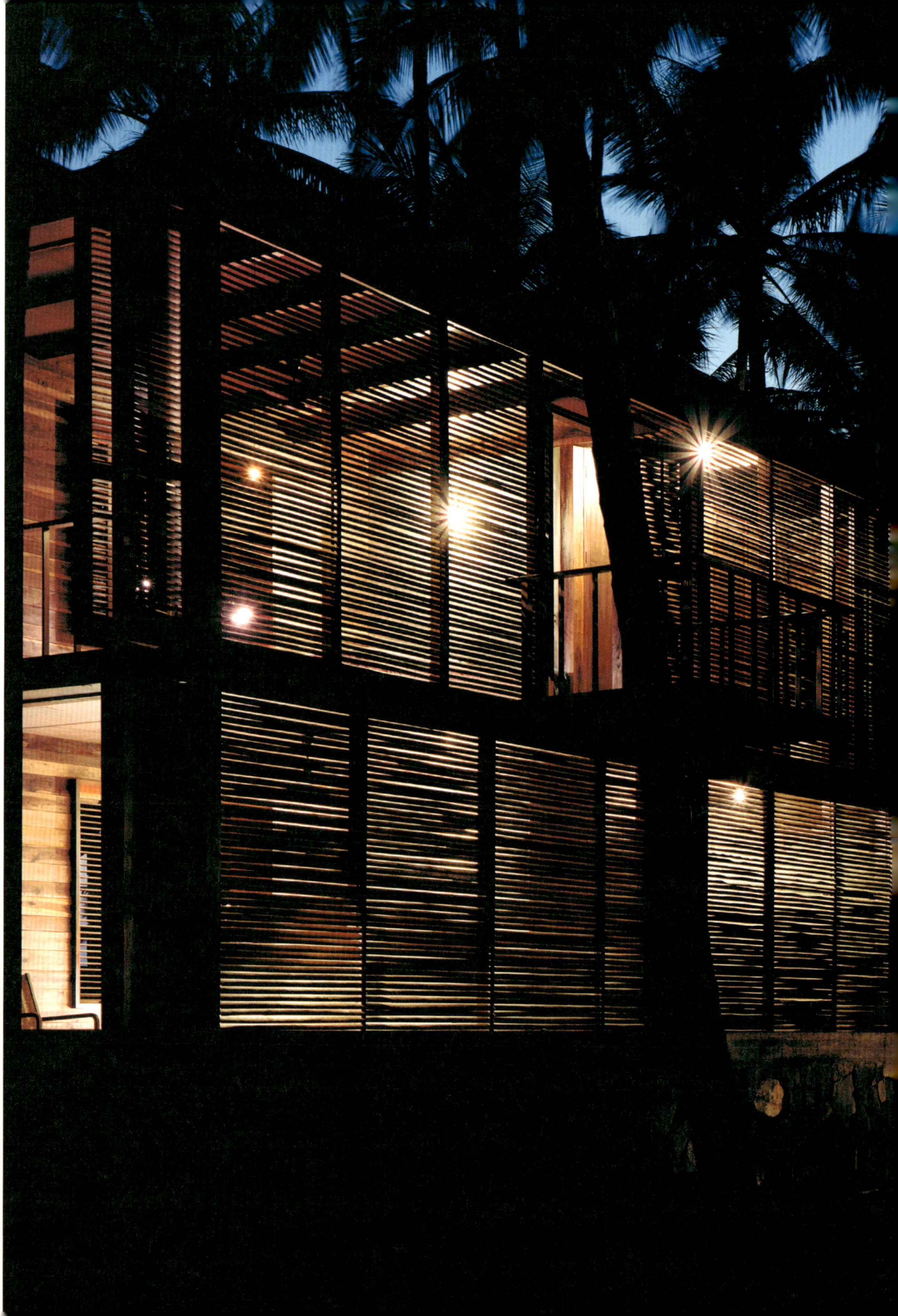

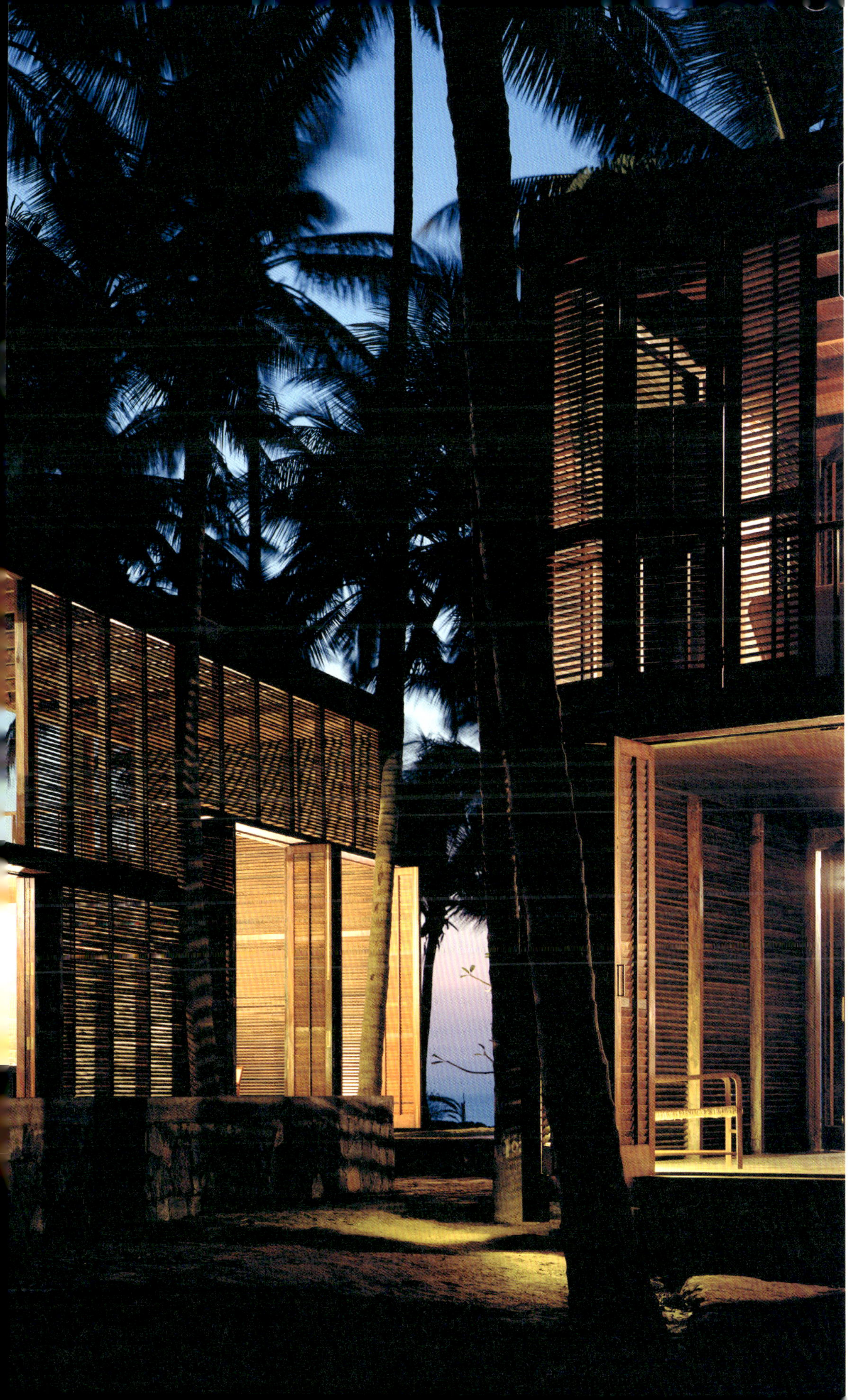

House on Pali Hill
パリ・ヒルの住宅

2008 Bandra, Mumbai, Maharashtra, India

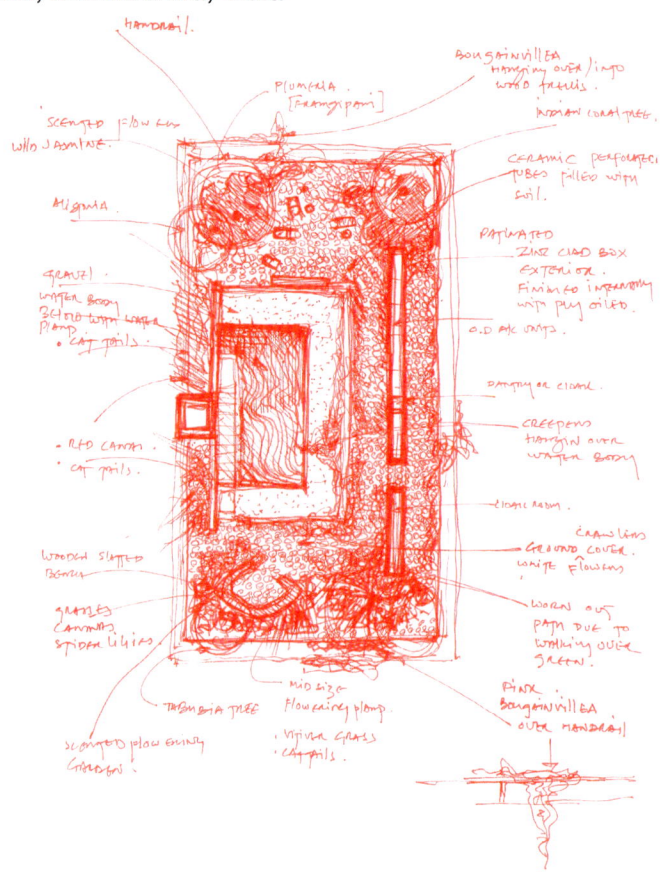

丘の斜面には、その地名にちなんだ住宅が建っていた。間口の狭いその古い住宅は、コンクリートの躯体のみを残して解体されたあと、ガラスや木製のスクリーン、吊り階段、蔓棚を挿入されて、ひとまわり大きく膨らみ、そしてプライバシーと囲い込まれた空間が縦列に並んだ間取りになった。

今回の改築では、増床とテラス増設のほかにも、動線や階段まわりに微妙な段差をつけたり、この都市住宅に光と風を取り込んだりした。ライムストーンを張った光沢のある床には外の景色が映り込み、かたや着色の漆喰壁は光を反射させ、主階の居間の吹抜けを照らす。居間は屋外の木製デッキに続いており、その先はもう公園である。1階の住空間には、高窓から光が降り注ぐ。また寝室へ至る廊下では、窓際につくり付けられた腰掛けがアクセントをつけている。書斎と主寝室は中庭の水盤に面しており、この水盤の潤いが都会の喧噪を忘れさせてくれるだろう。人目につかない上の階では、四季の変化が感じられる。続いて床から浮かぶように取り付けられた階段を上がると、屋上庭園に出る。そこは街の息苦しさから逃れて息抜きをするための、現代版マチャン*ならぬ樹上の隠れ家である。

* A machan is platform hidden in the trees, used for observing game in the jungle.
マチャンとは、ジャングルの樹上につくられた、トラ狩りのための見張り台。

Sited on a hillside plot, eponymous with its location, the existing house with its narrow footprint was stripped down to its structural concrete frame and expanded volumetrically with a series of insertions in the form of screens, glazed and wooden, floating staircases, and planted trellises, creating an enfilade of privacy and enclosure.

Reprogrammed with the addition of a floor and terrace and a series of carefully arranged changes in level around transitional spaces and staircases, light and air are drawn into the interior of this city house.

Reflective limestone floors mirror the landscape, while pigmented plaster walls diffuse the light in the double height living space on the main level which leads to a timber deck and a public garden beyond. Clerestory windows draw generous light into the family spaces on the first level, and the corridor leading to the bedrooms is punctuated with a window seat. The study and master suite open onto the water court, which provides a moist, still salve from a harried metropolitan condition. Located on the upper, more private level, it invites the seasons into the house, and a staircase planned as if suspended above it, leads to the roof terrace garden, providing a machan*-like arboreal retreat as a temporary and repeated release from the density of city.

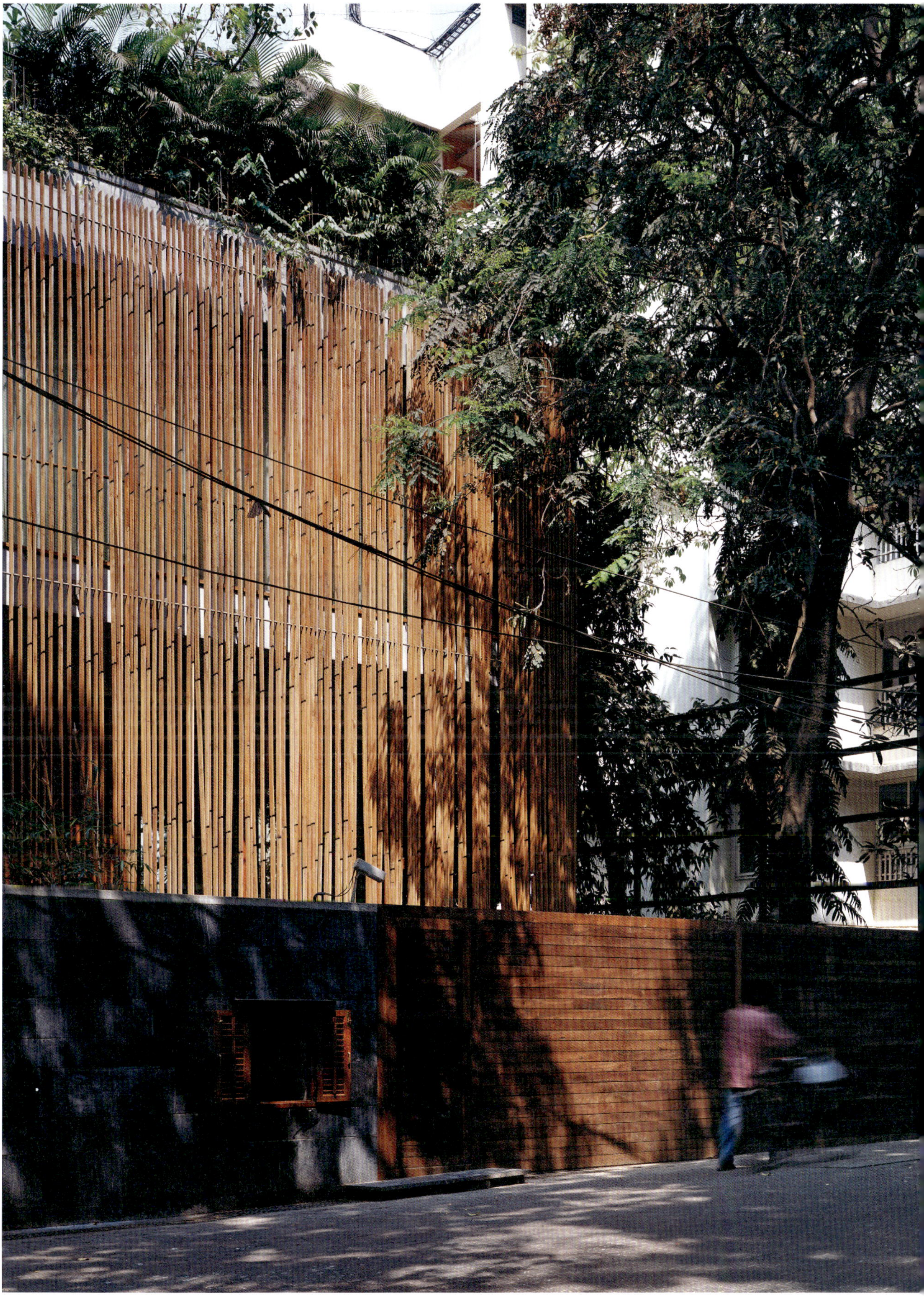

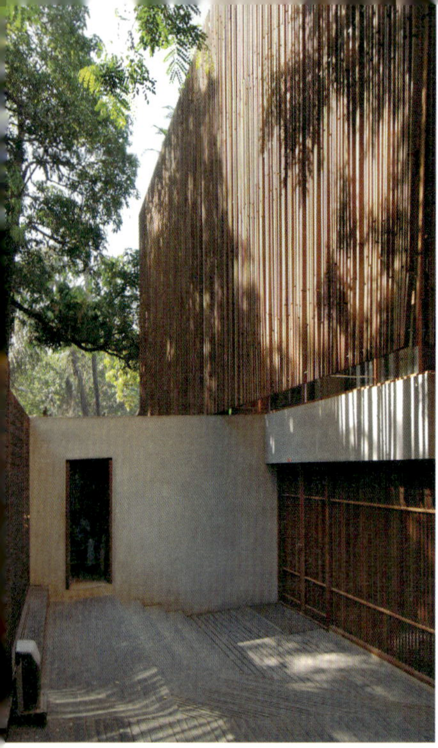

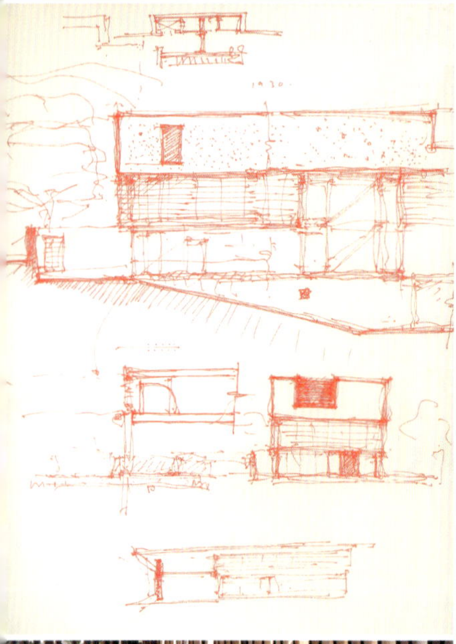

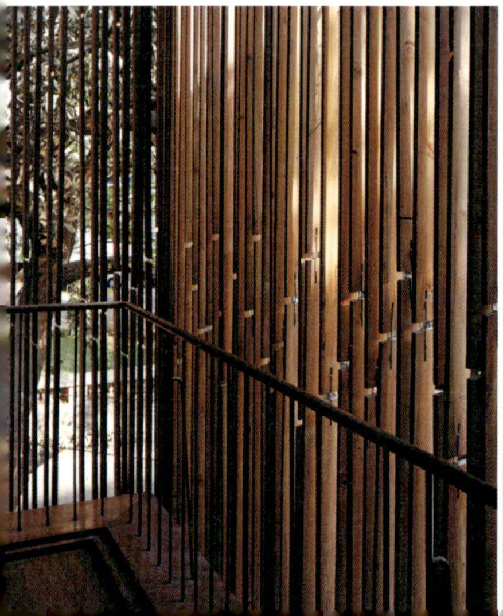

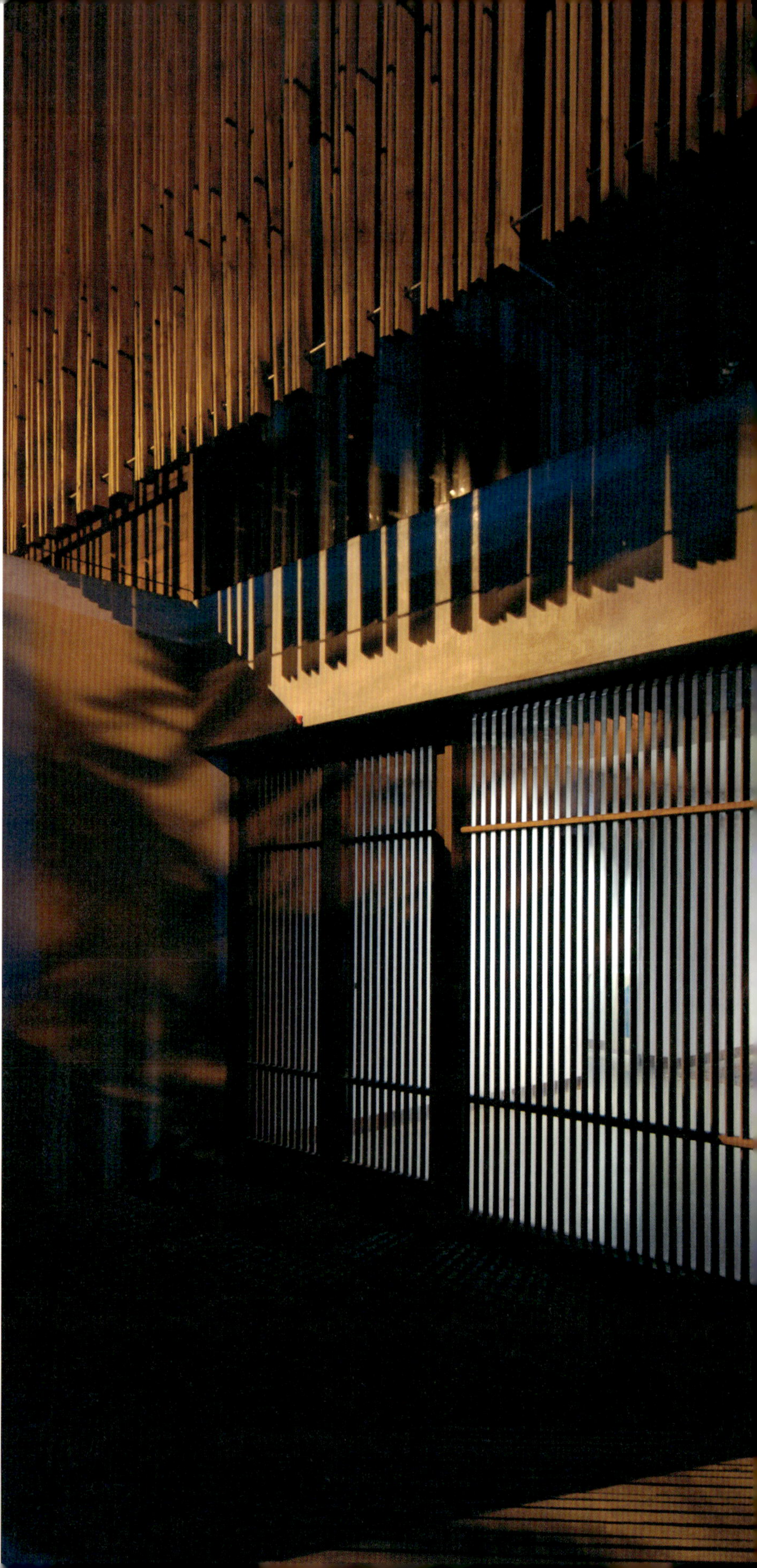

Sections

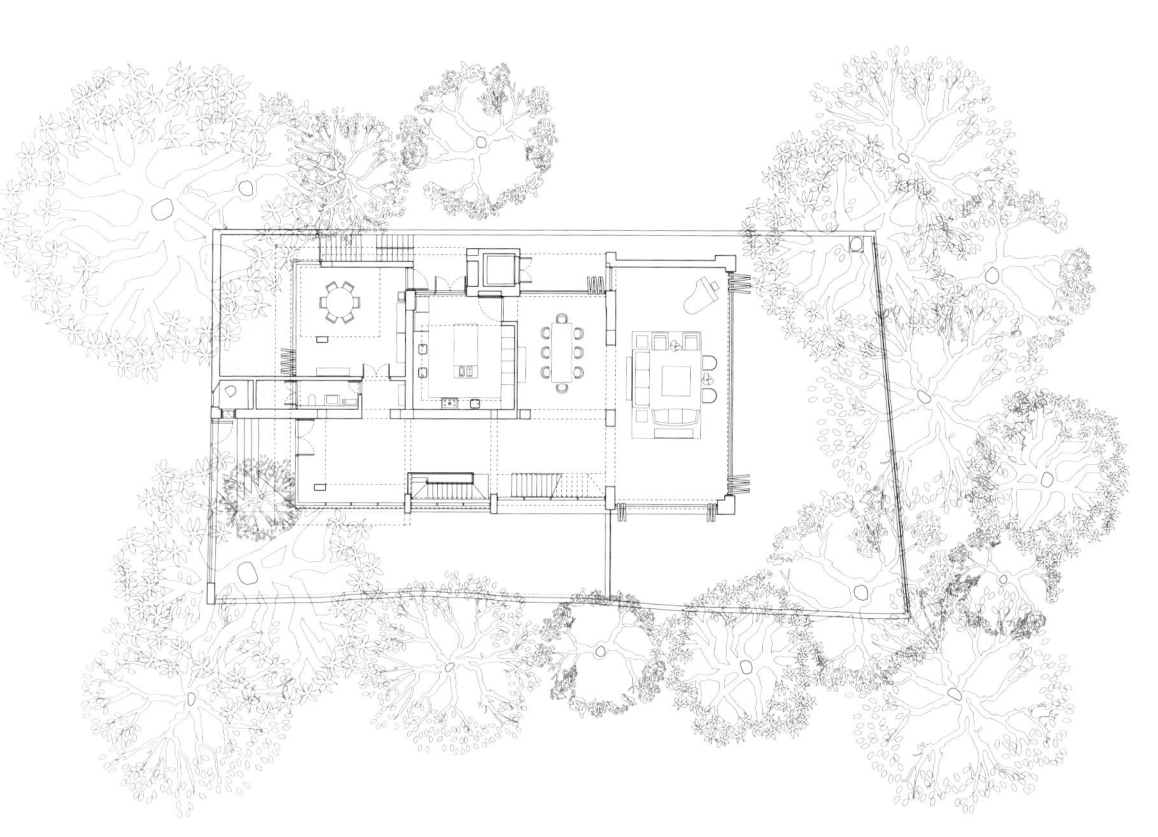

Ground floor plan

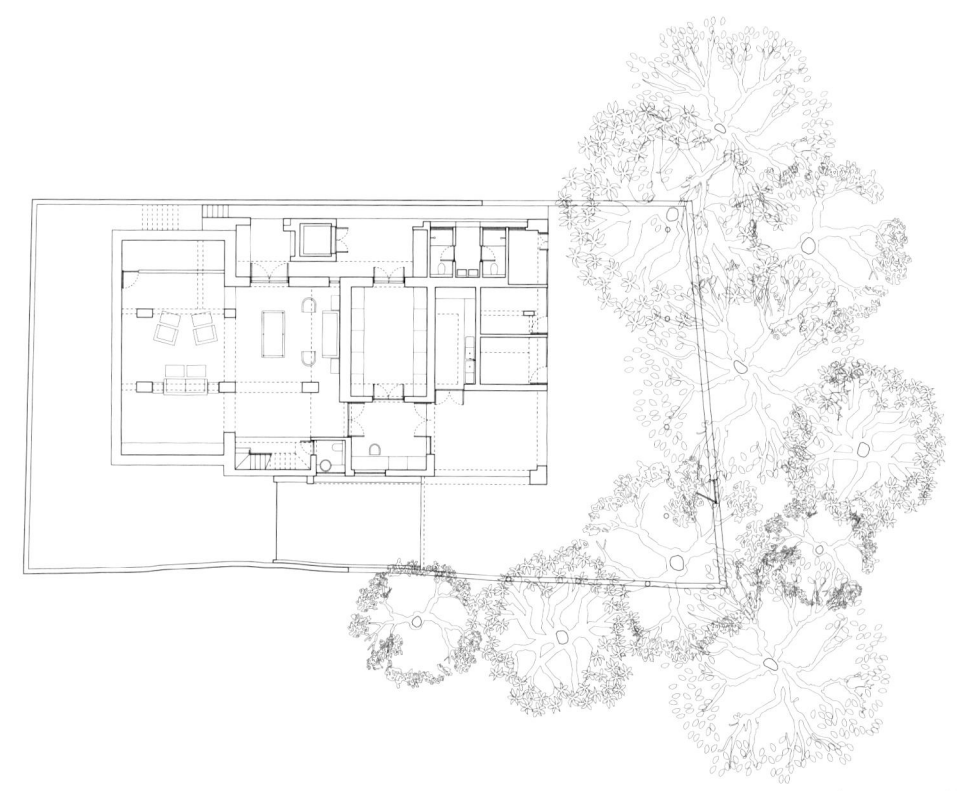

Lower ground floor plan

0 1m 5m 10m   N

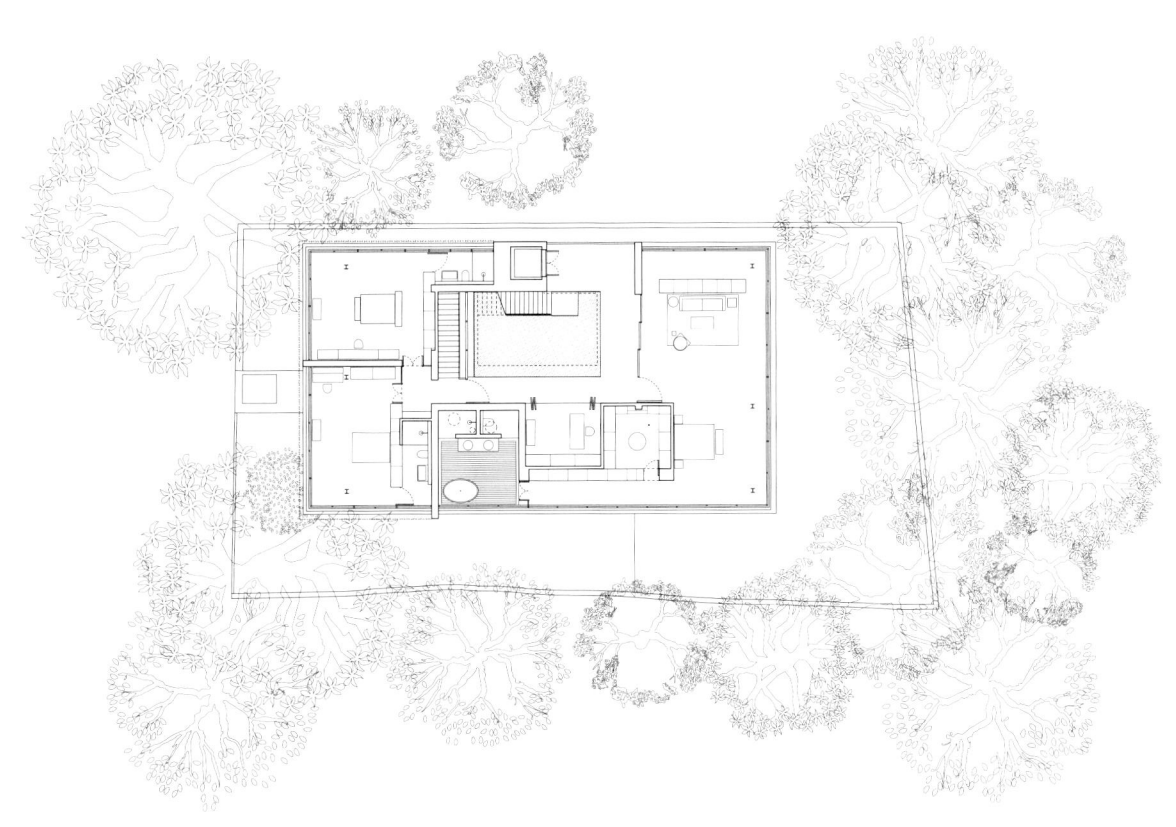

Second floor plan

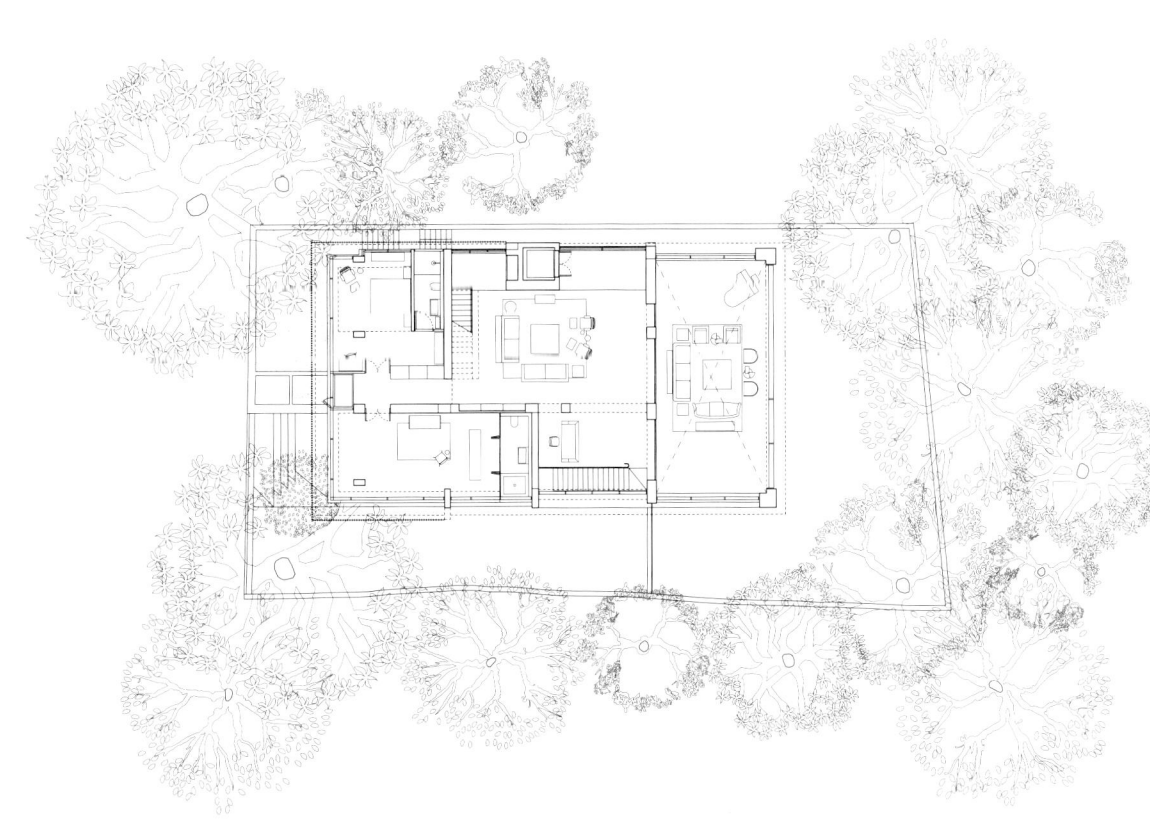

First floor plan

126

二層吹抜けの居間の内観および居間まわり。
Views from in and around the main double height living space.

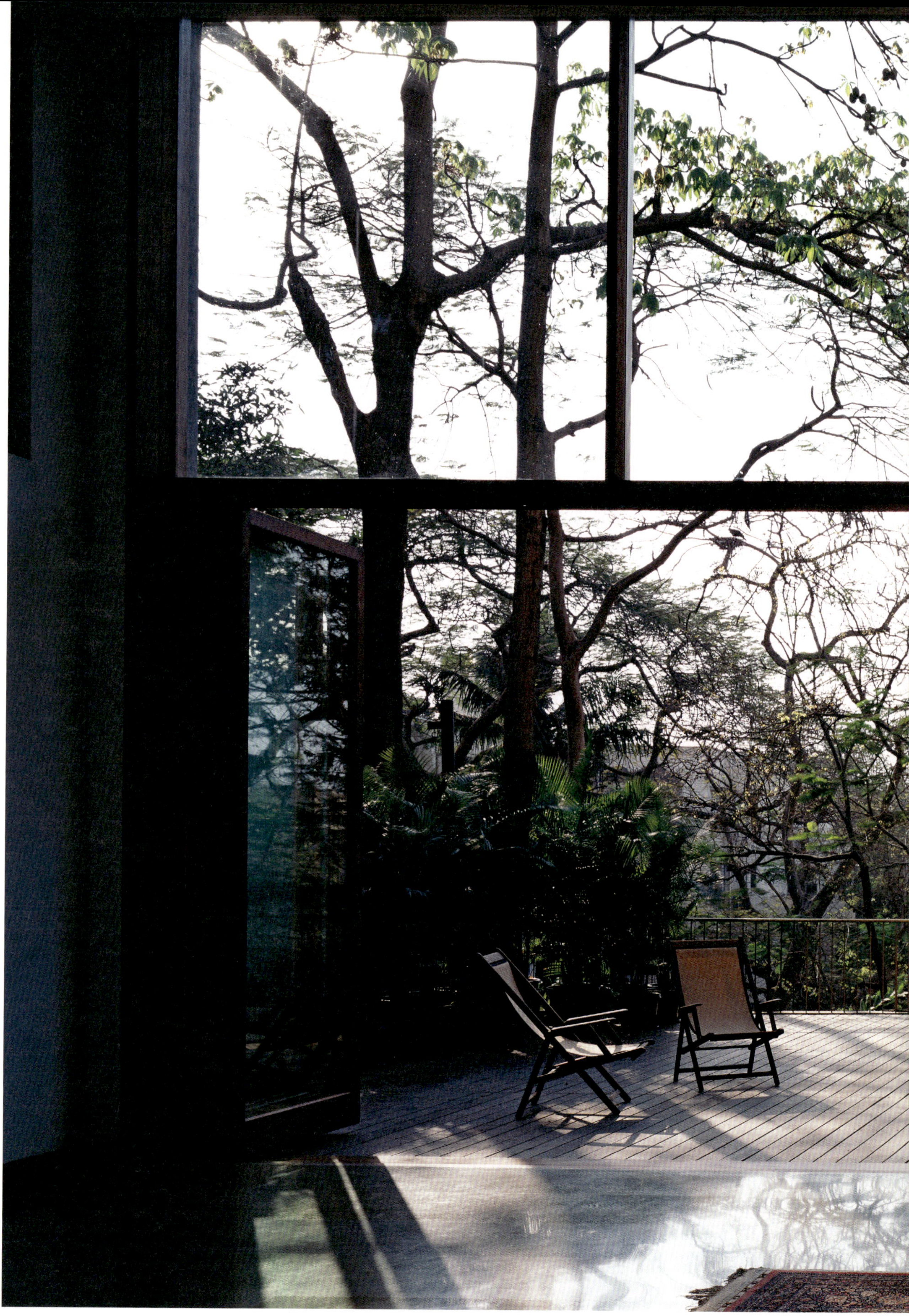

居間より西側テラス越しに公園を望む。
View from the living space facing west onto terrace and park beyond.

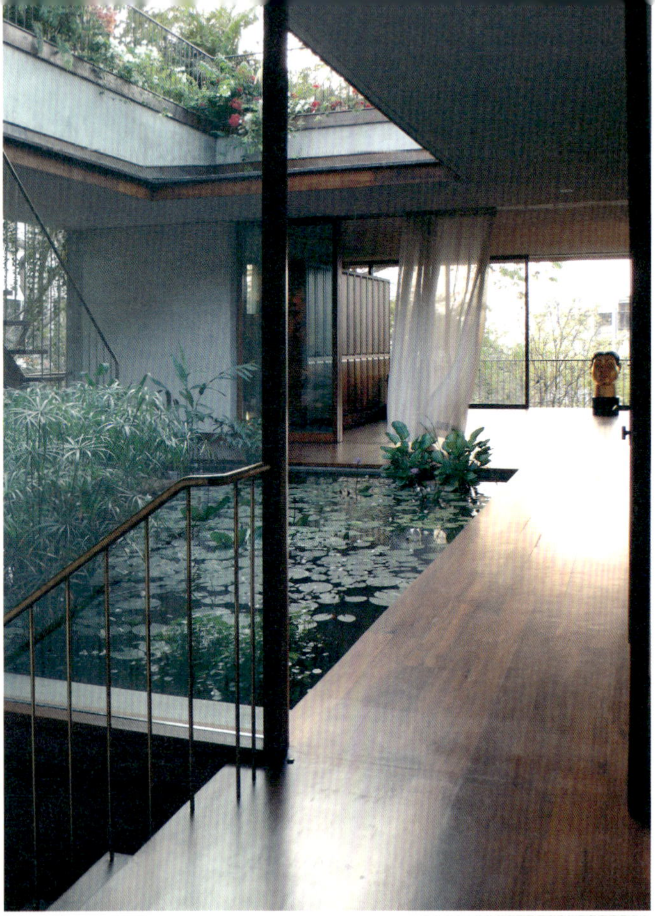

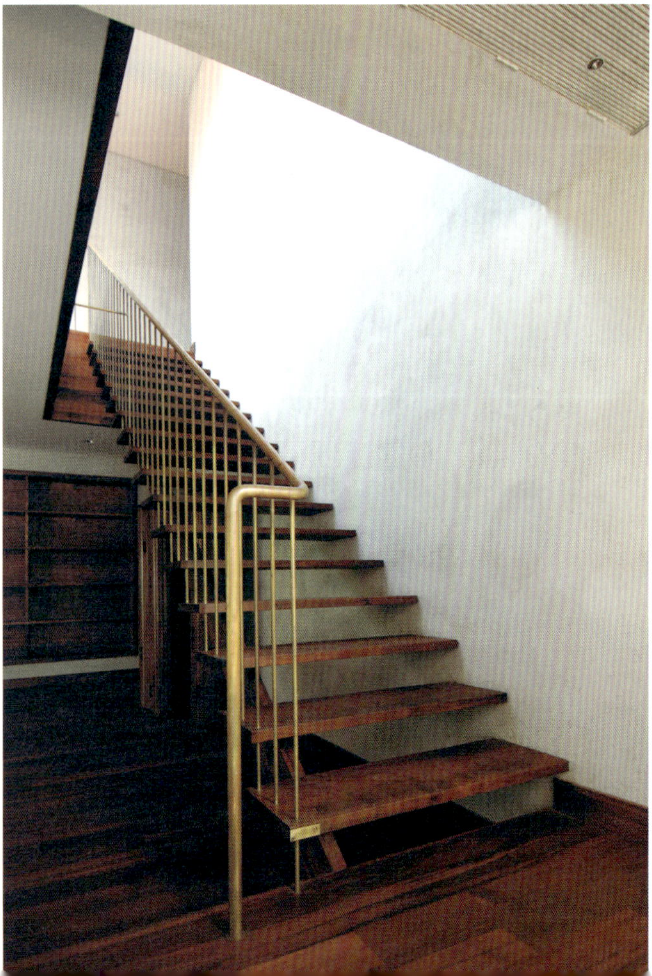

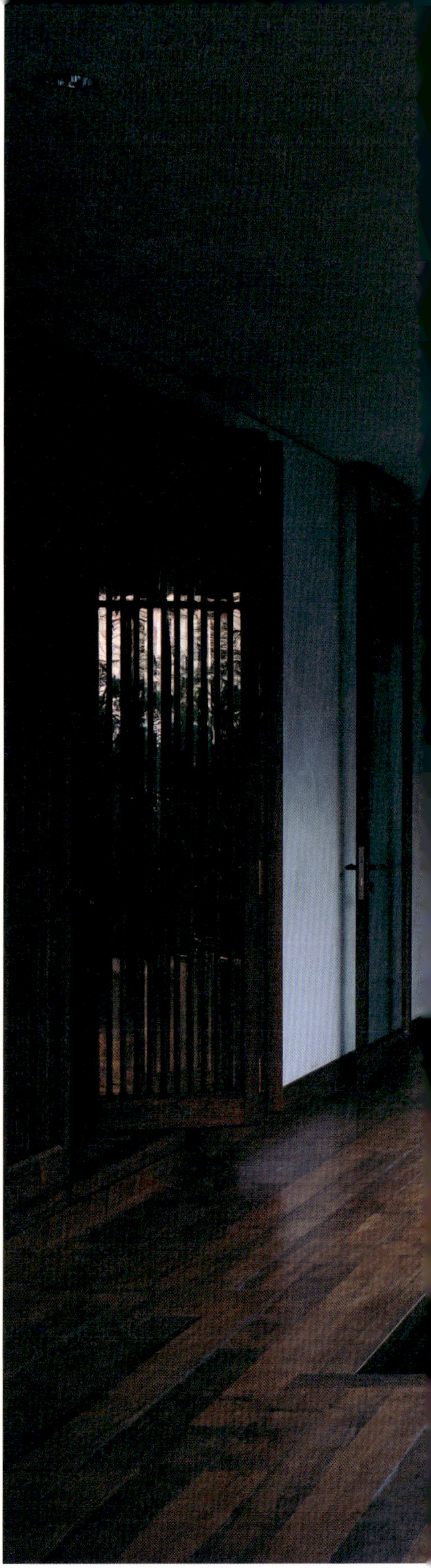

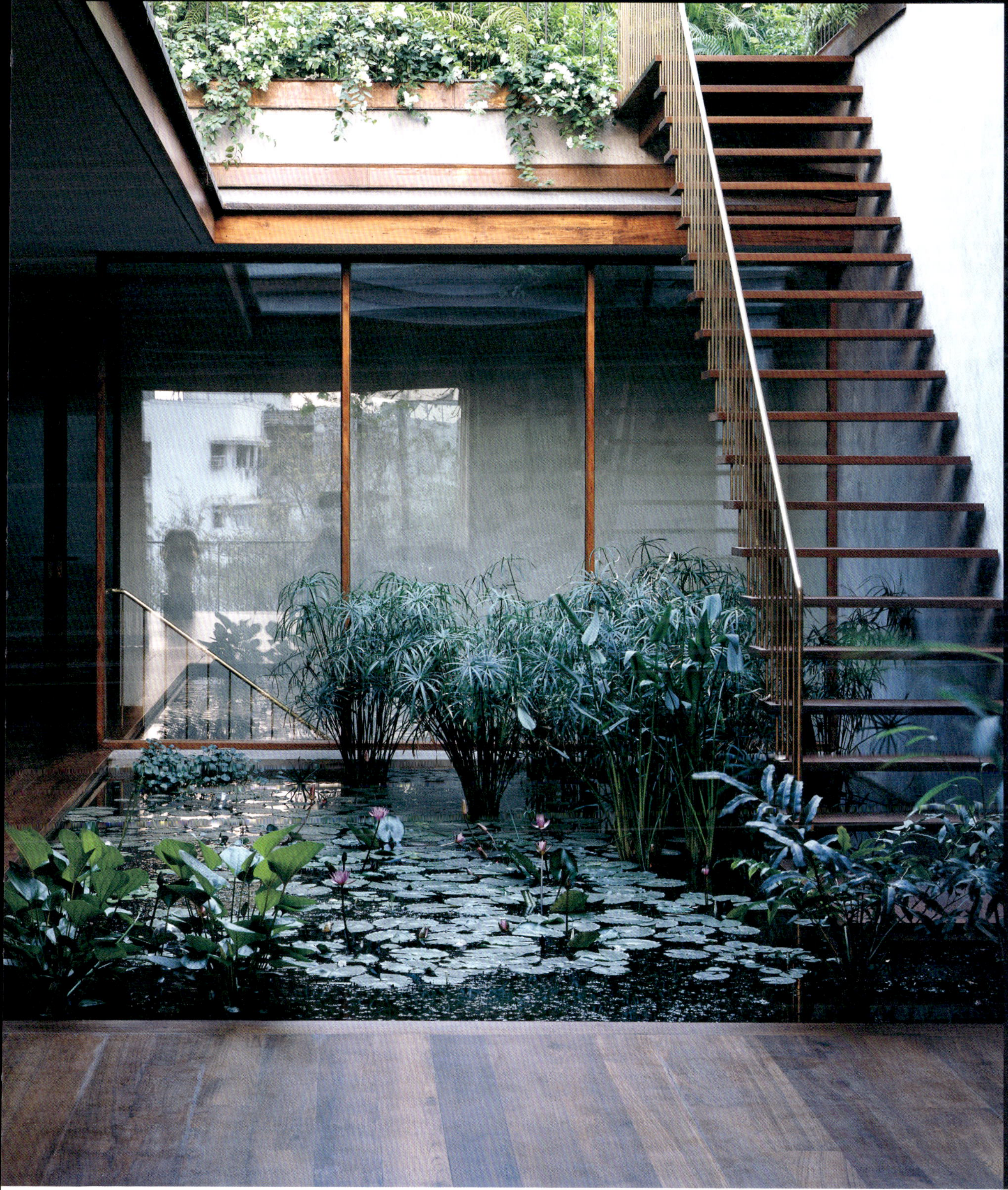

(左)階段から主寝室越しに公園を見下ろす。
(下)水盤の奥の階段は屋上へ至っている。
(右頁)公園から見た住宅の西側立面。

(Left) View from staircase looking through the master bedroom to the park below.
(Below) Water court with staircase leading up to roof terrace.
(Opposite page) The west elevation of the house seen from the park.

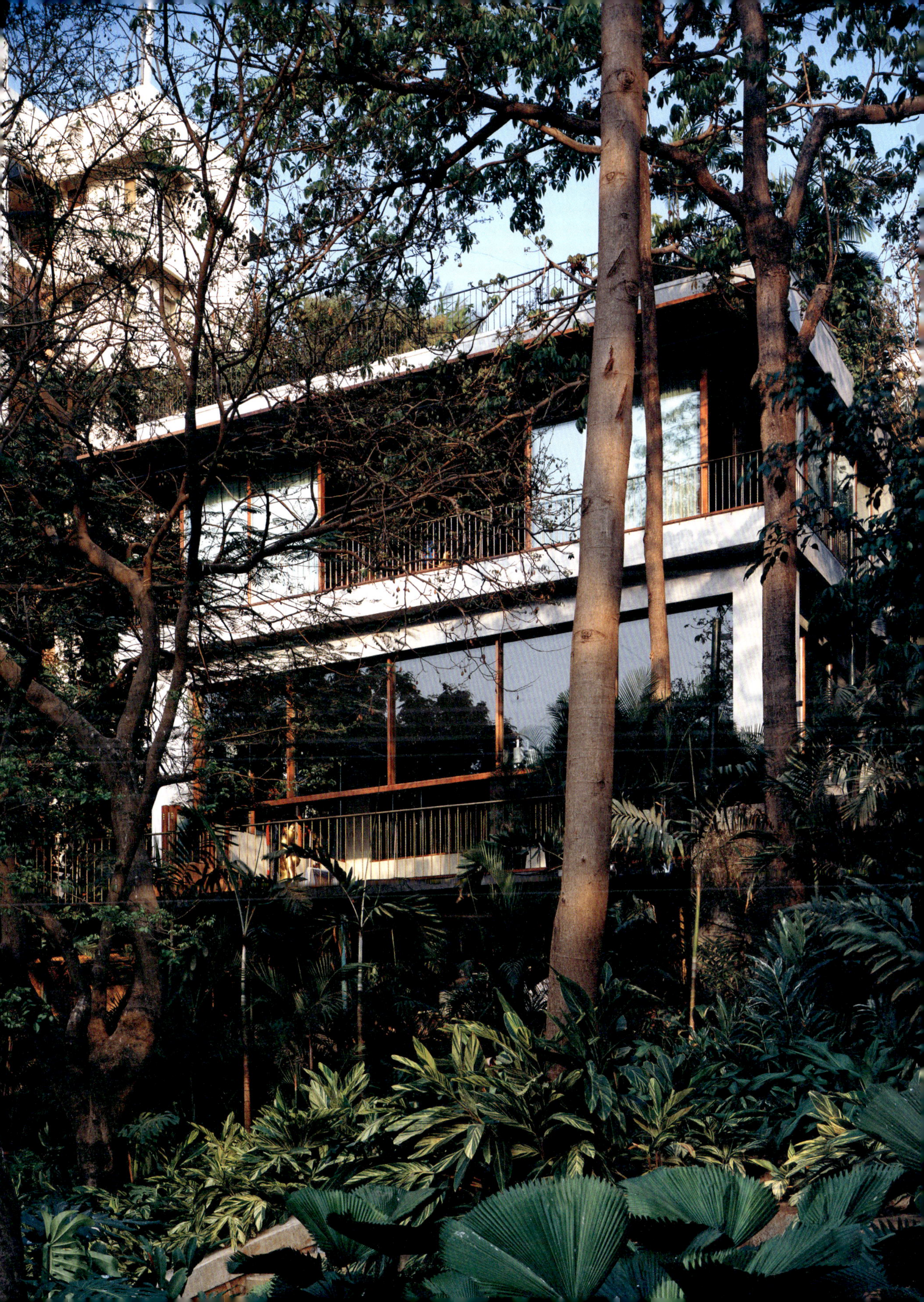

Belavali House
ベラヴァリの住宅

2008 Belavali, Maharashtra, India

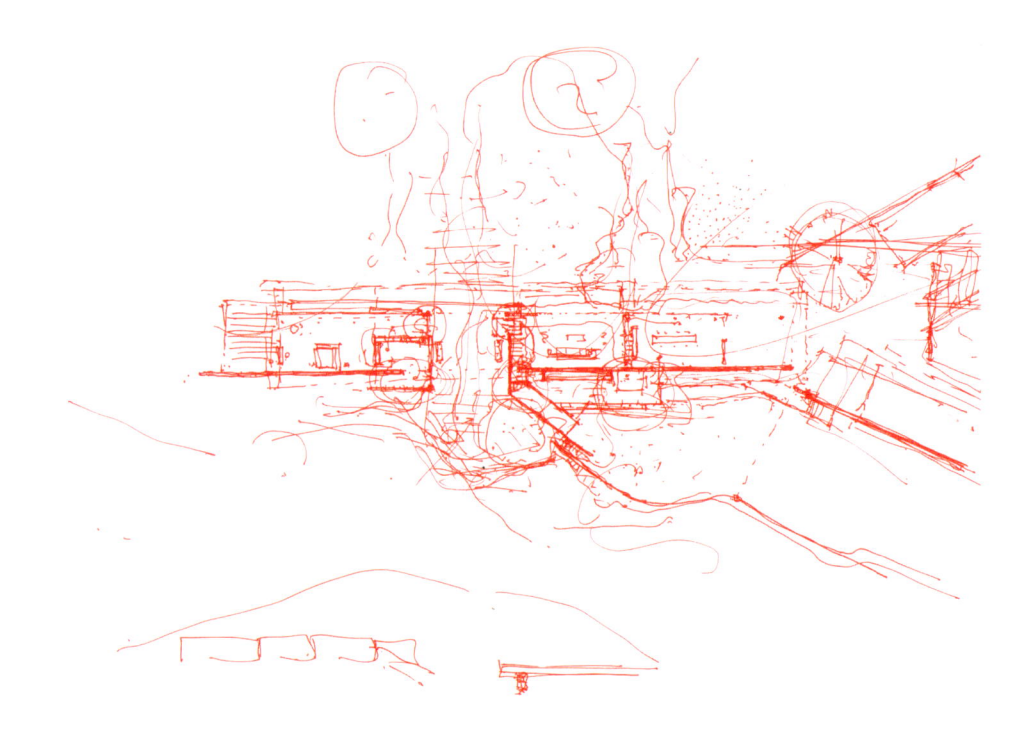

一面に農地の広がる中に、住宅の各部屋が鈴なりになって建つ。東には森が、西には棚田が広がる。その間にあるこの家は、自然という庭の中に佇むパビリオンとして構想された。石垣は排除と保護と庵の役目を担う。この石垣を、プライベートな住まいと自然や農地との間に巡らした。

住宅は、ちょうど棚田の段差を示す目印になっている。全体をすっぽりと覆う1枚の屋根は、ごくふつうの鉄骨柱に支えられている。この素朴な建物は、石と木とガラスの面を、着色モルタルで均一につないでできている。がらり戸は開閉式の壁面と化して、長い周期で繰り返されるアジア・モンスーンと夏の気候に応じて屋内気候を調節し、また丘の景色や畑の鮮やかな緑をフレーミングする。

この母屋に付属する客室・設備群は、いかにも農家風の佇まいである。5エーカー（約2万㎡）におよぶ広大な棚田の環境を損ねないよう、どの棟も環境負荷をかけないように設計されている。農地を海に見立てれば、足元の石畳は居住用の群島である。田んぼの中の畦道や石垣をここに再現したのも、田畑には自然環境と人工環境が見事に融和していると考えたからだ。

Into an open agrarian landscape is built a house as a series of clustered rooms composed as a whole, located between the eastern forest and terraced fields of rice in the west and imagined as a pavilion in a garden of nature. Stone walls act as elements of exclusion, protection and anchorage, drawn out together to form a mediating plane between private inhabitation and the natural and agricultural landscapes.

The house acts as a register for the changes in grade dictated by the rice paddies, and is united by a singular roof plane, supported by basic structural steel supports. This primary building is composed of masonry, wooden and glazed wall planes rendered seamless by a continuum of pigmented cement plaster. Louvered doors become operable facades for the control of interior climate, to tune with the cycles within the long Asiatic monsoon and summer, and framing views of the hill landscape and electric green cultivations beyond.

Archetypal farm-like building clusters for guest and service blocks are ancillary to the main dwelling. Each cluster economises its footprint to preserve the cultivable condition of the five-acre rice plantation, and decks of stone are islands of private inhabitation in this agricultural condition. Original walkways and walls which aided in the traversal of the paddies were enhanced and reconstructed in an attempt to bring closer together the natural and manmade environments which are best mediated in the agricultural condition.

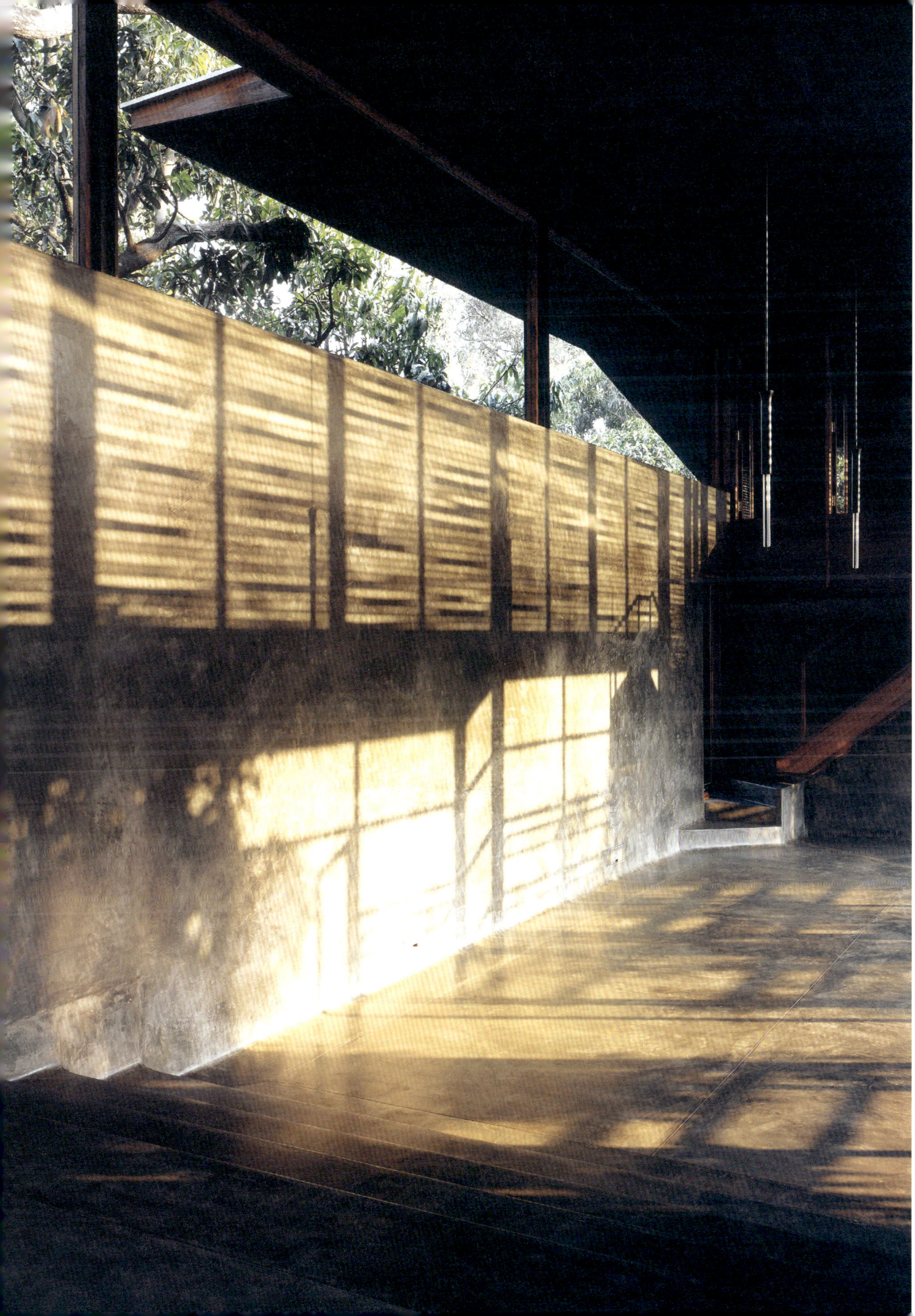

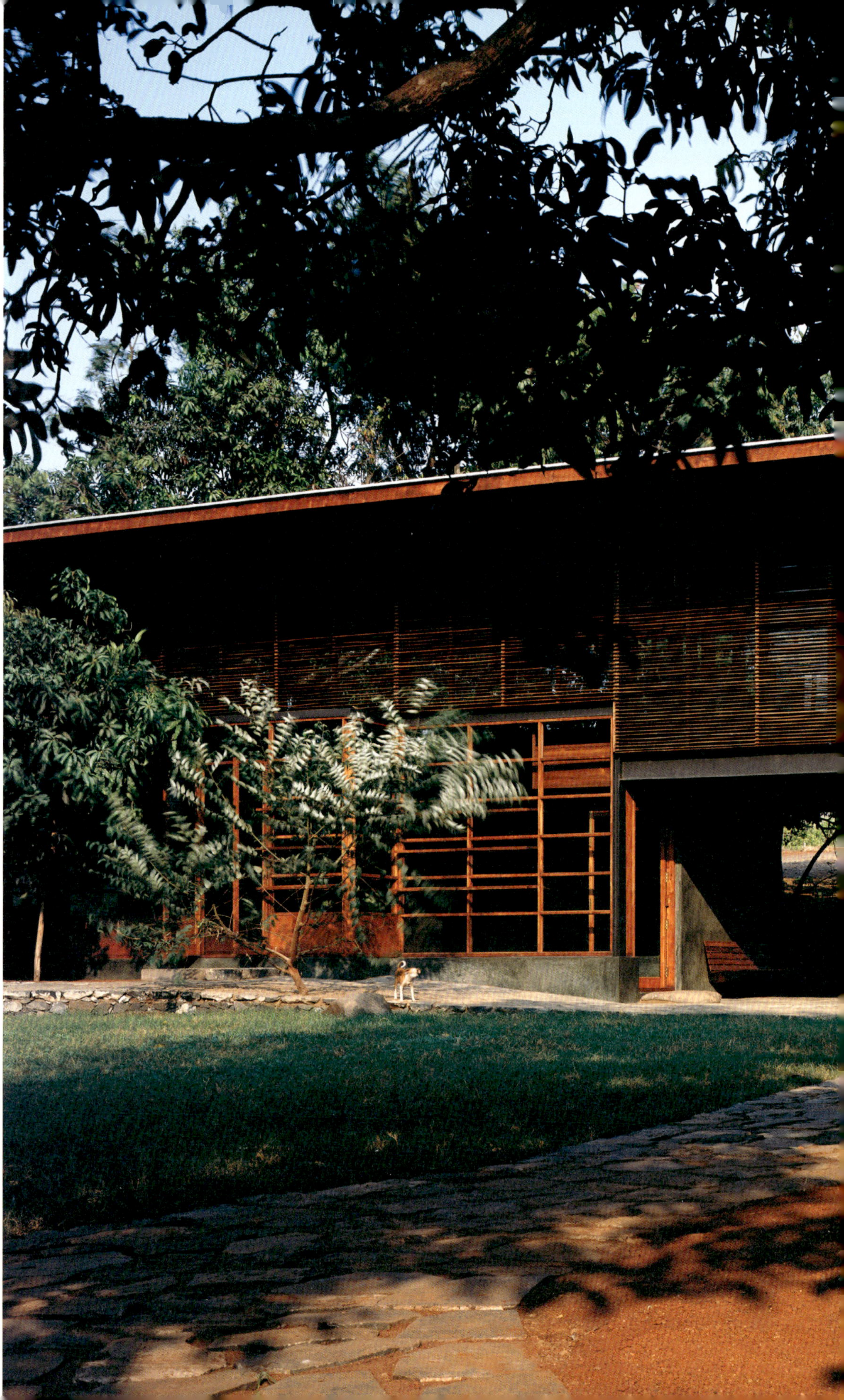

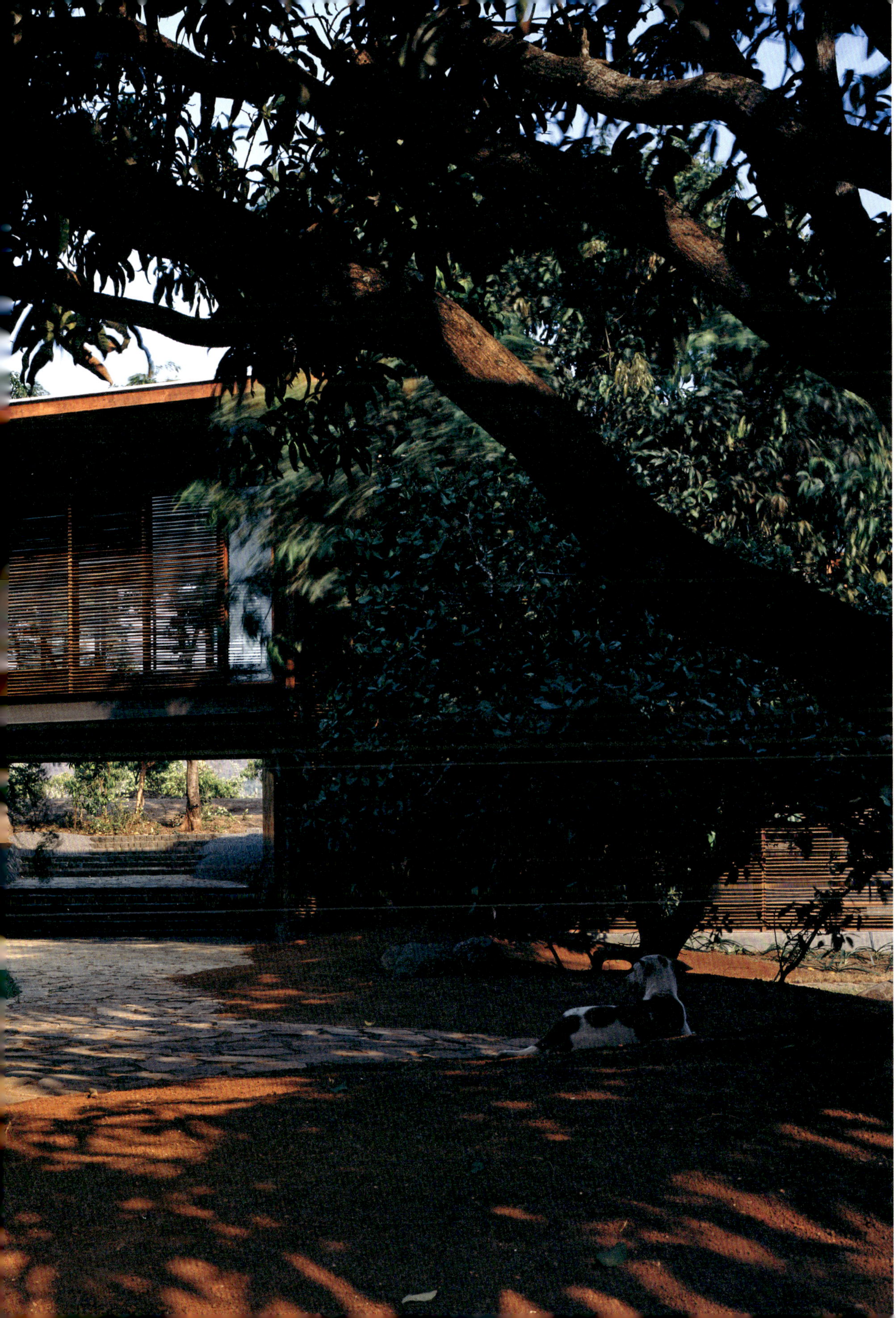

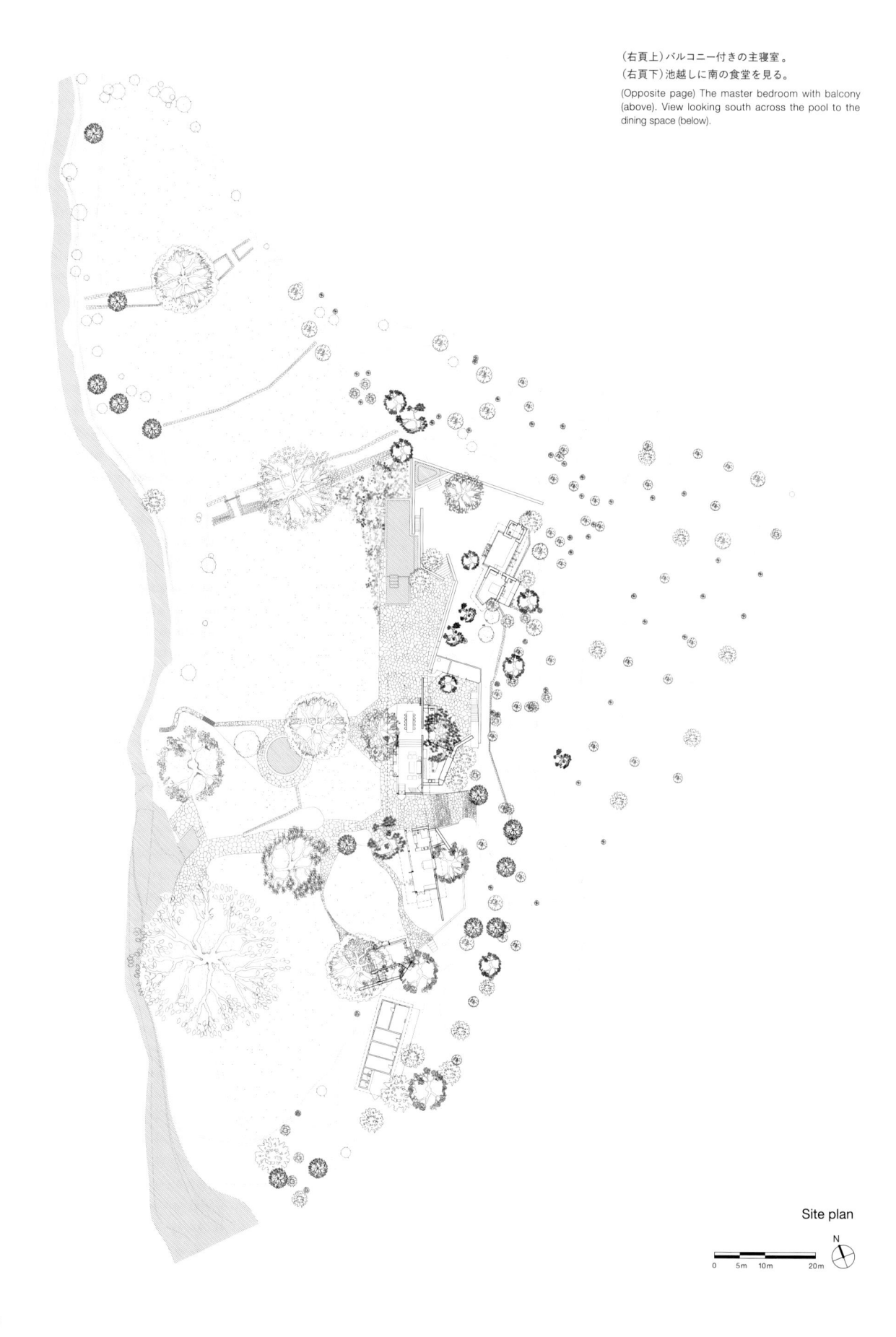

（右頁上）バルコニー付きの主寝室。
（右頁下）池越しに南の食堂を見る。

(Opposite page) The master bedroom with balcony (above). View looking south across the pool to the dining space (below).

Site plan

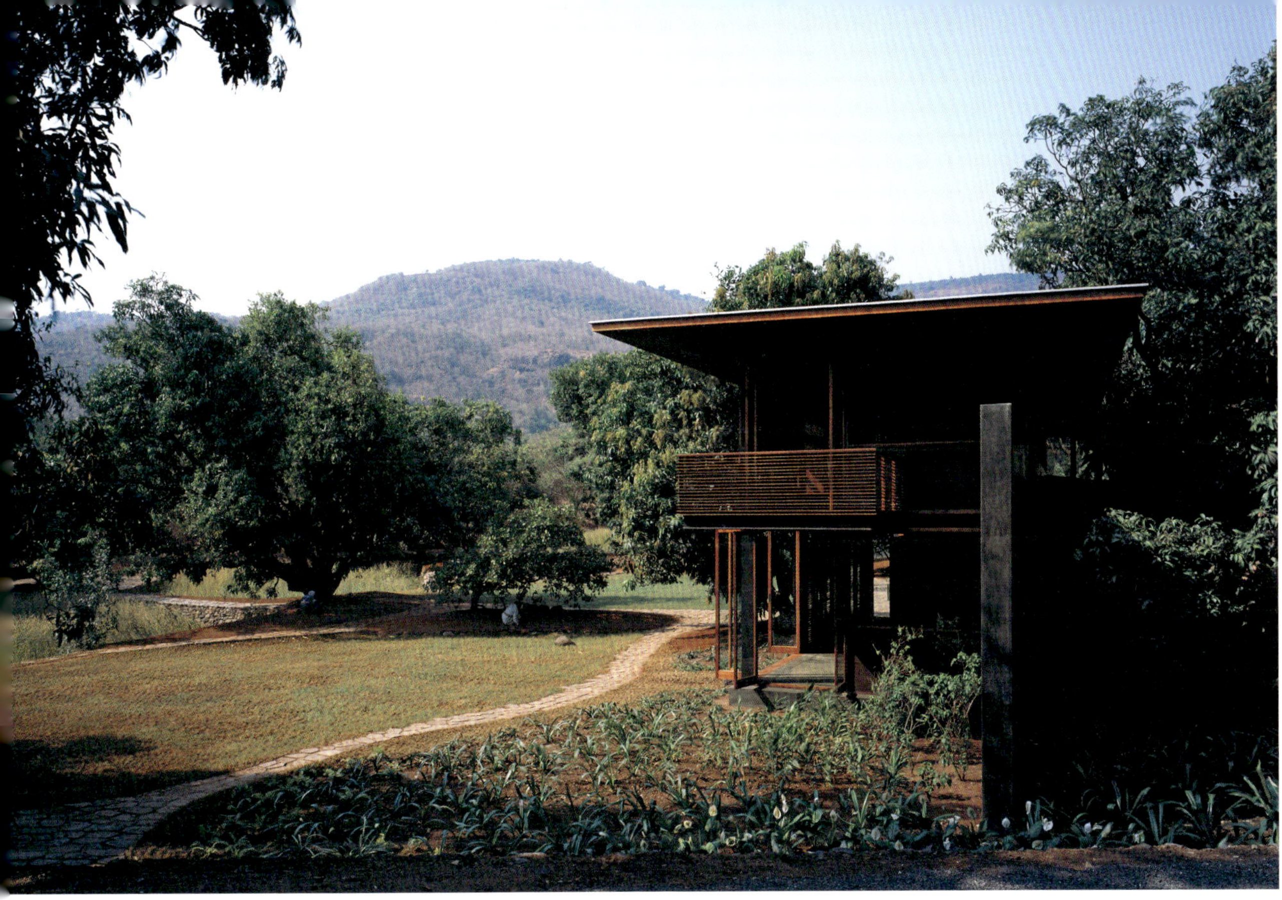

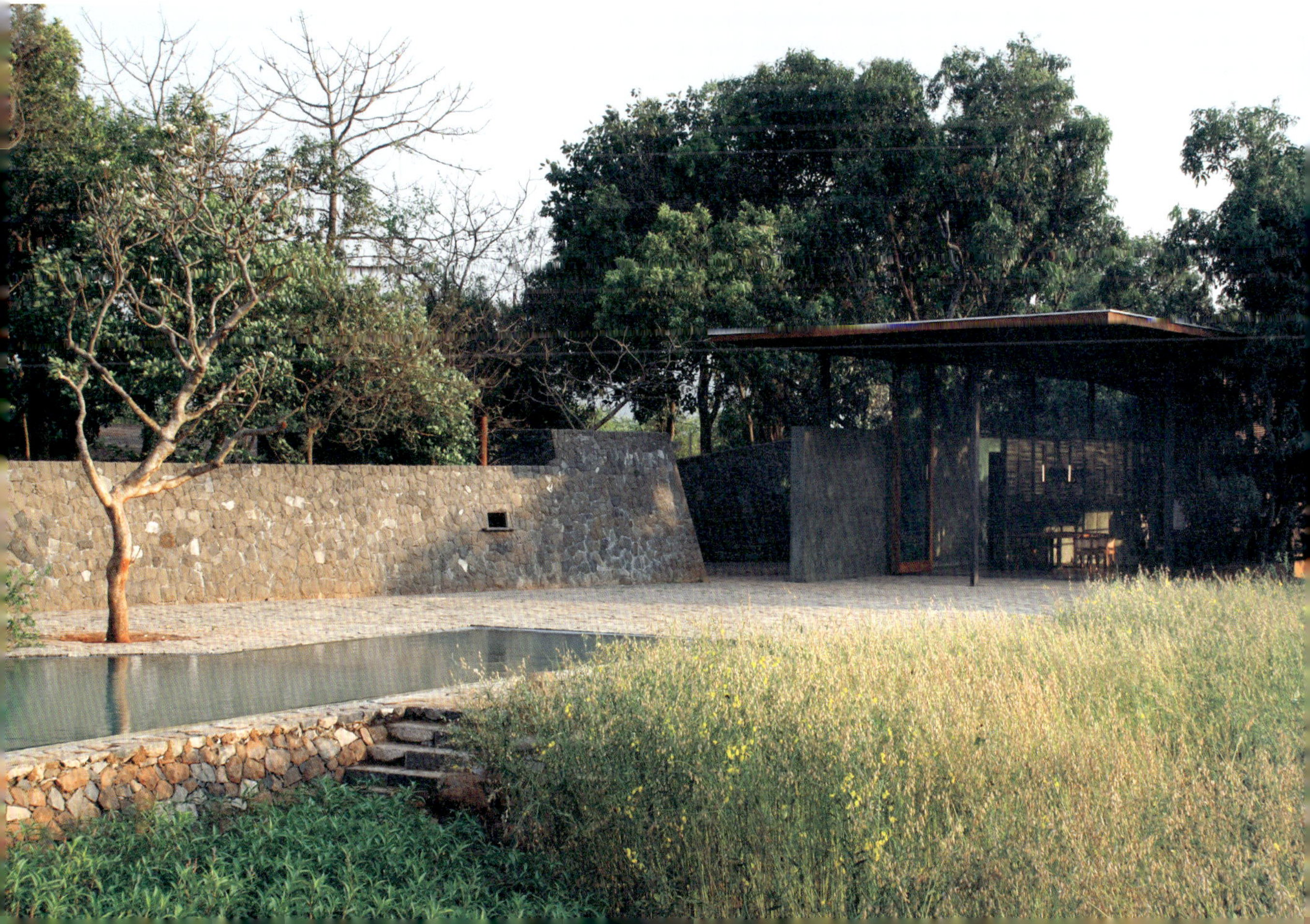

（上）軸組模型。（下）パティオから台所を見る。
（右）玄関前の再生玄武岩を敷き詰めた石畳と階段。
(Above) Structural framing model. (Below) Kitchen seen from patio.
(Right) Recycled black basalt stone paving and steps to the entry.

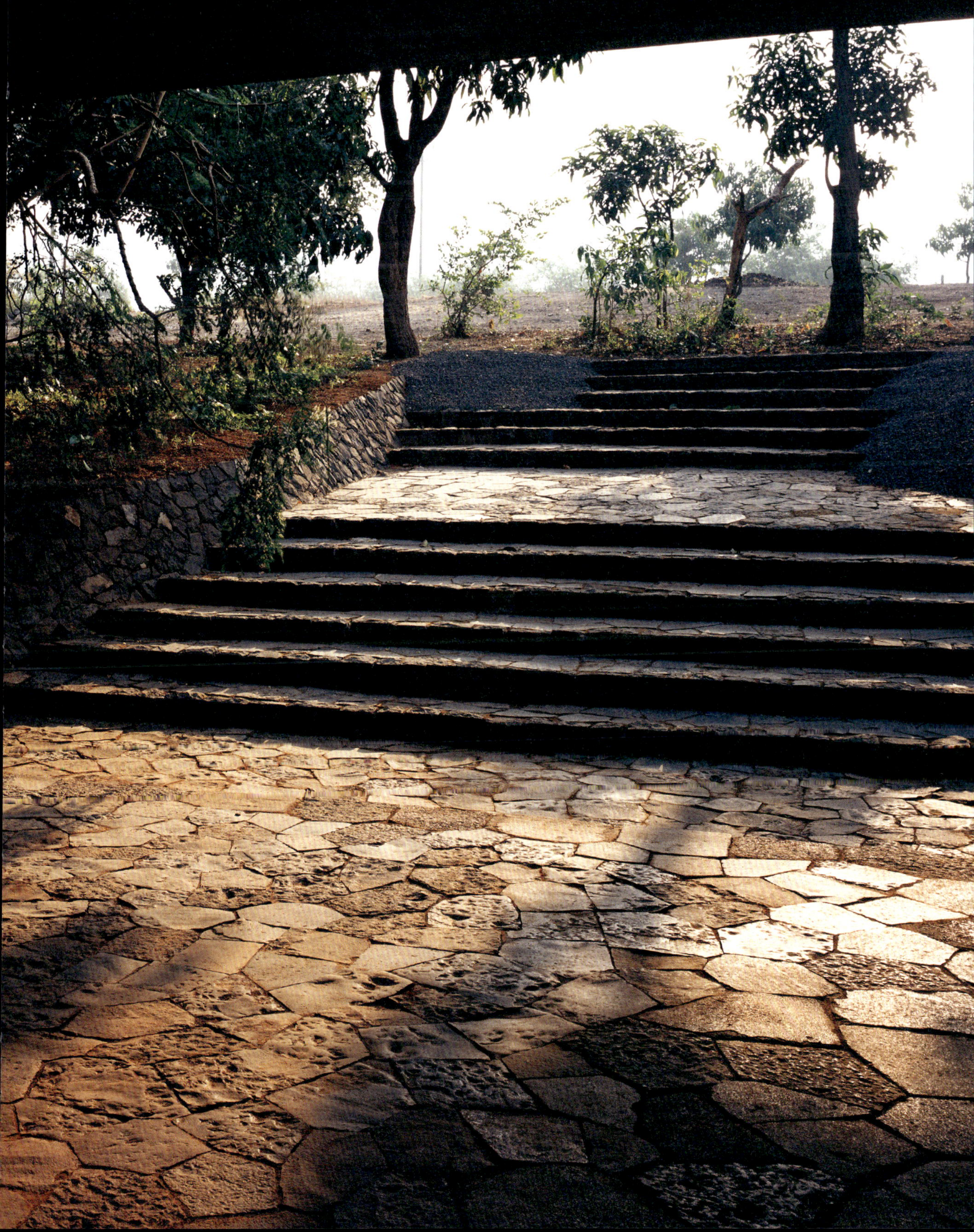

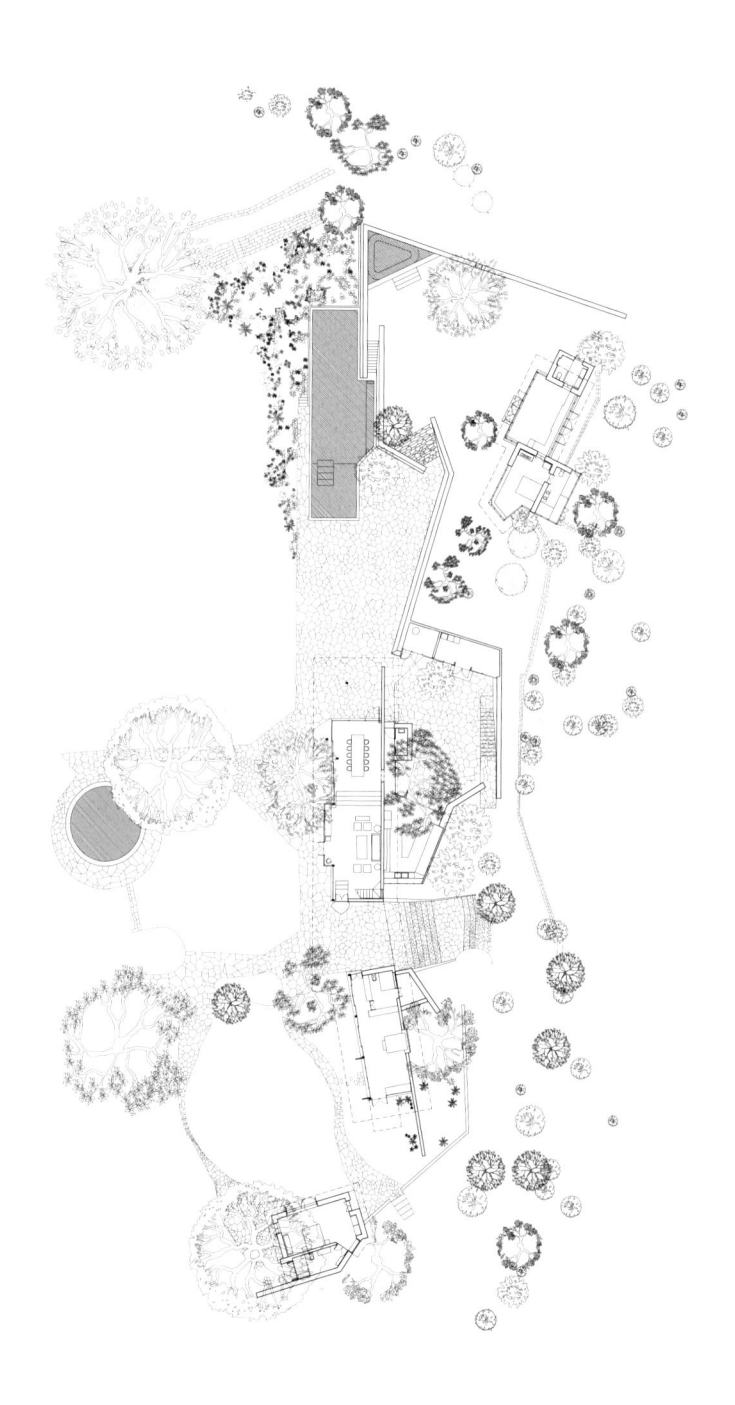

Ground floor plan

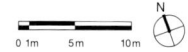

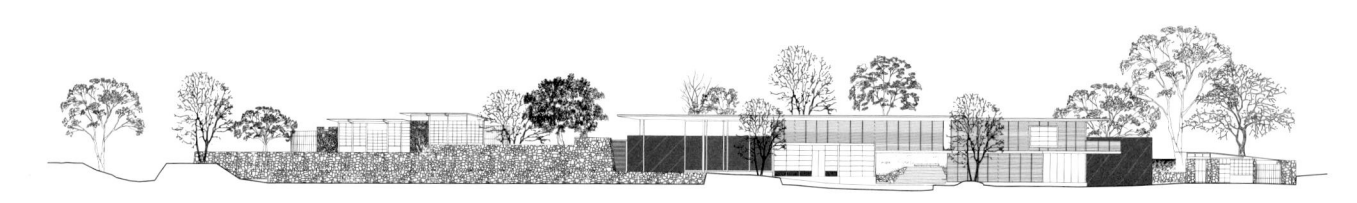

0 1m 5m 10m N

West elevation

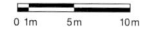

0 1m 5m 10m

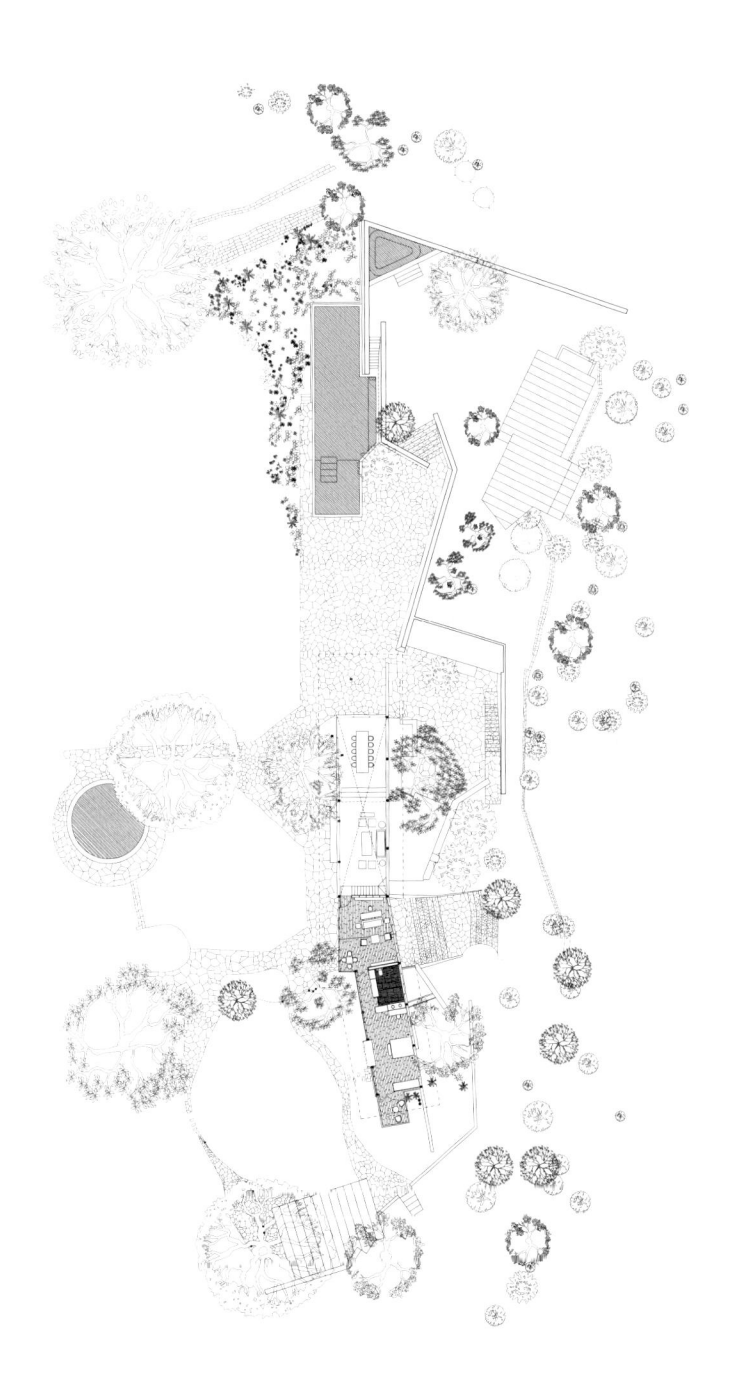

First floor plan

Site section east to west

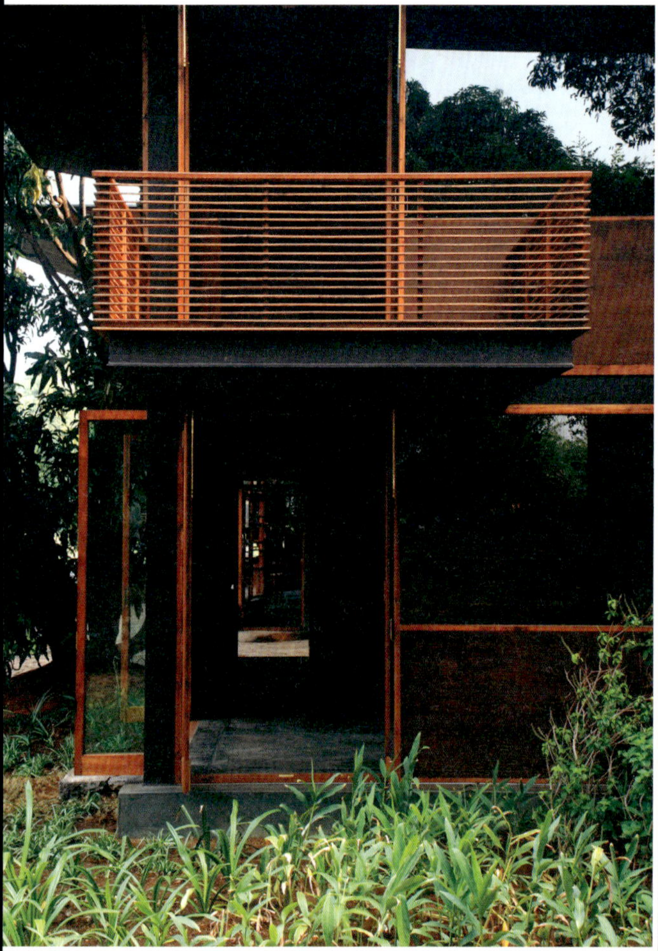
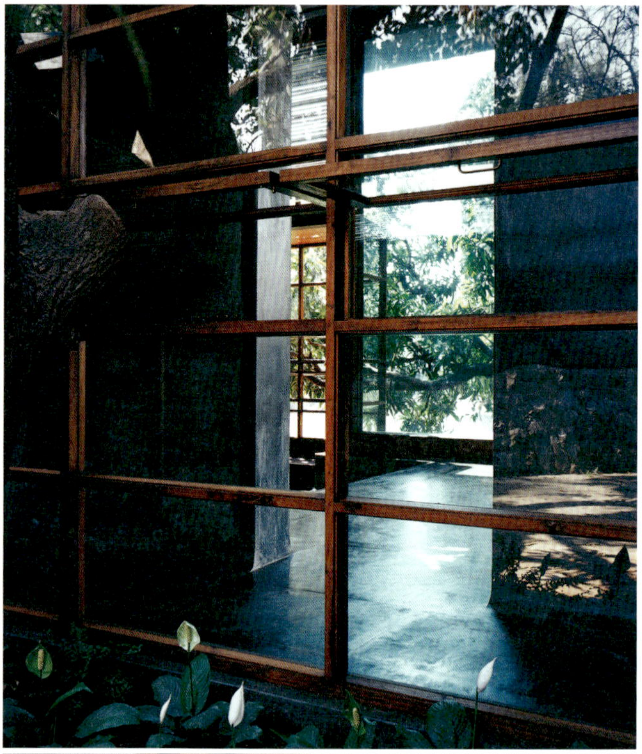
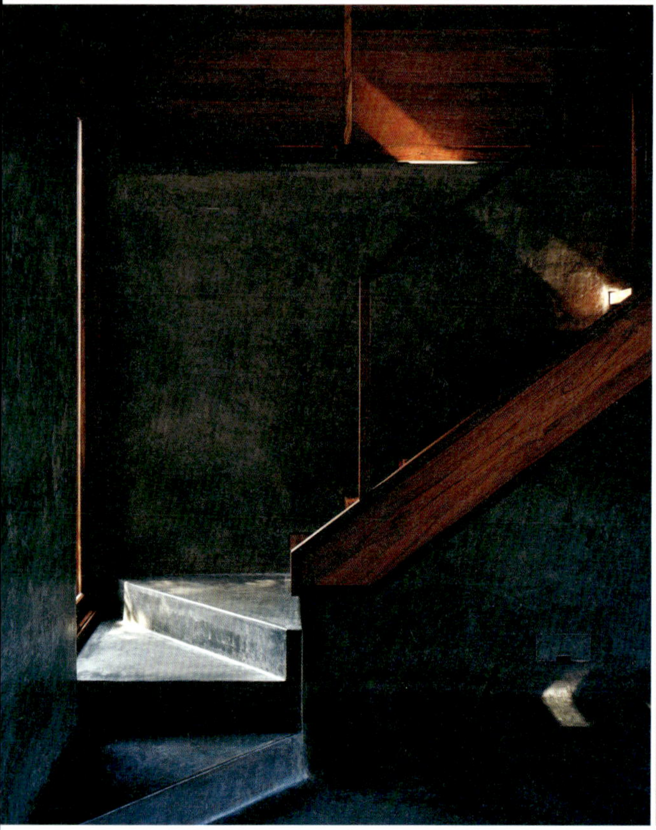
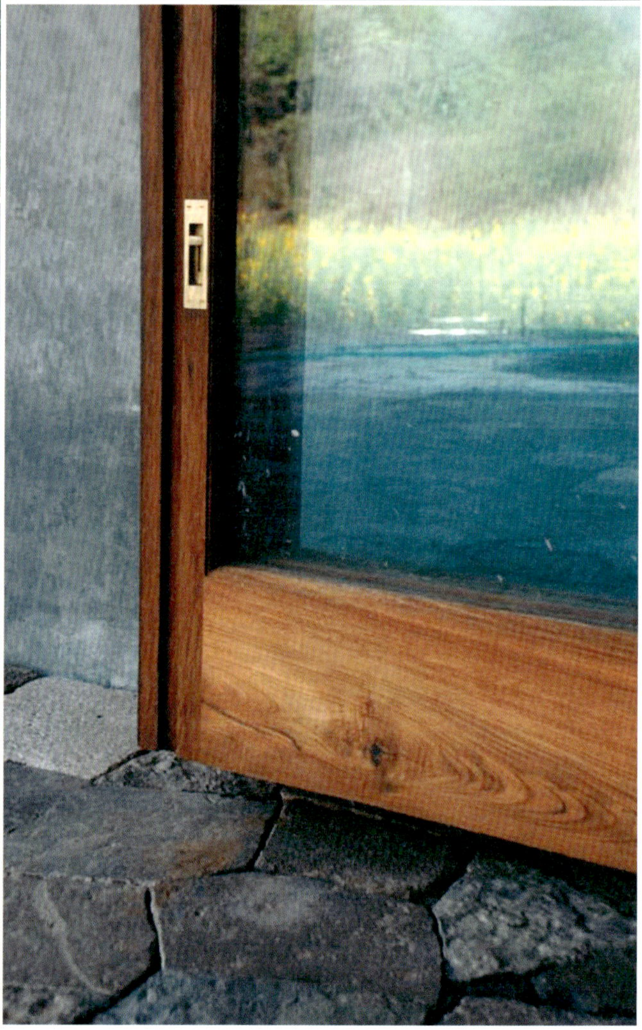

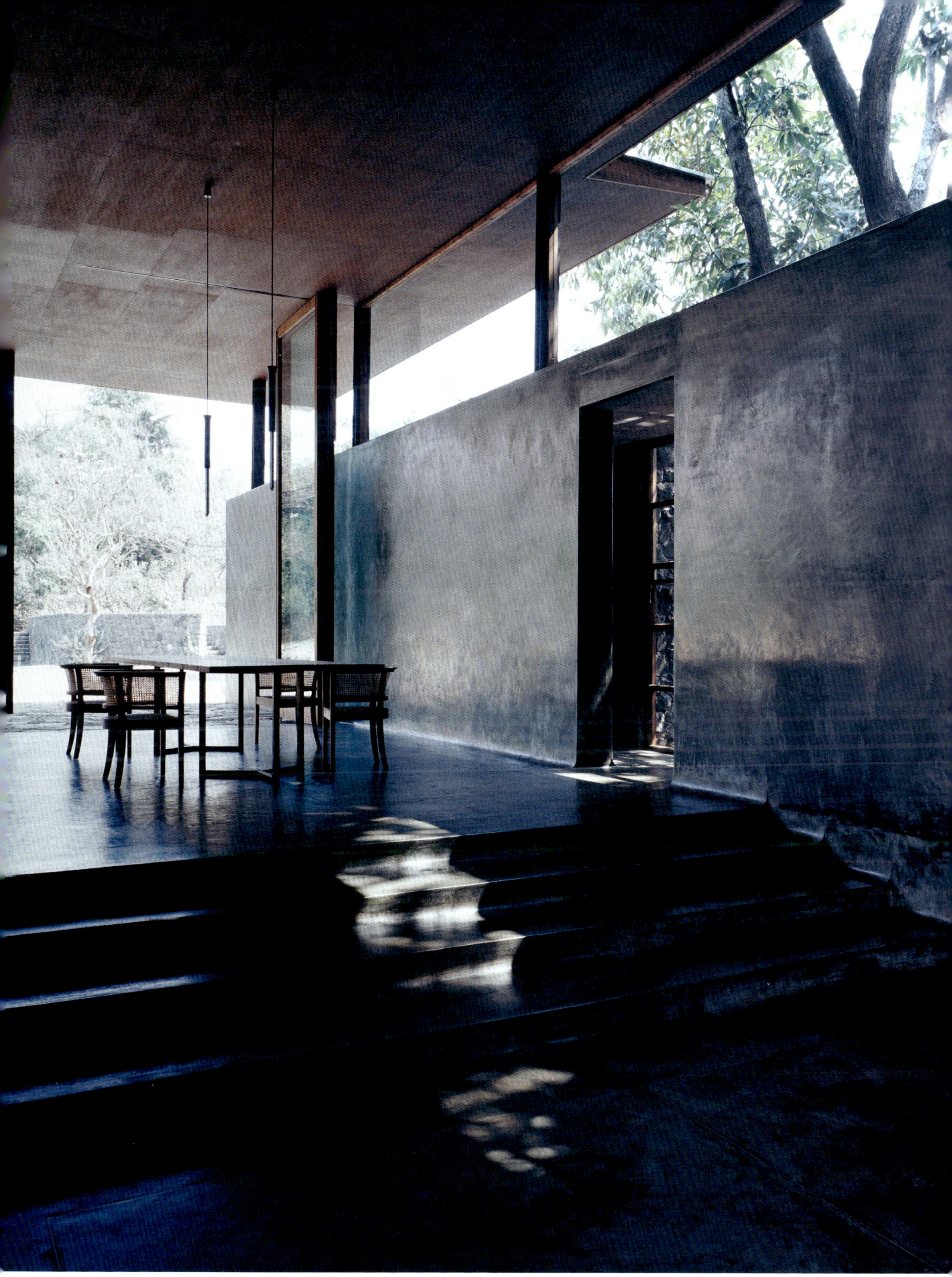

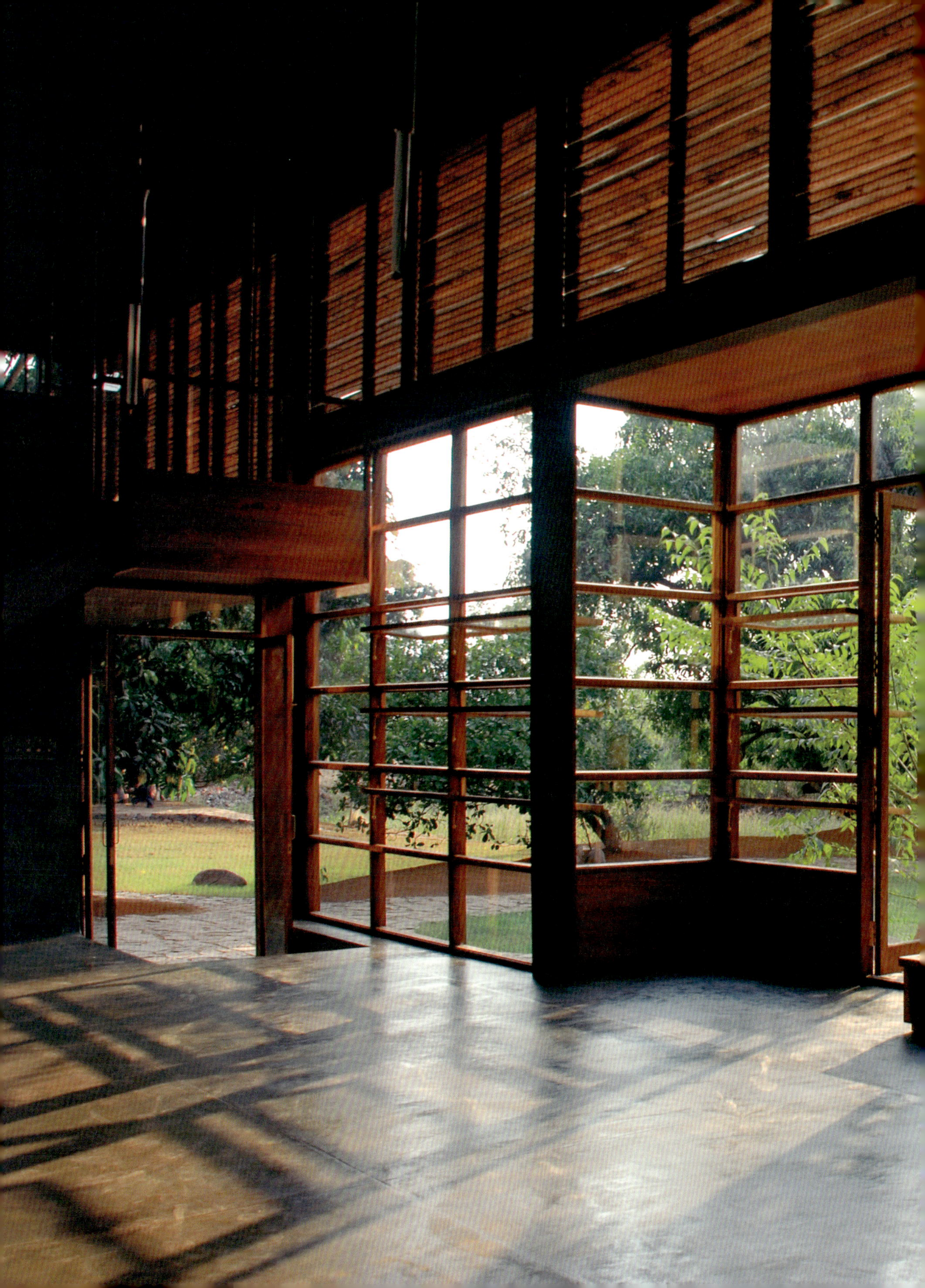

二層吹抜けの居間の出窓からは庭を見渡せる。

The double height living space with bay window overlooking the garden.

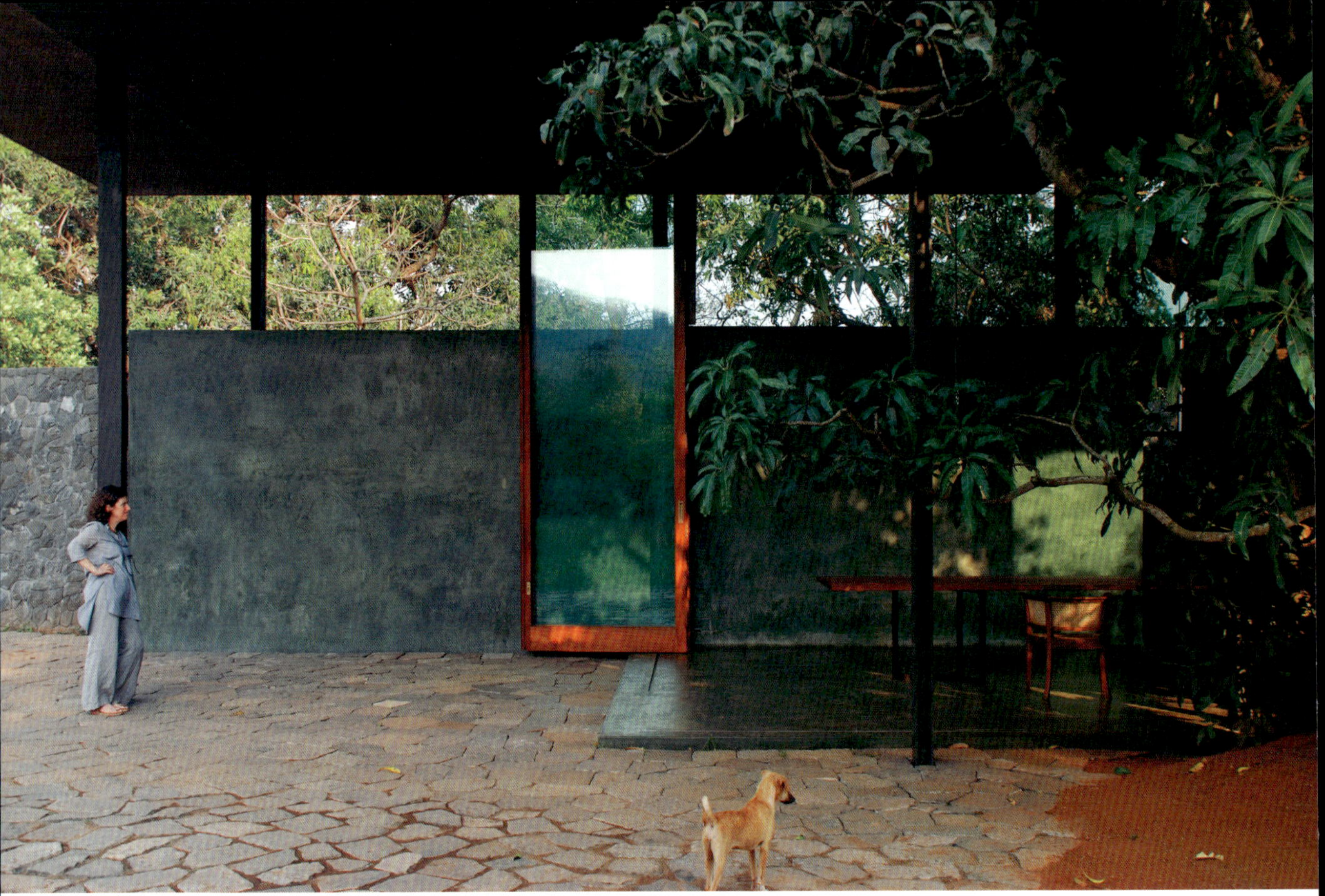

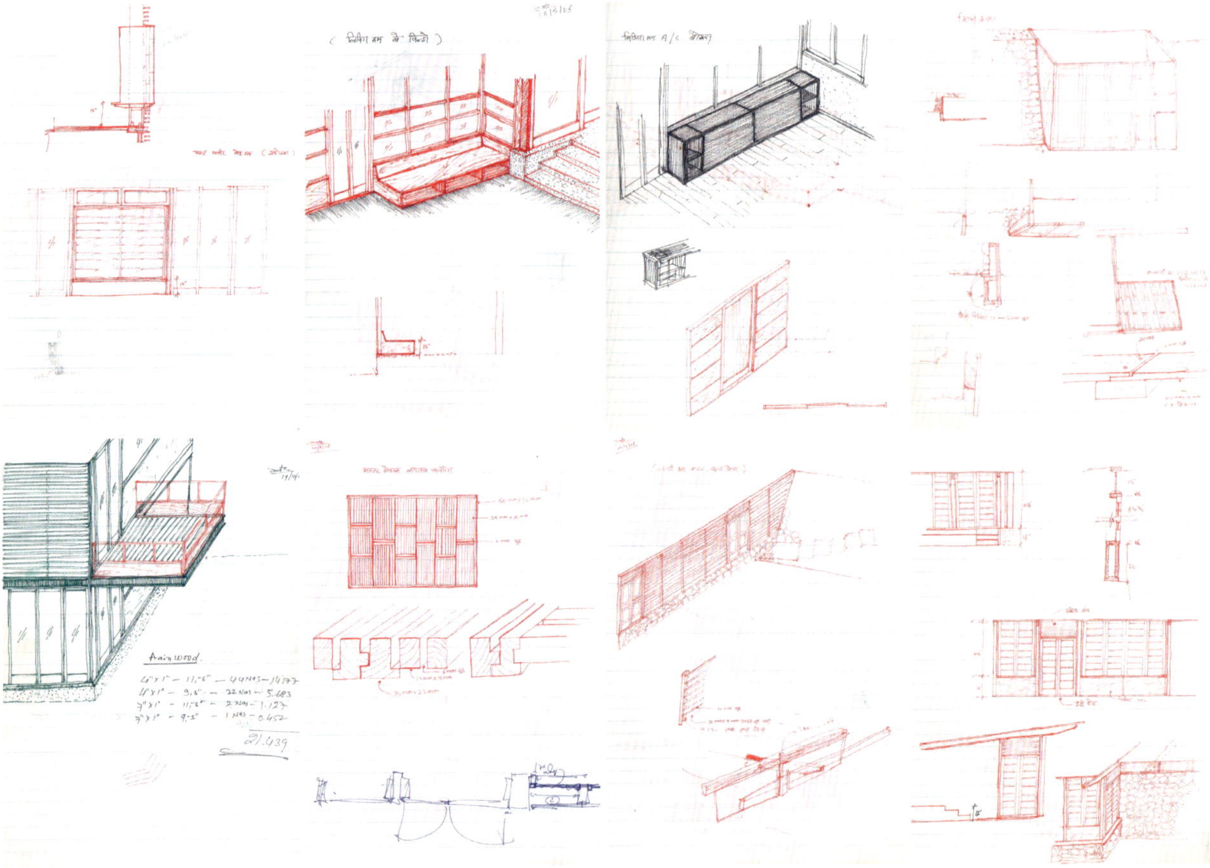

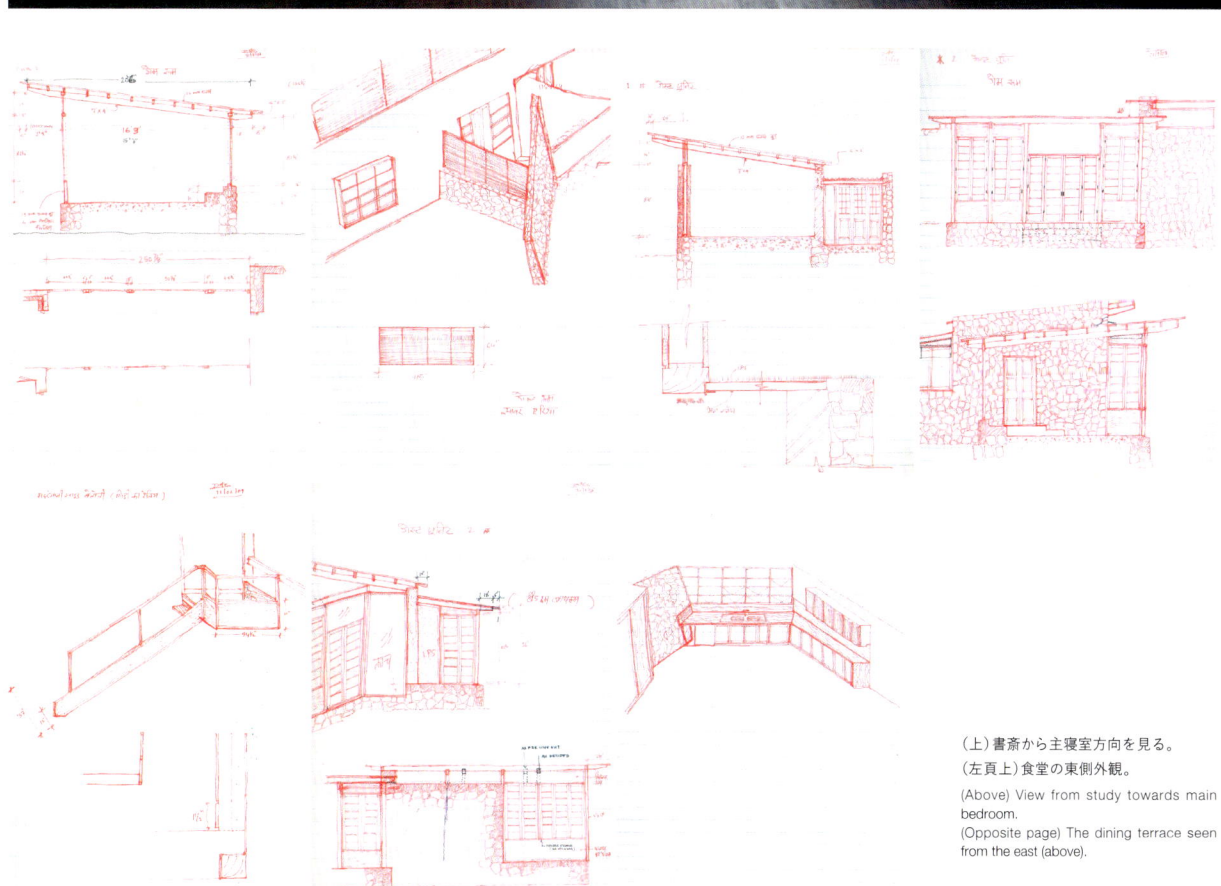

（上）書斎から主寝室方向を見る。
（左頁上）食堂の東側外観。

(Above) View from study towards main bedroom.
(Opposite page) The dining terrace seen from the east (above).

（上左）食堂から田んぼとその背後の丘を見晴らす。
（上右）庭から客室を見る。
（右頁）敷地西端の小川から眺めた建設中の住宅。

(Above left) Dining room overlooking paddy fields and the hills beyond. (Above right) View from the garden to guest bedroom.
(Opposite page) View of house under construction from the stream at the western edge of site.

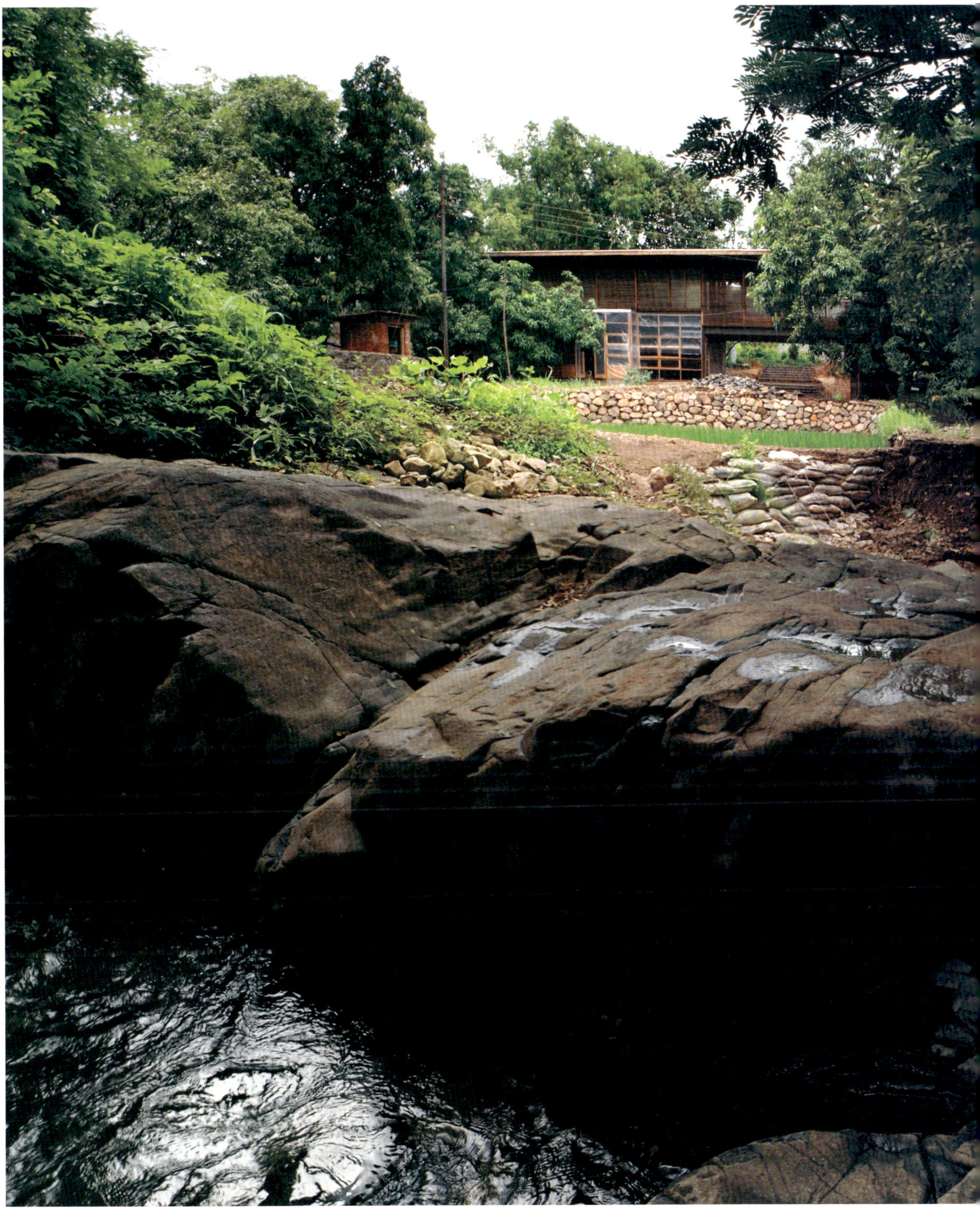

Utsav House
ウスタヴ邸

2008 Satirje, Maharashtra, India

ここでは、それぞれ床の高さも足元の荒地の高さもまちまちな各棟が連結され、住宅としては内向きに自己完結した配置となっている。地場の玄武岩を積み上げた黒く分厚い石垣が、まるで要塞のように四周に巡らされて住宅を囲み込む構造をつくっており、この家族住宅はその内側でいかにも住宅らしい佇まいで建っている。

インド亜大陸ではベランダは住空間の境界を定める一要素にすぎないが、それがこの住宅では主役を演じ、しかも伸び縮みする。つまり庇の長さと床の広さを操作できるので、必要に応じて屋内に光と風を取り込める。

住宅の主軸に沿って池と植え込みを配し、これにより高低差をつけ、屋根のつくりや明るさにも変化をつけた。中庭には昔ながらの貯水池を設け、あふれた水が庭に流れ出るようにしてある。

室内の壁と床には着色を施して、一帯に広がるサバンナの枯れ草を模し、いっぽうコンクリートと玄武岩は、各棟共通の素材言語である木枠と調和させた。

施主は、この住宅に暮らすようになってからというもの暗闇への恐怖心を克服した。部屋の奥まで夜のとばりに包まれてしまわぬよう、大地と空のバランスがかすかに保たれるようになるまで、家じゅうに昼のような光を夜の闇に灯したからである。

Arranged as a system of interlocked pavilions, continuous with one another and every change in grade both of the interior and the barren plateau on which it is situated, the house is defined in its inward relationship with itself.

Local basalt, thick and black, is used to create the four stone walls that form the bastion within which this single-family dwelling acts itself out, providing structure and enclosure for the house.

The verandah, an element that has been the defining space of housing in the subcontinent, here becomes the feature which is elasticated, as roof and ground planes are manipulated to capture and control light and air within the programmed volumes.

Pools and partial garden-like plantations are planned into the cardinal sections of the house, creating changes in height, roof systems and levels of light. The main courtyard contains a traditional catchment pool, training the water to overflow into the surrounding gardens.

Interior walls and floors are pigmented to imitate the savannah-like dry grasses of the surroundings, and concrete and basalt stone align with timber framing in the material language of this assemblage of pavilions.

The owner's fear of the dark was overcome in this house, disallowing as it does, the complete entry of the night into its depth, instead diffusing the diurnal elements of light and night until a delicate balance between earth and sky is negotiated.

154

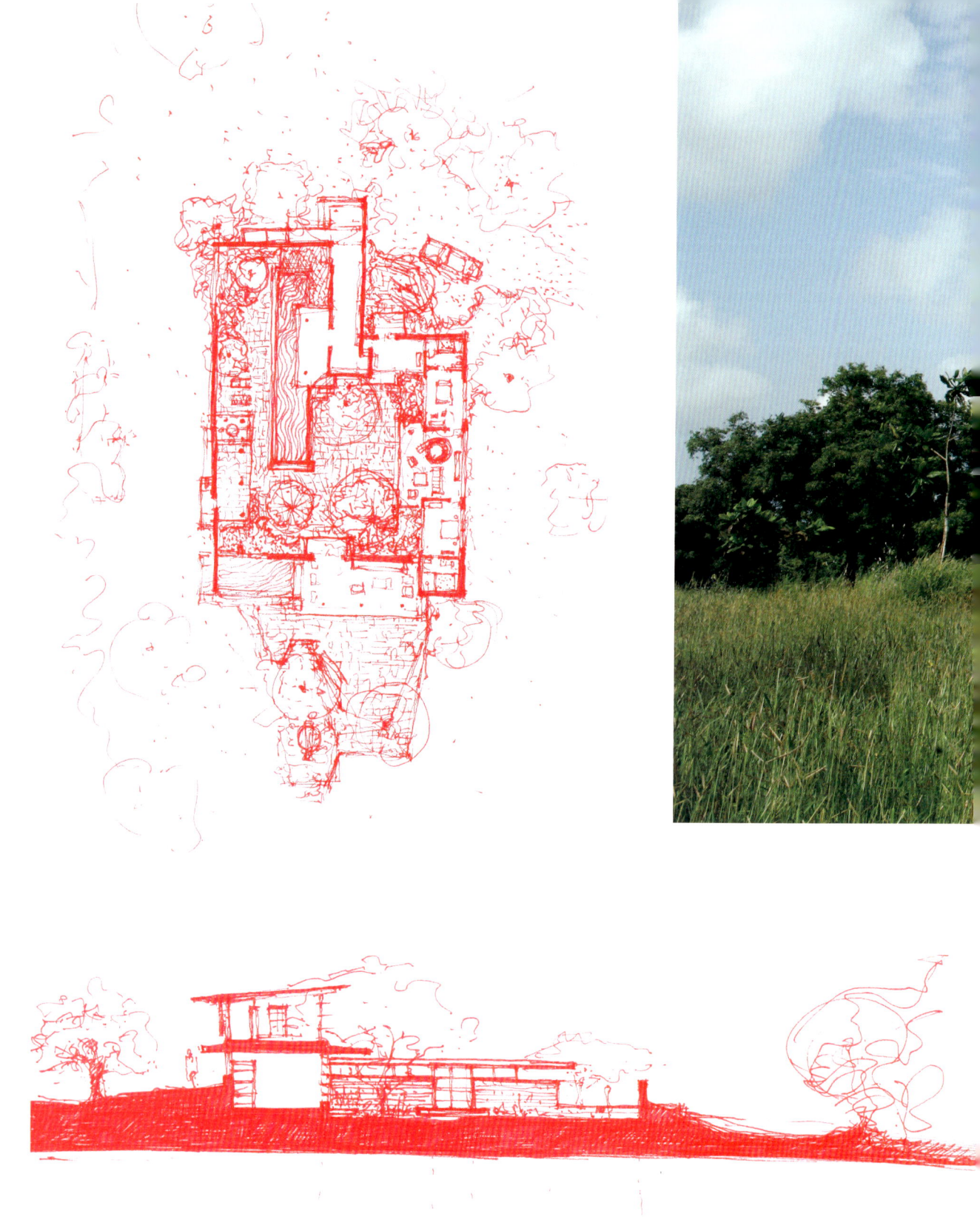

(上) 車道から南側立面を見る。
(右) 南東に位置する玄関口。
(Above) The south elevation seen from the driveway.
(Right) View of entrance from the south-east.

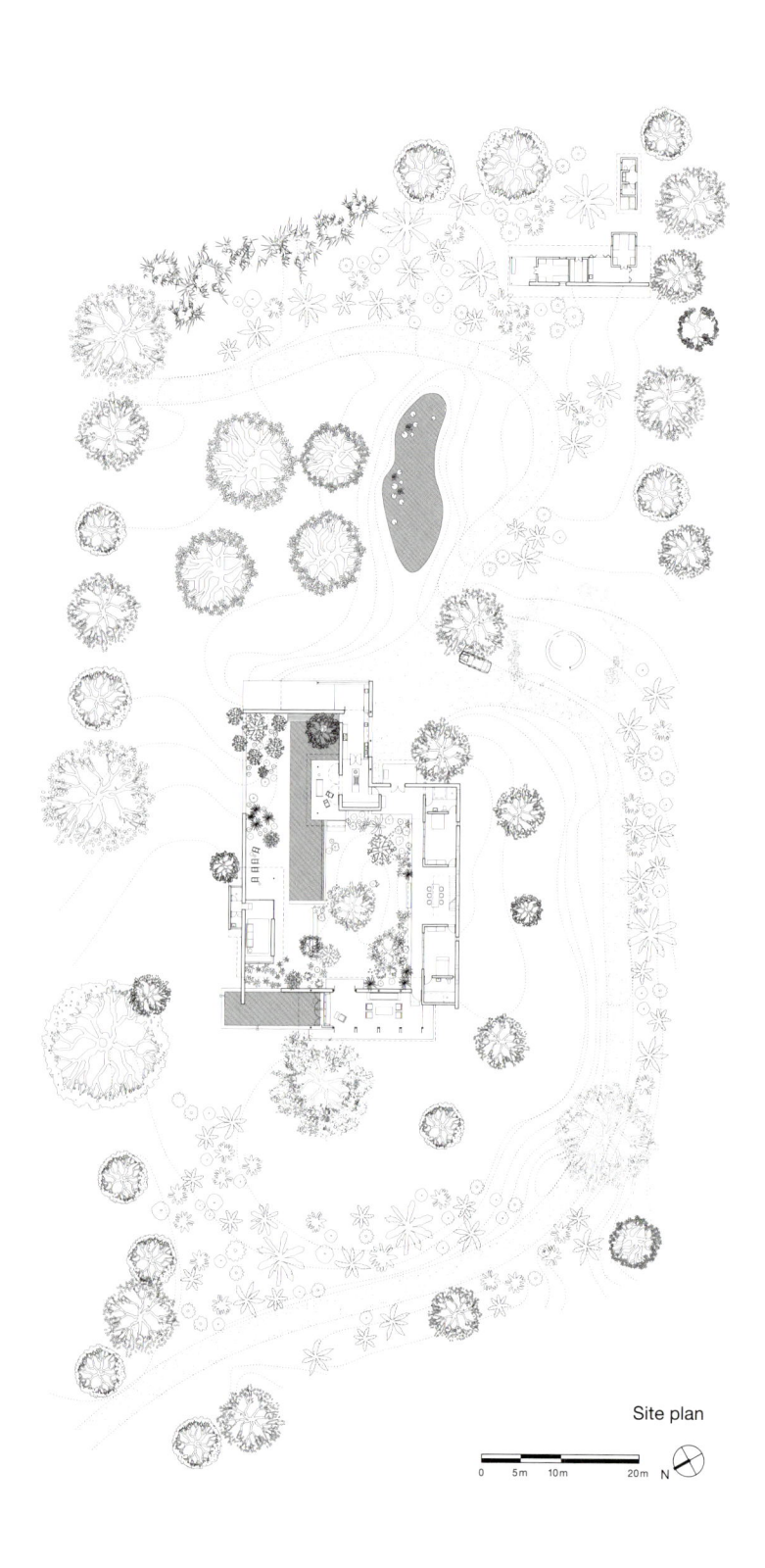

Site plan

0 5m 10m 20m N

プールと中庭越しに南側の寝室群を見る。　View looking south across the pool and courtyard to the bedrooms.

外周に巡らした分厚い石垣には、地場の黒玄武岩が使われた。石垣には通風と採光用に木製の枠をはめてある。 The thick peripheral walls are constructed from locally excavated black basalt. Wooden frames set into the stone provide ventilation and light.

First floor plan

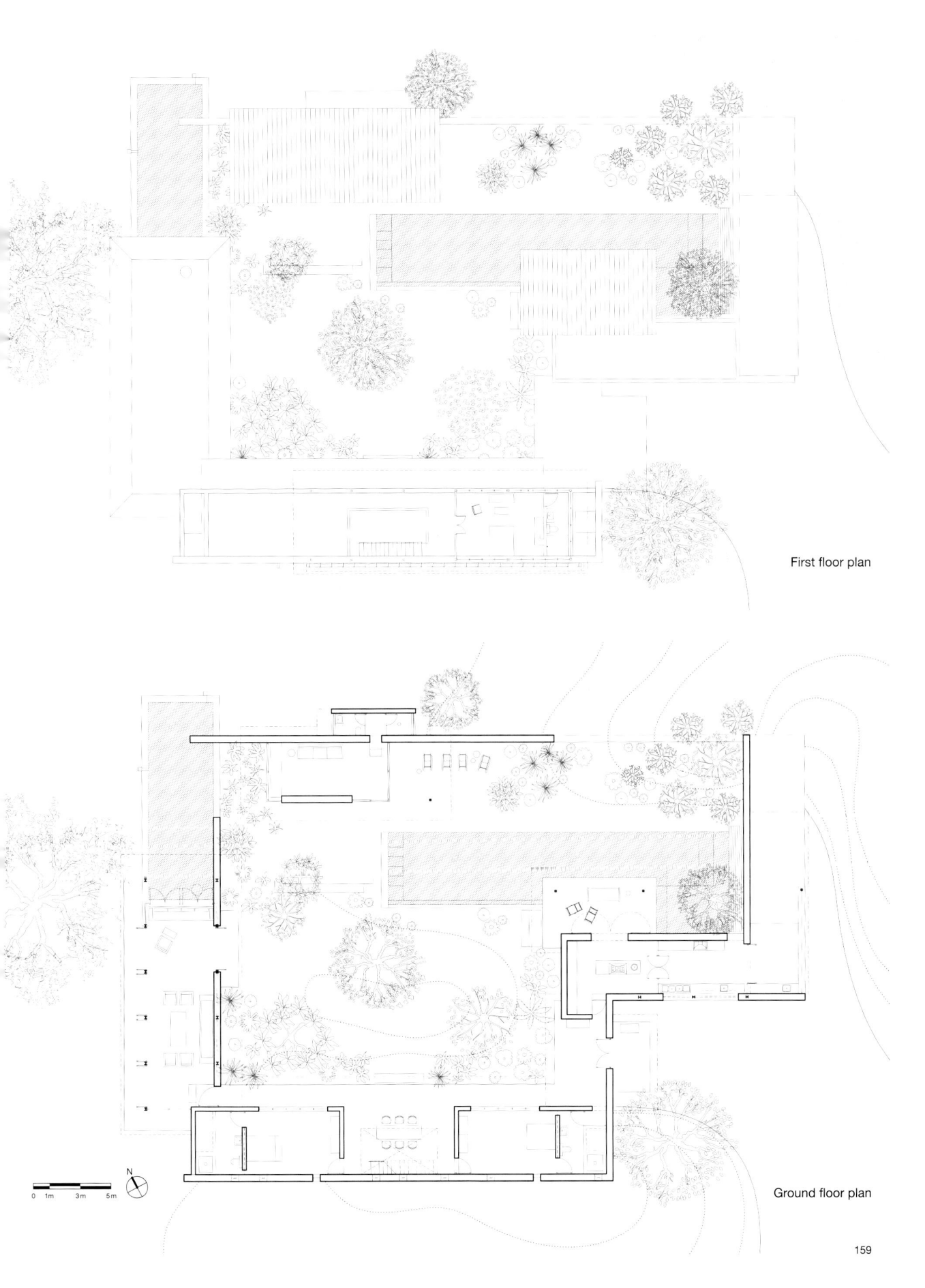

Ground floor plan

0 1m 3m 5m

159

(上)中庭から玄関を振り返る。(左2点)中庭内の池。
(右頁) 東から池と食堂を見る。その奥には居間と
メディア・ルームがある。

(Above) The entrance seen from within the courtyard.
(Left images) Views of the pool within the courtyard.
(Opposite page) Veiw of pool and dining room from the
east, looking towards the living and media rooms.

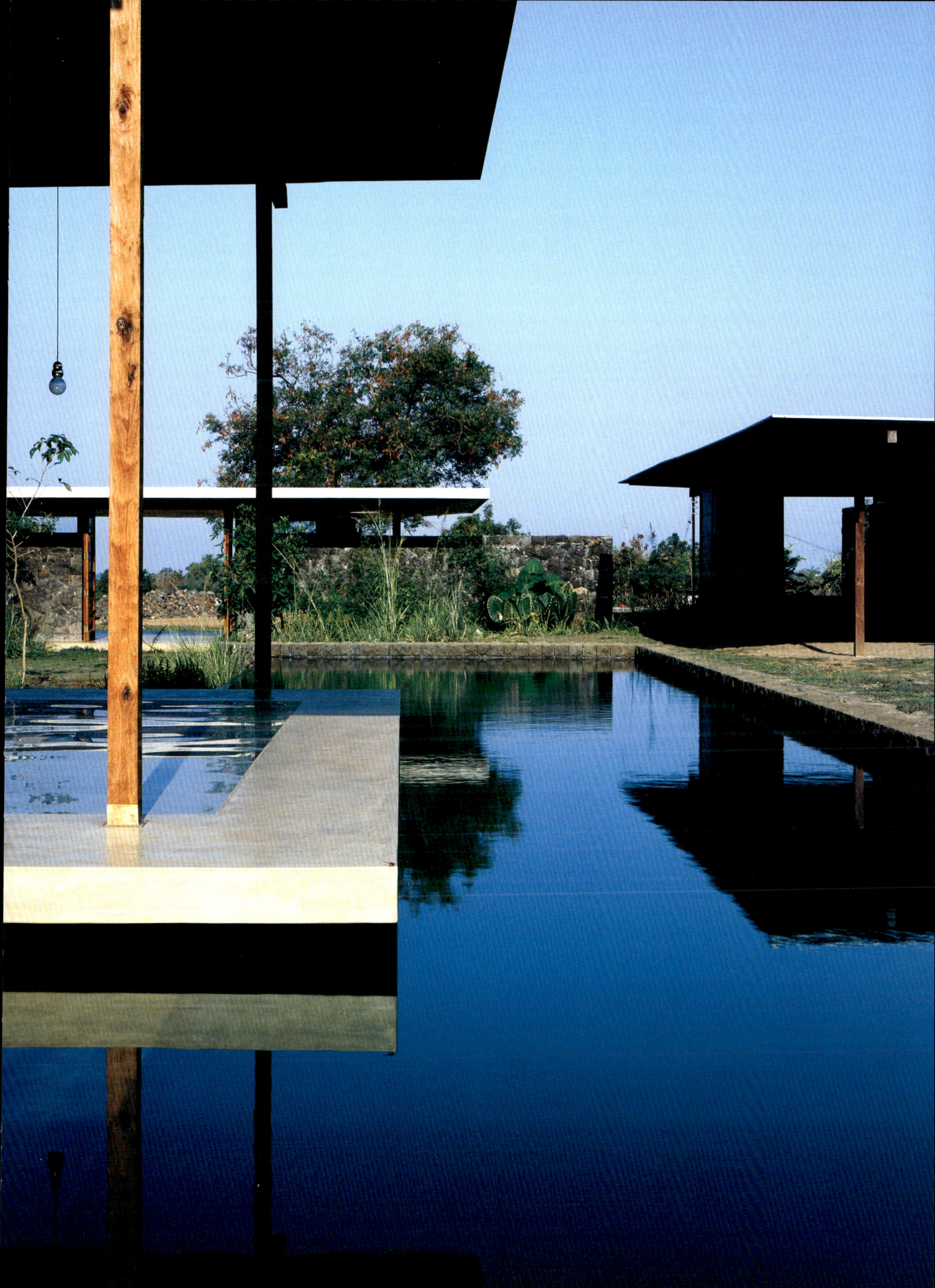

（上）南西のそよ風が吹く外廊下。溝型ガラスをはめたジャロジー窓は、プライバシーを確保しつつ、奥の寝室まで光と風を届けてくれる。
（右頁）主寝室から屋上テラスを見る。

(Above images) Exterior passages open to the southwesterly breeze. Louvered windows fitted with fluted glass provide privacy while still allowing air and light to enter the deep-set bedroom spaces.
(Opposite page) View of the rooftop terrace from the master bedroom.

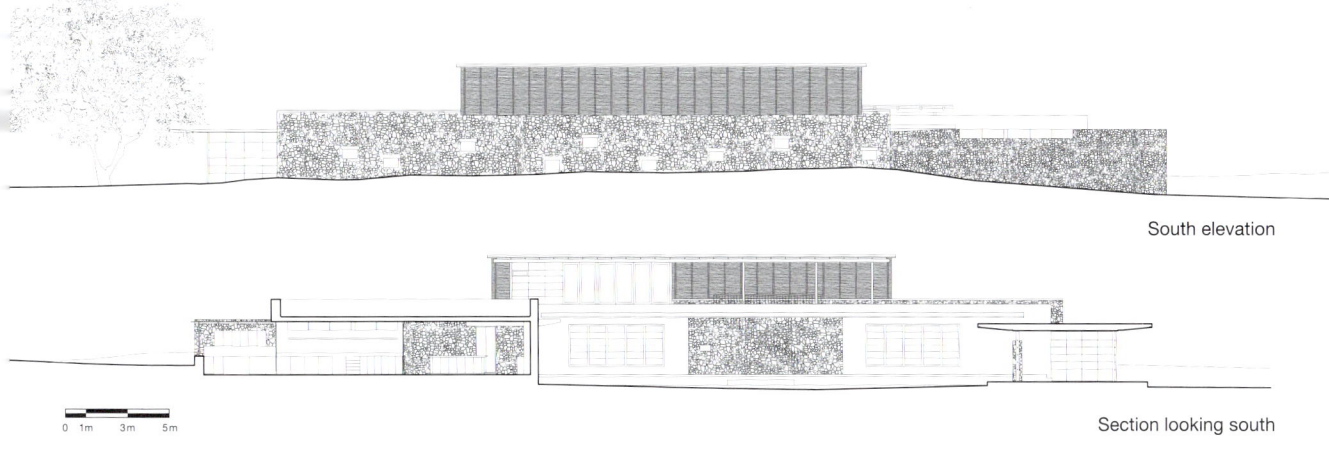

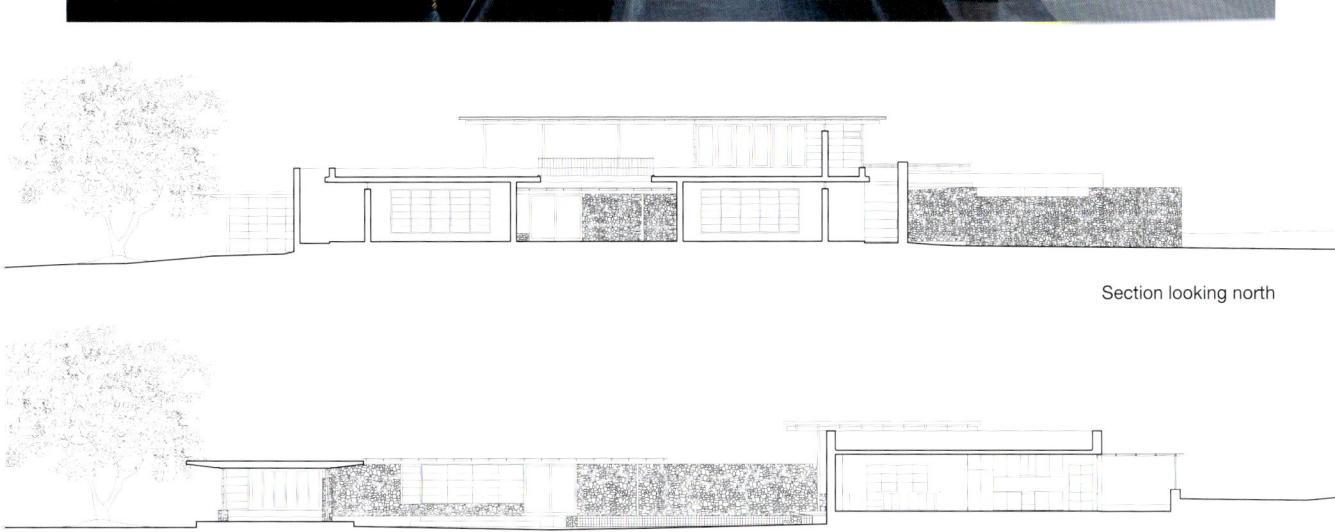

South elevation

Section looking south

Section looking north

Section looking north across courtyard

163

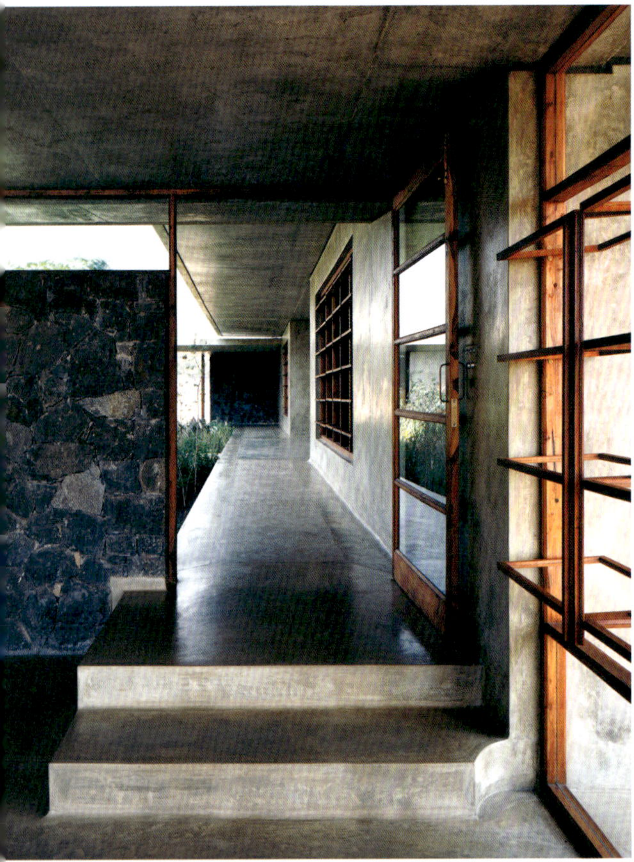

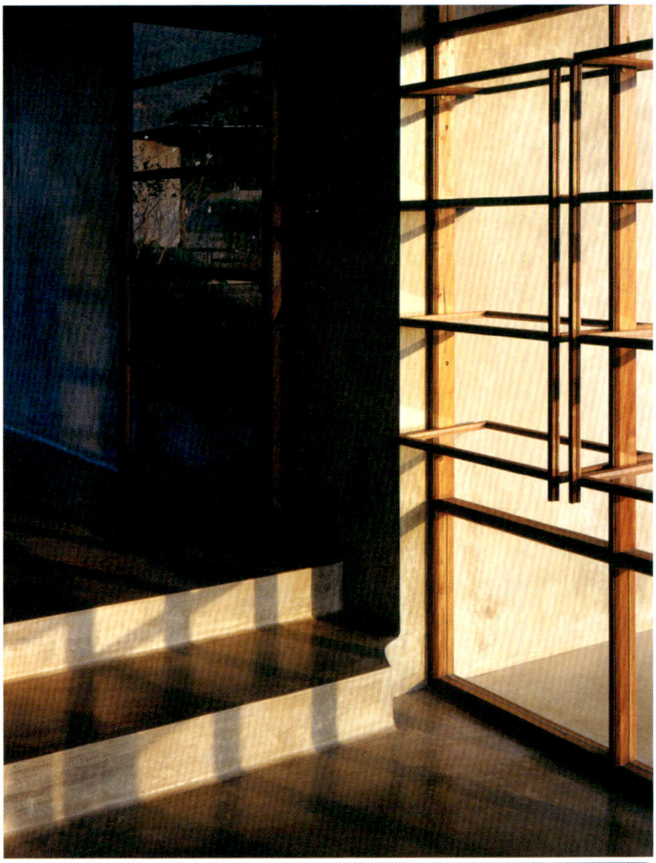

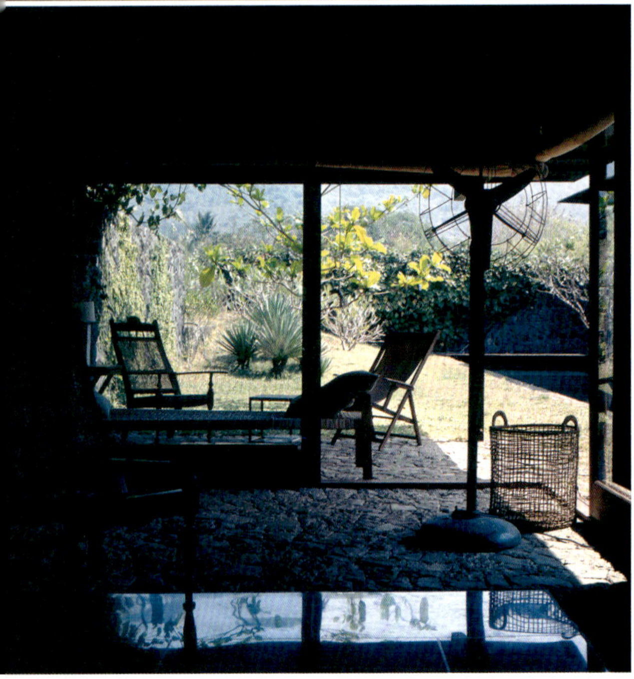

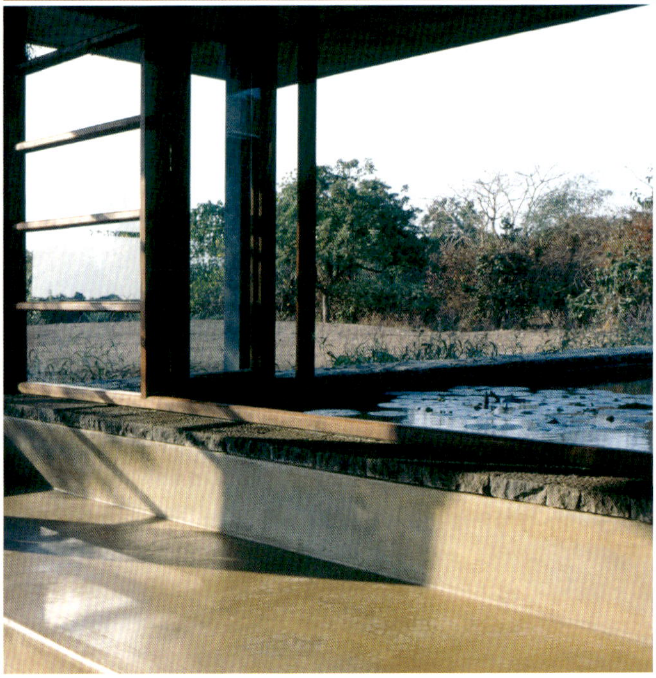

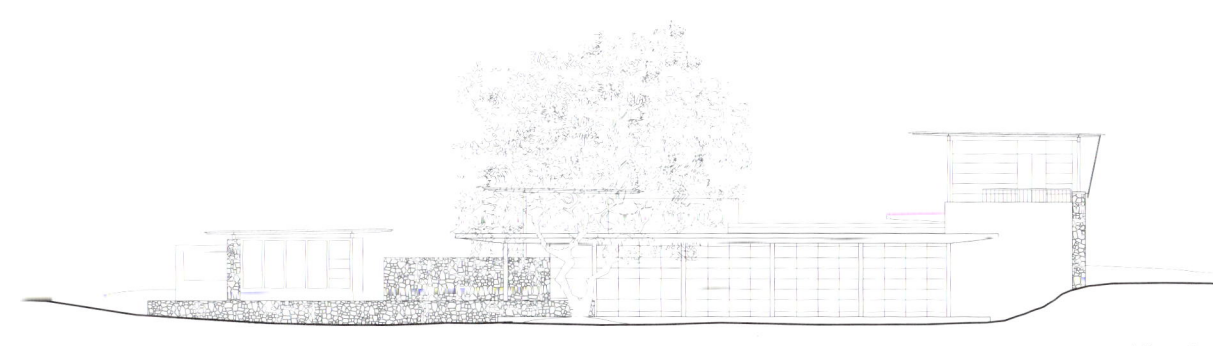

West elevation

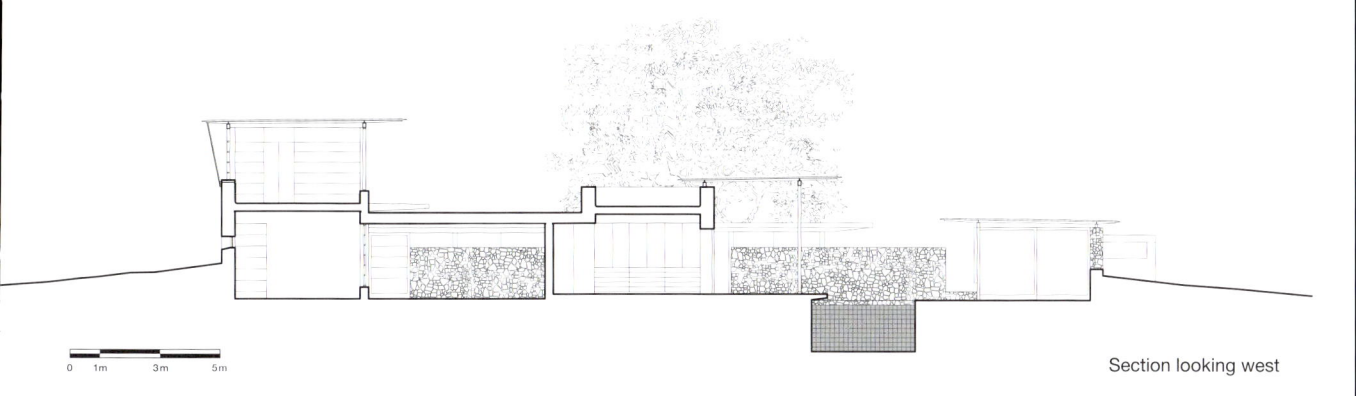

Section looking west

0 1m   3m   5m

165

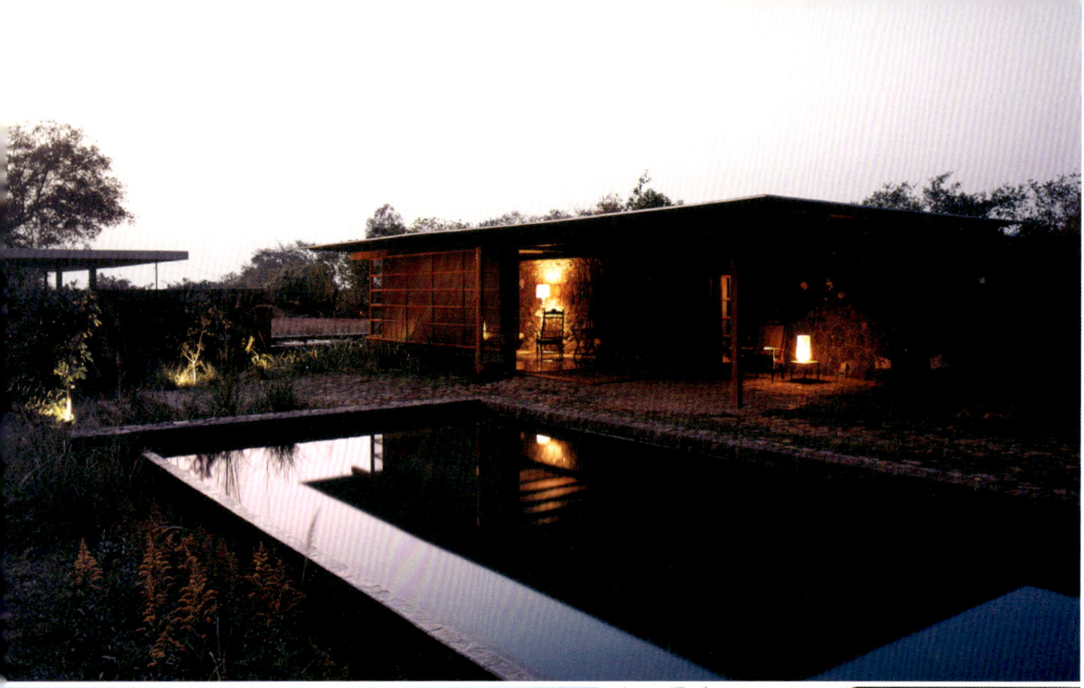
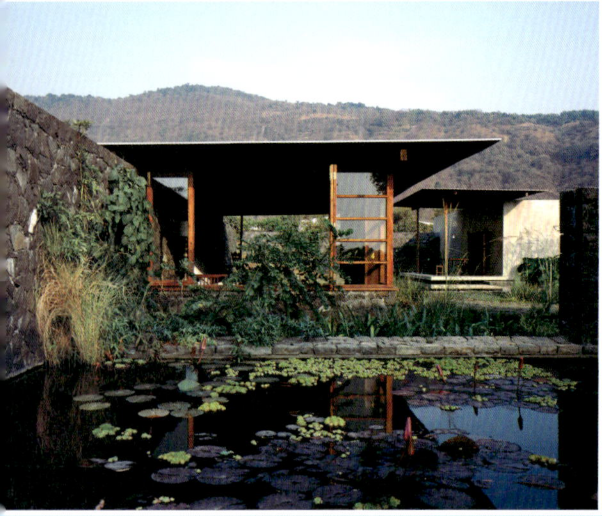
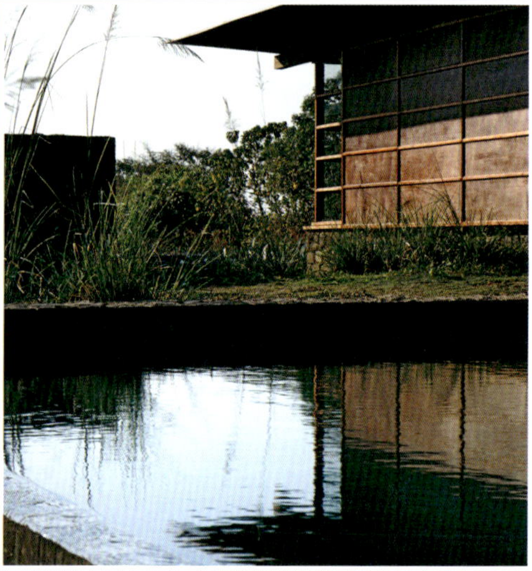
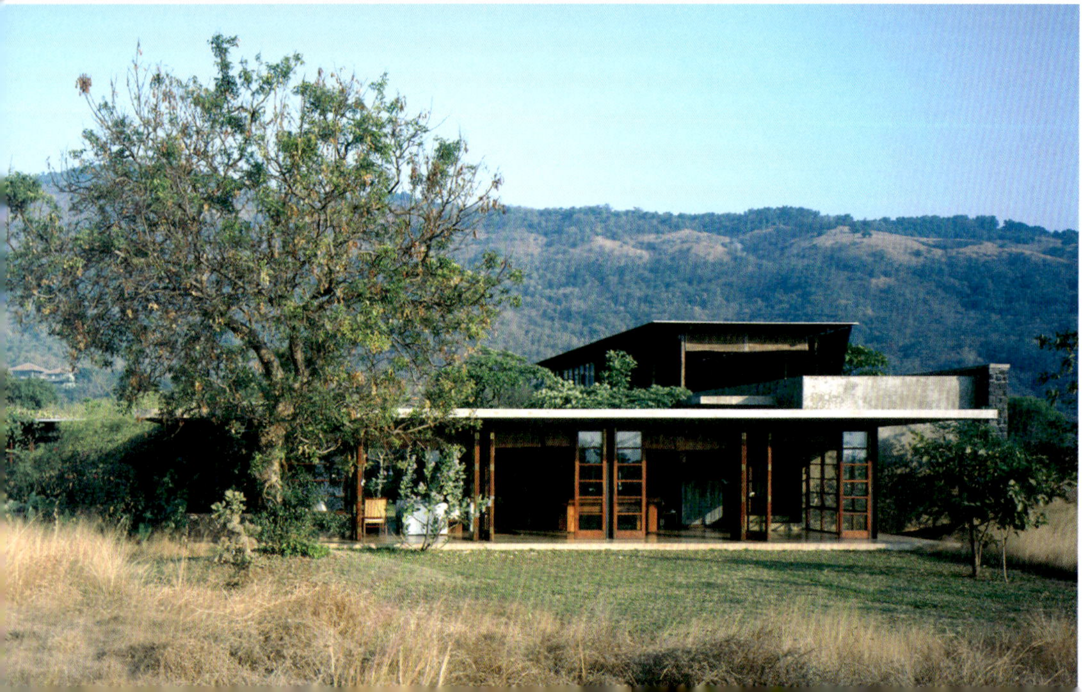

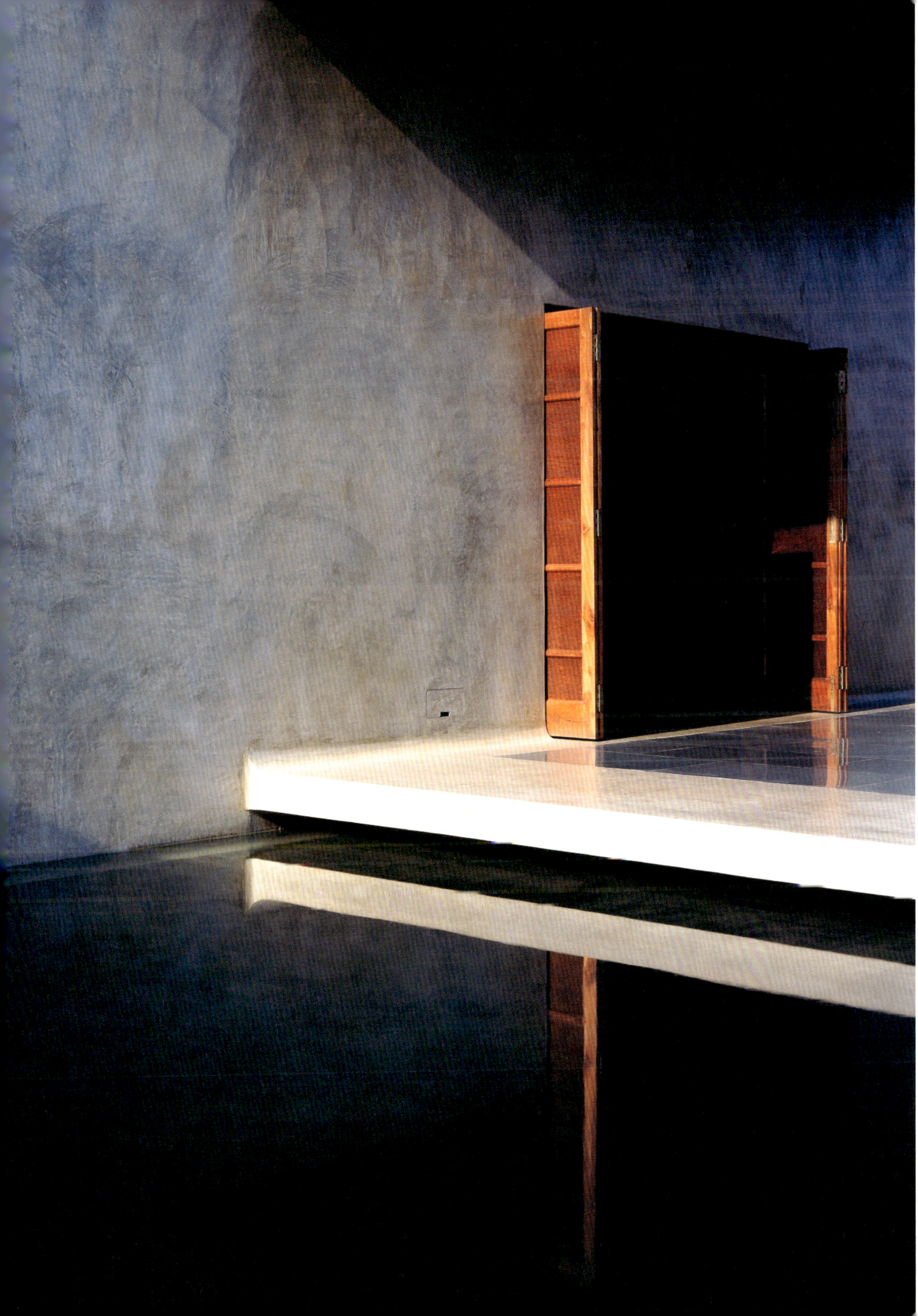

Copper House II
コッパー・ハウス II

2011 Chondi, Maharashtra, India

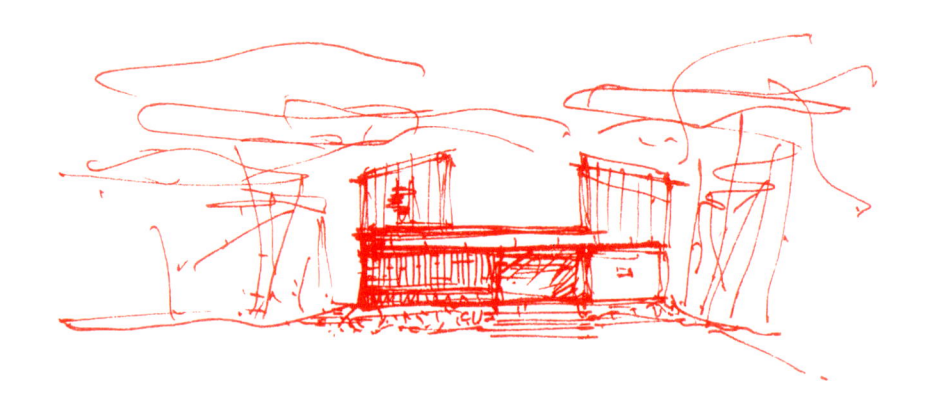

井戸を掘ったときに出た土をモンスーン期の雨で締め固めて、それを住宅の基礎に据えた。ムンバイが大洪水に見舞われた2005年、敷地内にあった古いポンプ室の水位標は最高位を記録した。この記録をもとに、基礎を杭打ちにして、住宅が最高水位より低くならないようにしてある。中央の盛土には井戸を掘削したときに出た土を再利用し、この中庭を囲い込むようにして住宅を高く築いていった。
建築をつくる手順は3段階に分かれている。その1、建物をふたつのブロックに分け、これらを石畳の中庭で隔てつつ、屋根は第2銅葺きで統一する。両ブロックの上階はそれぞれ私的な空間にあて、うち一方には寝室兼浴室のワンルーム、他方には書斎付きの寝室を設ける。下階には、家族室を併設した居間を配し、ほかのプライベートな空間ほど閉鎖的にならないようにする。このメインの空間は、ここでは文字どおりデッキとして機能するので、ここから外の景色と中庭を一望できる。上階の銅仕上げのプライベートな空間は、互い違いに配置されており、それぞれには家でくつろぐのに必要な、居心地の良さと独りになれる環境が用意されている。
その2、遮蔽装置によって光の層をつくる。これについては、昔ながらの木工細工でつくった枠に目の細かい網を張り、溝型ガラスをはめて、自然光と庭の緑を透過させつつ外の景色をぼかしたり、あるいは木枠の引窓や折畳み窓を取り付ける。以上は、家に引きこもるための仕掛けである。青磁色の漆喰壁が与えるはかない印象は、蓋に緑青を吹いた四角い陶製容器のかけらを思わせる。ひと続きになった銅葺きの屋根は、第2の基準面にあたり、これは屋上にも屋根にもなる。
その3、水を取り込む。その水とは、人を物心両面で打ちのめしてしまうモンスーン期の豪雨であり、井戸であり、小川であり、家の裏手にあるプールのことでもある。この住宅は、容器にもざるにもなるホルトゥス・コンクルスス*をそなえている。やはりここでも、隠遁と回遊と排除の形式が探られた。

* Literally, an "enclosed garden"; a courtyard.
 字義通り、「閉ざされた庭」すなわち中庭の意。

Using the monsoon to compact the soil that was the resultant material from the dig for the well, the foundation for the house was built. The severe flood of Mumbai in 2005 had marked its high-water mark on a pump-house extant to the site, and using it to register the datum for the house, a stilt foundation was built above the high-water line. The central fill came from the excavation for the well, and around a court, the house grew.

The logic of the building is written into three primary architectural moves. The first is the creation of two distinct blocks, separated by the stone-paved courtyard on the ground, and united by the cupric roof plane at the upper level. The two blocks function as discrete personal spaces on the upper level, one is a singular space of bedroom and bath, the other has an additional study. At the ground level, an indoor family room becomes an adjunct to the main living space which does not have the containment that the other more private spaces exhibit. This main space functions literally as the deck of the house, overlooking the landscape and the courtyard, creating a simultaneity of vistas. The copper-covered private spaces at the upper level are positioned in mutual tension, with the guarantee of simultaneous intimacy and isolation, so essential to the domestic interior.

The second definitive move is the layering of light which is articulated with screening devices made of fine netting framed in traditionally crafted wood, fluted glass which diffuses the light and greenery and hints at the absent city, and sliding and folding wooden windows, all of which allow for degrees of seclusion. The walls are finished in wa celadon-coloured traditional plaster, giving the transitory appearance of a fragmented ceramic container, rectilinear and encased with a lid of weathered copper. The continuous copper roof plane forms a secondary datum for the house, becoming a surface of potential occupation and cover.

The last is the inclusion of the element of water, in the form of the monsoon rain relentless as it is in its action on material and mood, the well, the stream and the pool beyond the house. In this house, with its hortus conclusus* acting both as container and sieve, the architect's exploration of the rites of retreat, passage and exclusion are tested again.

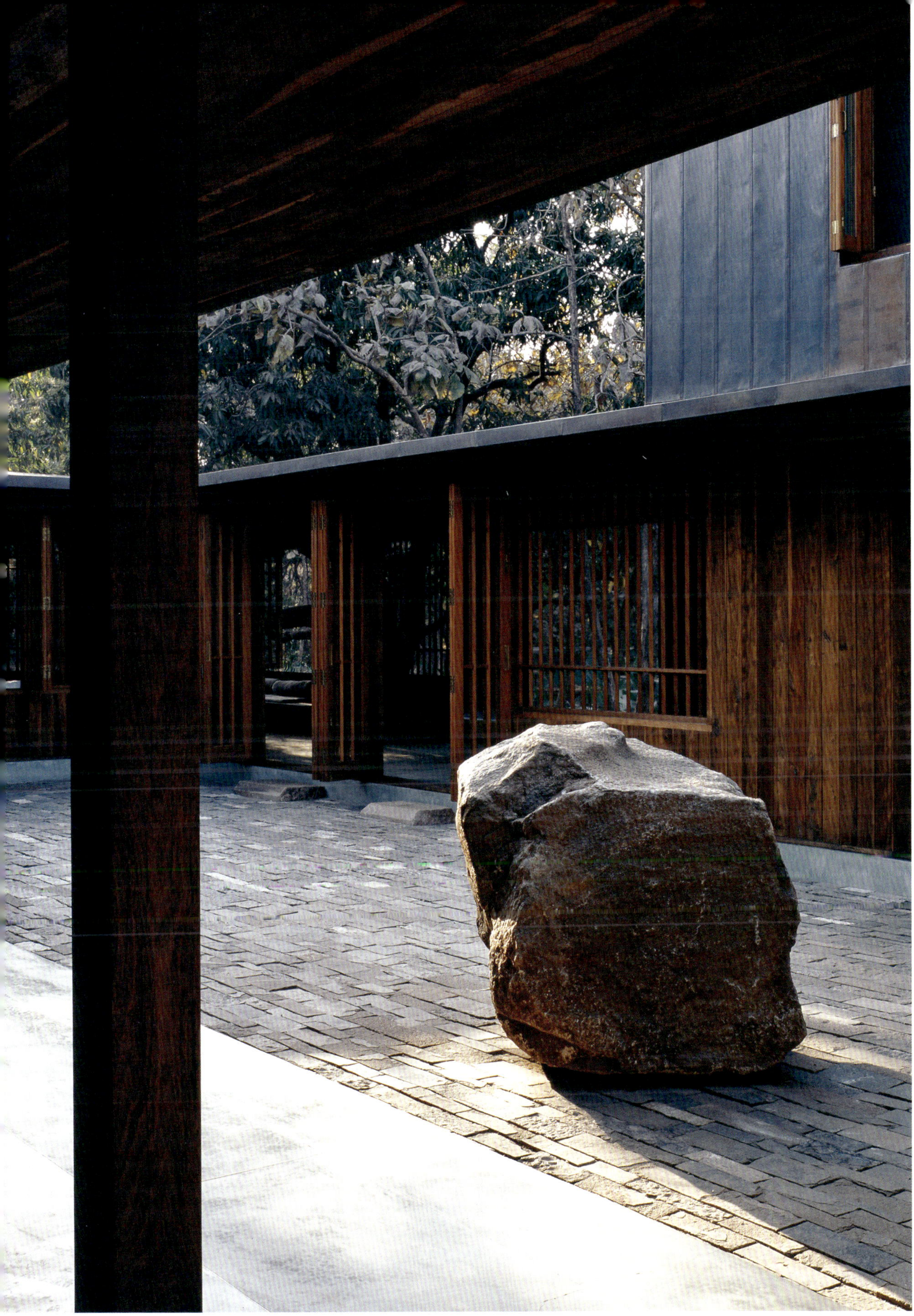

(上)南側の庭からの住宅全景。
(下5点)スイミング・プール、ジム、掘抜き井戸。

(Above) View of the house from the south garden.
(Bottom images) The swimming pool, gym and artesian well.

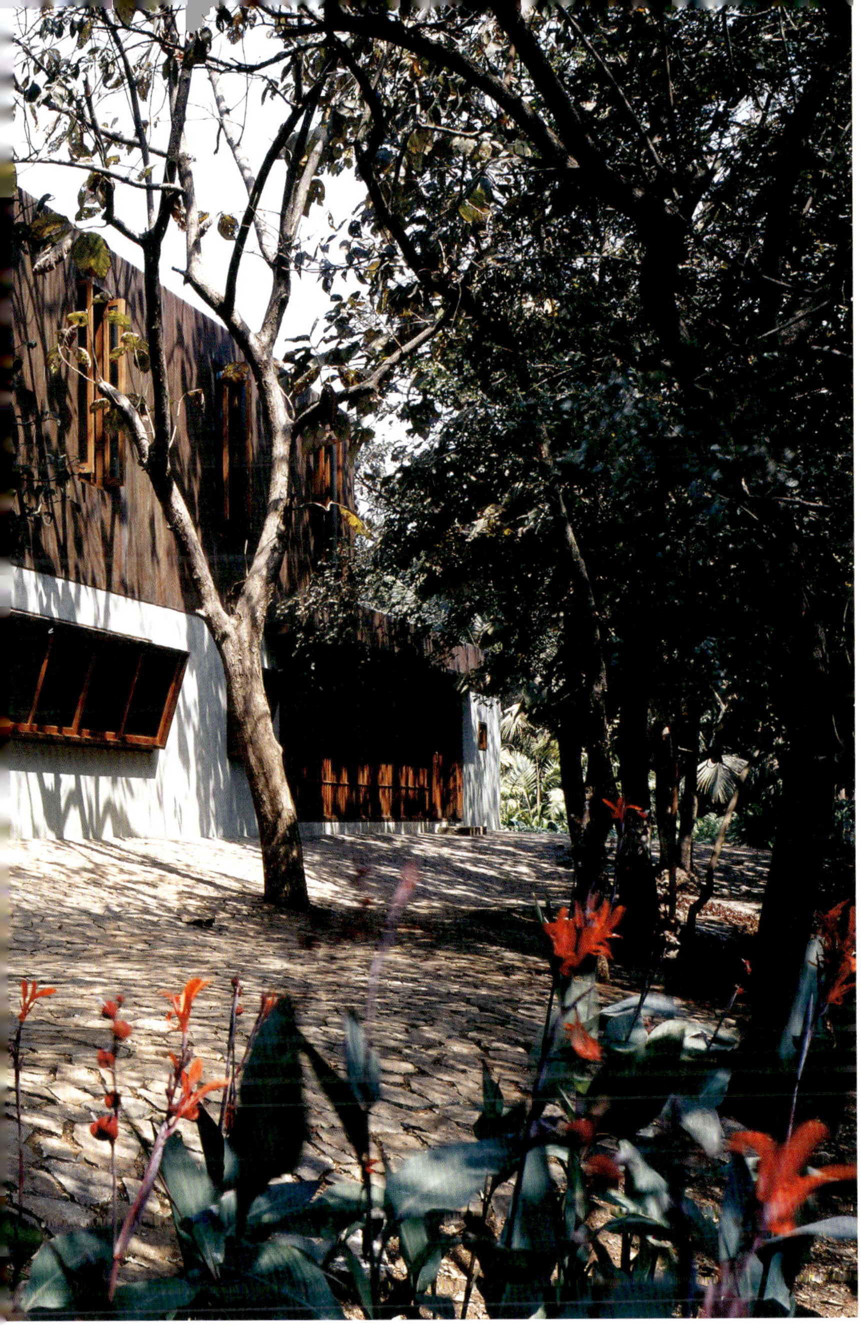
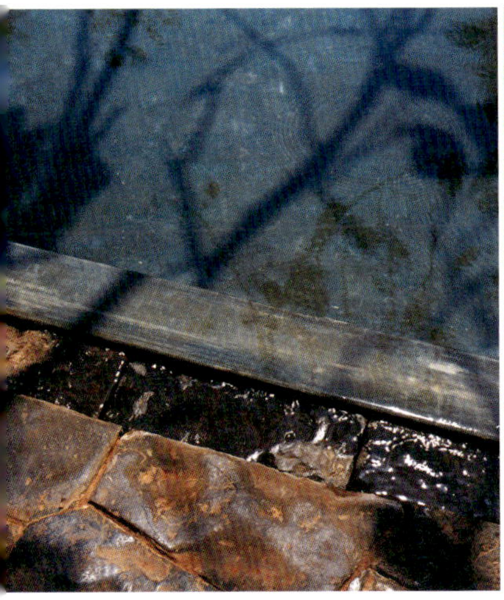
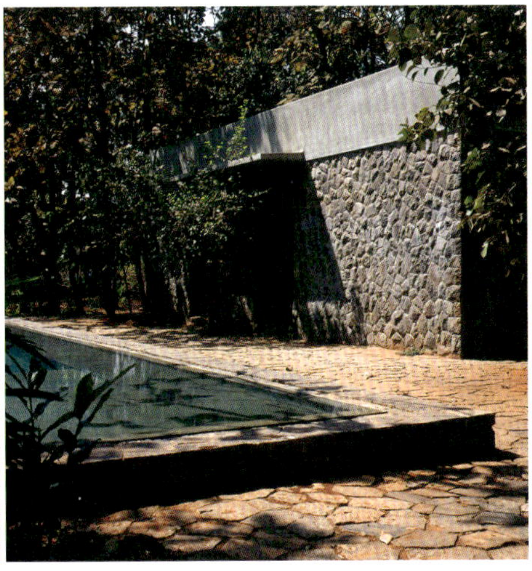
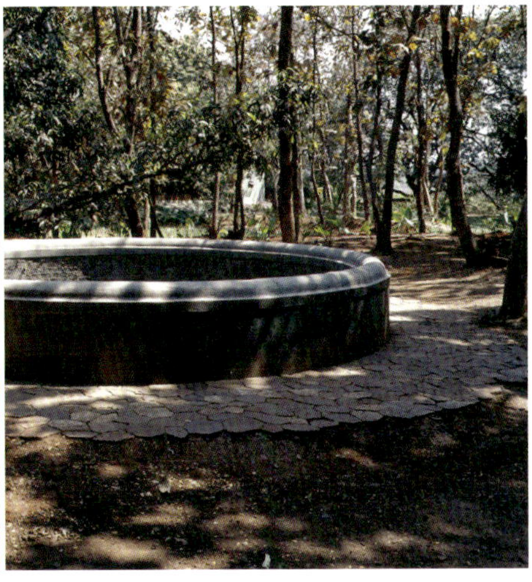

（上）敷地各所からの住宅外観。
（右頁）玄関先のベランダをくぐり抜けると中庭に出る。

(Above images) The house viewed from various parts of the landscape.
(Opposite page) The entrance verandah with a view through to the courtyard.

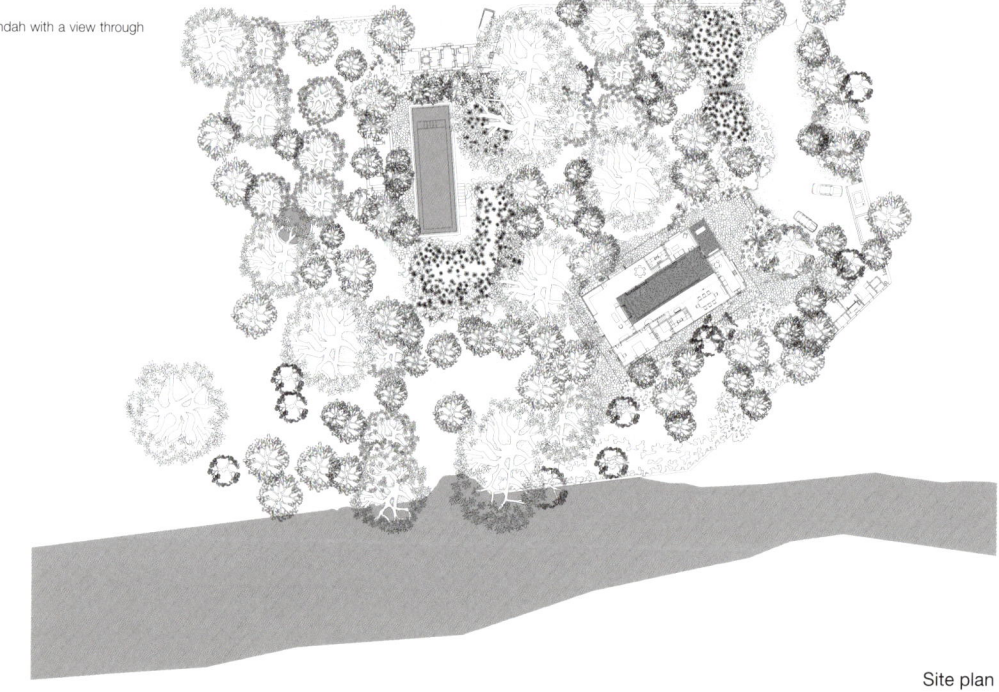

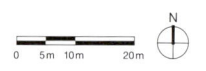

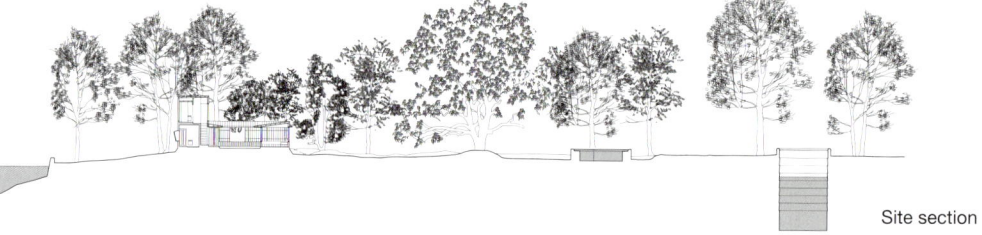

Site plan

Site section

172

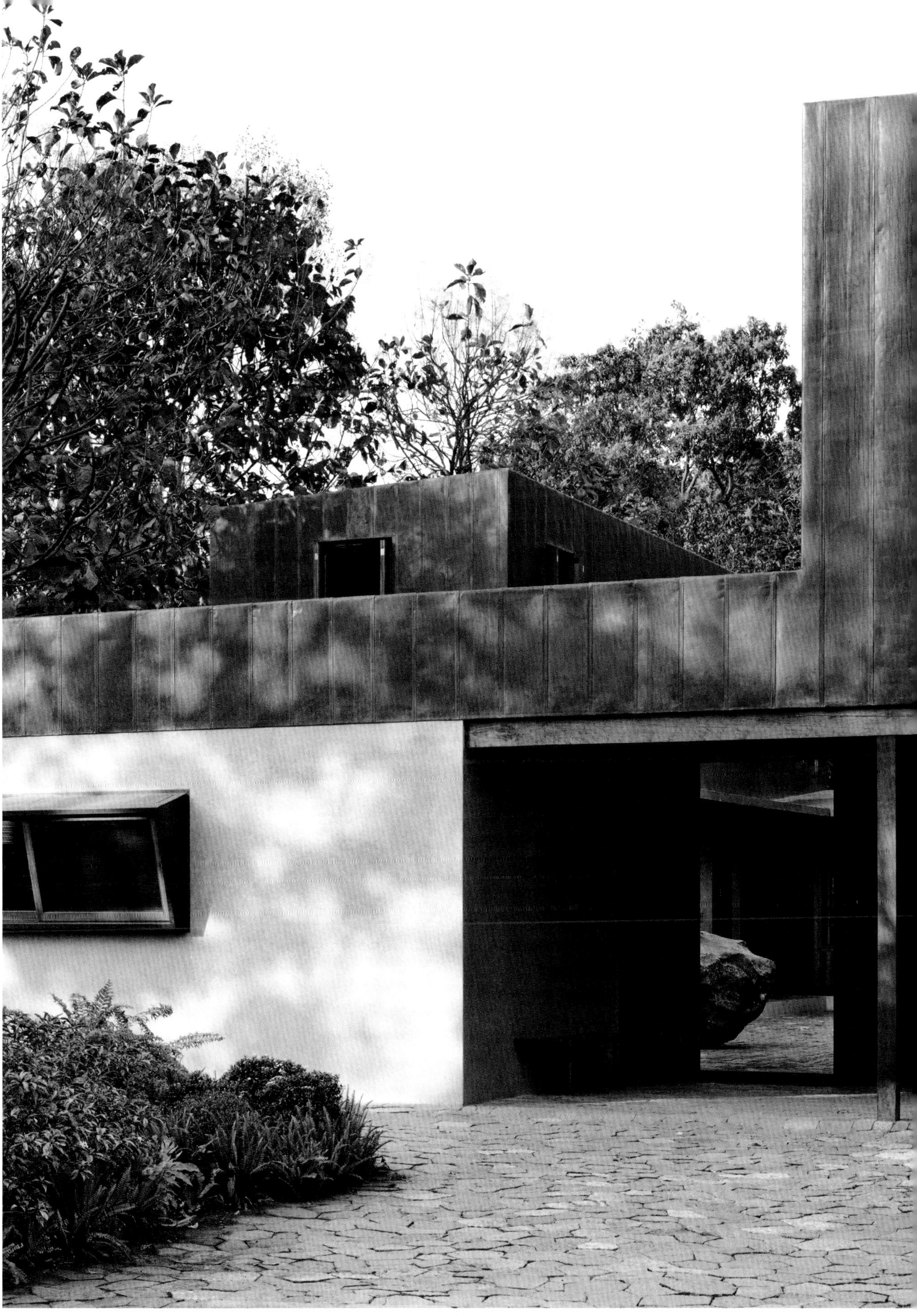

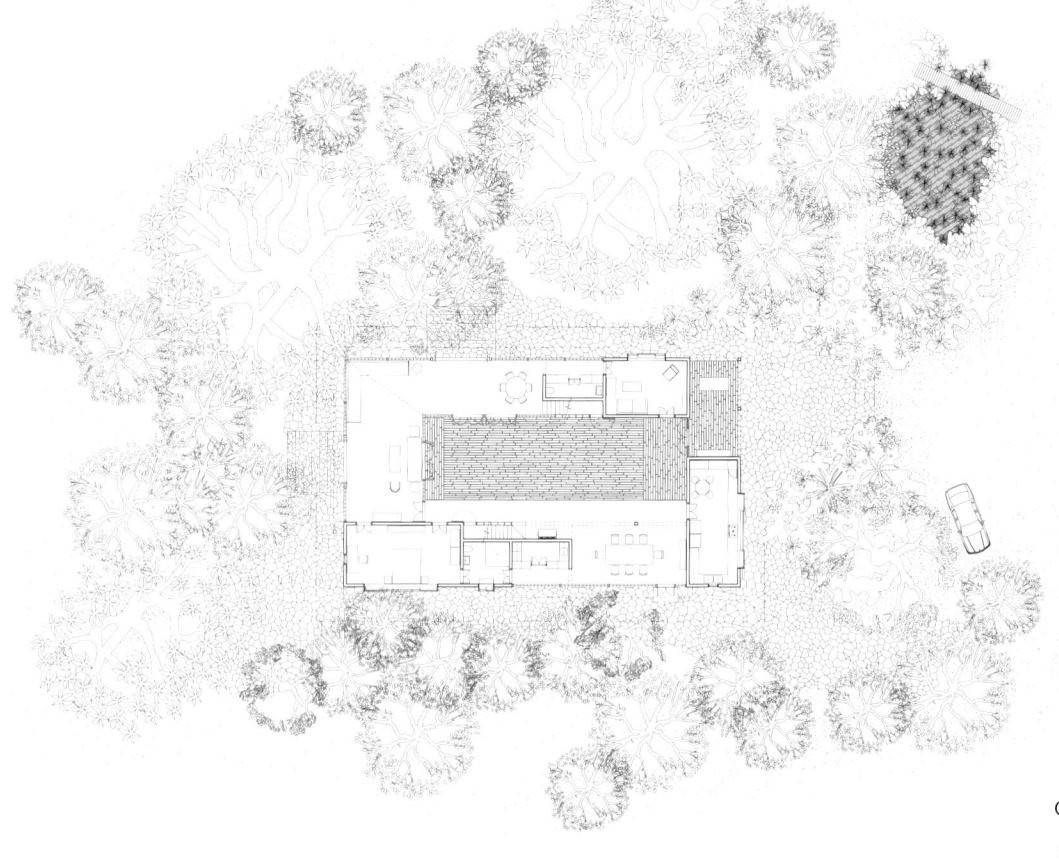

Ground floor plan

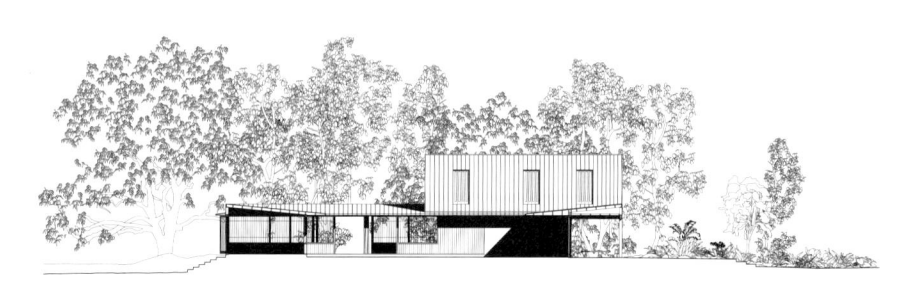

0 1m   3m   5m

Section looking north

Section looking south

0 1m   3m   5m

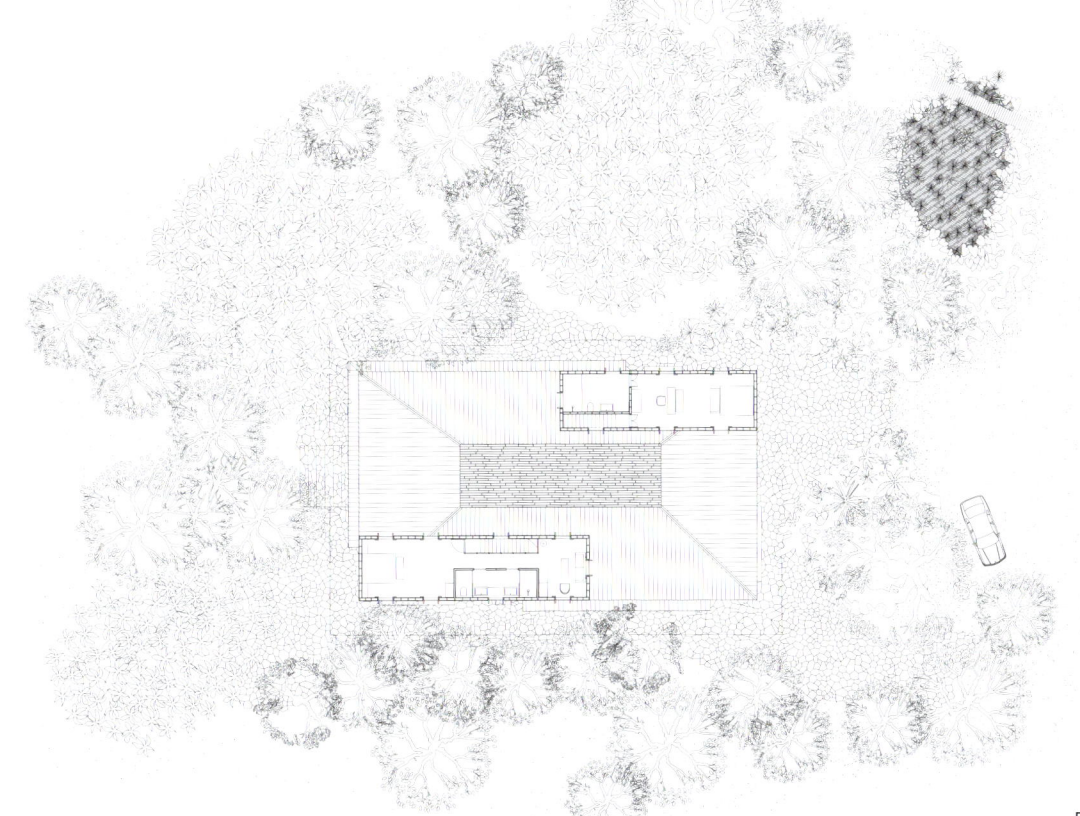

First floor plan

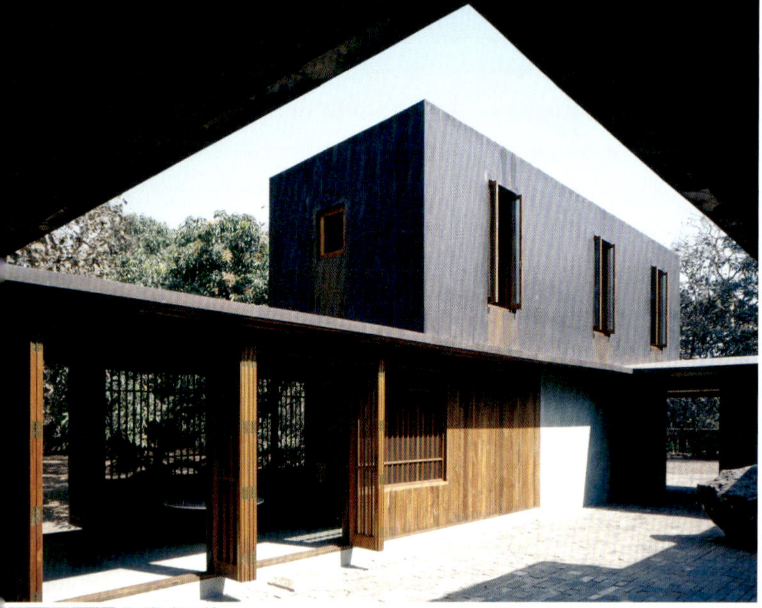
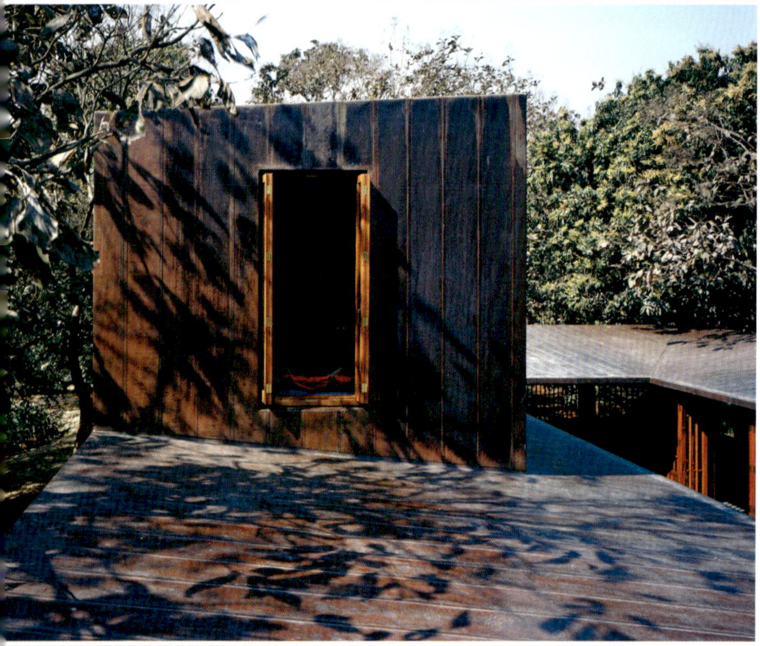
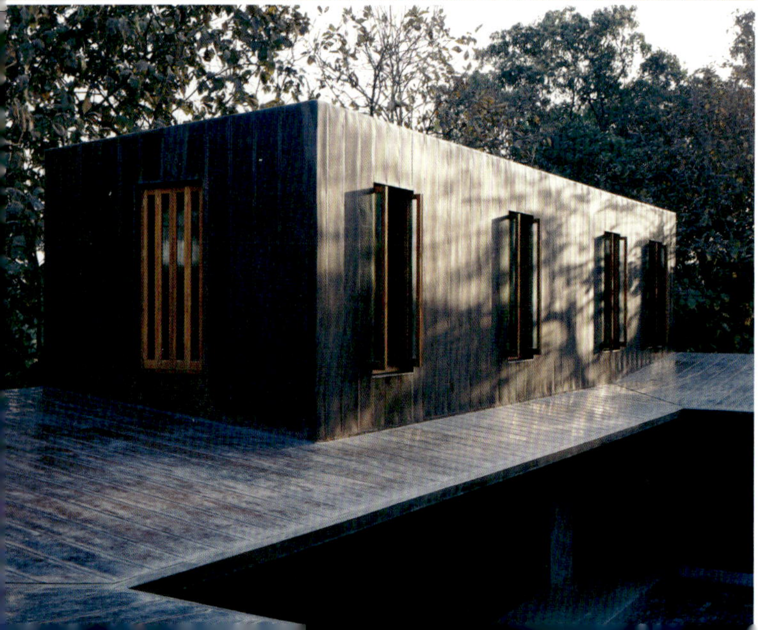
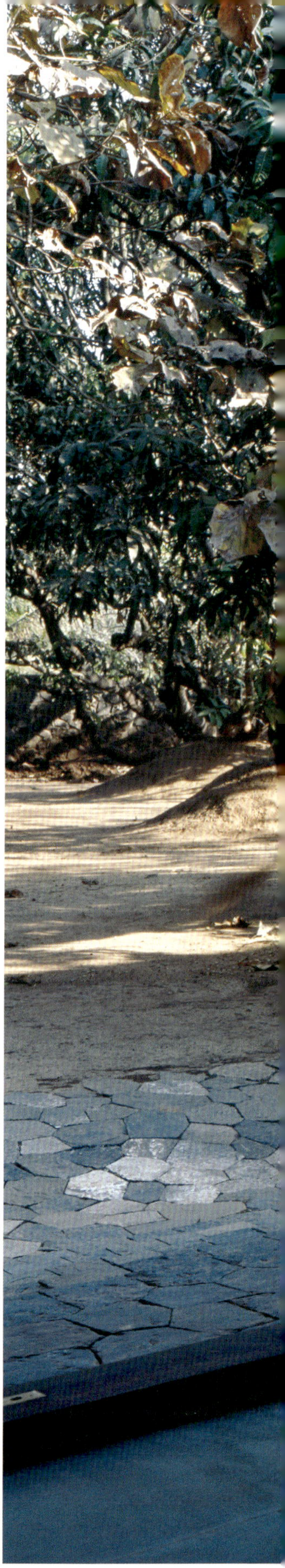

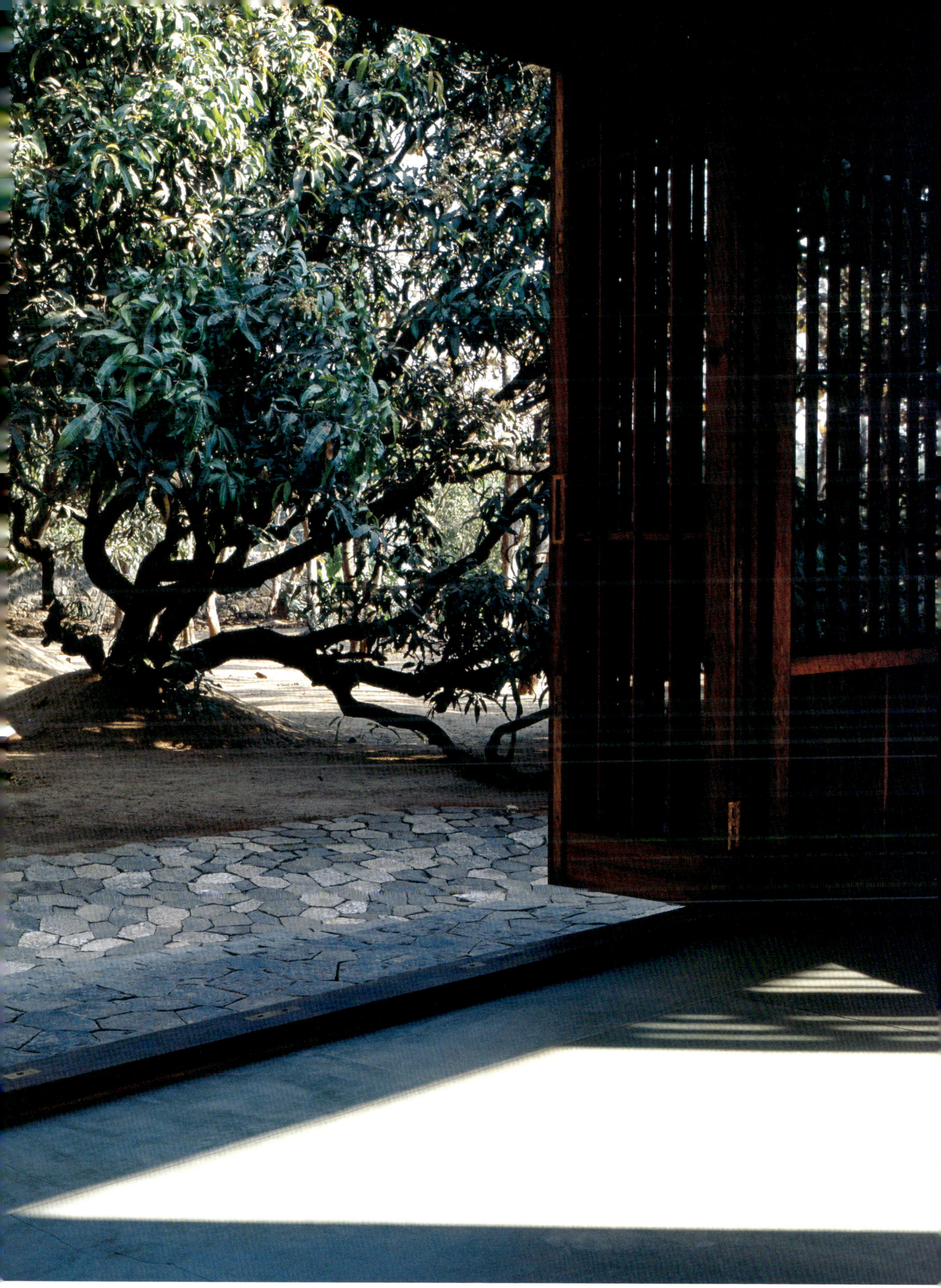

178

（上3点）ベランダ下の居間。
（左）開放的な食堂から居間を見る。
(Above images) Views from the verandah living space.
(Left) View from the open dining space towards the living room.

179

180

（上）居間から西の季節河川を望む。
（左頁）廊下と階段。

(Above) Looking west from the living space towards the seasonal stream.
(Opposite page) Interior passages and stairs.

181

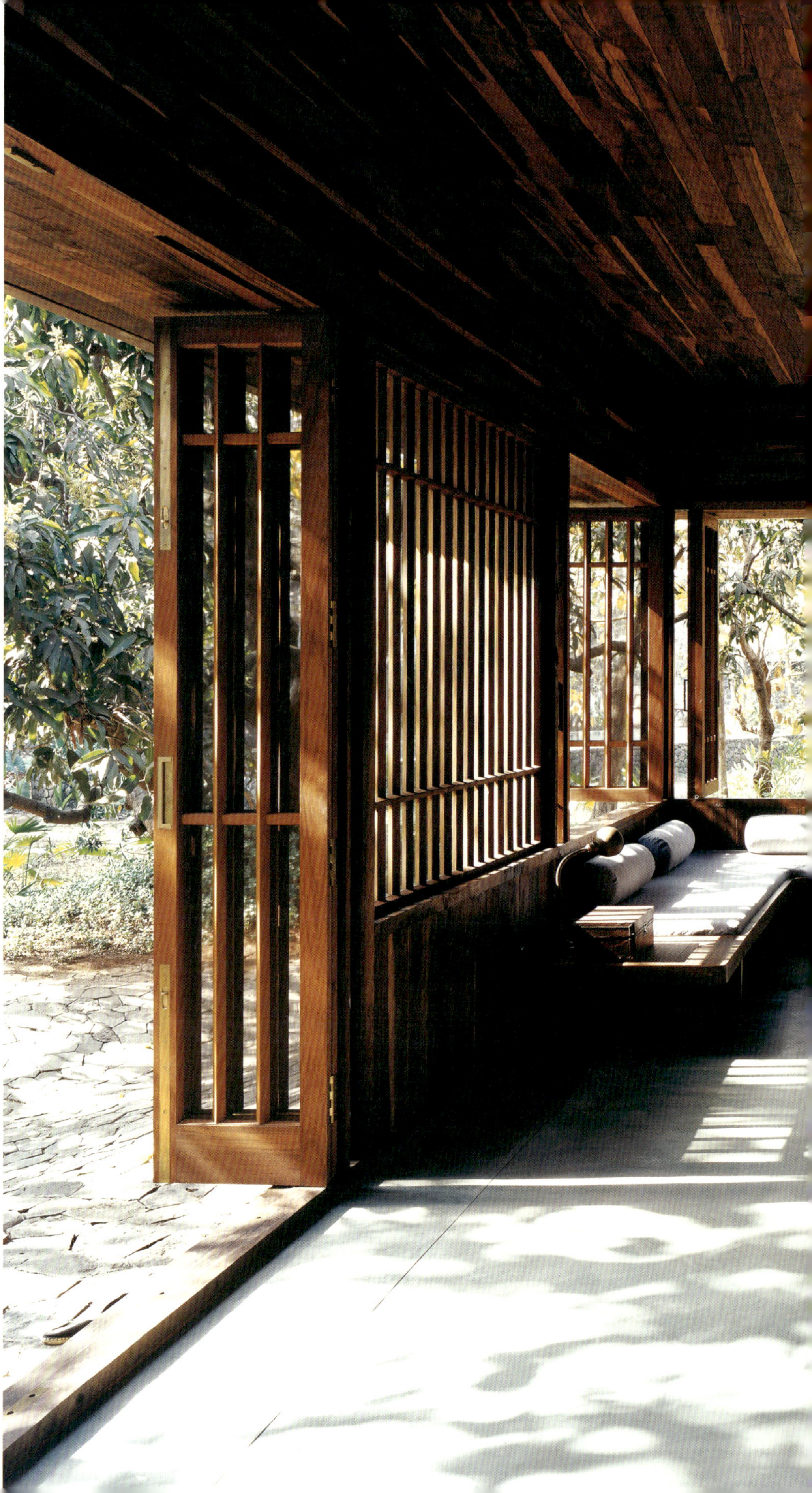

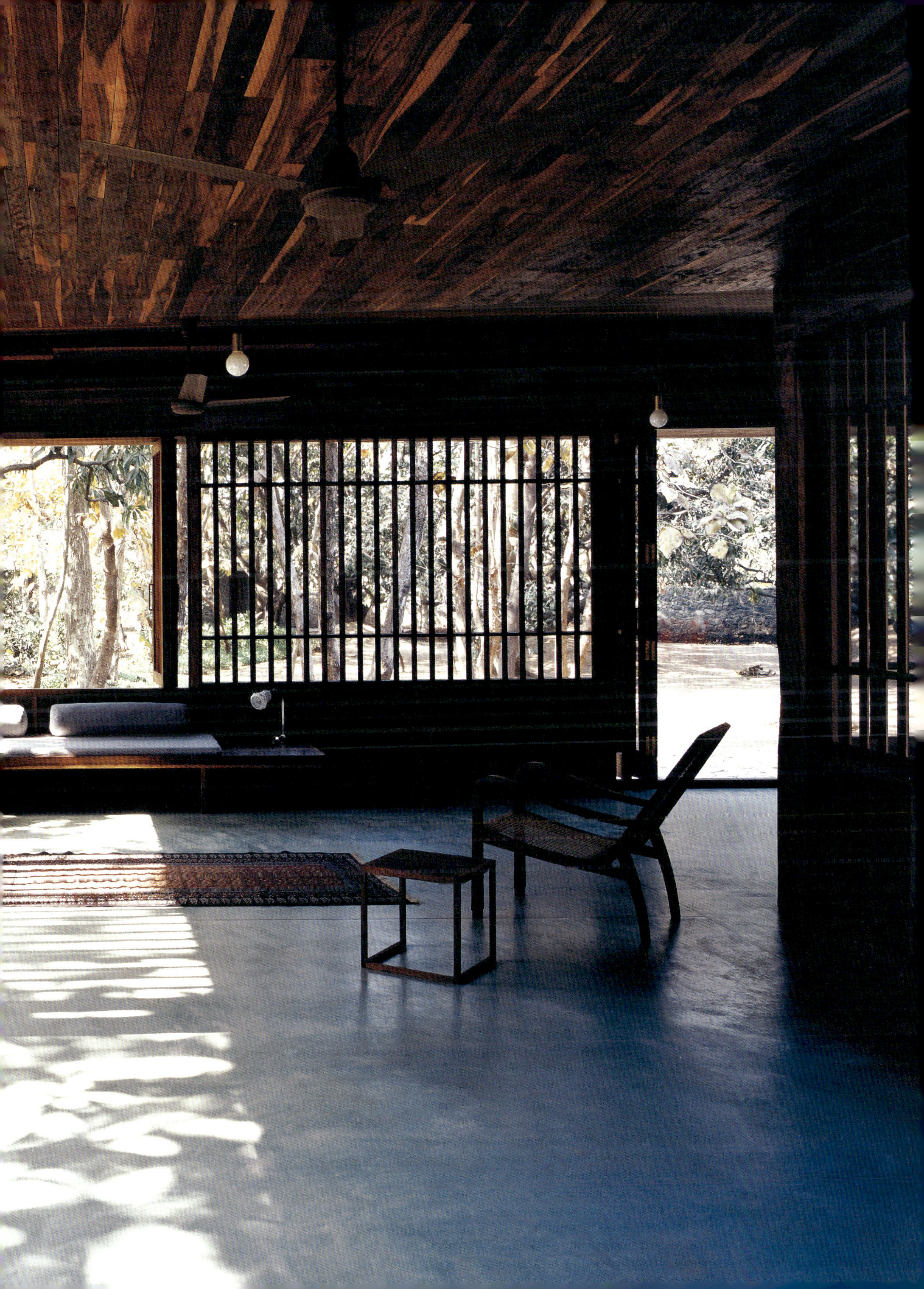

(上)主寝室。(下左)1階寝室。(下右)台所。
(右頁左)大工による窓と外装の収まりのスケッチ。

(Above) Master bedroom. (Below left) Ground floor bedroom. (Below right) Kitchen.
(Opposite page) Carpenter's sketches with window and cladding details (left).

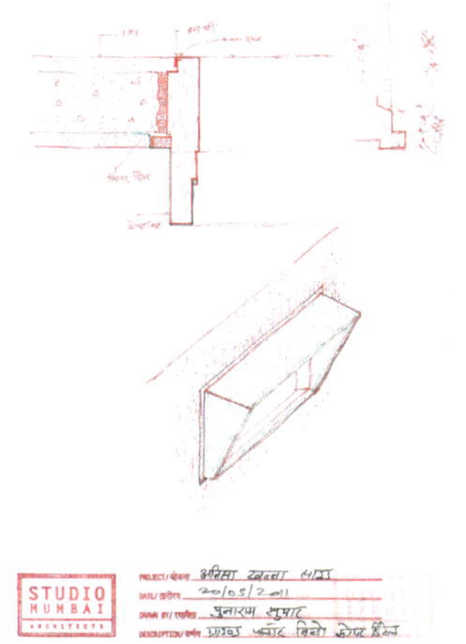
STUDIO
MUMBAI
ARCHITECTS

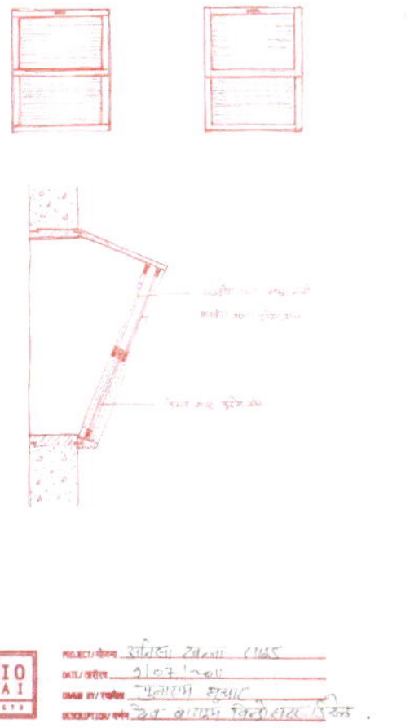
STUDIO
MUMBAI
ARCHITECTS

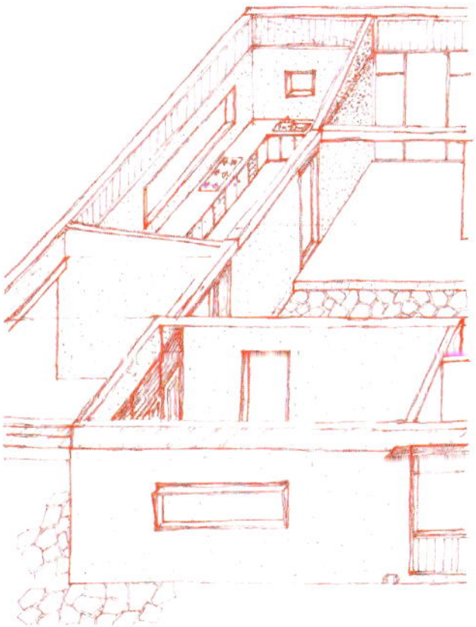

STUDIO
MUMBAI
ARCHITECTS

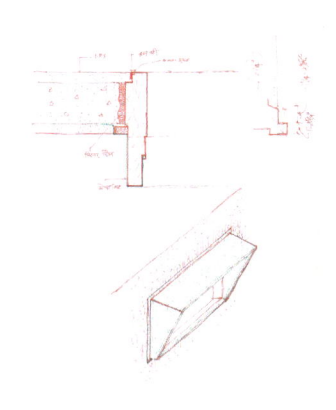

（左上）敷地に石を置くようす。
（下2点、右上）中庭に岩を設置するようす。
（右頁）玄関戸口から岩を見る。

(Above left) Placing a stone in the landscape.
(Bottom images and above right) Positioning of the rock within the courtyard.
(Opposite page) The rock seen through the doorway of the entrance portico.

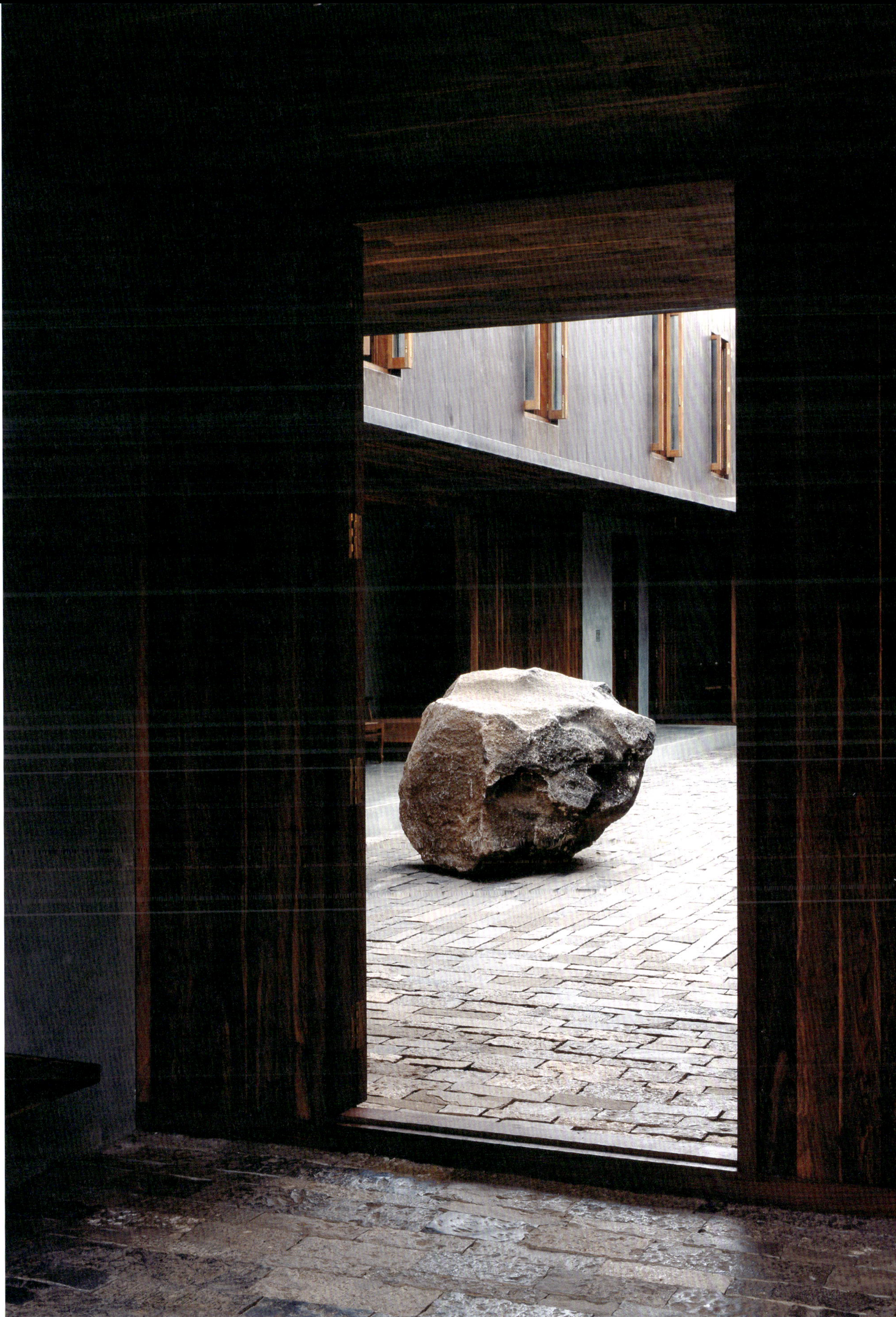

1:1 Architects Build Small Spaces, V&A Museum
「1:1 建築家がつくる小さな空間」展　ヴィクトリア&アルバート博物館
2010　London, UK

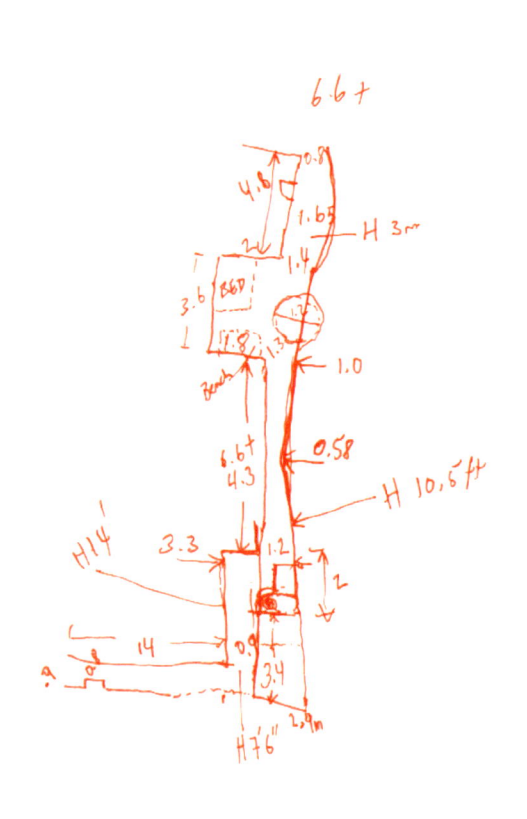

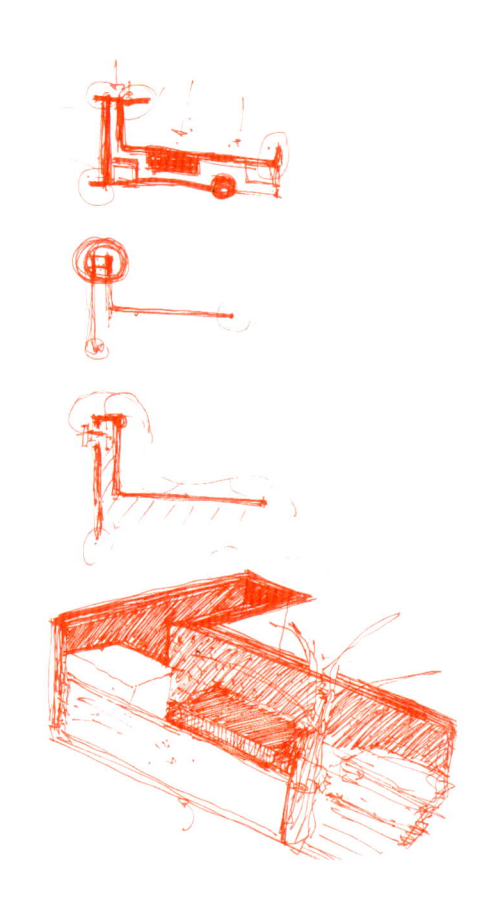

テーマは、既存の街並みの隙間につくられた建築空間である。この構造物は、私たちの現事務所とその隣の倉庫との隙間につくられた住居群を薄く切り取ったものである。現状からこれをひらめいたとはいえ、ここに現物をそのまま再現するつもりはない。

むしろここでは、住宅に関する建築スタディを純化した。多機能空間のいわば原点である住宅には、共用の住環境があり、退避と瞑想と祈りの場がある。その一連のこぢんまりとした規模の空間は、個人のニーズや気分に応えてくれる。そこにいると気分転換になり、精神は健全かつ穏やかに保たれ、また人としての尊厳も保たれる。

ここでは構造が曖昧なぶん、人工と自然の境界が抽象化される。それは、ふとしたことで現れるもうひとつの現実の姿なのだ。たぶんそれは一定の法則に従って現れるものではなく、見える人には見えるものなのだろう。私たちの狙いは、[建築の]真の力を発揮させることにある。窮屈な場所からの逃げ場をつくるには、まずは想像力と親しみと謙虚さをもってあたることだ。

Our proposal explores architectural spaces formed between the boundaries of existing buildings. The structure is a slice from a series of dwellings sandwiched between our current studio and the adjacent warehouse. Although it is inspired by a real condition, our aim is not to produce an exact replica within a museum environment.

This is a distilled architectural study of a dwelling, a home of multifunctional spaces consisting of communal living environments, places of refuge, contemplation and worship. They are a series of intimately proportioned spaces that are able to adapt to personal and emotional needs. They inspire versatility as well as order, calm and dignity.

The structure is ambiguous, creating an abstraction of the relationship between artificiality and nature. It is a depiction of another reality, seen almost by accident; we imagine it will be explored in ways other than specified, allowing for personal interpretation. Our purpose is to show a genuine possibility; to create a refuge from a constricted spatial condition that emerges from imagination, intimacy, and modesty.

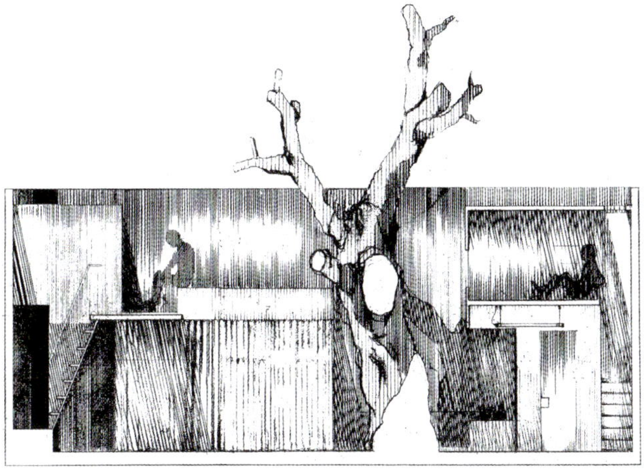

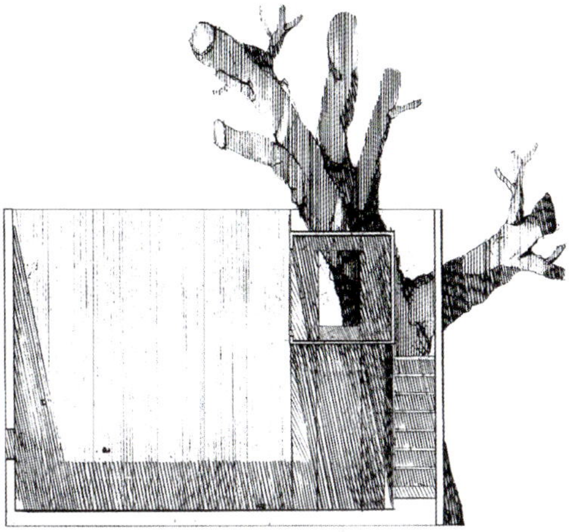

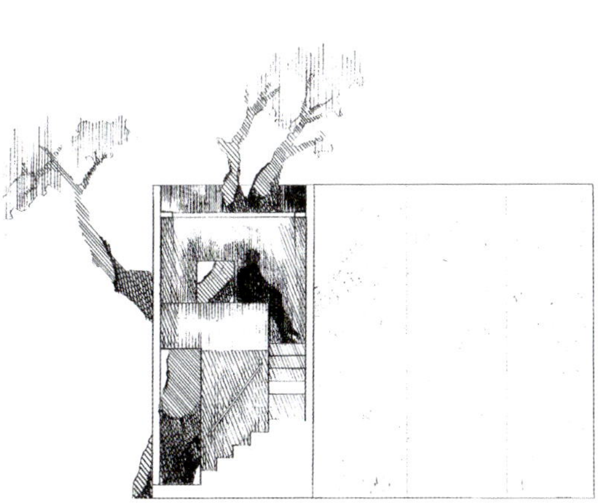

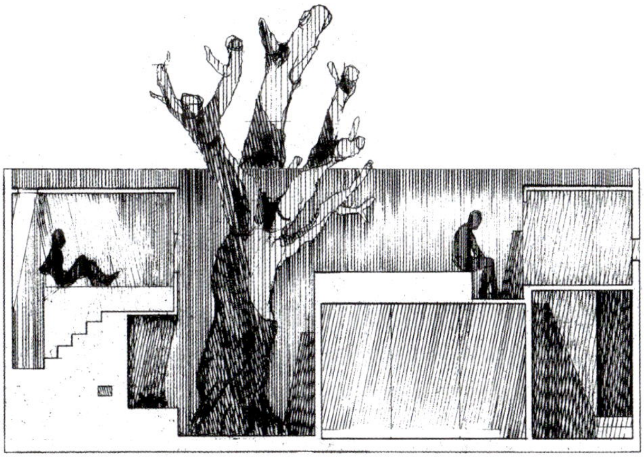

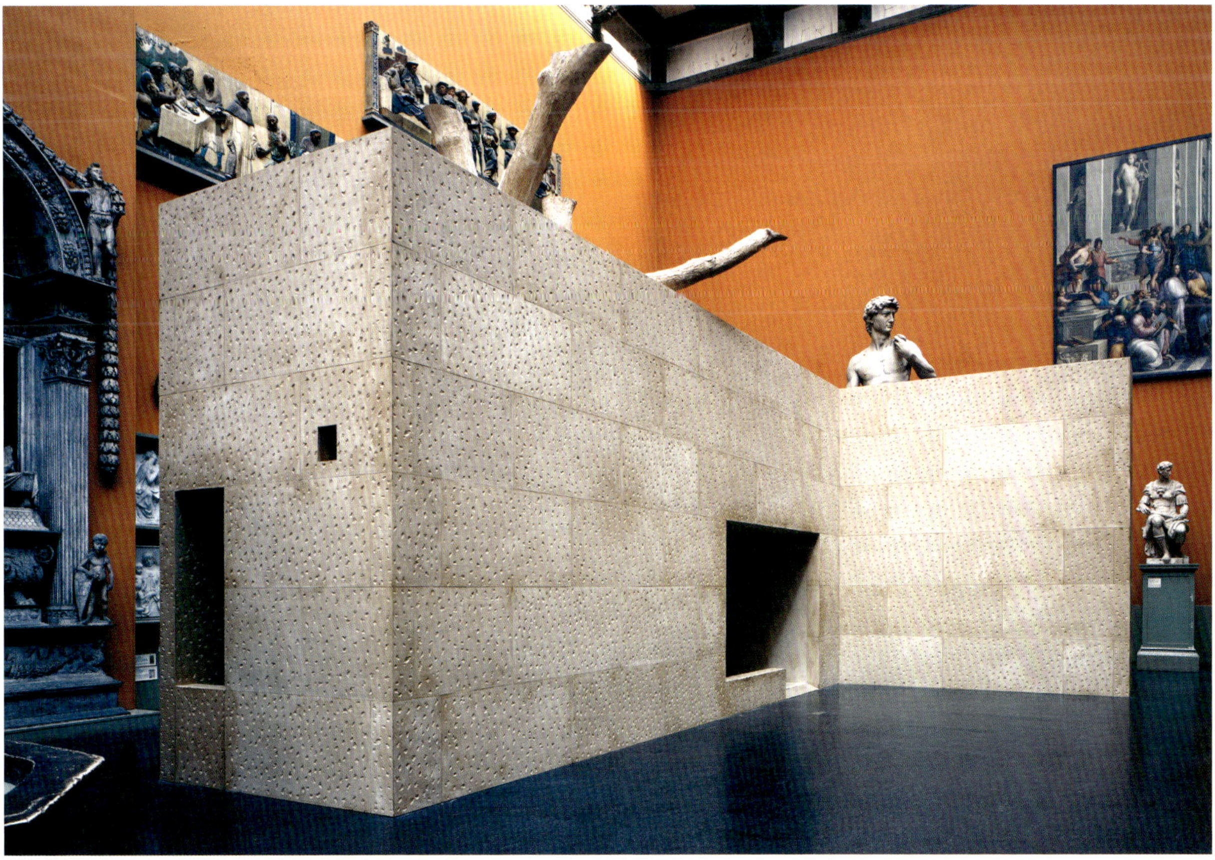

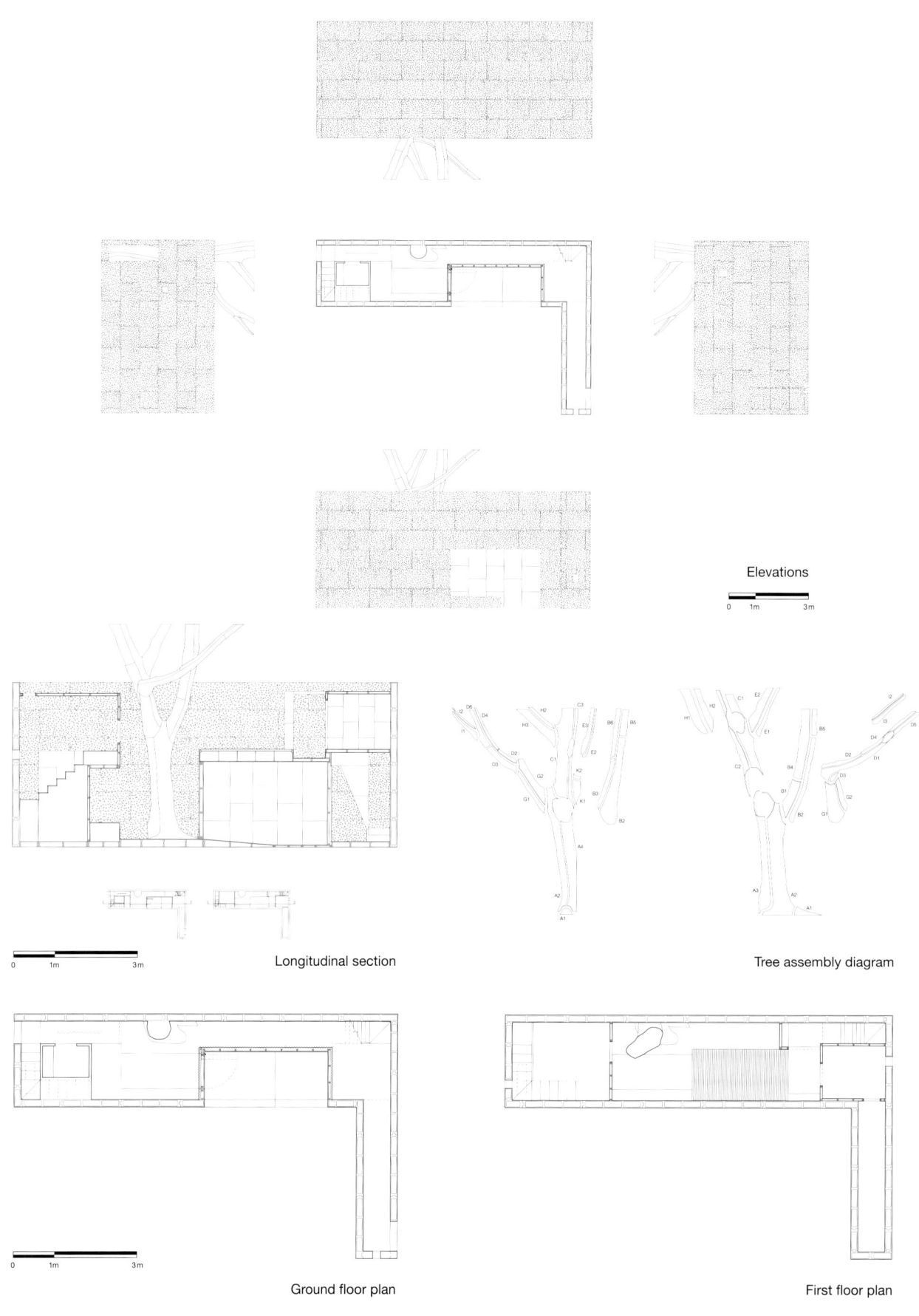

Elevations
0 1m 3m

Longitudinal section
0 1m 3m

Tree assembly diagram

Ground floor plan
0 1m 3m

First floor plan

石膏レプリカ展示室でのインスタレーション。　The installation in the plaster cast courts at the museum.

192

インスタレーション内に設けられた住空間、寝室、動線、寺。　Views of the living, sleeping, circulation and temple spaces within the installation.

Workplace, Venezia Biennale
ワークプレイス──ヴェネチア・ビエンナーレ展
2010 Venezia, Italy

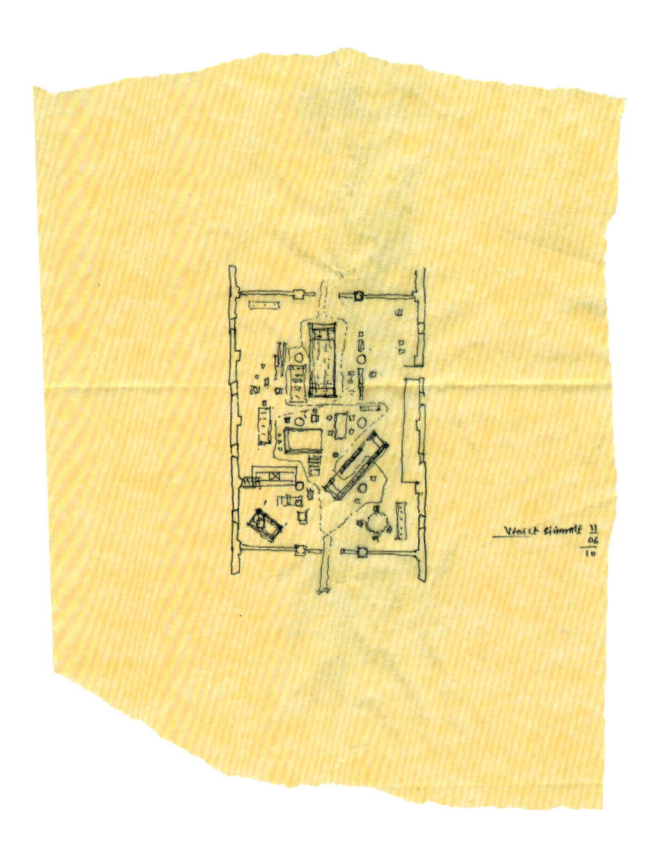

人間にとっていちばん身近な環境とは、人が半ば無意識にしつらえ、住まう空間のことである。そこを自分がくつろげるような空間にすることもできるし、あるいは見慣れないもので埋め尽くせば、刺激を受けて物の見方が変わるかもしれない。インスピレーションの源はいくらでもある。観察力さえあれば見つかるものだ。建築はかくあるべし、といった固定観念を抱くのもいいが、とりあえずその前に知っておくべきことがある。なぜ物事がそうなっているのかということを。「ワークプレイス」の環境は、モックアップ、模型制作、素材スタディ、スケッチや図面作成といった構想のための反復作業を通じて整えられていく。私たちは、場所を注意深く観察したり、伝統技術や在来工法、地場素材、限られた資源を相手に編み出された人間の創意工夫などに想を得ながら、プロジェクトを練り上げていく。

人びとの暮らしを観察することから始まったこうした建築スタディは、いまや私たちにとって欠かせないツールとなっている。そのおかげで、どのプロジェクトでもその複雑な細部にまで目が行き届くし、建物をつくりながらも、そのときどきの状況に臨機応変に対処していくことができるのだ。

建築の真の力を発揮させるためにも、私たちは対話を重ね、互いに想像力と親しみと謙虚さをもって顔をつきあわせて情報を共有するようにしている。

Our immediate environment is a space that we subconsciously create and inhabit. We can make this space very familiar or we can expose ourselves to unfamiliar elements that provoke our response and reevaluation. There are many sources of inspiration: one only has to observe closely. It is possible to have set ideas of what architecture should be, but first we need to understand why things are a certain way.

Work-Place is an environment created from an iterative process, where ideas are explored through the production of large scale mock-ups, models, material studies, sketches, and drawings. Here projects are developed through careful consideration of place and a practice that draws from traditional skills, local building techniques, materials, and an ingenuity arising from limited resources.

Inspired by observation of real life conditions, these architectural studies are vital tools that enable us to look at the complexity of relationships within each project and to respond and adapt freely through the practice of making. They are ambiguous, exciting as part and whole, between idea and reality.

Our endeavor is to show the genuine possibility in creating buildings that emerge through a process of collective dialog, a face-to-face sharing of knowledge through imagination, intimacy, and modesty.

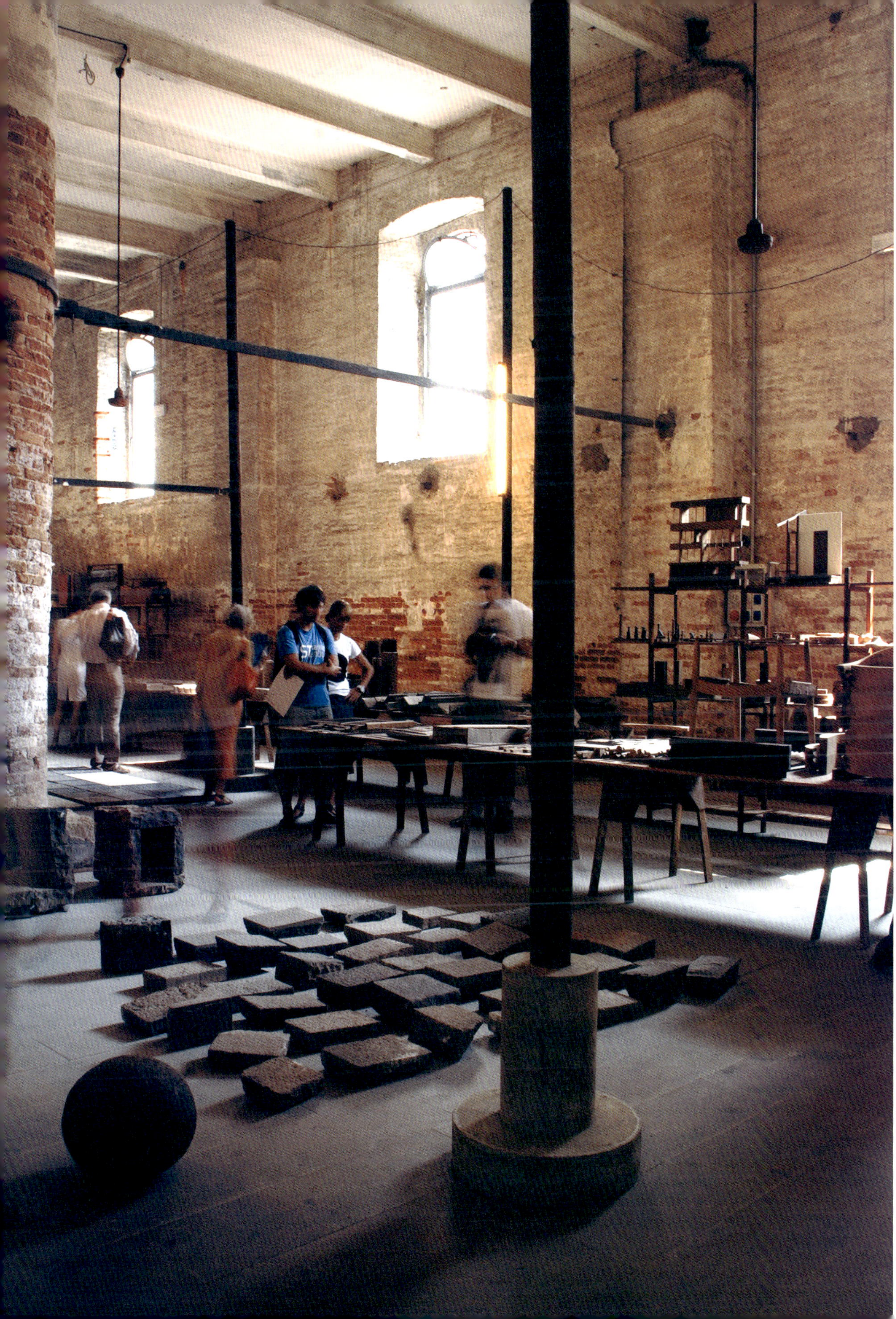

ワークショップにある模型やモックアップやオブジェをはるばるヴェネチアへ運び、アルセナーレに展示してワークショップの雰囲気を再現した。

Models, mock-ups and objects from the workshop were transported to Venezia and installed in the Arsenale to recreate the atmosphere of the workshop.

196

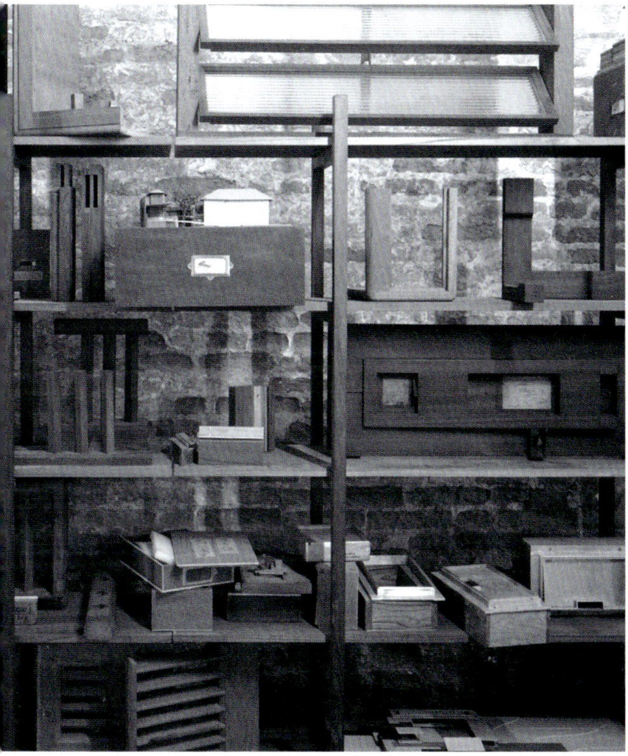
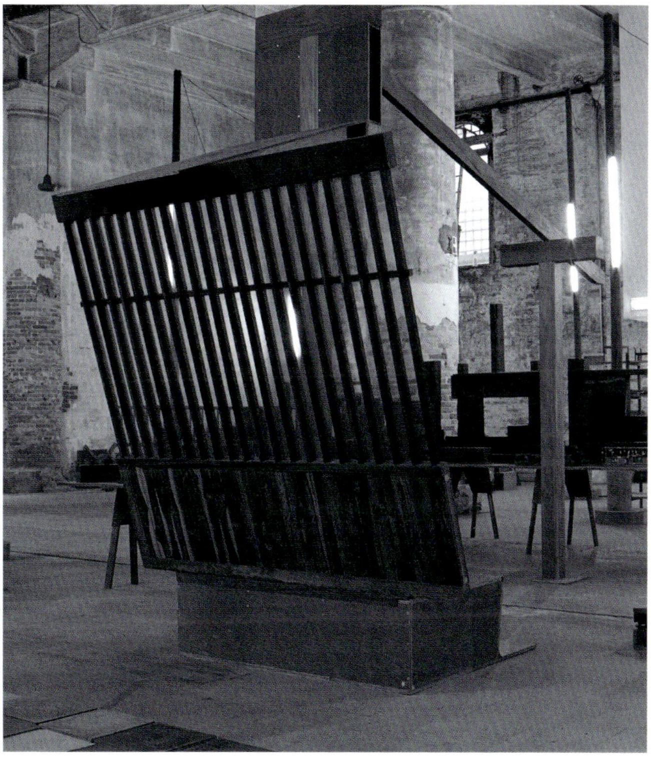
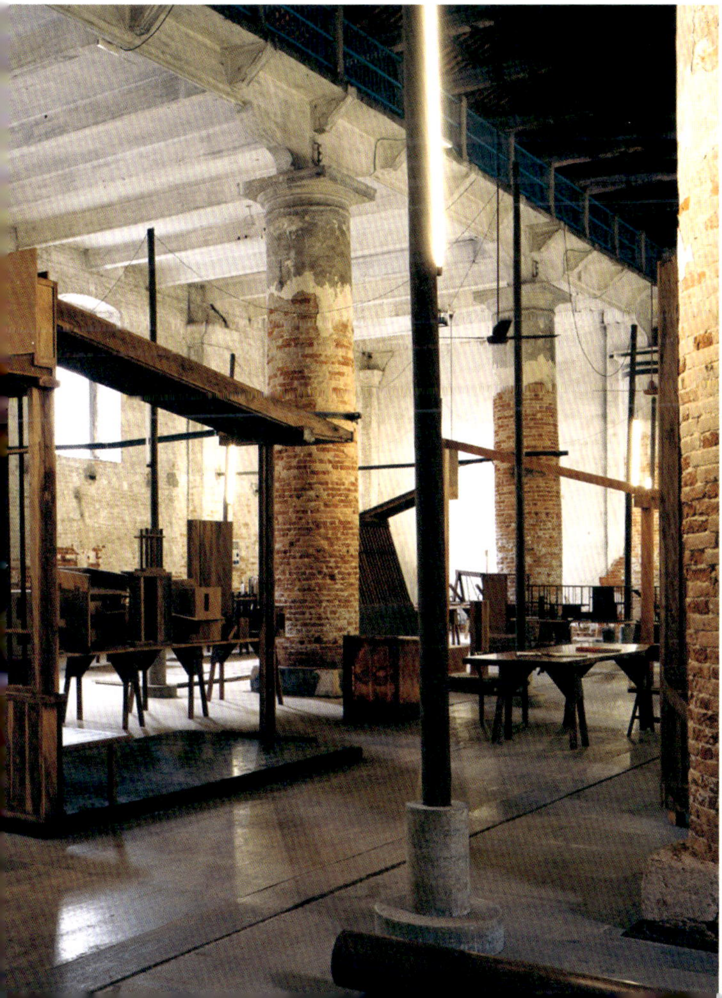
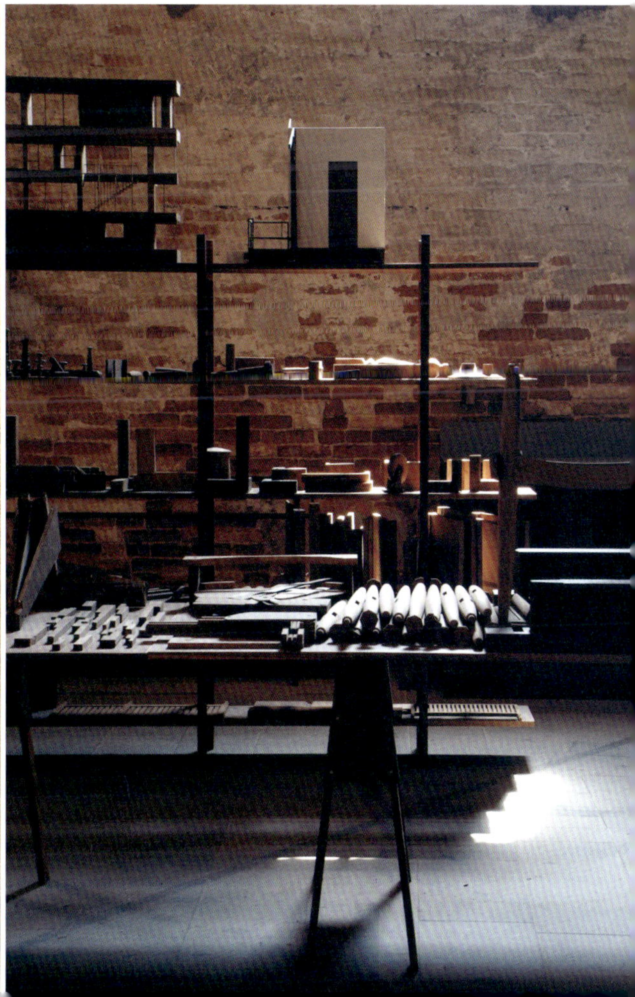

(左上)「パルミラの住宅」と「コッパー・ハウスⅡ」の模型。
(左下)「コッパー・ハウスⅡ」の窓のモックアップ。
(右頁、左上から時計まわりに) IPSの破片、木釘、椅子の型板、材料見本と左官工具。

(Left above) Models of Palmyra House and Copper House II.
(Left below) Mock-up of Copper House II window.
(Opposite page) Fragments of IPS, wooden pegs, chair templates, material samples and plastering tools (clockwise from top left).

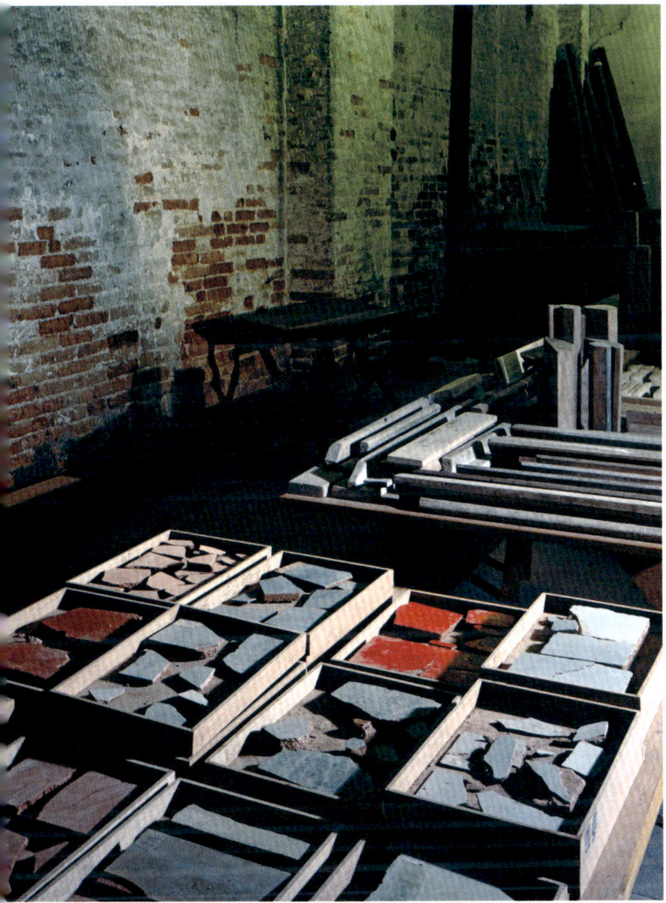
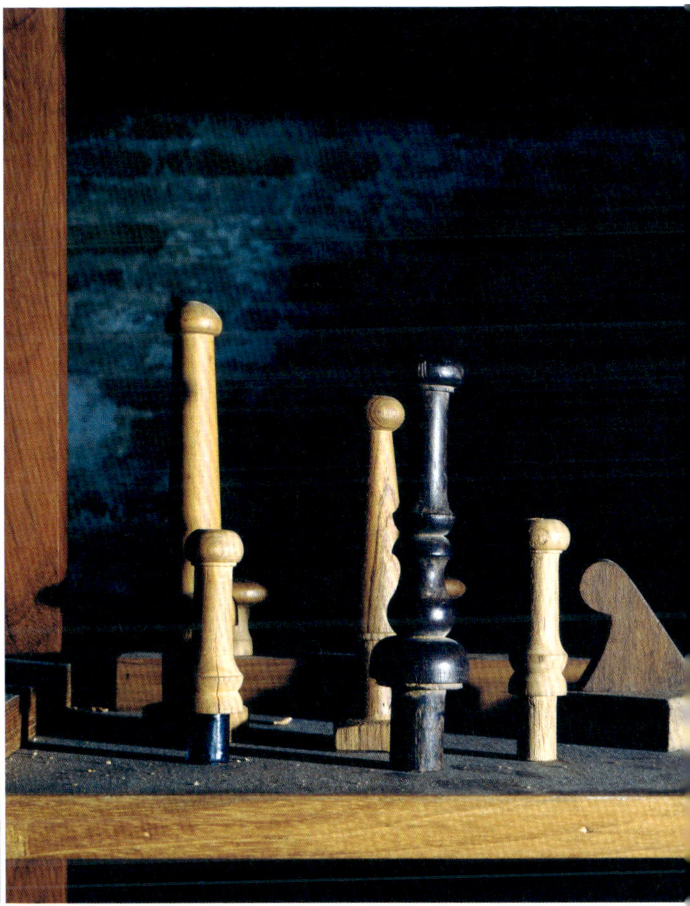
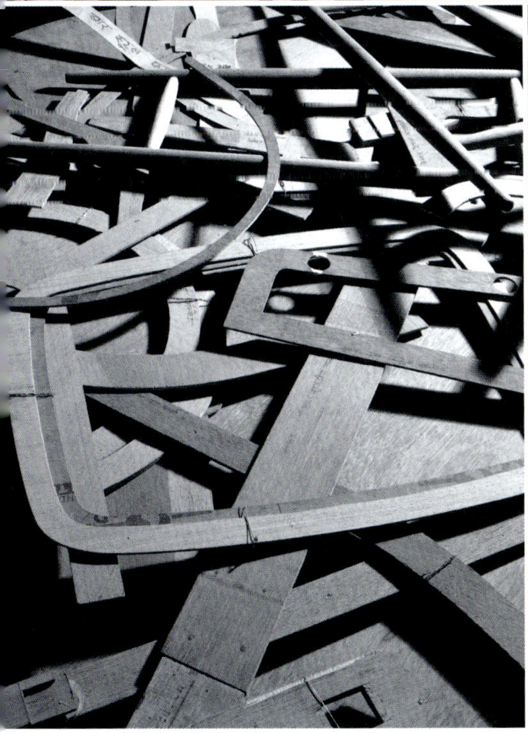
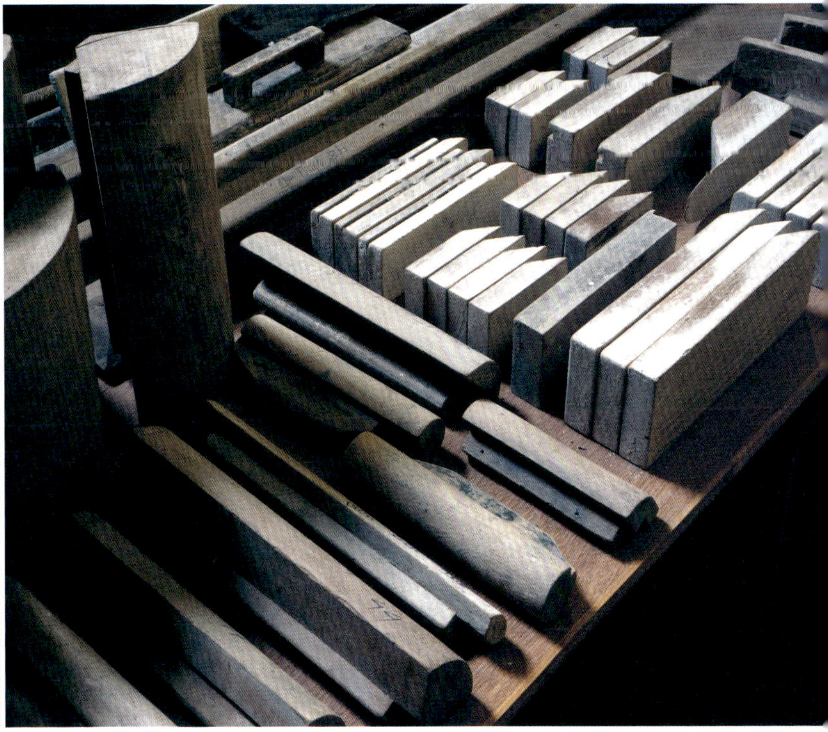

META Chile
META チリ

2011- Tumbes, Chile

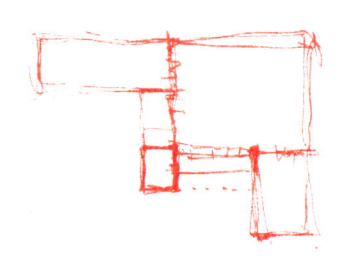

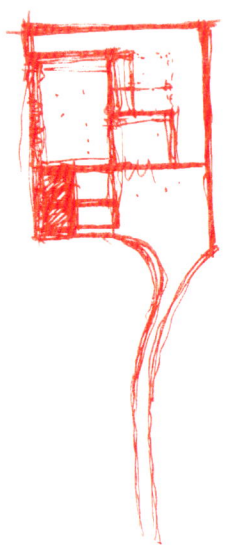

タルカワノ北部のトゥンベス半島は、もっぱら漁業に依存した地域である。コンセプシオンからは北に25km離れており、人口は1,344人。地元にある学校は地震とその後の津波によって壊滅的な損傷を被ったが、ここに仮設ユニットが建てられたことで、トゥンベス再建の努力もやっと目に見える成果を上げた。しかし自然災害は、建物ばかりか漁業にも打撃を与えた。

敷地は計画中の遊歩道の終点の、海岸のすぐ際にある。西には切り立った崖が、東には岩肌も露わな海岸が迫っている。海辺は北に向かって延び、かたや村落は南に広がっている。ここでは沿岸に浮かぶ漁船も、吹きつける強風や穏やかな気候と同じく、日常の光景である。都市計画ならびにインフラ整備の一環として、沿岸には敷地のすぐ手前まで津波対策の防潮堤が築かれるという。ここにパビリオンを建てるとしたら、海と陸とを隔てるわずかな境界線上に収まるよう、この防潮堤の上にじかに建設することになるだろう。

このパビリオンでは、隔たりを消したいと考えた。陸と海との隔たり、丘と海岸、記憶と期待、身近なものと異質なものとの隔たりを。1枚のプラットフォームを、堅固な防潮堤と崖の間に据える。そこはちょうど遊歩道の突き当たりの場所で、遊歩道沿いにはかつて船大工のつくった木造船の修復作業場がある。パビリオンは平らなテラスとなって沖に向かって張り出しながら、訪れる人をはるか高みにもち上げるかたわら、海の眺めや、反対側の陸地の気配や、眼下を往来する漁船の動きをとらえる。内部に設けられた窓付きのエントランスにせよ、広い矩形の部屋やドックを見下ろす柱廊にせよ、それぞれ明確な構造と用途をそなえている。外観のやや緑がかったくすんだ色のコンクリートには、古びた趣がある。中庭には、粗いセメントをつなぎにして、形状のまちまちな石が敷かれた。パビリオンをただのモノとして見れば、ごくありふれた形態をしている。これは、風の向きや、広大な海の眺めや、海辺のそこかしこにある建物の陰影を意識してつくられたせいだ。そのくせ異国風なところも目につく。その構造といい配置といい、どこか風変わりでぎこちない。まるで海岸に漂着したものが、風景に接ぎ木されたかのようだ。

Tumbes is a peninsula located north of the Talcahuano that depends heavily on the fishing industry. It is 25 km north of Conception with a population of 1344. The local school was irreparably damaged in the earthquake and resulting tsunami, but a modular replacement school was the first visible effort in reconstructing Tumbes. Along with buildings, the fishing industry was negatively affected by the natural disasters.

The site is situated at the end of a planned pedestrian promenade immediately facing the coast. It is bound tightly by both the steep topography to the west and to the rocky coast to the east. The beach extends towards the north, while the main part of the village spreads out along the south. Fishing boats are nearly always present on the coast, as are high winds and a temperate climate. In terms of planning and infrastructure, a new anti tsunami retaining wall will be built along the coast, ending near the site. The pavilion has the possibility to be built directly on the retaining wall in order to fit comfortably within the thin boundary of the coast and topography.

The pavilion is meant to negotiate the line that differentiates land from water, hill from shore, memory from anticipation and familiar from the alien. A single platform is poised in-between a very solid retaining wall and a prominent hillside, at the extreme of an artificial promenade that will be facing a new area for restoration of artisan wooden boats. The pavilion is firstly a flat terrace extending away, lifting the visitor out and above, while harnessing views of the sea, a hint of land on the other side and of the arrival and departures of fishing boats below. The main interior spaces include an entrance vestibule with a window, a generous square room, and a long colonnaded space over-looking the boat dock, each distinct in their structure and value. The construction has a dark concrete appearance, aged with a soft green texture. The central court has irregular blocks of stone embedded in rough cement. As an object, the pavilion has the familiarity of a universal form, relating to the way it catches the wind, as a frame for views of an infinite body of water, the shade and shadows of seaside structures everywhere. At the same time, it has the mark of a foreign hand, almost peculiar in its structure and disposition, uncommon and awkward. It is an object grafted onto this landscape, as if brought in by the sea.

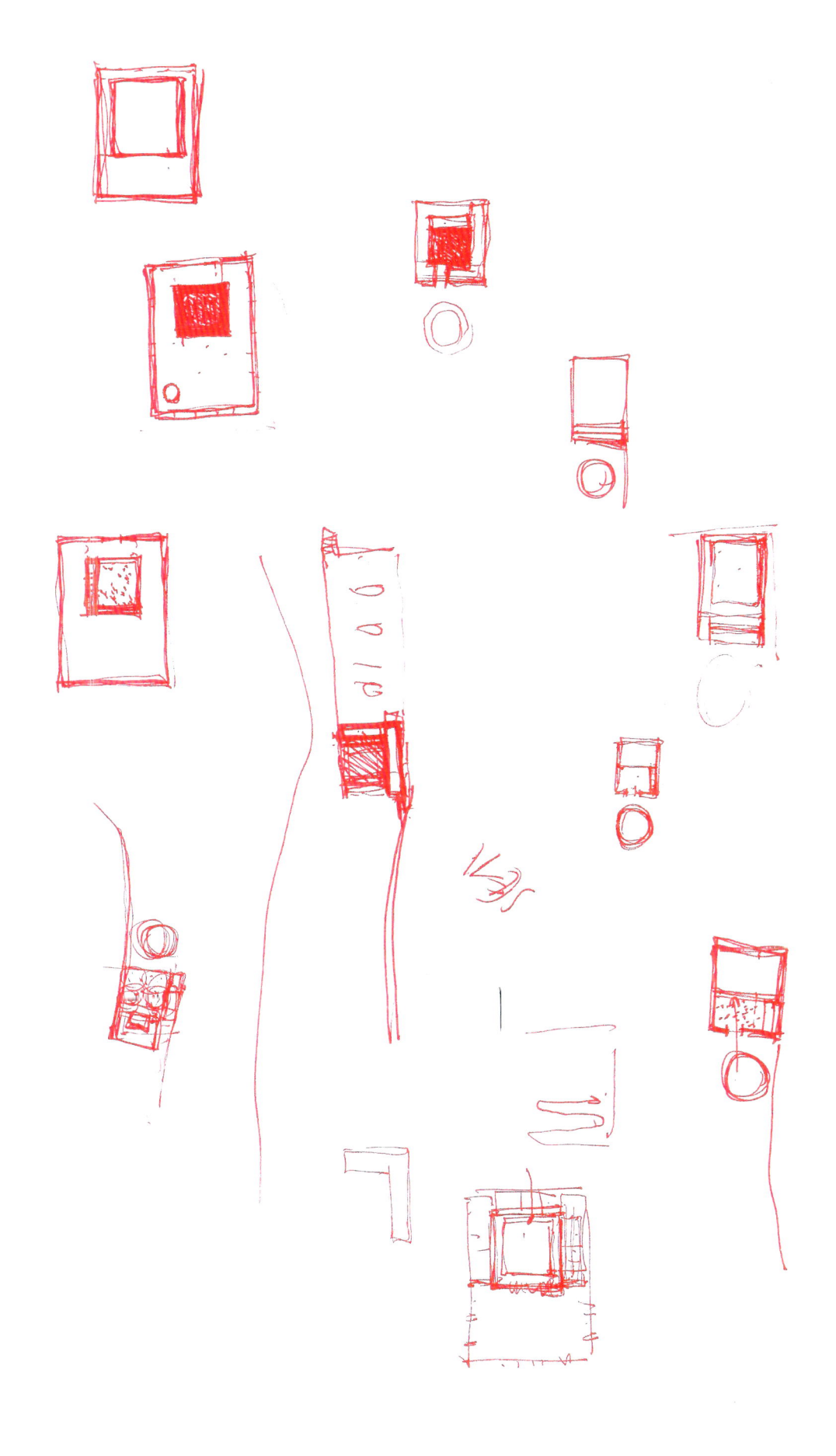

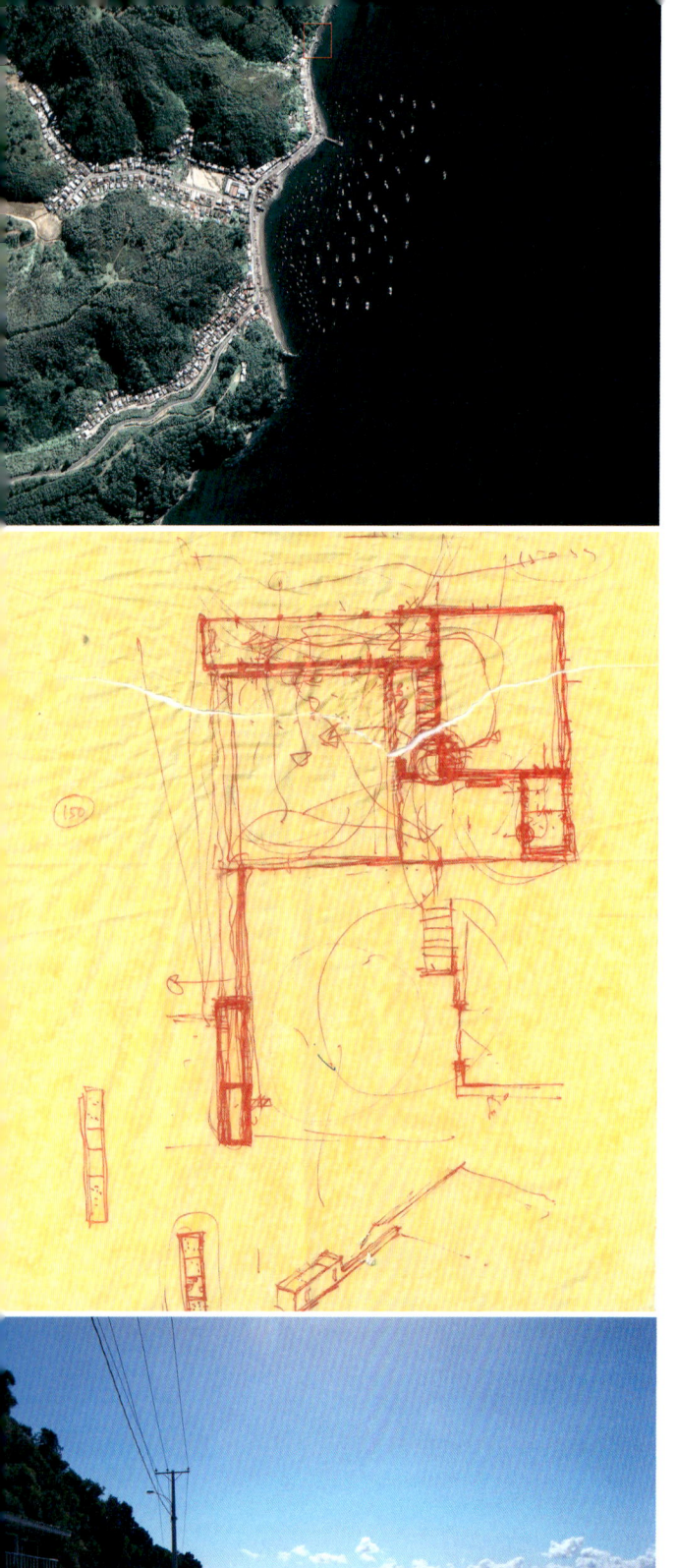

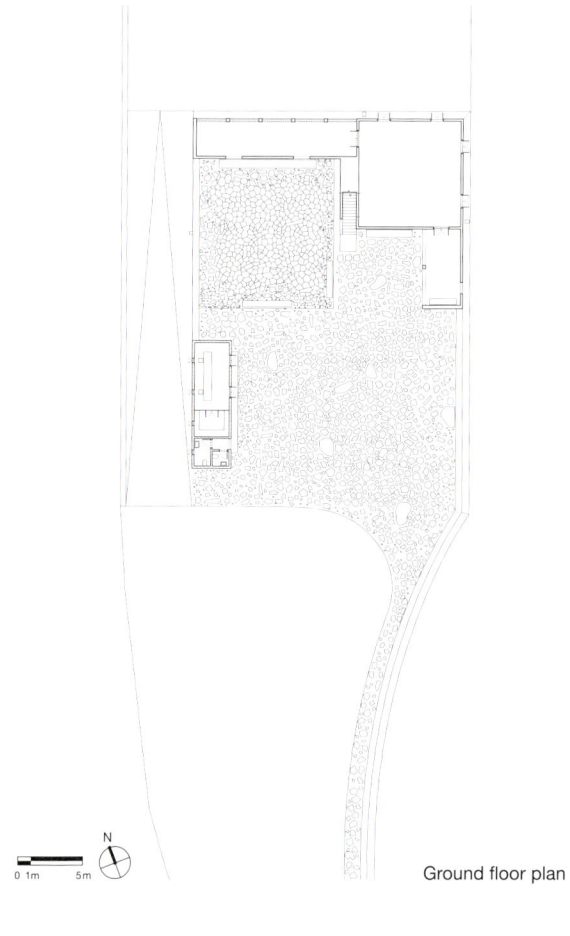

Ground floor plan

Site plan

North elevation

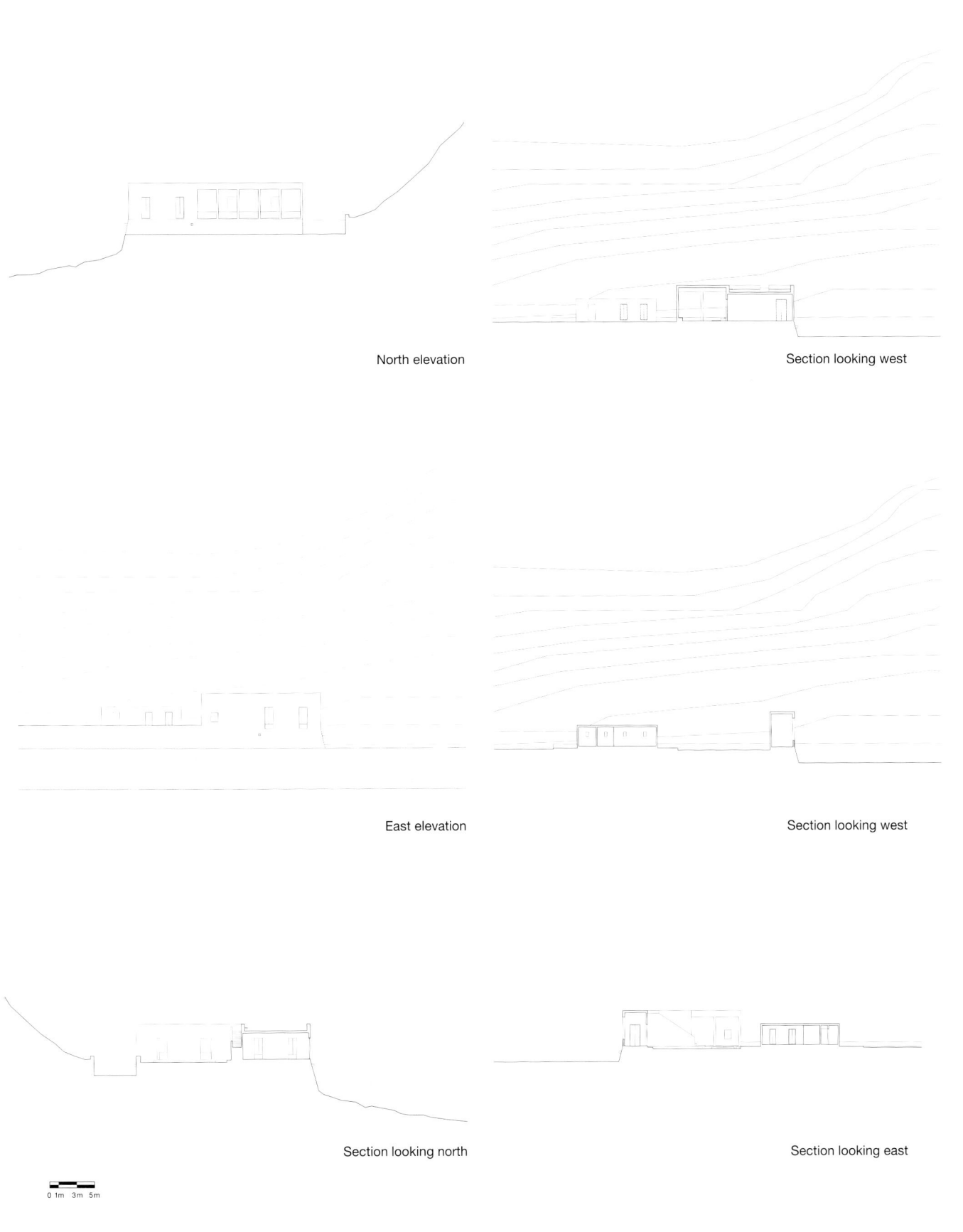

Section looking west

East elevation

Section looking west

Section looking north

Section looking east

0 1m 3m 5m

204

大小のスタディ模型。 Photographs of large and small scale study models.

Saat Rasta 561/63
サート・ラスタ 561/63

2010- Byculla, Mumbai, Maharashtra, India

ムンバイにある古い倉庫の壁の内側に、大小の7つのスタジオ／住居がそっと忍び込む。細長い隙間が、各住居を連絡する通路の役目を果たしている。

通路を歩いていると、中庭がかわるがわる現れて、そのたびに光の波が押し寄せる。各中庭の入り口に設けられたベランダは、隣家との交流の場でもある。

中庭に向かって下降する勾配屋根は陽射しと雨を遮り、雨を中庭に落とす。中庭に落ちた雨水は、夏に備えて地下の貯水槽に貯められる。鉄骨の細い柱は、屋内空間と中庭のフレームとなる。内装は白く統一されており、そこにはめ込まれた透明ガラスは室内を見せ、かたや溝型ガラスは眺めを遮る。この壁と、地場のライムストーンを張った灰色の床が、トップライトや窓から入る光を反射する。

目指したのは、内部空間を、居心地が良く安全でありながらも環境に対して開かれた憩いの場にすることと、その時々の都市の活力を取り込んでいくことである。

Seven studio/homes of varying size slip discreetly into a walled enclosure of an old Mumbai warehouse. A long narrow open space acts as a street connecting these dwellings.

Walking through this passage, one encounters the rhythm of different courtyards filled with undulating light. These spaces are entered through verandahs that interact with the neighbors.

The inward sloping roofs provide shelter from the sun and rain and collect the water through the courts into under ground storage tanks to be used in the summer months. A slender steel structure provides a frame to the interior spaces and courts. These interiors are rendered white, framing fluted and clear glass to obscure and reveal views within the enclosure, while floors are finished in local grey limestone, both reflecting the light drawn through the aperture of the roof and windows.

This project seeks to create an interiority that is intimate, secure yet open to the environment, providing respite, and absorbing through time, the ever changing forces of the city.

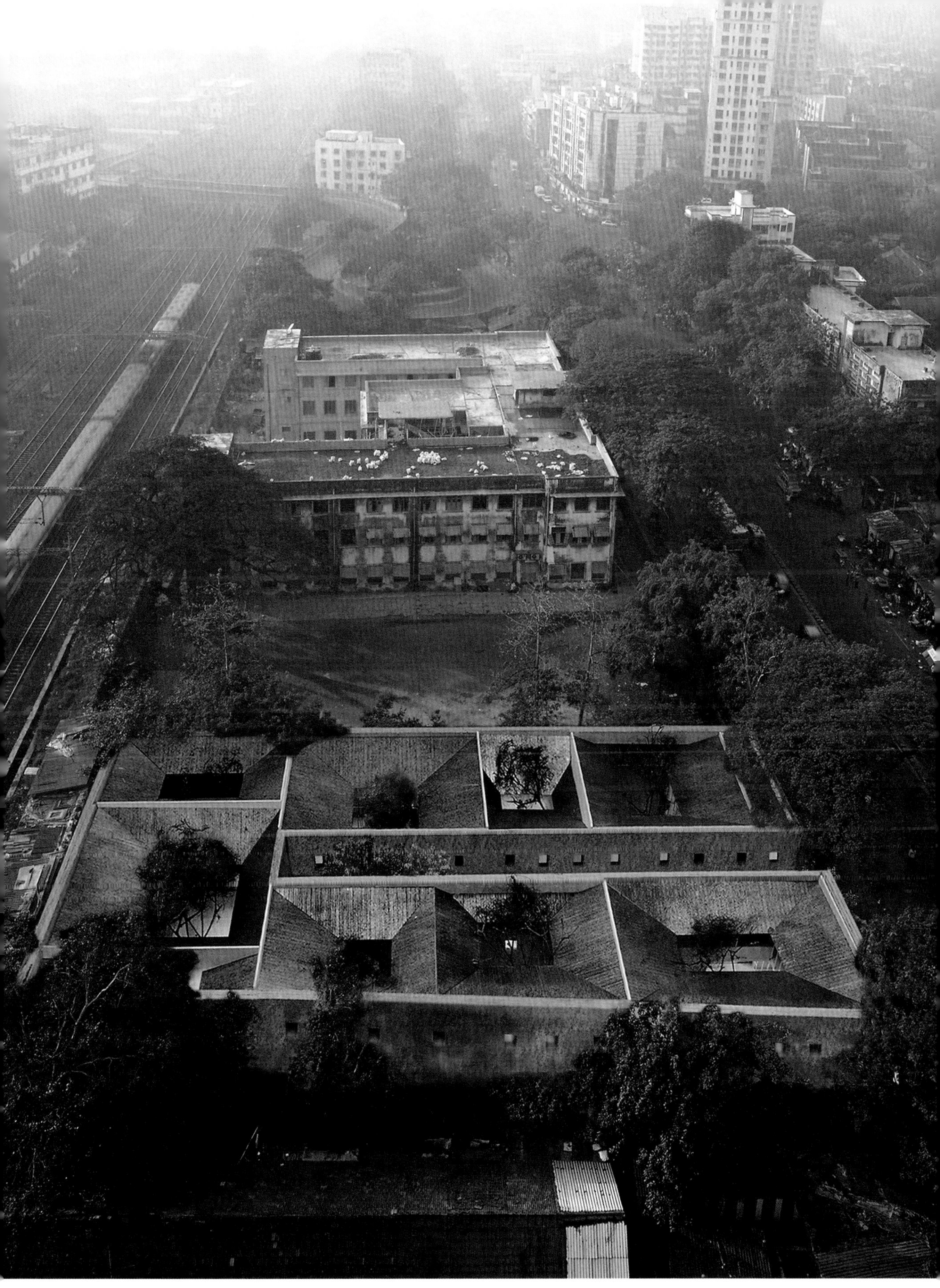

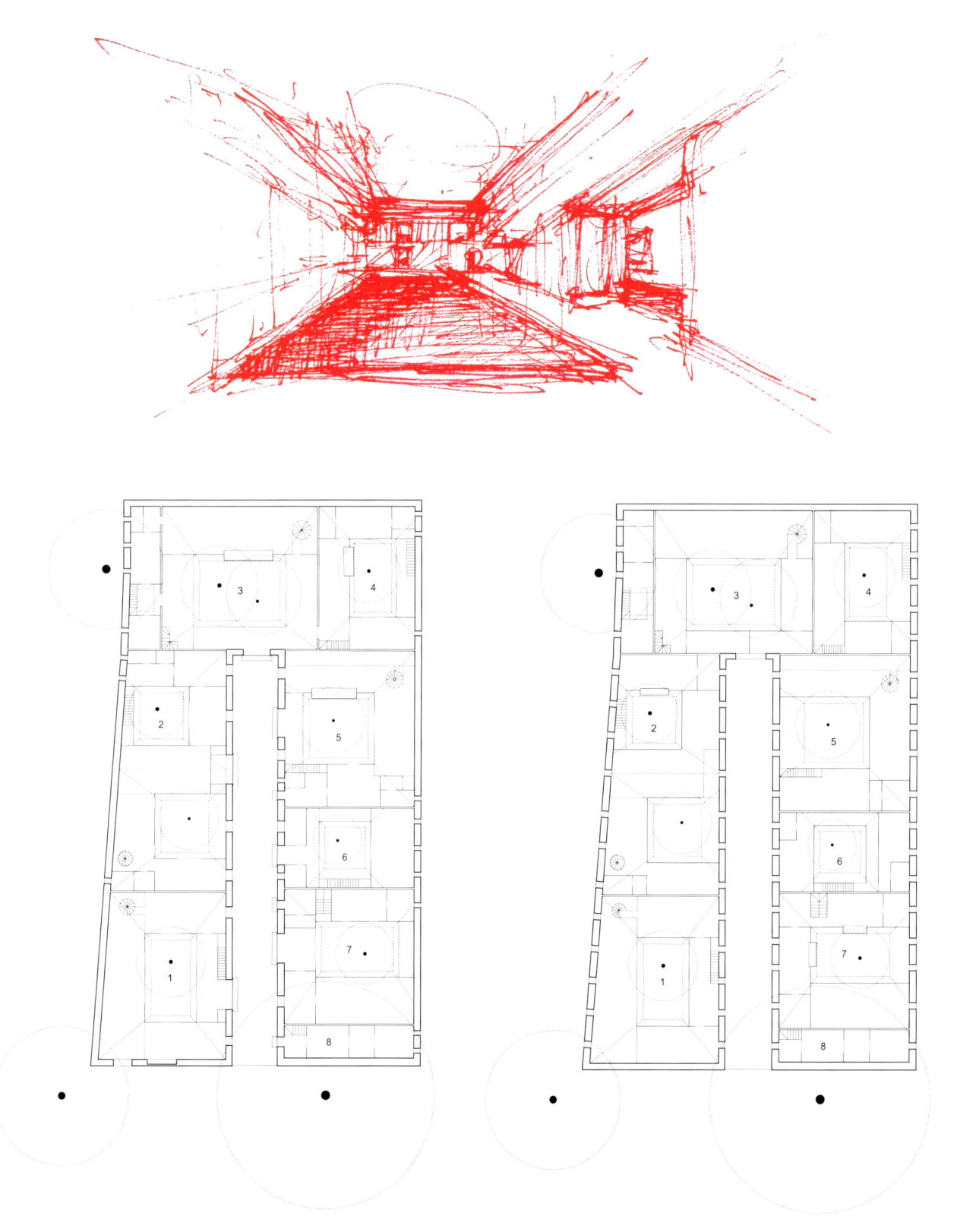

1-7 studio / home
8 shared utilities

Ground floor plan

First floor plan

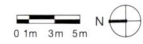

0 1m 3m 5m   N

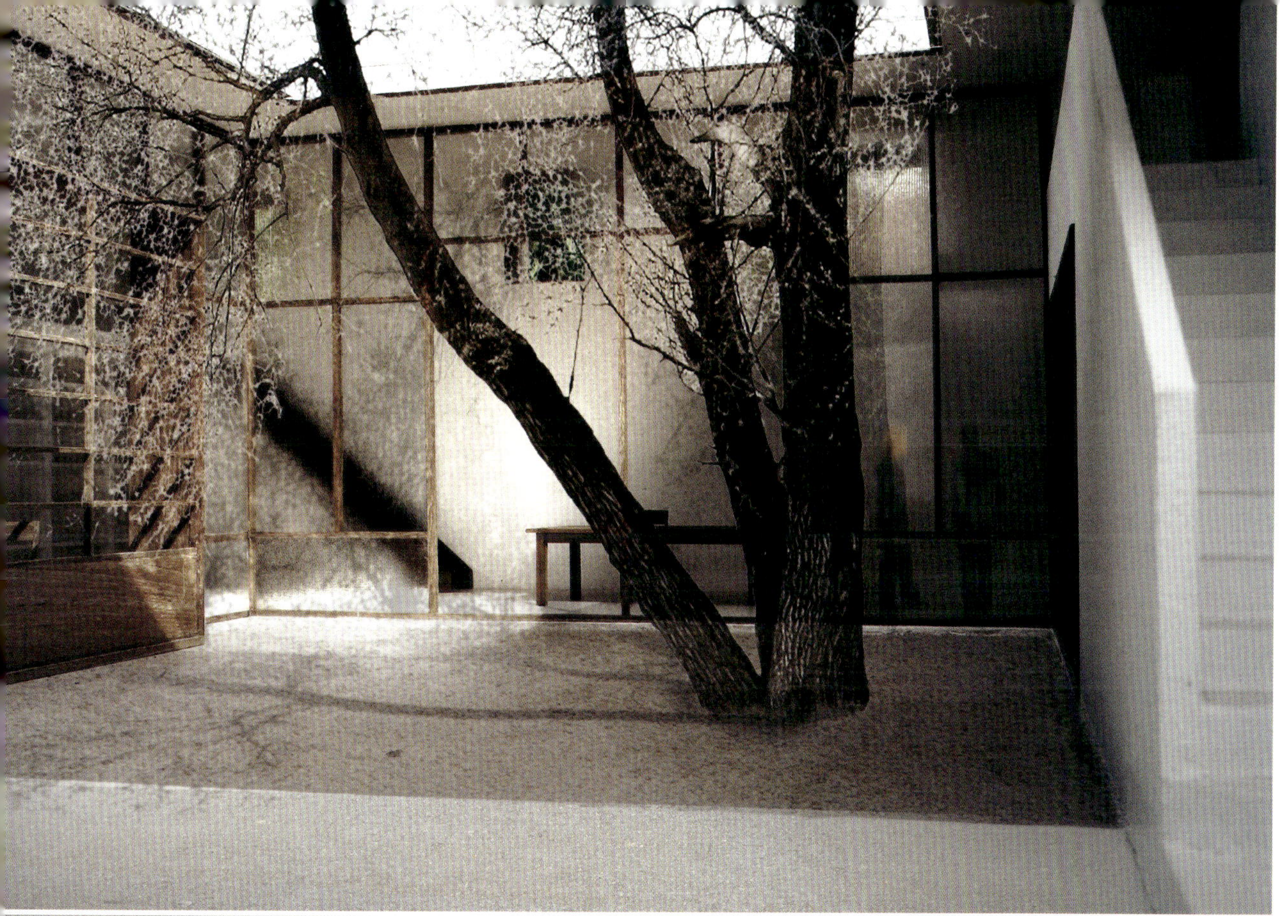

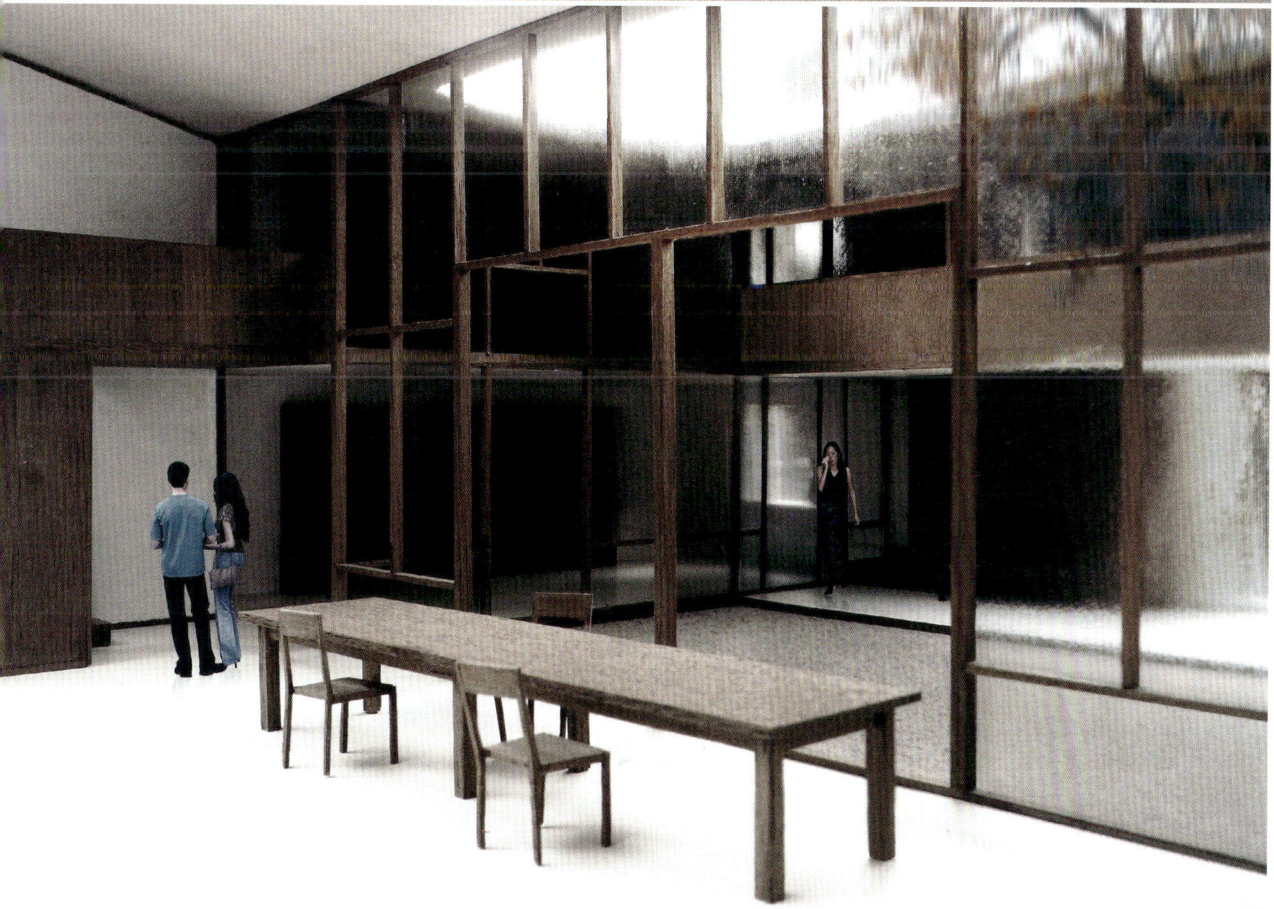

長手方向の断面模型を用いた採光スタディ。　Sectional models and light studies cut through the length of the building.

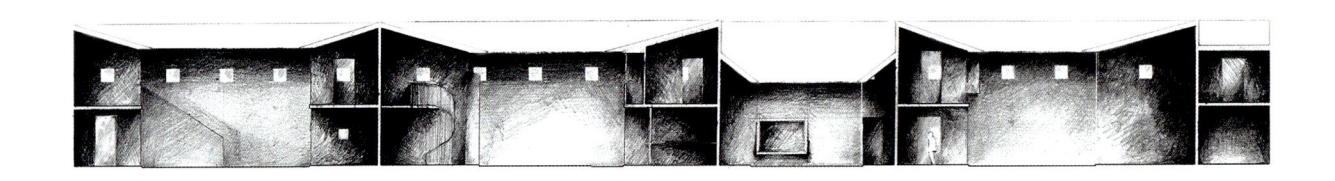

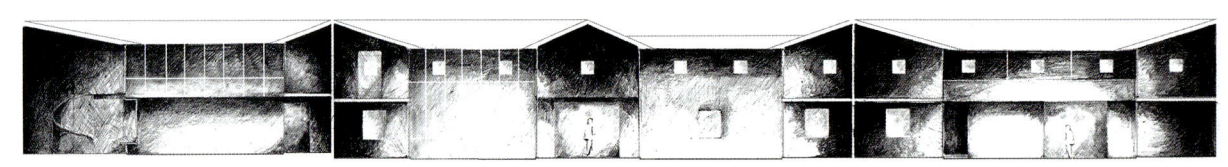

Light sections

(上)線路脇に建つ7つの中庭式住宅の初期模型。
(Above) An early model of the seven courtyard houses and the adjacent railway tracks.

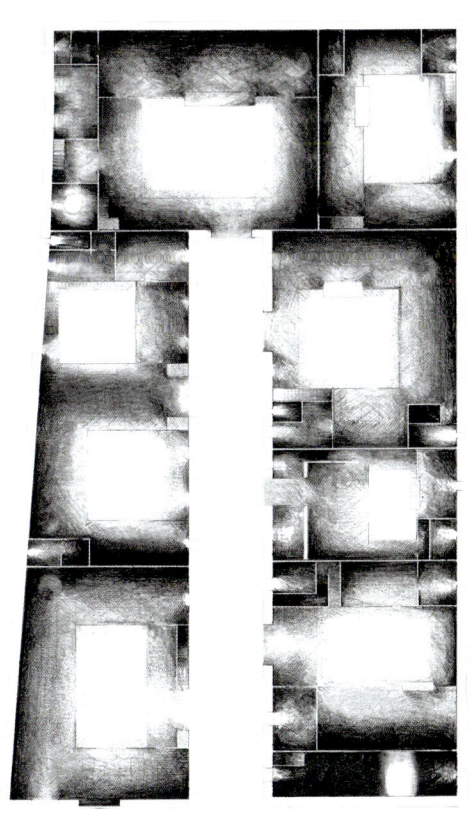

Light plan

スタジオ・ムンバイ
見ることと知ること

エルウィン・ビライ

私にはビジョイ・ジェインの声が聞こえる。

「私がしきりに考えるのは、スタジオをどのように組織すればいいのか、どんな体制で仕事をすればいいか、です。今のこの体制に行き着いたのも、ひとつには私自身が大工や石工たちとずっと顔をつきあわせてきたからです。今の私には、彼らの言語が話せるし、彼らは彼らでこちらに歩み寄ってくれた。私たちは互いに相手の視点に立って考えるようにしてきましたが、それでも完全に相手を理解するところまではいきません。だからとりあえずは互いの接点となるところから始めます。複数の視点が重なり合って厚みを増してきたら、しめたもの。こんな具合に私たちは日々仕事をしています。いずれにせよ型どおりのやり方では、事務所はつくれなかったでしょうね。これが私たちの仕事の流儀であり、逆にそうするしか建築をつくりようがない。そもそもうちにはマニフェストも議題もプランもない……。まったくの行き当たりばったりです。大工たちも、いまでは建築家として振る舞います。というのも、コンセプトについても彼らと話し合って決めるんです。材料の話に限らず、空間、軽さ、重さ、量塊、密度といった話も、彼らには通じます。こちらが〈物語〉を伝えると、彼らは自分の体験とか、背景、記憶、過去を語ってくれる。だから私も自分の過去と体験を打ち明ける。私たちはそんなふうにしてプロジェクトについて語り合うのです。」[*1]

以上の発言には、スタジオ・ムンバイならではの持ち味が端的に述べられている。それは、コミュニケーションの取り方である。人はふつう、自分は他人と共通の言語で話していると思いこみがちだが、実は人によって言葉はまちまちなのだ。だから人は知らず知らずのうちに相手の言語に合わせることで、会話を成立させながら、物語を紡ぎ、作品をつくり、人生を楽しむのである。

このプロセスを理解し説明しようとして行き当たったのが、ペーター・スローターダイク（1947年-）の考究である。彼はこの世界における人間の存在というものを、つぎのように解き明かす。「存在とは媒介的なものである〈中略〉ルネサンス心理学を提唱した人びとは、魂が、他者に霊感を与えて交流をするための工房にすぎないことをすでに知っていた。だがルネサンスにおいて獲得されたこうした認識は、はたして今世紀にはすっかり忘れ去られてしまい、新しい種類の心理学的空間に上書きされた。科学の様式にあてはめた、それもたいていは利己的で浅薄な心理学的空間に。」

そして私は、われわれが何者であるのかを悟り、またスタジオ・ムンバイとビジョイ・ジェインはその振る舞いにおいて、ワークショップや敷地において、あるいは自作を訪れる際において、「存在することは、関係することであり、空間となることであり、場所を開けること」[*2]だと、気づかせてくれる。「ウスタヴ邸」では、犬たちが来客を温かく出迎え、客に向かって吠えないどころか、手入れの行き届いた美しい住空間に先導してくれる。「パルミラの住宅」では、浜を洗う波の音も、家の中を抜けるそよ風も、身体に感じられる。内と外は別々なのに、ひとつの空間になっている。

会話をすること、物語を伝えること、プロジェクトについて話すこと、つくること、創造すること、すなわち、
「己の耳に聞こえたものに反応することによって、人は初めて存在たりうる。それは、共に聴き、識別し、探求し、最終的には共に暮らすことの幸せを味わうことである。このように、聴くのも、楽しむのも、志すのも、現れることも、いずれも同じ「こと」── 同じあなたである。最初の献身 ── 自分に関係のある音に耳を澄ませることができるように、己を覚醒させること。」[*3]
だから私たちは耳を澄まして、自分の興味を引くものを心に刻むのである。

ここでふと頭をよぎるのが、スティーブ・ジョブズ（1955-2011年）が『ホール・アース・カタログ』から引用した句「Stay Hungry, Stay Foolish」（貪欲であれ、愚直であれ）[*4]である。これはこの場合になにを意味するのか。人生に関心をもつということは、貪欲になるということであり、また愚直であるということは、自然体でいること、直観、知覚を信じることであり、そのうえにデザインも豊かな暮らしも成り立っているということだ。直観、視野の広さ、直観とデザインとテクノロジーと知識の融合があればこそ、アップル社製品は広く支持を集めた。おそらく知性一辺倒ではなく、そこには、人が感じるもの、心にずしりと響くもの、あるいは直観を信じる心があるのだろう。ビジョイ・ジェインとスタジオ・ムンバイもやはり「Stay Hungry, Stay Foolish」と言っているような気がする。

これを裏付けるように、バーナード・ルドフスキー（1905-88年）は「芸術と建築において、身体的快楽は知的快楽に優先されなければならない」と言う。また「私たちに必要なのは、新しい技術ではなく、新しい生活様式である」という彼の信念は、その晩年の著作『さあ横になって食べよう 忘れられた生活様式』の副題でもある。ルドフスキーは、家の中の部屋はそれぞれ身体機能に基づいてデザインされている（身体を横たえて休む場所、食事をとる場所、湯船に浸かる場所）との前提に立ったうえで、建築は五感を刺激し、日常文化を洗練させるのに役立つと考えた。[*5] 世界を見渡しては、名もない職人のつくった建築に注目したり、自然の営みや作者不明の建築からなにかを悟る

Studio Mumbai, Seeing and Knowing

Erwin Viray

I can hear Bijoy Jain

"I am very curious about how one builds a studio. How does one build a practice? Part of the reason we have shaped our practice in this way is because the people I have been with the longest are my carpenters and masons. They have a language that I am now able to speak, and they have met me halfway. I have to meet them from their point of view and they have tried to meet me from my point of view, but we do not quite get to each other's place. We work from places where we overlap. It is quite interesting when you start getting a multiplicity of layers coming from different points of view. That is really how we try to work in the studio. I could not have built a studio with a conventional background. We work this way because it is the only way we can produce architecture. It has not come from a manifesto, an agenda or a plan… it is an extremely free process. The carpenters are now acting as architects in the studio, because we have conceptual discussions with them, not only about materials but also about space, lightness, weight, mass, density, and they understand it. We tell stories, they talk about their exposure, their backgrounds, their memories, their history, and I discuss mine, and my experiences. We talk about projects." [1]

These words encapsulate a very special quality that is unique to Studio Mumbai, the process and act of communication. Often, we believe and take for granted that we speak the same language with everyone, but in reality we do not, we speak different languages. Unconsciously we adjust ourselves to meet the other language so that our language meets theirs. Eventually we are able to understand each other and create a story, make a piece of work, and enjoy what life reveals.

Trying to understand and explain this process lead to the discovery of Peter Sloterdijk's exploration, which sought to explain our presence in this world. "Existence is medial… the protagonists of Renaissance psychology had already realized that the soul cannot be anything other than a studio for transactions with inspiring others. These achievements of Renaissance knowledge have, admittedly, been almost entirely forgotten in our century, and overlaid with scientifically stylized and usually also individualistically shallowed new versions of psychological space." It makes me realize who we are, and Studio Mumbai and Bijoy Jain bring us to be conscious that "To be is to relate, to be space, to make room for" [2] in what they do, in their workshop, on site, and in visiting the works they have crafted. At Utsav House the dogs welcome you warmly, they do not bark at you but usher you into the beautifully tended and inhabited spatial enclosure. At Palmyra House, the sound of waves pounding the shore enables a presence to be felt, together with the breezes that flow through the house. Inside and outside are distinct and at the same time one space.

Conversations, telling stories, talking about projects, to make, to create, "To respond to what you hear is to come into existence, it is to experience happiness at inter-listening, filtering, pursuit, and finally, habitation — such that listening, enjoying, intending and emerging are the same "thing"— YOU. First devotion, rousing yourself to the state of alertness necessary to open up to the sound that concerns you. [3] And so we listen, we register those that are of interest to us."

This brings us tangentially to a quote from the Whole Earth Catalogue that Steve Jobs (1955-2011) quoted, "Stay Hungry, Stay Foolish" [4]. In this context what could this mean? To be interested in life is to be hungry, to stay foolish is being natural and having a belief in intuition, in man's perception as a basis for design and a good life. An intuition and a widening of knowledge, an intersection between intuition, design, technology and knowledge produced the widely admired Apple products. Perhaps it should be acknowledged that rather than over intellectualization, there should be a belief in what we feel, and our gut feeling, or intuition. Bijoy Jain and Studio Mumbai seem to say too, "Stay Hungry, Stay Foolish."

This is complimented by Bernard Rudofsky (1905-88) when he says,"I believe that sensory pleasure should take precedence over intellectual pleasure in art and architecture." And his espousal of "what we need is not a new way of building but a new way of living", which is the subtitle of one of Rudofsky's last works. Setting out from the assumption that the design of every single room in a house is based on a physical function: one place to lie the body down to rest, another to take in food, a third to step into a tub to bath, Bernard Rudofsky believed

傾向は、ビジョイ・ジェインとスタジオ・ムンバイにもみられる。ルドフスキーによるこうした文章は、100年前に自然や仕事や工芸について論じたジョン・ラスキン（1819-1900年）やウィリアム・モリス（1834-96年）の著作を思い起こさせる。

今朝方そんなことを考えつつニューヨーク・タイムズ紙を開くと、ダグ・エイケン（1968年-）の記事が目に留まった。「古い家の足跡をなぞるようにして建つこの新居を建てる間にも、やはり似たような疑問が頭をよぎった。『戸外でも屋内でもあるような暮らしとはいったいどんなだろうか。この場所だったら、思想や文化を、光、風、空気、動線をどう扱ったらいいのだろう。自分の世界をどう建築の中に収めたらいいのか。』エイケンいわく『僕らにとってはごくあたりまえのもの——椅子、テーブル、光——が、作品をかたちづくっていく……どうせなら、誰かと分かち合える場所、つまり誰かと一緒に働いたり、あるいは人を招いたり、一緒に体験できる場所にしたいでしょう？』」[*6]
これを読んで、「パルミラの住宅」やアリバグにあるスタジオ・ムンバイの作業場を思い出した。

目を凝らして観察する、それは「見ることとつくることは、最初の芸術行為」[*7]であるように、本来は生きる行為なのである。これを物語るのが、スタジオ・ムンバイに保管された、ビジョイをはじめ職人や大工たちの描いた膨大な数のドローイングやスケッチである。これらはノートに綴じられて、その赤い表紙には「スタジオ・ムンバイ」のゴム印が押されている。なるほど、ヴィーヤ・セルマンズ（1938年-）もこんな発言をしている。
「私にとってドローイングとは、考えること、ある考えが辿った軌跡、一点からまた別の点へと動いた痕跡なのです。人は、あるものを別のものと区別するためにドローイングを描く。プロポーションを描いて、スケールを調整する。ドローイングなくして絵を描くことなどできません。」[*8]
ドローイングとは、記録をし、資料を作成し、物語を伝え、プロセスを追うための手段である。ドローイングやスケッチは、自分の話す言語を顧みたり自分の言語領域を広げるための手段、あるいは建築のプレゼンテーションや表現の手段となる。ドローイングが原寸大の模型と化すこともあれば、その反対に、予めつくられた原寸大の模型の記録としてドローイングが起こされることもある。素材もまたひとつのツールとして、考える、定義する、つくるといった当初の行為を検証するのに使われる。

ビジョイに、同時代のどの建築家の作品が気になるかと問うと、彼はいくつか名前を挙げたあとに、「彼らがなにを見ているのか、どう見ているのかが気になる」と答えた。そこで私は聞き返した、「見るって？」。偶然にも私は河井寛次郎の自邸を訪れる機会に恵まれ、そこで目にした光景をきっかけに、「見ることと知ること」を知った。『The Unknown Craftsman』[無名の工人]に、こんなくだりがある。
「見ることと知ることとは屢々違う。一致すれば之より幸なことはない。（278頁）
美への理解に於ては直観は理知より、一層本質的なものである。（279頁）
見る力は内に入ってゆくが、知ることは周囲を廻ることに過ぎない。美への理解には分別より以前に働く直観の力がなければならない。（280頁）
見るということは具体界に関わり、知るということは抽象界に繋がる。（285頁）
［見る力］は生れてくるものであって、人為的に作ることができない。［知る力は］半ば勉学でその力を増大することができる。（287頁）」
そしてその忠告とは、
「ものを見た時、先ず審いてはいけないということである。謂わば批判を最初遠慮することである。この習慣をつけることは何より必要だと思える。ものを始めから知の対象として扱ってはいけないという意味である。〈中略〉之を他の言葉で言い現すなら、先ず受け容れよということである。自分を主張せず〈中略〉受身の立場に立つということが肝腎である。丁度鏡が、ものの姿を受け容れるのと同じである。磨かれた鏡が更にその機能を発するように、自分の心を無心になし得るなら更によい。〈中略〉無心というと、何ものもない消極的な態度のように取られるかも知れぬが、ものそのものにじかに触れる積極的な力はここから湧くのである。（287頁）」[*9]

ことによると、ビジョイ・ジェインは対談中ずっとこのことを話していたのかもしれない。そしてスタジオ・ムンバイという家族には、それがある。彼らの躍動が、葛藤が、悦びが、こちらにも伝わってくるように。ビジョイ・ジェインは言う、「それは実践であり、私自身であり、私の人生である」。その人生とは皆との会話であり、出会いなのだ。建築とは、そうした人生を、会話を、見ることと知ること、何百年来のプラクティスを取り戻す手段なのである。

エルウィン・ビライ　2012年3月31日、京都にて

*1. Excerpts from an ongoing dialogue: A conversation between Dr Balkrishna V. Doshi and Bijoy Jain, El Croquis, Studio Mumbai 2003-2011, p.15（バルクリシュナ V. ドーシとビジョイ・ジェインの対談より抜粋）
*2. Peter Sloterdijk, Bubbles: Spheres Volume I, Microspherology, Semiotext(e)/Foreign Agents 2011 p.124
*3. ibid., p.504
*4. Walter Isaacson, Steve Jobs, Little, Brown, 2011, p.59（邦訳：ウォルター・アイザックソン『スティーブ・ジョブズ』井口耕二訳 講談社2011年）
*5. Architekturzentrum Wein, Lessons from Bernard Rudofsky: Life As a Voyage,2007, p.262
*6. http://www.nytimes.com/2012/04/01/t-magazine/doug-aitkens-sound-garden.html?pagewanted=1&_r=1
*7. ibid., p.17
*8. Chuck Close, Vija Celmins interviewed by Chuck Close, Vija Celmins, ed. William S. Bartman, New York 1992, p.11
*9. Muneyoshi Yanagi and Bernard Leach. The Unknown Craftsman: An Japanese insight into Beauty, "Seeing and Knowing", Kohdansha America, 1990, pp.109-112（原典：柳宗悦『柳宗悦コレクション2 もの』日本民藝館監修 ちくま学芸文庫 2011年 278-287頁）

architecture served to stimulate the senses and refine everyday culture.*5 Looking at the world in pieces of architecture made by unnamed craftsmen and discovering from the processes of nature are traits of Bijoy Jain and Studio Mumbai. These writings by Rudofsky also bring us to texts by John Ruskin(1819-1900) and William Morris(1834-96), who explored nature, work and craft more than a hundred years ago.

Reading the New York Times paper this morning, I discovered an article by Doug Aitken: "The creation of the new house, which sits on the same footprint as the old one, proceeded with similar questions: "How does one live the outdoor-indoor life? How does one work with ideas and culture, with the light, the wind, the atmosphere, the foot traffic in this specific place? How do you frame the world around you within the architecture?" For Aitken, "These things that we take so much for granted — a chair, a table, a light — shape what you make… And you want to make places you can share, where you can collaborate and have people over, and have an experience."*6 These words bring me back to the Palmyra House, and the workshop in Alibag of Studio Mumbai.

Being observant, observing, "The act of looking and making as a primal act of art"*7 becomes a primary act of life. In Studio Mumbai, one manifestation of this is the drawings and sketches created by Bijoy, the artisans, carpenters and craftsmen, all recorded on the red covered notebooks stamped Studio Mumbai. Vija Celmins adds a few words to confirm, "I see drawing as thinking, as evidence of thinking, evidence of going from one place to another. One draws to define one thing from another, draws proportions, adjusts scale. It is impossible to paint without drawing."*8 Drawing as a means to record, as a means to document, to tell a story, to understand an unfolding process. Drawings and sketches as a means to probe the language we have, how we can extend the boundaries of our language, or a means of architectural presentation and representation. Drawings that become one to one scale models, or sometimes a process reversed, the one to one scale models comes first and the drawing to document it comes later. Materials also form a set of tools to probe the primal act of thinking, defining, making.

When I asked Bijoy about the contemporaries whose works he is interested in, he named a few, and said, "I am interested in what they see and how they see." And so I asked, "What is to see?" By chance, I visited Kanjiro Kawai's house and discovered some scenes that lead to a window of "On seeing and knowing". In the "*Unknown Craftsman*", we read a chapter stating: "Seeing and knowing are separate. Nothing could be more admirable than when they coincide. In understanding beauty, intuition is more of the essence than intellectual perception. To "see" is to go to the core; to know the facts about an object of beauty is to go around the periphery. Intellectual discrimination is less essential to an understanding of beauty than the power of intuition that precedes it. Seeing relates to the concrete, knowing to the abstract. Seeing is a born faculty. Knowing is acquired." And so an advice is given, "to put aside the desire to judge immediately and to acquire the habit of just looking. Second, do not treat the object as a subject of intellect. Third, just be ready to receive, passively, without interposing yourself. If you can make your mind void of all intellectualization, like a clear mirror that simply reflects, then all the better. This conceptualization — the Zen state of mushin ("no mind") — may seem to represent a negative attitude, but from it springs the true ability to contact things directly and positively."*9

Perhaps, this is what Bijoy Jain has been saying all along in conversations, and what is seen in the family that is Studio Mumbai. As one feels that life, that struggle, that joy; as Bijoy says: "it is praxis, it is I, and it is my life". And that life is a conversation with everyone and an encounter with all. Architecture is the means to bring us to that life, that conversation, that seeing and knowing, that praxis that has been there for hundreds of years.

Erwin Viray March 31, 2012 Kyoto

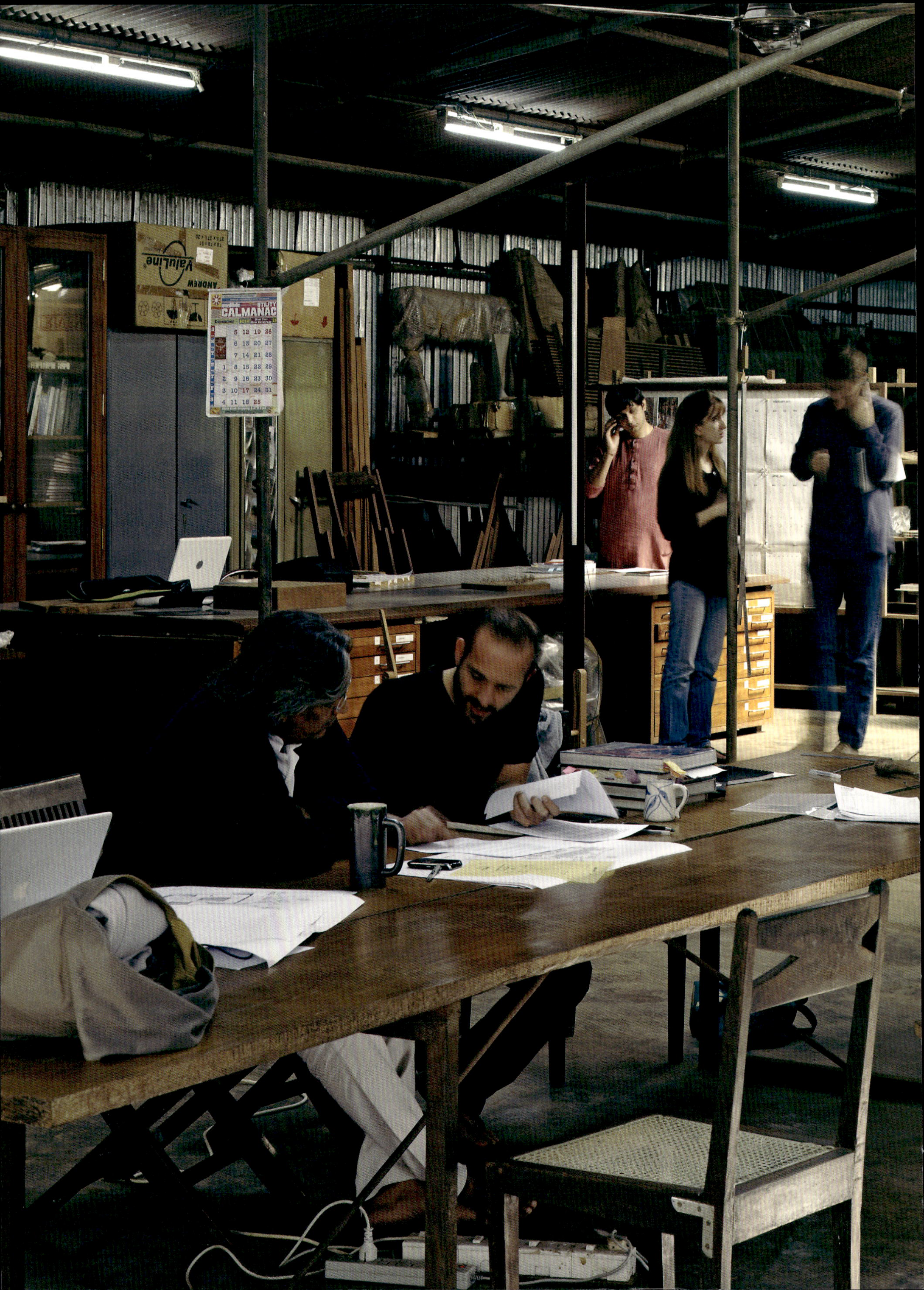
UTILITY
CALMANAC

Profile
略歴

Bijoy Jain
ビジョイ・ジェイン

1965年、インド・ムンバイに生まれる。90年アメリカ、セントルイスのワシントン大学で修士号を取得。89年からロサンゼルスとロンドンで実務経験を積んだ後、95年に帰国し、出身地ムンバイにてスタジオ・ムンバイを設立。スタジオ・ムンバイは、熟練職人と建築家からなる人的ネットワークにより設計・施工を一貫して行っている。
ヴィクトリア＆アルバート博物館（2010）をはじめ、「ワークプレイス」で特別賞を受賞した第12回ヴェネチア・ビエンナーレ（2010）に出展。作品はアルヴァ・アールト・シンポジウムやニューヨーク建築連盟などで紹介されるほか、2010年度アガ・カーン賞の最終選考にも残った。フランス建築協会（IFA）の世界サステイナブル建築賞（2009）、ならびに香港デザインセンターのアジア・デザイン賞（2009）を受賞。

Bijoy Jain was born in Mumbai, India in 1965 and received his M. Arch from Washington University in St Louis, USA in 1990. He worked in Los Angeles and London between 1989 and 1995 and returned to India in 1995 to found his practice. Studio Mumbai is a human infrastructure of skilled craftsmen and architects who design and build the work directly. The studio has built installations in the Victoria & Albert Museum (2010) and at the XII Venezia Biennale 2010, where the installation "Workplace" was awarded a Special Mention. Their work has been presented in venues such as the Alvar Alto Symposium and the Architectural League of New York and was a finalist in the Agha Kahn Awards 2010 Cycle. Studio Mumbai received the Global Award for Sustainable Architecture from L'Institut Francais D'Architecture (2009) and the Design for Asia Award from the Hong Kong Design Center (2009).

Credits
クレジット

Photographs 写真

Hélèn Binet
pp. 54; 56; 59; 61 bottom right; 63; 65; 67; 73; 74-75; 77; 78; 79 top; 80 bottom; 82-83; 85; 90; 91 bottom; 93 center, bottom; 94-97; 99; 101; 103; 105 top; 106 bottom; 108; 110-111; 112 bottom left; 113; 114 top; 115 bottom; 118-119; 121; 122 bottom left; 126; 127 top; 128-129; 131; 132-133; 135; 136-137; 139 top; 141; 144 bottom left, top right; 145; 152-153; 157; 160 center, bottom; 161; 162 bottom; 163; 164-167; 169; 170-173; 175; 176-187; 189; 191; 192; 193 bottom; 197 top and bottom left; 198-199;

Mitul Desai
pp. 26-35

Prabuddha Dasgupta
p. 115 top

Ariel Huber
p. 155 bottom

Photos provided by Studio Mumbai unless otherwise noted.
上記以外はスタジオ・ムンバイ

Texts テキスト

Wolfgang Fiel
Berno Odo Polzer
pp. 46-57

Mitul Desai
pp. 26-35

Radhika Desai
pp. 36; 58; 68; 84; 100; 120; 134; 153; 168

Erwin Viray
pp. 8-25, 212-215

Texts provided by Studio Mumbai unless otherwise noted.

Japanese Translations 和訳

Jun Doi 土居 純
pp. 6〜45, 58〜217

Emiko Hayakawa 早川恵美子
pp. 46〜57

Cooperation 協力

Studio Mumbai Architects
Michael Anastassiades   Collaborator V & A, In-between Architecture
Dr. Muirne Kate Dineen   Collaborator V & A, In-between Architecture
Emiko Hayakawa 早川恵美子

STUDIO MUMBAI : Praxis　スタジオ・ムンバイ：プラクシス

2012年7月11日　初版第1刷発行
2024年6月10日　初版第6刷発行

監修：ビジョイ・ジェイン＋ジョセフ・ファン・デル・ステーン
発行者：渡井 朗
編集：TOTO出版
協力：スタジオ・ムンバイ
アートディレクション＆デザイン：AOYL（佐藤直樹＋菊地昌隆）
印刷・製本：株式会社東京印書館
発行所：TOTO出版（TOTO株式会社）
〒107-0062 東京都港区南青山1-24-3 TOTO乃木坂ビル2F
[営業] TEL: 03-3402-7138　FAX: 03-3402-7187
[編集] TEL: 03-3497-1010
URL: https://jp.toto.com/publishing

落丁本・乱丁本はお取り替えいたします。
本書の全部又は一部に対するコピー・スキャン・デジタル化等の無断複製行為は、著作権法上での例外を除き禁じます。
本書を代行業者等の第三者に依頼してスキャンやデジタル化することは、たとえ個人や家庭内での利用であっても著作権上認められておりません。
定価はカバーに表示してあります。

© 2012 STUDIO MUMBAI

Printed in Japan
ISBN 978-4-88706-328-0

STUDIO MUMBAI
ARCHITECTS

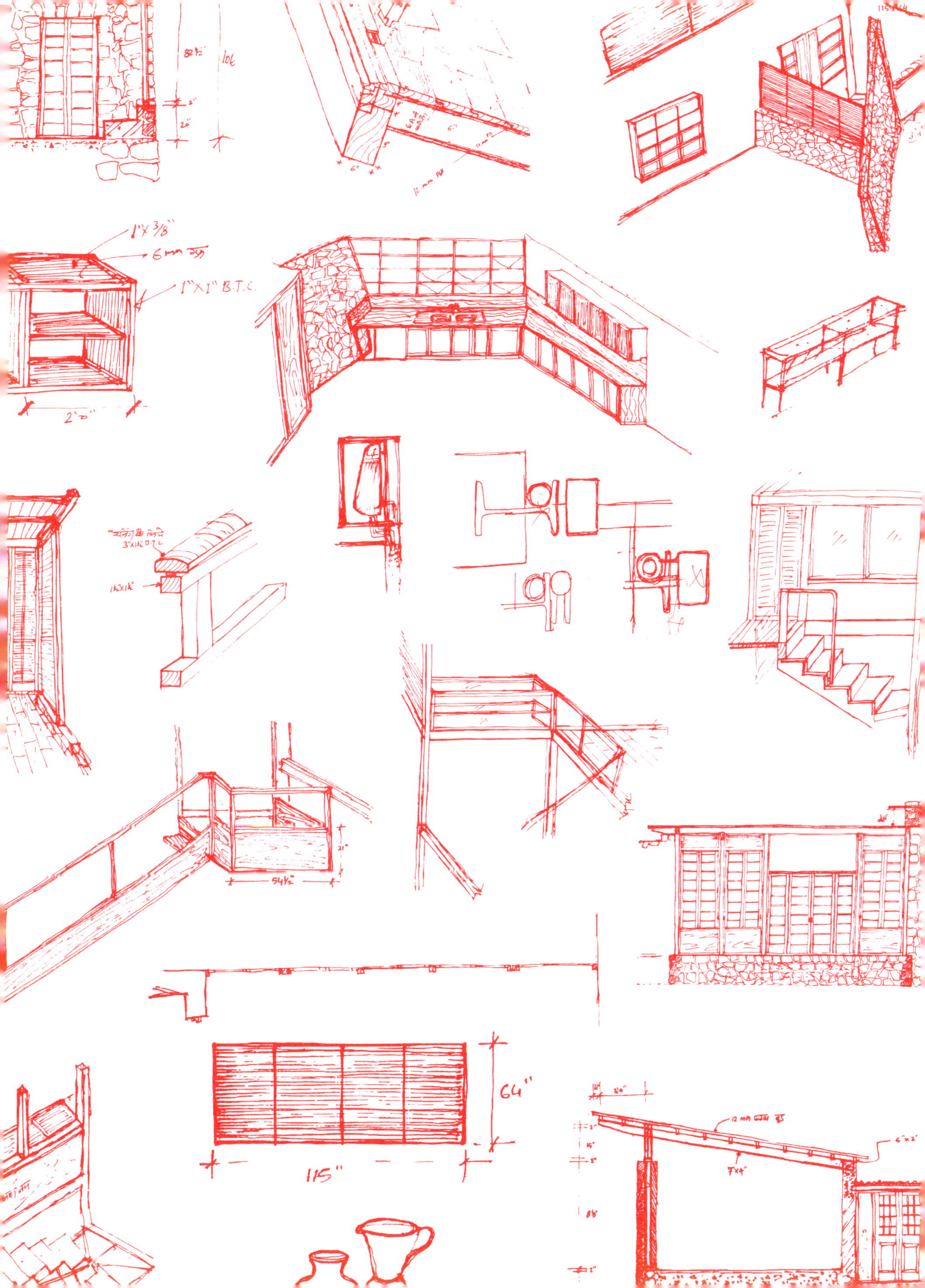

C.D — COW DUNG.
T.W.S — T. WOOD SLAPS.
L.S — LOCAL STONE.